THE
COCAINE
WARS

THE COCAINE WARS

Paul Eddy · Hugo Sabogal · Sara Walden

W· W· NORTON & COMPANY
NEW YORK · LONDON

Published simultaneously in Canada by Penguin Books Canada Ltd., 2801 John
Street, Markham, Ontario L3R 1B4.
Printed in the United States of America.

The text of this book is composed in Primer, with display type set in Helvetica
Bold Stencil. Composition and manufacturing by
The Haddon Craftsmen, Inc.
Book design by Marie-Helene Fredericks.

First Edition

Library of Congress Cataloging-in-Publication Data

Eddy, Paul, 1944–
   The cocaine wars: murder, money, corruption, and the world's most valuable
commodity/Paul Eddy, Hugo Sabogal, Sara Walden.
     p. cm.
     Bibliography: p.
     Includes index.
     1. Cocaine. 2. Narcotics, Control of—Florida—Corrupt practices.
I. Sabogal, Hugo. II. Walden, Sara. III. Title.
HV5810.E33 1988
364.1′77′09759—dc19

ISBN 0-393-02579-9

W. W. Norton & Company, Inc.
500 Fifth Avenue, New York, N.Y. 10110
W. W. Norton & Company Ltd.
37 Great Russell Street, London WC1B 3NU

1 2 3 4 5 6 7 8 9 0

Additional reporting: Justine Picardie, Dorothy Wade, and Michael Graham.

To the memory of "Kojak":
source, guide, staunch ally, and true friend.
He died the day this manuscript
was due to be completed.

And to Neysa,
his wife, who did not deserve to lose him.

Contents

CONTENTS

Cast of Characters

ALBARRAN FERNANDEZ, OLGA   Miami River Cops-case juror who was lobbied by the defendants' relatives and told them "I'm not going to convict."

ALVAREZ, ALEX   Lead investigator for Centac 26 in the Miami River Cops case, nicknamed "Clintino."

AMARALES, ANDRÉS   Colombian guerrilla leader who led bloody attack on Palace of Justice in Bogotá.

AMILCAR   *See* Rafael León Rodríguez.

ARCE GOMEZ, LUIS   Bolivian minister of interior, cousin of trafficker Roberto Suárez Gómez.

ARIAS, LEONELA   Medellín cocaine trafficker, known as Leonela de Brand, who was an associate of Griselda Blanco. She was murdered in Medellín while on her way to a funeral.

ARIAS, RODOLFO   Corrupt City of Miami police officer known as "Rudy," who became the government's star witness in the Miami River Cops case.

BAEZ, PEDRO   Survivor of the Jones Boat Yard rip-off in which three of his colleagues drowned.

BANNISTER, EVERETTE   "Mr. Fixit" for Bahamian Prime Minister Lynden O. Pindling.

BANNISTER, GORMAN   Son of Everette who defected to the United States and revealed the inside story of massive corruption in the Bahamas.

BANZER SUAREZ, HUGO   President of Bolivia when the economy collapsed and landowners decided to plant "one heck of a lot" of coca trees.

11

CAST OF CHARACTERS

BARBER, FRANK Florida marijuana smuggler who was in league with corrupt DEA supervisor Jeffrey Scharlatt and tried to frame Luis "Kojak" García.

BARDWELL, STANFORD Federal prosecutor in Baton Rouge, Louisiana, who pursued Adler "Barry" Seal.

BECKWITH, CHARLES Sold his home on Norman's Cay to Carlos Lehder.

BENSINGER, PETER Former Administrator of the DEA who approved Raúl Díaz's proposal to create Centac 26.

BETANCUR CUARTAS, BELISARIO President of Colombia when justice minister Rodrigo Lara was murdered by drug traffickers. He forced the Cartel leaders into hiding.

BLACK CARLOS Kojak's favorite "boatman."

BLACK, ROY Leading defense lawyer in the Miami River Cops case.

BLANCO, GRISELDA TRUJILLO DE the "Ma Barker" of Medellín cocaine trafficking whose ruthless methods led to the cocaine wars in Miami.

BLUM, JACK Special counsel to a Senate subcommittee investigating links between drug traffickers and the CIA.

BOWE, NIGEL Nassau attorney who ripped off Carlos Lehder. Lehder threatened to have him "removed from the population count."

BURSTYN, SAMUEL Miami defense attorney nicknamed "Wild Man," who represented Rudy Arias.

CARDONA SALAZAR, RAFAEL Organizer of Jorge Ochoa's distribution network in Miami. He assisted in the plot to murder Barry Seal.

CARTWRIGHT, K. C. Known as the "white Everette Bannister." He is alleged to have involved Robert Vesco in drug trafficking.

CID, JUAN Cuban trafficker betrayed to the IRS by his wife, Nancy. He attempted to frame Raúl Díaz.

COELLO, OSVALDO Corrupt Miami police officer who plotted to murder government witnesses. He fled to Jamaica and the Bahamas, where he was finally arrested.

COS-GAYON, FERNANDO Head of Madrid drugs squad who arrested Jorge Ochoa.

CROSBY, JAMES Chairman of Resorts International, which operated gambling casinos in Nassau and Freeport. He paid hundreds of thousands of dollars to Everette Bannister and Prime Minister Pindling.

CUMBAMBA *See* Miguel Vélez.

DANGOND, JULIO Colombian marijuana trafficker who supplied Kojak García.

DE LA VEGA, ARTURO Corrupt City of Miami police officer.

DIAZ, JOE Centac 26 detective.

DIAZ, RAUL Founder of Centac 26 turned private investigator. Now described as "the most dangerous man in Miami" by a federal prosecutor.

DICKSON, CLARENCE Chief of the Miami Police Department, which has suffered the most serious police scandal in America since Prohibition.

DRAGIN, BOB Hit-man who was given the first contract to kill Barry Seal in Baton Rouge, Louisiana.

ECHEVERRIA BRAND, HUGO Medellín killer who briefed police on Dadeland murders.

ESCOBAR GAVIRIA, PABLO A leader of the Medellín Cartel.

ESTRADA, ARMANDO Corrupt City of Miami police officer.

FERNANDEZ, LUIS Undercover narcotics detective in Miami, a real-life "Sonny Crockett" of "Miami Vice."

FERRE, MAURICE Mayor of Miami when the massive hiring of police recruits took place.

FRANCAR, GENE DEA agent in Miami and Kojak's case officer.

GARCIA MEZA, LUIS President of Bolivia who succeeded General Hugo Banzer after a bloody coup. His administration dispelled any lingering doubts about the government's involvement in drug trafficking.

GARCIA, ARMANDO Corrupt City of Miami police officer who fled, together with his father, after Centac learned of their attempts to murder witnesses.

GARCIA, LUIS Known as "Kojak," legendary Miami trafficker turned DEA informant.

GARMIRE, BERNARD Former Miami police chief who attempted to drag the department into the twentieth century.

GARY, HOWARD Miami's first black city manager, who fired then Miami police chief, Kenneth Harms.

GIMBERNAT ORDEIG, ENRIQUE Jorge Ochoa's respected Spanish

attorney, who was drawn to his case by "the Nicaraguan factor."

GONZALEZ, ARMANDO Known as "Maleta," hit-man for Amilcar. He gave Raúl Díaz the evidence he needed to make Amilcar Centac's first target.

HARMS, KENNETH Former Miami police chief, fired unceremoniously by city manager Howard Gary at 2:47 A.M.

HEADLEY, WALTER Former Miami police chief who ran the department for almost twenty years as his personal fiefdom.

KIBBLE, JIMMY DEA agent in Madrid who resisted pressure from Washington to have Jorge Ochoa arrested "right away."

KILLINGER, RUSSELL State prosecutor assigned to the Miami River Cops case.

KOJAK See Luis García.

LARA BONILLA, RODRIGO Colombia's justice minister, murdered by drug traffickers in 1984.

LAMAZARES, GERMAN Raúl Díaz's first important informant, murdered by a fellow trafficker.

LAMAZARES, NANCY Germán's widow and Raúl Díaz's lover. Later she married Cuban trafficker Juan Cid and attempted to frame Raúl Díaz.

LEHDER RIVAS, CARLOS ENRIQUE Colombia's most prolific transporter of cocaine.

LEON RODRIGUEZ, RAFAEL Known as "Amílcar," Centac 26's first target. Raúl Díaz wanted him dead.

LLERENA, FE Mother of corrupt Miami police officer Arturo De la Vega. She tried to influence the jury.

LUCAS, PRESTON Undercover narcotics detective, a real-life "Ricardo Tubbs" of "Miami Vice."

MADRID PALACIOS, CARLOS Miami enforcer for the Ochoas, author of the "trafficker's bible."

MAILLIS, ATHANASIOS Known as "Tommy the Greek." He worked for the CIA and the DEA in the Bahamas. He claims Prime Minister Pindling attended Lehder's weekend parties on Norman's Cay.

MAJOR, LAWRENCE Assistant Commissioner of police in the Bahamas and a virtual one-man task force.

MALETA See Armando González.

MARTINEZ, FAUSTINO   Pedro Martínez's son, who told Kojak Miami police officers had caused his father's death.

MARTINEZ, JOSE   Hit-man hired by corrupt Miami police officers to kill government witness Armando Un.

MARTINEZ, PEDRO   Miami drug trafficker who drowned in the Miami River during the raid at Jones Boat Yard.

MCDUFFIE, ARTHUR   Black insurance salesman whose death spurred the 1980 Miami riots.

MEIE-LINNEKOGEL, MARGIT   Carlos Lehder's German mistress on Norman's Cay.

MERMELSTEIN, MAX   Cartel's man in Miami turned government witness. He arranged the first contract to kill Barry Seal.

MILIAN RODRIGUEZ, RAMON   Major money launderer for the Medellín Cartel who claims drug traffickers financed the Contras.

MOLINET, OSCAR   A survivor of the raid at Jones Boat Yard.

MONKEY   *See* Ricardo Morales.

MORALES, JORGE   Colombian trafficker who wanted to have Kojak murdered. He claims to have donated $4.5 million to the Contras.

MORALES, RICARDO   Known as "Monkey," legendary Cuban terrorist, drug trafficker, and informant for Raúl Díaz. He was shot dead in a sordid bar fight.

NOGUERA, JUAN   Colombian marijuana trafficker who supplied Kojak.

NOVAK, RICHARD   New York oceanography professor who resisted Carlos Lehder's attempts to force him off Norman's Cay.

NOVICKI, TRUDY   State prosecutor assigned to the Miami River Cops case.

OCHOA RESTREPO, FABIO   Father of Jorge Ochoa.

OCHOA VASQUEZ, FABIO   Jorge's young brother. He and Pablo Escobar placed the contract on Barry Seal's life.

OCHOA VASQUEZ, JORGE LUIS   The principal leader of the Medellín cartel.

OCHOA VASQUEZ, JUAN DAVID   Jorge's eldest brother.

OCHOA, MARGOTH VASQUEZ DE   Jorge's mother.

OCHOA, MARIA LIA DE   Jorge's wife.

PACO   *See* Miguel Sepúlveda.

PANESSO, GERMAN   Griselda Blanco's rival and one of the victims of the Dadeland massacre.

PINDLING, SIR LYNDEN OSCAR   Prime Minister of the Bahamas.

PINDLING, LADY MARGUERITE   Pindling's wife.

PLASENCIA, GEORGE   Centac 26 detective who participated in the Miami River Cops investigation.

POLOZOLA, FRANK   Louisiana federal judge who sent Barry Seal to the halfway house in Baton Rouge where he was killed.

QUESADA, CARLOS   Cuban trafficker and close friend of Ricardo "Monkey" Morales. Morales betrayed him.

QUINTERO CRUZ, LUIS CARLOS   Hit-man for the Medellín Cartel. He shot and killed Barry Seal.

RABIN, SAMUEL, JR.   Centac's former prosecutor who defended one of the Miami River cops.

RAMIREZ GOMEZ, JAIME   Colombian police colonel who led the raid on the massive Tranquilandia cocaine laboratory. He was killed for his temerity.

RAMOS, PEDRO   Miami drug trafficker who worked with corrupt police officers.

RODRIGUEZ, FELIX ISMAEL   CIA contract operative, also known as Max Gómez. He is alleged to have been the link man between drug traffickers and the Contras.

RODRIGUEZ, LUIS   Cuban drug trafficker who proposed the rip-off at Jones Boat Yard. A small man with big ideas, he ended up in a pine box.

RODRIGUEZ, ROMÁN   Corrupt City of Miami police officer and Armando Estrada's nervous partner.

RODRIGUEZ GACHA, GONZALO   A leader of the Medellín Cartel.

RODRIGUEZ OREJUELA, GILBERTO   Cali drug trafficker who was arrested with Jorge Ochoa in Madrid. Like Ochoa he later won freedom in Colombia.

ROUNTREE, WILLIAM   Juror whose stubbornness led to a mistrial in the Miami River Cops case.

RUIZ, ELADIO ARMANDO   Cuban trafficker accused of the murder of Germán Lamazares. He was killed by Monkey Morales.

RYSKAMP, KENNETH   Federal judge who presided over the Miami River Cops trials.

SARON, PETER   DEA special agent assigned to Athanasios "Tommy the Greek" Maillis.

SCHARLATT, JEFFREY   Senior DEA agent, bribed by Florida trafficker Frank Barber.

SEAL, ADLER BERRIMAN   Known as Barry. Drug smuggler and pilot turned DEA informant, he penetrated the Medellín Cartel and implicated the Sandinista government in drug trafficking. Murdered by the Cartel in Baton Rouge, Louisiana.

SEGURA, VICTOR   Cuban trafficker who gave Kojak his start as a smuggler.

SEPULVEDA, MIGUEL   Known as "Paco," he was a member of the Griselda Blanco gang.

SINGLETON, ALAN   Detective Sergeant for Metro-Dade Homicide and supervisor of Centac 26.

SMITH, GEORGE   Bahamian cabinet minister accused of taking bribes from drug traffickers.

SMITH, HOWARD   Corrupt assistant commissioner of police in the Bahamas. He was on Kojak's payroll.

SOMOZA, ANASTASIO   Deposed president of Nicaragua who paid Everette Bannister $320,000 to secure refuge in the Bahamas.

SUAREZ GOMEZ, ROBERTO   Bolivian drug trafficker and head of the most powerful cocaine ring in that country.

SULLIVAN, MICHAEL PATRICK   Federal prosecutor assigned to the Miami River Cops case.

UN ROQUE, ARMANDO   Luis Rodríguez's lieutenant, turned government witness in the Miami River Cops case. The defendants attempted to have him killed.

VAUGHAN, FEDERICO   Alleged senior official in the Sandinista government who arranged for Barry Seal to land and refuel in Nicaragua. He was photographed by Seal helping to load a plane with cocaine.

VELEZ, MIGUEL   Known as "Cumbamba," hit-man for Griselda Blanco and the Medellín Cartel.

VESCO, ROBERT   American swindler who bought refuge in the Bahamas and went into partnership with Carlos Lehder.

VISUÑA, HIPOLITO   Gave Raúl Díaz information about Amilcar's involvement in Miami double homicide.

VON EBERSTEIN, CHARLES   Edward Ward's partner in marijuana smuggling ring.

CAST OF CHARACTERS

WALSH, MIGUEL   Author of the most comprehensive DEA report on cocaine trafficking in Colombia.

WARD, EDWARD   Marijuana smuggler who operated from Norman's Cay, and bribed a government minister.

WARD, EMILIE   Ward's wife.

WILLIAMS, DOUGLAS   Former state prosecutor who defended one of the Miami River cops. He was Raúl Díaz's nemesis.

WITT, DICK   Aide to police chief Bernard Garmire. He later witnessed the panic hiring of new police recruits, and feared the consequences.

YOCHELSON, ROGER   Attorney for the Justice Department who monitored the lost battle to extradite Jorge Ochoa from Spain.

Prologue:
The Education of Jack Blum

I n the early days of March 1987, a middle-aged Washington lawyer named Jack Blum flew to Miami, Florida—to what its boosters call the Shining City—to begin an investigation into some of the more Byzantine aspects of international drug trafficking. He had hoped to begin by interviewing the United States Attorney for the Southern District of Florida, and since Blum had been sent by a US Senate subcommittee and was vested with all of its great authority, he anticipated no difficulty in getting an appointment. But the US attorney was unavailable: he was in hiding, driven there by the threats of drug traffickers in Colombia to have him killed, guarded around the clock, it was said, by a police SWAT team. Blum thought it an extraordinary situation, but in the Shining City it was not regarded as an event of any great significance.

Blum checked into the Intercontinental Hotel, one of only two hotels in all Miami that his sources at the US Customs Service would recommend. At all of the others, they said, there were people on the traffickers' payroll who searched the rooms of government men. The claim carried the ring of exaggeration but, as Blum soon learned, Miami is a city of startling assertions: that no matter where you live, a drug dealer lives nearby; that the revenues from drug trafficking are greater than those from tourism, exports, health care, and all other legitimate businesses combined; that *most* of the currency in circulation in Miami carries traces of cocaine.

From the newspapers, and from talking to people in law enforcement, Blum learned that there were police officers in Miami and in some of its satellite cities in Dade County who did not always arrest drug traffickers. Instead they stole the traffickers' cocaine, and sometimes they killed them. They also stole confiscated drugs from the police property department and confiscated drug money from the police safe. As a result, some were millionaires. True, some were also in jail, but at least they could afford the fat fees paid in cash to the best criminal defense lawyers, many of whom were once Miami's best prosecutors. They could also afford the services of private detectives who knew how to find flaws in the prosecution's case; the best of them were once some of the best narcotics detectives in town.

But the smell of corruption extended far beyond that. It seemed to Blum that there was scarcely a police department in the whole of Dade County that was not under investigation or that was not investigating itself, and that there was scarcely a federal law enforcement agency that had not been shaken by drug-related scandal. Then there were judges who had taken bribes from traffickers, and a city official who sat on the board of a bank that laundered drug money. Blum was told that traffickers regularly bought zoning permits for the office buildings and shopping malls in which they invested some of their proceeds; they paid city and county employees to search the waste bins in sensitive departments; and, they contributed generously to the re-election funds of some prominent local politicians. A writer for *The Miami Herald* had once said that a good day at city hall was one on which the FBI did not arrive with a subpoena—and Blum thought he was only half joking.

All of this was going on in a place that, as Blum well knew, had the greatest concentration of law enforcement manpower and resources ever assembled in the United States to tackle a specific problem of crime. Besides the twenty-eight municipal police forces in Dade County, each of which had its own narcotics squad, and specialized units of the Metro-Dade Police Department, the Florida Department of Law Enforcement, and the Florida Marine Patrol, there was a list of federal agencies and departments engaged in what Washington called "the war

on drugs" that was as long as Jack Blum's arm: the US Customs
Service, the Coast Guard, and the US Navy; the Drug Enforcement Administration (DEA), the FBI, the IRS, and the CIA; the
Bureau of Alcohol, Tobacco and Firearms; the Secret Service,
the departments of Justice and Treasury, the Border Patrol, and
the Immigration and Naturalization Service (INS). To coordinate the efforts of this exceptional army, there was the South
Florida Task Force, reporting directly to Vice-President George
Bush. Yet in February 1987, five years after "the war" began,
there was more cocaine on America's streets than there had
ever been, and it was cheaper and purer, and more people were
using it. Those who were primarily responsible for these conditions were not in jail, nor even sought in their own countries.
Understanding that phenomenon, and its causes, was the mission that took Jack Blum to Miami.

He began his investigation—in effect, his education—at the
Metropolitan Correctional Center in western Dade County, on
what used to be swampland. He drove there from Miami in a
rental car that he had difficulty in parking because the prison
lot was filled with Porsches and BMWs and other top-of-the-
line examples of automobile engineering: "It's lawyers' day," a
guard explained. Once inside, Blum sat in a small visitors'
room and carefully took notes as one of the prisoners, a former
drug smuggler, calmly recounted a story which, if true, perhaps explained why the federal government had so comprehensively failed to win the war on drugs: because the federal
government—or elements of it—was itself actively involved in
drug trafficking.

In a small but expensive house by the water in Miami's Coconut Grove, Blum listened to another former smuggler, who had
never been to jail, describe how he and others had literally
bought a sovereign nation that sits just fifty miles off the coast
of Florida; how members of a government supposedly friendly
to the United States had allowed its territory to be used for the
transshipment of tons of cocaine en route to America, and
profited from it. Yet the US State Department still supported
that government, and even made excuses for it. Blum, who is
far from being an advocate of bellicose or belligerent foreign
policy, eventually closed his notebook and told the smuggler

that if his allegations were true, then the United States should mount an invasion.

In coffee shops and bars and dimly lit restaurants, law enforcement officials told Blum what they would not say in their offices: that the head of the armed forces in Panama was up to his neck in drug trafficking yet he counted among his friends the State Department, the CIA, and even the DEA. They also told Blum that despite five years of effort and the expenditure of enormous sums of money, they had failed to even identify most of the people who organize and direct the massive cocaine trade: Colombians who are known collectively as the Cartel. And of those leaders of the Cartel they had managed to identify—and harry and pursue and indict—only one was in jail. The rest were free and very much in business. They had intimidated the government of their own country into virtual submission. And if the rumors were true, they were still sufficiently potent to be able to send the US Attorney for the Southern District of Florida into hiding, for fear of his life.

On the plane back to Washington, D.C., Jack Blum drafted the first report of his investigation, which attempted to summarize what he had been told. The next day he tore it up. He was afraid that any senator who read it would find its contents unbelievable; that they would say, "Poor old Jack's been in the sun too long." He did not really believe it himself.

Now he knows better.

PART ONE

THE COCAINE EXPLOSION

In Colombia and Bolivia, cocaine
trafficking was revolutionized. And on
the streets of Miami, there was war.

1

The Kingdom of the Ochoas

On a hillside near the northwestern Colombian city of Medellín, in the shade of jagged, bluish mountains, is a handsome country estate where herds of cattle graze on lush grass and purebred horses are free to roam. *Finca la Loma,* "the ranch on the hill," is swept by light breezes from the Cordillera Central and enjoys a climate which is like a year-long English summer's day.

The inhabitants of this pleasant retreat are the Ochoas, an old family of cattle breeders and landowners. Headed by Fabio Ochoa, one of the wealthiest and most influential men in the province of Antioquia, the Ochoas are a close-knit family. Don Fabio, as he is known to all, and Doña Margoth Vásquez de Ochoa, the family's tiny and wizened matriarch, insist that when their six children, their children's spouses, and their children's children are at home, they all sit down to eat together every day.

The Ochoas present themselves as a large, aristocratic Catholic family of good, old stock, directly descended from the second wave of settlers to Colombia—mostly refugees from the Basque region of Spain—who founded Medellín in the Río Aburrá valley in 1616. These early Spanish settlers encountered fierce resistance from small groups of seminomadic Indians of the region who chose to hang themselves rather than become slaves. Some tribes were entirely annihilated; others abandoned their homes and land, as well as an extensive network of

25

gold mines, some of which are still productive three centuries later. Thus, the Ochoas of Antioquia trace their ancestry back to pure-blooded Spaniards who rarely intermarried with hostile Indians and whose community grew exponentially.

The Ochoas made their first fortune from cattle raising, as any one of them will tell you. According to family folklore, Don Fabio's grandfather, Abelardo Ochoa of Salgar (a small town south of Medellín), received the highest distinction offered by the Colombian government, the *Cruz de Boyacá,* for his enterprise in importing new types of cattle from the Netherlands to strengthen local strains. Further back in time, Abelardo's father, Tulio, raised the finest purebred racehorses in Antioquia.

Continuing the traditions of his ancestors, Fabio Ochoa, the still-dapper but now corpulent paterfamilias, keeps one of the finest stables of horses anywhere, and spends much of his time buying thoroughbreds to stock it. The courteous old gentleman—shod, clad, and hatted entirely in white—is a familiar sight at almost every horse fair in Colombia. But, as he is desperately afraid of flying, Don Fabio must travel extremely long distances by road in automobiles that have been specially adapted to accommodate his bulk. He is rarely seen without his wife on his arm, or without a security guard of a dozen young men around him.

The Ochoa family business is inextricably tied to bullfighting and Don Fabio has invested, along with other local grandees, in a bullring near *Finca la Loma.* There, one of his sons, his namesake, often demonstrates his skills on horseback as a picador, whose part in the drama is to enrage the bull and weaken its shoulder muscles with a lance.

The Ochoas have three daughters and three sons. Fabio, at age thirty, is the youngest and the best looking. His reputation as a skillful rider extends throughout Colombia and to Spain, where he buys most of his horses for undisclosed sums of money, and where the family had an aircraft customized to transport them. Young Fabio also has a well-publicized reputation as a philanthropist. He is committed to offering food and shelter to thousands of Medellín's street urchins.

The eldest brother, Juan David, in his early forties, prefers motor cars. He owns a prized collection of fine performance automobiles and tinkers with them whenever he has the time. He is quiet and exceptionally reserved, and prefers those social engagements where only family and very close friends are present.

The middle son, and by far the most prominent, is thirty-eight-year-old Jorge Luis. He is small and stocky, with a full head of black wavy hair and a trim mustache. He likes to wear fine clothes and gold jewelry, and enjoys elegant restaurants. As much if not more than anybody in the family, Jorge's passion is for horses and bullfighting. He owns large tracts of land in Medellín where young horses are reared and trained, and a horse-breeding farm near Bogotá. In the northern district of Repelón, not far from the old colonial city of Cartagena on Colombia's Atlantic coast, he owns an arena where young bulls are initiated and prepared for their eventual slaughter. The arena sits in the middle of Ochoa's *Hacienda Veracruz,* a vast ranch that incorporates several small towns, a private zoo, and a paved airstrip long enough to accomodate commercial airliners.

Ochoa travels frequently: to Panama, where he keeps much of his money and where he obtains passports and identity papers, and major credit cards in any name he chooses; to Brazil, where he has made some of his largest investments; and above all, to Spain, the fatherland.

The Ochoas' obsession with things Spanish—bullfighting, Spanish horses, Spanish art (Don Fabio has bought several Picassos)—is typical of the Colombian nouveaux riches. Despite their claims to pure Spanish descent untainted by Indian blood, the hallmark of Colombian aristocracy, nouveaux riches is what the Ochoas are; part of a peculiar subculture which has flourished in Medellín in the last decade.

Set high on a saddle of rock, Medellín, Colombia's second largest city, was once renowned for its unrivaled production of orchids; it is now better known for the violence of its inhabitants. Since the late 1970s and throughout the 1980s, homicides in Medellín have averaged five per day. People are killed not only in back alleyways and on isolated roads, but on busy street corners—with occasional massacres of up to ten people at a time—during funeral ceremonies for murdered relatives, and at Sunday mass. "This is a city at war," said one overworked physician.

In fact, much like Chicago, Detroit, or New York during Prohibition, Medellín has nurtured its own version of *La Cosa Nostra—la mafia criolla,* as the locals call their own brand of gangsterism—over which the Ochoas preside. Along with its modern office blocks, majestic views of the surrounding hills, and brightly lit cafés, Medellín has a school for pickpockets who, at one time or another, have plagued most of the world's major cities. It is also a place where assassins are trained in a variety of techniques such as *asesino de la moto:* one man steers a motorbike while the passenger, riding pillion, delivers the fatal blow.

The reason for the violence and the gangsters is that many of the inhabitants of Medellín have invested the same single-minded effort they once put into mining gold, growing coffee, producing textiles, or smuggling contraband into developing a new source of prosperity: cocaine. By the most conservative estimates, every year forty-five tons of cocaine are channeled through Medellín to the United States; ten more tons, usually of inferior quality, go to Europe.

Medellín, in short, is the boiler-room of the international cocaine trade, and the Ochoas of Antioquia are among a handful of families that dominate it. "Bomb Medellín," said one veteran agent of the DEA in Miami, "and the war on drugs is over."

By commercial airliner, Medellín is a mere two hours from Miami. The city is served by one of the most modern airports in Latin America, a fortuitous fact since the approach to the airport is hair-raising. As a plane prepares for landing, it has to negotiate imposing hillsides. The noise of the landing gear locking into place may suggest an imminent touchdown, but there is no flat stretch of land—let alone an airport—in sight. There are more sharp turns and another daunting hillside to avoid before the pilot finally sees the runway. Landings were even worse at the old terminal, which was situated in the middle of town, 4,500 feet above sea level. This may explain why Don Fabio is so afraid of flying.

The Kingdom of the Ochoas

Less than an hour from the airport, around an unexpected bend, the first glimpse of Medellín is of *Cinturones de Miseria.* This aptly named scattering of settlements resulted from a mass flight from the countryside prompted by *La Violencia,* the bloody nationwide civil war that lasted from 1946 to 1957. Antioquia and its neighboring provinces bore the brunt of the violence, and the road from the airport passes through two of its most lasting memorials: *Comuna Nororiental* and *Comuna Noroccidental*—huge shanty towns infested with poverty, drugs, violent crime, and prostitution. What people call "homes" here are unhealthy shacks, not fit for habitation, lying next to open sewage canals.

Downtown Medellín is a tribute to noise and disorder, bisected by wide and busy avenues, where crossing the street safely is an art. Hundreds of privately run buses stop at random, collecting more and more passengers until they hang from doors and windows. Life on the sidewalks is intense and loud, with street vendors working in the shadows of modern skyscrapers, offering everything for sale from dogs and underwear to herbal remedies. Churches, which meant so much in the past, stand almost empty, their precincts no longer the meeting place of friends and lovers, but the active hub of petty criminals, alcoholics, and drug pushers and abusers. The chaotic *Parque de Berrío,* opposite Medellín's revered cathedral, has become a sanctuary for everything that the imposing building it faces so bitterly opposes.

Most of the park's habitués live west of the downtown in *Barrio Antioquia,* unquestionably Medellín's most dangerous zone. Declared a red-light district several decades ago and located next to the old airport, *Barrio Antioquia* harbors prostitutes of both sexes and people dispossessed of any values. The perpetrators of the most shocking crimes in Medellín come, almost always, from *Barrio Antioquia,* and it was largely emigrés from this slum who served in the vicious "Cocaine Wars" experienced by both Miami and New York City between 1979 and 1982. Together with the district of Itagüí in southern Medellín, *Barrio Antioquia* is the easy recruiting ground of paid killers. Customers interested in a *trabajito*—"a little job"—can stop, literally, at any corner and recruit an assassin.

Fees vary: $100 for an unfaithful lover; $20,000 for a government minister. The potential killer usually demands a photograph of the victim and asks about habits, place of work, and so forth, then, depending on the difficulty of the assignment, sets the price. Because the *barrio* is also infested with confidence tricksters, it is acceptable for customers to require a *muerto de prueba,* a test killing, that can be of anybody.

There are, of course, large areas of Medellín where the prevailing atmosphere is of normalcy: apartment blocks where working families and young professionals struggle to give their children a straight start and hope for the best; office blocks where normal businesses are conducted, though rarely in isolation from drug trafficking and its subsidiary crimes; universities where young people question the validity of instant rewards and easy money, but often around a table on which sit lines of cocaine. That is all because the temptation to become a part of Medellín's largest industry is enormous and apparent: the visible dividing line is the Medellín River, and, across it, the tree-lined paradise of *El Poblado.*

The main boulevard of *El Poblado* is flanked by exclusive restaurants, bars, boutiques, and art galleries, and it is invariably jammed with the latest imported automobiles bearing sticker prices that very few Colombians can afford. The spectacular mansions and apartment buildings on *Las Diagonales* and *Las Lomas* seem to be replicas of the palatial homes that can be seen on such American television programs as "Dallas" or "Dynasty," and some of them bear those names. Colombia's best architects and designers have been hired to blend Italian marble facades with huge bullet-proof windows. There are white stucco villas obviously inspired by location shots on "Miami Vice," and starker, more modern houses built of brick and largely concealed by thick woods. Almost every house in *El Poblado* is surrounded by a high fence and guarded by heavily armed men of the kind who ask questions later.

For entertainment, *Poblado* residents can drive up a hill to restaurants such as Kevin's, which have stunning views of Medellín and its surroundings. Kevin's offers fine wines, gourmet food, and, ensuring the privacy of their conversations, cellular telephones for every diner. (Cellular telephones cost up to

$10,000 apiece in Colombia.) Outside the restaurant's main door, young men wearing awkwardly knotted ties keep an eye on their employers through glass walls. Under their arms they carry elongated bags containing powerful submachine guns. The obsession with security in *El Poblado* is understandable because many, if not most, of its residents—including the Ochoas, who have a family pied-à-terre there—are members of the flourishing cocaine mafia. Their potential enemies include kidnappers, guerrillas, money-hungry policemen, corrupt army officers, and each other.

To the people who live on the wrong side of the Medellín River, those who succeed in crossing it are known as *los mági-cos,* the magicians. "All of a sudden they have a house in *El Poblado,* an apartment in colonial Cartagena, another in Miami, the latest Mercedes-Benz for him, the latest BMW for her, a house in the country, horses, boats, you name it," said a young university professor. "If that isn't magic, what is?"

Very few of Medellín's two million inhabitants remain wholly untouched by the magic. "There is no family in this town that is not implicated either through a brother, a cousin, or a relative," said a local observer. "And my relatives," added a young professional, "keep telling me to join them."

Carlos Julio Gómez Gutiérrez ("Papi" as he is known to his friends), a trafficker who claims to speak for the most powerful cocaine families including the Ochoas, argues that drug money has created thousands of jobs in light industry and on construction sites and ranches. "And we want to create more jobs," said one of his assistants in a television interview. "Real jobs, not the type that governments always promise." The claim is corroborated by economists and researchers in Medellín, who add that cocaine traffickers also support an army of runners, drivers, bodyguards, and assassins. Indirectly, they support bankers, accountants, lawyers, realtors, builders, shopkeepers, and others. "They pay good money, and I take it," said Luis Mesa, an interior designer who has done work for all the leading traffickers. "And they never ask for credit."

Their economic power reaches far beyond Medellín. Just how much drug money is repatriated to Colombia is anybody's guess, but a senior official of *Banco de la República* readily admits its importance: "We need that money to keep the economy going. That's a sad but unequivocal reality."

But there is also a dark side to the magic. Medellín's traffickers have established control over the city and its authorities through fear. No criticism is brooked: when *El Espectador,* Colombia's second largest newspaper, published a series of articles in the summer of 1983 about one of the city's most prominent mafiosos, an army of men simply confiscated all copies of the offending paper sent to Medellín's vendors and distributors. They terrorize debtors and eliminate officials and critics who they perceive are out to get them. In Bogotá they murdered the minister of justice and, subsequently, the judge who was investigating his death; they killed the head of the national drugs squad, the editor of *El Espectador,* and the attorney general. They regard no one as beyond their reach: a former government minister who had offended them and was given a diplomatic posting abroad for his own safety, was hunted down in January 1987, and shot five times—in Budapest, Hungary. In all, the traffickers are estimated to have killed more than two hundred Colombian government officials, police officers, soldiers, judges, and journalists; almost one hundred have died in Medellín alone.

No section of Colombian society has been more intimidated than the judiciary, which, even without the constant threat of violence, operates under enormous strains. Poorly paid judges labor under absurd workloads: any one of the thirty "superior" judges in Bogotá might have as many as *three thousand* unsolved violent deaths on his docket, with, if he is lucky, firm suspects in no more than fifty of those cases. (In the Colombian legal system it is normally the judiciary and not the police who investigate crime.) Bringing a case to trial can take five years and then, in all probability, the witnesses will not show up. In the overwhelming majority of cases there is no indictment and no trial. Even those who are supposed to administer it describe the Colombian justice system as "a joke."

To that chaos, drug traffickers have added the elements of corruption and brutal harassment. Those judges who cannot be bought are threatened by means of "telephone terrorism" and, if they persist, are killed, no matter what their rank. Eleven of

Colombia's twenty-four Supreme Court justices discounted warnings not to enforce an extradition treaty with the United States that was aimed specifically at drug traffickers; in November 1985, they paid with their lives in a massacre at the courthouse. To nobody's surprise, the justices who have replaced them are mainly opposed to extradition—and who can blame them.

Occasionally the major traffickers have suffered defeats—even the Ochoas of Antioquia: Don Fabio has been arrested, though briefly; in December 1987 Jorge, his most prominent son, was in prison in Colombia, facing the threat of extradition to the United States until a judge set him free—an act that outraged the Reagan administration. But even if Jorge Ochoa was extradited, such action is now unlikely to make much difference to Colombia's cocaine trade. A DEA official, who will not be named, says there is no hope for the country; it has become "custom-made for criminals." Gonzalo Guillén, a Colombian investigative journalist, claims there was a time when almost every Colombian was disgusted by the traffickers and their actions; now, he says, everybody "and I mean *everybody,*" is attempting to share in the fruits of the trade.

Another observer in Medellín who insists on anonymity reports a conversation with a city official in which he asked about the complicity of the authorities in cocaine trafficking. "How far does it go?" said the official. "If you tell me that the church is involved, I could not deny it."

What the Ochoas now preside over, with two other Colombians, is a loose federation of tightly controlled underground corporations they call simply *la compañía,* "the company," but that is known to the outside world as the Cartel. In the last five years it has become structured and highly organized.

There are groups that specialize in obtaining the necessary raw materials and delivering them, in precise quantities, to select clandestine laboratories throughout Colombia and lately, in Panama, Venezuela, Argentina, Brazil, and even the United States. There are groups responsible for security and, if necessary, for subverting law enforcement agents, the military, judges, lawyers, politicians, and even former presidents. There are yet other groups specializing in the transportation of the refined cocaine to its markets around the world, principally America.

But these days the Cartel's interests extend far beyond that. Once their cocaine successfully reaches the United States or Europe, profit margins multiply several times over. Because of that, the Ochoas and others have seized—often through great violence—a major stake in distribution, relying on a pool of thousands of Colombian aliens in Miami, New York, Chicago, and Los Angeles—and, increasingly, in Madrid, London, Paris, Hamburg, Rome, and Rotterdam.

These supporting groups, organized by special envoys from Medellín, work under a strict code of discipline, from the need to survive in a hostile environment. Security arrangements are entrusted to experts, such as Carlos Madrid Palacios, a former Venezuelan naval officer whom the Ochoas sent to Miami to "sort out" their operation after they had suffered a number of seizures and rip-offs. Madrid Palacios developed a "plan of action" that he wrote down and that came to be known as the "traffickers' bible." It left little to chance:

Houses:
The house represents the operating center 'par excellence.' Therefore it must have: Functionality, comfort and, above all, security.

Who shall subsidize the house?
It must not be left up to the financial discretion of who is occupying it. The company must provide for all the expenses pertaining to it, making sure that it complies with all the details necessary for the tasks to be carried out. Therefore, the rent, payment of services and maintenance will be taken care of by the company.

Who shall live in the house?
Preferably a couple with children. Said couple must be medium age so as to justify the investment and because of his age the man can be used for distributing activities.

The Kingdom of the Ochoas

Obligations of the occupant:

To live a normal life. To try to leave the house always at the same time (to go to a predetermined location where he shall receive instructions for delivery).

Try to imitate an American in all his habits, like mow the lawn, wash the car, etc. He must not have any extravagant social events in the house, *but may have an occasional barbecue, inviting trusted relatives.*

It is recommended that every occupant have a well-maintained dog. Preferably a great dane. Therefore, the house must be selected with the appropriate conditions.

Minimum standards which a house must follow:

Residential location, preferably in a low traffic street.

Lots of green space.

Garage for two cars.

Garage hopefully not within the neighbors' sight.

Swimming pool (arguable).

Who must give the O.K. for the selection of the home:

Without any argument, the prospective occupant. His point of view and his hunches must be respected. He must never be imposed upon, only recommended.

Who must come and go into the house?

Ideally it should be whoever lives there. If that is not possible then only one person.

What must the occupants of the house have ready?

Tickets for another city in the U.S. and for abroad.

Money for emergencies (it can't be used for anything else).

A predetermined address to go to in case of emergency (refuge).

A trusted lawyer must be introduced to him. He must have all the telephone numbers where [the lawyer] can be reached.

A vehicle ready for escaping.

Things the occupant of a house must not do:

Fill it up with unnecessary furniture which he will be sorry to leave behind in an emergency.

Give his address to strangers.

Not stay in the house unless during activities of the company.

Use work vehicles for personal activities.

Go out with his wife, leaving the house unguarded when there is something to guard.

The Cartel invests heavily in the latest communications equipment such as state-of-the-art radios and pocket-sized digital encryption gadgets which encode a message so thoroughly it might take up to eighteen months to crack it, even with the aid of powerful computers. Mechanics and pilots outfit smuggling aircraft with long-range navigation equipment, radio altimeters, beacon-interrogating digital radars, and communications scramblers. The Cartel has ensured, through bribery and pay-offs, that there are no countries in Central or South America where those planes cannot land safely.

In short, from their ranch on the hill, the Ochoas have molded what was once a group of disparate and rival gangs into a sophisticated, determined, and ruthless multinational conglomerate. The Cartel has effectively brought Colombia to its knees through fear and intimidation, and, as we will see, its effect on the patterns and rewards of criminal activity has extended far beyond Colombia's borders.

The Third Scourge of Mankind

It is often argued in Washington, particularly on Capitol Hill, that the only way to curtail Colombia's cocaine traffickers is to deny them the raw material of their trade: the leaf of the coca plant. Coca does not grow abundantly in Colombia. It is better suited to the more fertile slopes and valleys of the higher ranges of the Andes to the south, in Bolivia and Peru. So, Washington has long believed, the solution to the cocaine problem lies in the hands of the governments of Bolivia and Peru: if they were to strictly limit or better still, eliminate the cultivation of the coca plant, they would limit or eliminate cocaine.

Faced with a carrot—the promise of increased American aid—and a stick—the threat to reduce or cut off what aid exists—the governments concerned have, from time to time, taken steps to reduce the coca harvest. The belief persists that they could do much more. But there are simple truths, not widely understood in Washington, that defy such an easy solution.

Coca is the oldest stimulant known to man and chewing the dried leaf to extract the alkaloids it contains has sustained humankind in the Andes since prehistoric times. In Peru, gourds containing coca leaves, and even a partially chewed quid of coca, have been unearthed from burial middens dating back to 2100 B.C. In Colombia, some of the idols standing in San Agustín's mysterious Valley of the Statues, idols dating back to 600 B.C., display the characteristic distended cheek of the coca chewer.

In more modern times, the great Inca civilization believed the plant was divine, brought from heaven by the first Inca emperor, Manco Capac. Throughout the Inca empire, from Ecuador to Chile, coca was at the center of their religious and social system. The right to chew it was a sovereign gift, bestowed on priests, doctors, young warriors, the relay runners who traveled 150 miles a day to deliver messages, and the scholars who kept the empire's accounts. Solid gold coca sprigs adorned the temples of the sun, whose altars could be approached only by those with coca in their mouths. If coca was the last thing a dying man tasted, he went to heaven.

Even today it has a touch of the miraculous. Coca is the gift that Peruvian Indians give to the parents of a prospective bride. It is the talisman put under the cornerstones of new houses and it is an abundant source of vitamins. Throughout South America, an estimated eight million people chew coca leaves, and millions more drink *mate de coca,* "coca tea," which is sold in almost every supermarket.

So the people of the Andes do not take kindly to foreigners telling them they should not grow coca. The first to try were the Spanish conquistadores. In 1567 the Council of Lima, established by Spain, condemned coca as "a worthless object, fitted for the misuse and superstition of the Indians." During the rule of Francisco de Toledo, the fifth Spanish viceroy, over seventy ordinances were issued against coca.

But as Father de Acosta, a Jesuit missionary in Peru, wrote in 1590: "I think it works and gives force and courage to the Indians, for we see the effects which cannot be attributed to imagination, so as to go some days without meat, but only a handful of coca . . ." It was not long before the Spanish were paying the Indian mine workers in coca leaves—and the Church collected tithes from them in coca.

Almost 400 years later when, under US pressure, the Peruvian government began a coca eradication program and prohibited the chewing of coca below an altitude of 1,500 feet (it is beneficial in combating altitude sickness), the country faced strikes and demonstrations in the coca-producing centers of Quillabamba and Tingo María. In 1980 in Cuzco, with the blessing of the local archbishop, the coca growers held the first of what has become an annual congress. By 1984, Cuzco's renowned agricultural college had become the focus of scientific opposition to American "crop substitution" projects, pointing out that one of the suggested substitutes, tobacco, was vastly more harmful to mankind than coca.

Cocaine, the principal alkaloid in the coca leaf, was also once regarded as practically divine. Who first isolated cocaine remains a matter of controversy because, by the mid-nineteenth century, there were a number of doctors and scientists in Europe conducting experiments to understand the remarkable qualities of coca. Some of them clearly enjoyed the work. "Borne on the wings of two coca leaves, I flew about in the spaces of 77,438 worlds, each one more splendid than the other," wrote Dr. Paolo Mantegazza, an eminent Italian neurologist in 1859. "I prefer a life of ten years with coca to one of a hundred thousand without it."

In any event, cocaine had been successfully isolated by 1880, when a German army doctor prescribed it for Bavarian troops on autumn maneuvers and noted a "marvelous increase in their energy and endurance." The doctor's report aroused the curiosity of Sigmund Freud in Vienna, who induced one of his young interns to experiment further with cocaine. The intern discovered that it had qualities useful for surgery: the ability to numb tissue while simultaneously constricting blood vessels, which limited bleeding. As a result, the discovery of the first local anesthetic was announced at a medical conference in Heidelberg, Germany, in September 1884. Freud, in the first of five essays on cocaine, eulogized it as "a magical drug." He recommended it for the treatment of depression, nervous exhaustion, hysteria, hypochondria, severe anemia, phthisis, and febrile diseases; as an aphrodisiac; and as a cure for syphilis, asthma and alcoholism. The pharmaceutical companies were swamped with orders.

Freud's enthusiasm for cocaine was soon tempered by his realization that "for some people" it had awful side effects. He gave it to a friend, Ernst Fleischl von Marxow, a fellow doctor, in the hope of weaning him off morphine. The "cure" succeeded, but only in transferring von Marxow's addiction from morphine to cocaine. Within a year he was injecting himself with one gram a day—one hundred times the original dose—and eventually suffered acute cocaine poisoning and psychotic delusions in which he imagined white snakes creeping over his skin. But Freud's reservations about cocaine's negative side came too late to save his friend—and other users. In as little time as word took to spread, coca and cocaine achieved enormous popularity in Europe and America, and Freud was accused of launching "the third scourge of mankind." (The first two scourges, according to his accusers, were alcohol and morphine.)

In Paris a young Corsican chemist named Angelo Mariani put coca leaf extract in wine and, between 1891 and 1913, collected thirteen volumes of testimonials from satisfied consumers of Vin Mariani. They included the czar and czarina of Russia, the Prince and Princess of Wales, the king of Norway and Sweden (then combined in unhappy union), King Norodom of Cambodia, the commanding general of the British army, and Pope Leo XIII, who awarded Mariani the Papal Gold Medal. Over 8,000 doctors, including physicians to all the royal households of Europe, testified to the wine's virtues, along with great artists, writers and performers of the time: H.G. Wells, Jules Verne, Émile Zola, Henrik Ibsen, Sarah Bernhardt, and Auguste Rodin. From America, Thomas Edison sent a note and a picture of himself for Mariani's endorsement album, and President McKinley's secretary wrote to say that a case of Vin Mariani had been enthusiastically received.

In Atlanta, Georgia, John S. Pemberton, a manufacturer of patent medicine, adapted Mariani's idea. He combined coca leaf extract with caffeine-rich kola nuts to produce a sweet syrup that he carbonated. Thus the world received its first taste of what Pemberton promoted as his "intellectual beverage and temperance drink": Coca-Cola. There were soon half a dozen imitation drinks, and coca cigarettes. Cocaine became an ingredient in hundreds if not thousands of elixirs, cordials, and quack medicines. In England, William Martindale, who was to become president of the Pharmaceutical Society of Great Britain, recommended an "infusion of coca" as a substitute for tea and coffee; he thought the use of it, in moderation, might prolong life.

There were those, however, who preferred to *enhance* life—or so they thought.

Concentrated cocaine, slammed into the bloodstream by injection, by snorting into the mucous membranes of the nasal passages, or by inhaling its vapors, has an almost immediate and unique effect upon the brain: it dramatically accelerates the speed of transmission of messages between the billions of neurons that comprise the central nervous system. In most people, the first result is a "cocaine high"—a sensation of euphoria and dazzling clarity of thought. "Like being on the roof of the world," is a typical description from first-time users; "like a thousand orgasms," is another. But the human brain is not meant to race at such prodigious speed and it is equipped with a safety mechanism. Overactivity of the neurotransmitters causes the brain to produce chemicals, called neuro blockers, which wash over the nerve cells and suppress their turmoil, as a wave of water might douse a fire. Because the amount of brain activity caused by cocaine is so extreme, so, too, is its reaction: swamped by neuro blockers, the nerve cells have difficulty communicating with each other at all.

The resulting "cocaine crash" can be as dramatic and almost as abrupt as the "high," though for some it is no worse than a mild hangover. For others, the journey down from "the roof of the world" results in acute psychological distress: depression, anxiety, and irritability—and a craving for more cocaine to relieve the very symptoms it has caused. Some consumers appear to develop a tolerance for cocaine, and, in the lexicon of medical researchers, become "recreational users" who seem to suffer no great harm. Others become psychologically addicted to the point of compulsion: they cannot eat or sleep; they lose interest in family, friends, and sex; they "binge" on cocaine, using it continuously for days at a time.

Cocaine is a drug that laboratory animals, given unlimited access, will select over and over again in preference to food and water, until they die. Few humans have that kind of unlimited access to cocaine, but, among those that do, there are reported instances of similar compulsion. In short, cocaine has the potential to steal the mind; there is no other drug like it.

Of course, little of this was known to nineteenth-century

medical science. But by 1895 there had been sufficient reports of systemic intoxication and deaths—most commonly from respiratory failure—to cause cocaine to be included in the United States Codex as a "poisonous substance." Added to that injunction were largely scurrilous yet widely published accounts of "coke-crazed" black men raping white women. Most of the propaganda came from segregationists, but such august bodies as the American Pharmaceutical Association endorsed these "findings": "Use of cocaine by negroes in certain parts of the country is simply appalling," the society declared in 1901. "The police officers of questionable districts tell us that the habitués are made wild by cocaine, which they have no difficulty at all in buying." That a survey of Georgia's penal institutions turned up only two cocaine users out of 2,100 black detainees did not deter a Georgia official from asserting that "many of the horrible crimes committed in the southern states by the colored people can be traced directly to the cocaine habit."

The mood of the times was with him and in 1906 Congress passed the Pure Food and Drug Act, which effectively ended the sale and use of cocaine as an ingredient in food products. One result was that The Coca-Cola Company was obliged to remove the cocaine extract from its formula. (Coca-Cola did not, however, cease to depend on the coca leaf for its success: according to two modern-day scientific detectives, George Andrews and David Solomon, the "secret" ingredient of "Classic Coke" is probably cuscohygrine, one of the less potent alkaloids contained in the coca leaf.)

In 1914—the year the creator of *Vin Mariani* died—cocaine was misclassified as a narcotic, and formally banned in the United States by the Harrison Act (misclassified because cocaine is, of course, a stimulant and not a suppressant). The rest of the western world slowly followed suit. By the mid-1930s, cocaine had virtually disappeared from drug literature and from most of the streets. In 1934 Cole Porter captured the American temper in one of his timeless lyrics:

> I get no kick from cocaine.
> I'm sure that if
> I took even one sniff,

It would bore me terrifically, too.
But I get a kick out of you.

But many serious historians of the subject contend that cocaine's decline in popularity had little to do with public opinion and nothing to do with law enforcement. Rather, they say, it was caused by the introduction of synthetic amphetamines, which also stimulate the central nervous system, and which, from the early 1930s, were much cheaper and much more available than cocaine. For a while, and like cocaine, these man-made palliatives enjoyed official grace, and, during World War II, were given to Allied troops in their daily rations.

After the war the official attitude towards amphetamines changed—perhaps inevitably, because there is a constant history of drugs of all kinds being initially tolerated or sanctioned by the state only to be condemned later and eventually restricted or prohibited. Witness morphine, which hundreds of thousands of Allied troops were given during World War I, and then denied, legally, on their return home.

It is because of such official ambivalence that drug traffickers thrive. They do not create markets; they profit by serving markets that already exist but where regular and legal supply has been cut off or prohibited. Their advantage is that their customers—their victims, perhaps—are willing coconspirators in the crime.

There is no better example of a successful conspiracy between traffickers and consumers than Prohibition, the forlorn attempt by a United States government to proscribe the use of alcohol. Prohibition did more than any other single factor to establish organized crime, the Mafia, in America. It was the Mafia that first recognized the potential renaissance of cocaine and the role that might be played by the legendary smugglers of Medellín.

Smuggling has been a major industry in Antioquia, and a way of life, since the first Spanish settlers arrived and began to mine gold. The Spanish crown granted to itself the sole right to buy gold in Colombia, in order to fix the price. Antioquians, therefore, smuggled their gold to Jamaica to sell it, for higher prices, on the open market. In much the same way, contemporary Colombian governments have insisted on a monopoly of coffee in order to regulate and protect what is the country's leading legal export; so, Antioquians smuggle coffee. They also smuggle quinine, tobacco, and emeralds out of the country—and, into the country, home appliances, motor vehicles, electronic equipment, computers, high-fashion clothes, perfumes, and watches, all of which are prohibitively expensive in Colombia because of import duty.

Even so, it came as something of a shock to the citizens of once-pleasant Medellín when, in 1959, two US federal agents arrived in their city to reveal that it had become one axis of international drug trafficking. According to the agents, contraband smugglers from Medellín were regular visitors to Havana, Cuba—the bawdy Havana of pre-Castro days—where they met and mingled with American mobsters. From them they learned that there was a great demand for heroin in the United States, but a serious shortage of supply. There was also a new and burgeoning interest in cocaine, but almost no illicit supply at all.

The men from Medellín could obviously help. From Ecuador they could obtain opium poppies with which to make heroin, and virtually unlimited supplies of coca leaves, with which to make cocaine, from Bolivia and Peru. Plus their smuggling routes and expertise were solidly established. Hence, the first drug laboratories were established in Medellín, supposedly with Mafia money and know-how. The product, mainly heroin, was smuggled to the United States via Havana and Mexico.

Fidel Castro's revolution in Cuba naturally put a dent in that trade, though it never ceased entirely. Then an event occurred in the late 1960s, that, though disastrous for Medellín's official economy, was supremely beneficial to the trafficking trade. Medellín had developed a large textile industry, which accounted for much of its booming prosperity since the early 1940s. Then, almost overnight, punitive import tariffs in Europe and strong competition from emerging nations in the Far East sent the textile industry in Medellín into deep recession. Thousands upon thousands of unemployed textile workers from the city headed for New York, where they sought employment in the garment industry; they slept ten to a room in Queens, and there were so many of them that Antioquians became by far the largest group of Colombian immigrants in the United States.

So, there was no shortage of witnesses from Medellín when America began to experience extraordinary fallout from the Vietnam War: the "flower-power" of the protest generation and blatant advocacy of drug use. At first the "drugs of choice" during the Vietnam era were marijuana, amphetamines, and LSD, which were the ones most readily available. Gradually, as law enforcement agencies began cracking down on these substances, making them more difficult and riskier to buy, a group of people described by medical researchers as "circumstantial users" turned, increasingly, to cocaine.

"Circumstantials" are people in high-stress jobs who say they use drugs in order to perform. Since many of them are professional athletes, popular musicians, and movie actors, they set trends, whether they like it or not. Beginning in 1969, the "circumstantials" endorsed cocaine as though they, like the Incas, thought it was divine.

John Lennon, Taj Mahal, Steppenwolf, and Jefferson Airplane were among those who sang about their own use of cocaine, and in New York a popular radio talk show was called "Kokaine Karma." In California prominent actors including Peter Fonda and Dennis Hopper gave cocaine, or "snow," wide social status by using it openly at parties, and Phil Spector, the record producer, sent Christmas cards bearing the greeting: "A little snow at Xmas time never hurt anyone." Hollywood, the worst offender, produced so many movies in which cocaine was taken that Art Murphy of *Daily Variety* was driven to complain: "Coke scenes are as *de rigueur* as explicit fuck scenes, so numerous these days they are sleep-inducing."

In 1973 the *New York Times* carried more stories about cocaine than it did about heroin, and, in response to the growing alarm, Congress passed tough new laws threatening drug traffickers with the possibility of life imprisonment, without parole. In 1974 the National Household Survey reported that 5.4 million Americans had tried cocaine at least once.

In Medellín the traffickers who attempted to feed this exploding market found they simply could not cope with "gringo" demand.

3

Walsh's Warning

On September 24, 1979, at the headquarters of the Drug Enforcement Administration in Washington, D.C., a young intelligence analyst named Miguel Walsh completed a paper that attempted to describe a startling growth in cocaine trafficking both within and through Colombia. Since the paper was intended for internal purposes, the sources available to him were extensive: the DEA's own voluminous files on seizures and arrests; reports from its agents in the field; Colombian police reports from Bogotá and Medellín; and nitty-gritty reports from confidential informants—"CIs" in the jargon— who trade information for immunity and are sometimes permitted to remain in the trade.

Walsh's resulting paper was part history, part analysis, and was intended to be "the most extensive consolidation of available data" on Colombian cocaine trafficking ever assembled. Above all else, it was a prescient warning of the danger Colombian traffickers posed.

Cocaine trafficking, Walsh wrote, had achieved "quasi-industrial status." It employed thousands of people and had "a substantial spillover effect in many other sectors of Colombian life." Disciplined groups were operating as underground multinational corporations, vertically integrated from clandestine laboratories in Colombia to tightly controlled distribution networks in the United States. Walsh warned of "the critical importance of the venality of government officials, police, judges, lawyers and politicians" who used their power and influence to support the traffickers. Their growing affluence allowed them to employ more and more sophisticated "talent," and "they thus incur increments of power both real and perceived. This is the principal aspect of the current state of narcotics trafficking in Colombia which many individuals find especially disconcerting. The cumulative effect of this problem is such that, in some regions of Colombia, narcotics traffickers command more power and respect than the central government in Bogotá."

Money, of course, was at the root of it—sums of money so vast as to be almost meaningless even to Walsh's sophisticated readers unless reduced to an equation. Employing a hypothetical model developed by other federal government analysts in 1977, Walsh attempted to estimate how much cocaine was flooding into the United States.

Since the leaf of the coca plant is the basic ingredient of cocaine, and since most of the world's coca is grown in Bolivia and Peru, Walsh began by estimating the amount of land those two countries dedicated to coca cultivation. Multiplying by a factor of 1,000 per 2.4 acres gave the amount (in kilos) of coca leaf produced annually. Simple subtraction of the amounts of leaf used for more or less legitimate purposes—medical use, Coca-Cola, coca tea, and chewing—gave the amount "unaccounted for" and therefore available for cocaine production. That amount, according to Walsh's calculations, was some thirty-one million kilos of coca leaf.

Refining coca leaves into cocaine hydrochloride is a three-step process. In the initial stage at least 200 kilos of coca leaf are needed to produce one kilo of crude coca paste. The next step, producing a kilo of cocaine base, requires 2.5 kilos of coca paste. The final transition, turning base into hydrochloride, requires just one kilo of base for each kilo of cocaine hydrochloride.

Walsh, adopting the natural conservatism of his profession, allowed for careless chemists and "slippage" and "wastage." He allowed for accidents and seizures and stockpiling. He allowed for much more "domestic production" of cocaine hydrochloride in Peru and Bolivia than any extant intelligence estimate suggested was the case.

Having allowed for every contingency, Walsh's paper estimated the annual production of cocaine hydrochloride in Colombia at 13,800 kilos, or a little under 14 metric tons. To demonstrate how much those kilos were worth, and the fabulous profits to be earned from them, Walsh next devised a model of his own.

Coca leaves cost fifty cents per kilo in Bolivia or Peru: though more than one thousand kilos of leaves were required for each kilo of cocaine—and more than three acres of land to grow them—the maximum cost of the basic ingredient was $625. By the time they had been turned into paste, then base, and finally into one kilo of cocaine hydrochloride, in Colombia the leaves had become worth $9,550, an increase in value of 1528 percent; modest by what was to come. While in transit to the United States—smuggled aboard an airliner or delivered by boat or plane to some convenient off-shore island—one kilo of cocaine was worth $24,000, according to Walsh's figures. Once inside the United States the value rose to $37,000.

At this stage, the mathematics of production were reversed: whereas before entering the United States, each step in the *manufacturing* process reduced the amount of product, each step in the *distribution* process increased it.

The one kilo of almost pure cocaine delivered to Miami or New York would be adulterated or "cut" with lactose, or some other neutral substance, by the "wholesaler" and sold to a "distributor" as *two* kilos, 50 percent pure, for $37,000 each. The distributor in turn would "cut" it again to produce four kilos. At the next step in the chain, the "retailer" would turn that into eight kilos, selling them at $70 or more a gram. What had started out as $625 worth of coca leaves could fetch $560,000 on the streets of America. Walsh calculated that if Colombia was indeed processing fourteen metric tons of cocaine a year, it was producing $7,784,000,000 a year in potential revenues from raw material that cost a mere $8 million. Seen in that context, cocaine had to be the most valuable commodity on earth.

The warnings contained in Walsh's paper created no great stir in Washington, though they should have. Perhaps the careful language of his paper served to disguise too well the truly alarming message it contained, which in essence was this: in just three years, the amount of land in Bolivia given over to the cultivation of coca had *more than trebled.* In other words, those of another DEA intelligence analyst speaking in 1986: "Someone out there had planted one heck of a lot of trees."

Indeed they had—and vastly more than Walsh's already alarming figures imagined. Within one year of his report, the best estimate of the size of the Bolivian coca crop was 58,275 metric tons, almost twice his figure. What his paper described as "a classic commodity market in a state of equilibrium, with adequate supply, steady (if slightly increasing) demand, and price stability," was about to explode.

Bolivia is twice the size of Spain, the fifth-largest country in South America, yet its population is less than seven million. It is completely landlocked, a place of prodigious mountains and unhealthy valleys that have isolated it from the rest of the world—and, for most of its turbulent history, that have isolated Bolivians from each other.

There are really three Bolivias: the Altiplano, a harsh, strange plateau, much of it at least 13,000 feet above sea level where most of the population lives, and most of whom are Indian; the lower valleys of the Andes, called the Yungas, Bolivia's agricultural heartland and the traditional center for coca growing, where the majority of people are *mestizos* ("of mixed blood"); and then there is the Bolivia of the eastern lowlands, which occupy 70 percent of the country's land area but contain only 20 percent of its people. The principal city of the lowlands is Santa Cruz de la Sierra, founded by the Spanish in 1561, though it more resembles a set built for a Hollywood western. Santa Cruz is the power base of Bolivia's minority "Europeans," who are mainly of Spanish and German descent. In 1975 the Europeans of Santa Cruz decided to plant "one heck of a lot of trees" in the Chaparé valleys of the lowlands.

Until the 1950s Santa Cruz was virtually inaccessible from the capital, La Paz, except by air. (The official capital of Bolivia is Sucre, but all of the instruments of government, save for the Supreme Court, are located in La Paz.) Road and rail links from La Paz to Santa Cruz ended the city's isolation at a fortuitous time because the country's economy was about to enter a steep decline.

Minerals—principally tin—are Bolivia's natural wealth. In

the early 1970s, when the productivity of Bolivia's tin mines began falling, successive Bolivian governments turned increasingly to the newly accessible Santa Cruz region in the hope of finding economic salvation through oil exploration, and sugar and coffee exports. When these attempts to rescue the economy failed, the landowners of Santa Cruz were induced to plant cotton: in 1974, the government-run *Banco Agrícola* invested 52 percent of its liquid resources in new cotton fields in the Santa Cruz region, most of it in unsecured loans. But just as those cotton fields matured, world cotton prices plummeted. As a result, most of *Banco Agrícola's* clients in Santa Cruz went into default. They saved themselves, and perhaps Bolivia, by replanting the cotton fields with coca.

This novel crop substitution program was conducted by the Santa Cruz chapter of *Asociación de Productores de Algodón*, the cotton producers' association made up of large and wealthy landowners. But the crop substitution was on such a colossal scale that it is inconceivable it happened without the knowledge and, at the very least, dereliction of duty of the Bolivian government. For one thing, in order to make transportation of the crop feasible, the producers needed to carry out the first step of the cocaine conversion process, extracting the alkaloids from the leaf and turning them into paste. To do that they needed to import vast quantities of sulfuric acid, alcohol, and acetone. That in itself was a major commercial undertaking which required the aid of the state. The implications of state aid, however, go far beyond that.

Bolivia's president in 1975 was General Hugo Banzer Suárez, a diminutive forty-four-year-old army officer who had seized power in a violent coup in 1971; what was the 188th coup in the 146 years since Bolivia's independence. Banzer, the grandson of German immigrants, was born and raised in Santa Cruz, and as he advanced in the ranks of the army, and then to the presidency, he was careful to maintain good relations with the producers' association in his hometown. As the nation's economic problems overwhelmed him and he was forced to introduce harsh fiscal policies that produced serious labor unrest, he turned more and more to his old friends in Santa Cruz to provide a solution.

When the cotton crop failed, his options had simply run out.

That does not mean Banzer sanctioned Bolivia's contribution to a massive expansion of the cocaine industry; there is no direct evidence of that. But individual members of his government, his army, and even his own family became directly and heavily involved.

The principal architect of the "coca revolution" in Bolivia was Roberto Suárez Gómez, then aged fifty-five, a cattleman with vast estates in Santa Cruz and in the north of the country, on a luxuriant green plateau called the Alto Beni. It may be that Suárez was already a drug dealer because he provided the contacts with the traffickers of Medellín, who were to be the recipients of most of Bolivia's new harvest. His edge in a country so large and so deprived of adequate roads was that he owned perhaps the largest private fleet of aircraft in Bolivia; their original purpose was to transport meat from the Beni region and Santa Cruz to market in La Paz, but they would soon carry other cargoes to different destinations.

Suárez formed a syndicate of well-connected landowners to grow and market coca whose members included: José Roberto Gasser, of German descent like Banzer, and whose family financed Banzer's coup in 1971; and, Guillermo "Willy" Banzer Ojopi, President Banzer's cousin. For logistical support, the Suárez syndicate recruited to its cause the commander of the army garrison in Beni, two army generals, and the head of customs at Santa Cruz.

It takes three years for the coca plant to reach maturity, so it was not until 1978 that the sheer extent of what had been done became apparent. By then, and bowing to great pressure from the United States, President Banzer had signed a United Nations agreement promising to limit what was already considered to be Bolivia's excessive coca crop of 11,800 tons, when domestic consumption required only 4,000 tons. In 1978, a year after he signed that agreement, the crop soared to 35,000 tons.

So perhaps it was sheer embarrassment that persuaded Banzer, in July 1978, to step down as president of Bolivia. By then his private secretary, his son-in-law, his nephew, and his wife had all been arrested for or were suspected of cocaine trafficking in the United States or Canada. And Banzer's attempt to appoint Guillermo, his cousin—and a leading member of Roberto Suárez's syndicate—to the consul's job in Miami had caused outrage at the DEA and a lot of distasteful publicity.

Or, perhaps he wanted to distance himself, and the army, from the opprobrium that was certain to come when Bolivian coca became Colombian cocaine, and hit the streets of America. In announcing his own resignation, President Banzer called for free elections and a return to democracy.

But such faltering steps as Bolivia took towards the restoration of civilian government were abruptly halted on July 17, 1980—one month before that government was to have been inaugurated—when General Luis García Meza staged the 189th coup. With him in power, any doubt about the government's direct involvement in drug trafficking disappeared entirely.

Garciá Meza appointed as his minister of the interior Colonel Luis Arce Gómez, Roberto Suárez's cousin. Arce favored a tightly run ship, and he imported from Argentina military advisers to help him set up an apparatus that would, by terror, stifle any dissent. Meanwhile, under his direction, the Bolivian army entered into arrangements with his cousin and other traffickers whereby they paid a "tax" on their shipments, and were left alone to get on with them.

It was so blatant, and the increase in the world's supply of cocaine so apparent, that the administration of Jimmy Carter and an outraged Congress agreed to suspend all US aid to Bolivia. This move did not matter too much to *some* Bolivians because their earnings from drug trafficking were estimated to be worth four times the country's legal exports. In a speech Arce responded to Washington's protest with what was his customary arrogance: "Complete responsibility for the inherent problem of trade in hallucinogens and the rise in the export of drugs falls on President Carter since, at the present time, having cut aid, he is the sole author of the increase in consumption of cocaine in the United States."

For most Bolivians however, the consequences were disastrous, as normal agriculture went into decline and President García Meza proved himself to be an incompetent administrator. One year and eighteen days after he took power, he was removed from it by his fellow officers, and with Arce, allowed to seek sanctuary in Argentina.

By then the damage had been done.

Coca paste poured into Colombia: direct by air from any of the 3,000 airstrips in Beni; by trucks riding the Pan-American Highway, passing through Peru and Ecuador; by boats sailing up the wild Pacific coast. So much of it reached Medellín that the established traffickers were forced to accept help from almost anybody who cared to join: they became known as *los apuntados* ("the enlisted") and there were hundreds of them.

Don Fabio Ochoa had fallen on hard times and had gone to Venezuela to sell some of his horses, when he received an urgent summons to return home. Jorge, his middle son, had just returned from the United States where he had seen for himself the growing appetite for cocaine. Indeed, he had helped to feed the demand, according to the DEA. In 1977 Ochoa, at the age of twenty-eight, was running the Sea-8 Trading Corporation in Miami, an import-export company that was allegedly bringing into the United States regular loads of cocaine for Ochoa's uncle, Fabio Restrepo Ochoa. In October 1977, Jorge narrowly escaped falling into a trap set by the DEA in the parking lot of a shopping mall. He abandoned his business and apartment in Miami and fled to Medellín where he decided that his own family should get into the lucrative cocaine business. According to local legend at least, he telephoned his father in Venezuela and said: "Papa, come home. The problem's solved." Given Don Fabio's status in Medellín, his extensive contacts, and his large close-knit family, the Ochoas were soon "enlisted" in the trade.

But it was not necessary to be well-connected in order to get a foothold in trafficking, nor, indeed, to achieve spectacular success. Pablo Escobar Gaviria would become a member of the House of Representatives in Bogotá, a legendary social benefactor in Medellín, and, when the Cartel came to be formed, second in importance only to the Ochoas. Yet he got his start as a petty thief.

About the same age as Jorge Ochoa, Escobar was born to parents of more modest means in Rionegro, a small hillside town about twenty-five miles from Medellín. His father was a farmer and his mother a schoolteacher, and he did receive a high school education, which put him above millions of others in Colombia. He was, however, unable to go to university, and entered instead into a criminal career that began with stealing headstones from cemeteries, under the cover of darkness. Escobar and his associates would shave them down to remove the inscriptions and sell them to newly bereaved relatives.

In the mid-1960s Escobar entered the United States illegally and did all kinds of menial jobs while he, like Jorge Ochoa, experienced at first hand America's growing enchantment with drugs. In the early 1970s he returned to Colombia, and Medellín, hoping to put that experience to use. He continued to steal—usually automobiles—but he also found occasional employment, traveling to Ecuador and Peru to buy coca paste and base, which he smuggled back to Medellín in trucks.

In 1976 when Escobar was already a small but established dealer in Medellín, controlling a small group of "mules" who traveled south to collect drugs for him, he was arrested with five other men and charged with attempted bribery in connection with a thirty-nine-pound shipment of cocaine that police found inside a spare tire—Medellín's largest cocaine seizure at that time. Although he spent three months in jail, Escobar's case was dropped because of a conflict of jurisdiction between two courts. Subsequent manipulation of the legal system led to the disappearance of his criminal record from the courthouse. Later, two of the police officers who arrested Escobar were assassinated.

So when the cocaine explosion began a couple of years later, Escobar was more than qualified to go into the trafficking business for himself. As he made money, he invested much of it in an aircraft fleet, allowing him to collect his own paste from Beni, instead of relying on other "transporters."

His wealth grew dramatically and he displayed it. He bought large ranches in Antioquia and the neighboring province of Chocó, as well as several houses and apartments in Medellín, and he invested in legitimate businesses, among them a bicycle factory he named *El Osito*—the nickname of his brother, a professional bike racer. For the poor of Medellín, he built over four-hundred houses and financed the construction of eighty soccer fields for the young.

His favorite residence became *Hacienda Nápoles,* three hours from Medellín, where he stocked a private zoo with four giraffes, two Indian elephants, and ten hippopotamuses. The estate had twenty-four artificial lakes and a network of roads sixty miles long. At dusk Escobar liked to sit by the swimming pool—flanked by a statue of Venus and a mortar platform—and watch his guards shoo hundreds of doves up into the trees until the branches appeared to be covered with snow.

His proudest possession at *Hacienda Nápoles* was a bullet-riddled 1930s touring car that he swore was the vehicle in which Bonnie Parker and Clyde Barrow ("Bonnie and Clyde") died at the hands of the FBI. That, and a statue he commissioned from Rodrigo Arenas Betancourt, one of Colombia's most renowned sculptors. It is the life-sized figure of a woman, Escobar's favorite prostitute.

Escobar, the Ochoas, and others like them were able to obtain such extravagant wealth because they revolutionized cocaine trafficking. In part this was because the sudden abundance of coca allowed them to deal in hundreds of kilos and then tons of cocaine. There was a time, before Escobar and the Ochoas became involved, when one or two kilos of cocaine was a significant shipment. There was a time (1979) when the confiscation of 110 kilos of cocaine in the Bahamas represented the most valuable police seizure of drugs ever made. But there would come a time when Escobar and the Ochoas, among others, could lose fourteen *tons* of cocaine in one police raid—and America was already so awash with drugs that nobody noticed.

There was another revolution that Escobar, the Ochoas, and others perpetrated—a second upping of the stakes, which had dramatic consequences for the American cocaine market.

Before the Ochoas and others, Colombia's traffickers were, in the main, merely producers and suppliers of cocaine. They smuggled the raw materials into Colombia, manufactured the finished product, and sold it, in Colombia, to whoever wanted to buy. If the client required delivery in the United States, he paid an additional smuggling charge; what happened after that was not the Colombians' affair.

But the new generation of traffickers, most of whom had spent time in America, were well aware that cocaine in Colombia was worth a fraction of its value in America: what

would sell for less than $10,000 a kilo in Colombia would fetch
$30,000, $40,000, sometimes as much as $65,000 a kilo in Amer-
ica—and that at wholesale prices. Of course, what was one kilo
of practically pure cocaine in Colombia became *two* kilos of 50
percent pure cocaine in the hands of the wholesalers. In other
words, what was selling in Colombia for less than $10,000 was
fetching the middlemen in Miami and New York as much as
$130,000.

The Ochoas and other rival groups decided to take a larger
share of the profits by establishing their own wholesale networks in America. From their actions, it is clear they expected
to have to fight for the territories. As new supplies of Bolivian
coca began to fuel the cocaine explosion, they quietly prepared
for war.

4

Dadeland

In 1961 when thirteen-year-old Raúl Díaz arrived in Miami from Havana, Monumental Properties Incorporated of Baltimore, Maryland, was busy expressing its "great faith in the future of South Florida" by building what it described as a "regional shopping center" eight miles south of the city in what was then pastoral Dade County.

It seemed more like blind faith. The rest of America might have been on the move, but few people from Miami ventured *that* far south into surrounding Dade County, except to hunt squirrels and quail. US Route 1, the major highway heading south, was sufficiently deserted that, after 8 P.M., local teenagers could stage drag races on the highway with little risk of encountering any traffic. In hopeful anticipation of a boom yet to come, Monumental Properties named its creation "Dadeland"; youngsters like Raúl Díaz and his friends scoffed, and called it "Deadland."

The developers were right, of course. As Dadeland took shape so, too, did events in Cuba—about 200 miles away, as the crow flies—events that were to change the face of Miami more profoundly and more swiftly than anyone could have imagined.

The true nature of Fidel Castro's revolution had become undeniable in 1960, when he abruptly established military tribunals to imprison hundreds and then thousands of his political opponents, had confiscated land and property, and all American-owned assets. Then, on January 3, 1961, the United States broke relations with Cuba in protest, and Cuba forged a new alliance with the Soviet Union. Thus, a fragile young democracy died in its infancy, and what had been a steady stream of emigration to the United States, in particular to Miami, swelled into a tidal wave.

In the revolution's first two, benign, years, the total number of refugees fleeing Cuba was a mere 64,000. Beginning in 1961 and for the next twenty years, legally or illegally, on officially sanctioned "freedom flights" or on rafts made from inner tubes, risking the currents of the Gulf Stream or via Mexico and even Spain, tens and then hundreds of thousands of Cuban refugees arrived in Miami. By 1981 there were enough of them for the city to make what stands as a unique claim in modern times: that the *majority* of its inhabitants were foreigners, born in a foreign land.

Raúl Díaz came to Miami on one of the early waves in July 1961, leaving behind in Havana his mother, a seamstress, and his father, a physical education instructor. His father was also "the best baseball coach in Cuba" according to Díaz and, therefore, "indispensable" to the revolution; it took him until the end of 1961 to wangle his exit visa, by which time Monumental Properties' "great faith" in the future growth of the region was beginning to look like a sure bet.

When Raúl arrived in Miami, the Cuban emigre's ghetto, known, inevitably, as Little Havana, was a compact appendix to the city, roughly twenty-six blocks long and twenty-two blocks wide, covering an area of less than four square miles. With new refugees arriving at the rate of 1,700 a week, *every* week, Little Havana was soon unable to contain them. Miami began to spread west towards the Everglades and south towards Dadeland, until new development burst the city boundaries and continued unchecked into the no-longer pastoral Dade County.

By 1971 Dadeland was no longer out of place, since it was surrounded by new and thriving communities. Reflecting that growth, the authorities formed the Metro-Dade Public Safety Department to police these unincorporated parts of Dade County, and Raúl Díaz became one of its first Hispanic recruits. Eight years later these communities were large and lawless enough to merit their own Vice, Intelligence, and Narcotics Squad—of which Díaz was made the head—and Dadeland was well on its way to becoming, in terms of volume, the busiest shopping center in America.

This phenomenal growth of Miami and its environs owed much to the skills and energy of the Cuban exiles, whose advancement in the community was startling by any measure. Miami's expansion also owed much to the steady growth in drug trafficking, which, to any but the blind, was clearly becoming more and more important to the city's economy.

Watching the impact on Miami of these three tidal waves—people, drugs, and untold amounts of cash—Raúl Díaz waited, with professional interest, for "something to give." Looking back now, he finds it appropriate and symbolic that the first rude shock came at Dadeland.

In the early afternoon of Wednesday, July 11, 1979, at the height of the summer sales, a white delivery truck bearing the legend "Happy Time Complete Party Supply" was driven into Dadeland's parking lot. Two men, passengers from the truck, entered the busy mall and walked into the Crown Liquors store carrying a paper grocery bag. From it they removed two .45-caliber Ingram submachine guns and without warning or pause, opened fire. Their specific targets were two male customers in the process of buying Chivas Regal whisky, but their fire was indiscriminate. Having killed their victims, they sprayed the store, the mall as they left it, and then the parking lot. When their weapons were empty they simply dropped them and produced new ones, and kept on firing. Morgan Perkins, who had been stocking the shelves in Crown Liquors when the mayhem began, escaped to the parking lot only to find himself being pursued by the truck and by gunfire from its windows. He was eventually hit in both feet as he sought cover under a parked car.

In the next day's *Miami Herald*, witnesses and officials competed to describe what had happened. "This was just like an Elliot Ness movie," said a woman who had been eating lunch in Cozzoli's Pizzeria, next door to Crown Liquors, when the shooting began.

"This was just like a Wyatt Earp movie," said Charles Diggs, Dade County's assistant medical examiner. "This is another Chicago," he said, seeking a more modern image. "This reminds me of Al Capone." Dr. Diggs had not been present at Dadeland, but he had examined the bodies of the two victims, which he likened to Swiss cheese. He told the *Herald* he had started counting the holes in one of the corpses and had given up.

Dadeland was not the first battle in what became known as the "Cocaine Wars." What shocked police about Dadeland, however, was the utter recklessness of the gunmen. What stunned them, when they discovered it, was the lengths the gunmen had taken to ensure that nothing and nobody got in their way.

The "Happy Time" party truck was found abandoned in another section of Dadeland's parking lot, three hundred yards from where the shooting had occurred. It had been purchased new, three weeks before, for $10,000 in cash, and then expertly "customized": lined with quarter-inch armor plate, fitted with gun ports and one-way glass, and equipped with six bulletproof vests. It was also equipped with a machine gun, two carbines, five handguns, and a 12-gauge shotgun—all of which had been fired—and ammunition for all of them. The shells for the shotgun had been modified by replacing the buckshot with steel ball bearings.

"Can you imagine what would have happened if some traffic cop had tried to pull that truck over?" said a police spokesman to reporters. He asked the media to warn the public to be on the look-out for any similar "war wagons," and, since there were several party caterers in Miami with names like "Happy Days" and "Party Times" with trucks to match, his warning created panic all over Dade County.

Raúl Díaz remembers Dadeland as "a swift kick up the ass." For him, it was the first solid evidence that something very significant was happening in the drug business. He did not then understand the cause, but it was clear to him that the drug business in South Florida was becoming so vast, so pervasive and, above all, so lucrative, that it had become so much a part of Miami's fabric, so commonplace, that those who engaged in it no longer felt constrained by any rules; that, like gangsters during Prohibition, they would go to any lengths to seize and expand their share of the trade. Díaz also believed that law enforcement had lost control, that it was outmanned and outgunned. He hoped for the opportunity to do something about it. In 1980, at the age of thirty-two, he was promoted to lieutenant and moved to the front line: Homicide.

Nobody was ever charged with the "Dadeland massacre" and, officially, the case remains open. The proximate cause of it was simple enough to establish: a settling of scores between two rival trafficking gangs, both of them Colombian. But precisely what and who lay behind this act of extreme violence did not become clear to the police for some considerable time—until November 16, 1982, when a "confidential informant" (CI), sat down with a Metro-Dade narcotics detective and described the details of his short but eventful criminal career.

The CI was a young Colombian named Hugo Echevarría Brand. His account was fascinating, not merely because it helped to explain Dadeland and place the "massacre" in context, but because he also described the inner workings of a Medellín cocaine trafficking "family"—a family remarkable both for its violence and for the fact that it was run by a woman.

Echevarría was fourteen years old and the member of a Medellín street gang when he first killed. The killing—of a member of a rival gang—was sufficiently well executed that it impressed Miguel Sepúlveda, known to all as "Paco," who was only twenty-four but already a leading member of a major trafficking gang. Paco sought out Echevarría, who was in hiding, and suggested that he "meet the boss."

Griselda Blanco de Trujillo liked to think of herself as "the Godmother" of cocaine trafficking, and she named her fourth son Michael Corleone after the character portrayed by Al Pacino in *The Godfather*. The U.S. federal judge who eventually sentenced her and her first three sons to long terms of imprisonment, thought she was more like "Ma" Barker, an American gangster of the depression era who ran what was literally an organized crime family: "If there ever was a case, other than the 'Ma' Barker case, that truly has demonstrated what a mother's influence ought not to be, it's this one," said the judge. "This is the most incredible thing I have ever seen."

"Ma" Blanco was a pickpocket in Medellín who got into cocaine trafficking and advanced in the trade through marriage. Each of her husbands was a trafficker of more importance than the last and each was killed in Colombia: in all, she was widowed four times. Her last husband (to date, at least) was Paco's brother; Paco, therefore, was a trusted member of her organization. When Paco brought her an adept fourteen-year-old killer as a potential recruit, she accepted him without question, and young Echevarría found himself on his way to the United States. Since the Colombian authorities were looking for him for murder, he was given false papers identifying him as a steward for Avianca Airlines, the national carrier. He performed a steward's duties just once, en route to Panama. There he was met and flown by private aircraft to the Bahamas and from the Bahamas he was taken to Miami Beach by fast boat. He was met on the beach by a group of Colombians, who demanded and destroyed his false documents, and he was then taken to the airport and put on a commercial flight to New York. Once more he was met by a group of his fellow countrymen, and this time taken to a *caleta,* a "stash house"—in fact, an apartment—in New York where cocaine was stored. For the next eight months, while he proved himself, Echevarría served as a guard of consignments of cocaine that averaged ninety kilos and arrived approximately every three weeks.

As Echevarría later described it to the police, the Blanco organization operated as "a brotherhood" of independent gangs, sharing the risks and Griselda Blanco's resources, and operating under her writ. But from time to time some of those gangs would break away from Blanco, and some of them would be perceived by her as rivals; in that event there was war.

On this point, Echevarría's account was confirmed by another informant who talked to the police in August 1982, in his case, out of fear. He owned a pet shop in Miami and had sold a number of expensive dogs to a woman named Leonela Arias, though she called herself something more grand: Leonela de

Brand. The pet shop owner began an affair with Leonela's daughter, and almost before he knew it, he found himself embroiled in the family's affairs. He became Leonela's escort to public functions and, to his alarm, her confidant. She told him she was in the cocaine business, and she also told him of $20 million rip-offs and machine-gun battles and bodies in the trunks of cars.

What Leonela did not tell him—fortunately, perhaps, for his nerves—was how she had got her start in the cocaine business, in Medellín. She bought a contract on her husband's life and, after he had been killed, used the insurance money as her stake to join the Blanco "brotherhood." The two women were close, until Leonela became a little too independent and Blanco began to regard her as a threat. She was killed on August 17, 1982, in Medellín, while en route to the funeral of a woman friend who had been killed the previous day. Her daughter, who was with her in the car in which she was shot but who was not hurt, said she was not surprised; she felt her mother "had it coming."

Meanwhile, having proved his reliability, Echevarría was given more responsible jobs in the Blanco organization and was transferred from New York to Miami. He made the journey with Paco, his mentor, in a car containing $2 million. Neither Paco nor Echevarría was armed on this trip, for fear they might be stopped by the police. In case anybody else tried to stop them, however, they were escorted by a Blazer wagon filled with Colombians who carried machine guns and other automatic weapons.

Echevarría's new assignment was in another *caleta,* this one in Miami and devoted to the storage of money. He was the guardian of the house for a year and saw untold millions of dollars packed into false-bottomed suitcases to be carried out of the United States by "mules" or hidden in the innards of refrigerators labeled "For Export" to Colombia. He was also on hand to witness the jealousies and rivalries that would plunge the Blanco organization into two bitter internecine wars.

The first began with outright treachery in 1975, when Juan Guillermo, one of Blanco's trusted supervisors, stole a little over $2 million of her money from the Miami *caleta,* and fled to

Colombia. Guillermo used that money to recruit workers and gunmen, and he returned to Miami with them, determined to take a share of Blanco's market. Blanco ordered Paco to stop him.

Echevarría's detailed account of the resulting war, some of it told from first-hand experience, is all the more chilling for its matter-of-factness: two men executed on Miami Beach, and their bodies disposed of; the killer in his turn killed, lured into a trap by a pretty girl; three attempts in Miami to ambush Guillermo, all of which failed—one of them because he used his girl friend as a shield. She was shot, but he got away. The Blanco organization finally caught up with him in Medellín, where they killed him.

The second internecine war was far worse. It began in Miami in 1978 when, once again, one of the gangs in Blanco's brotherhood attempted to break away and, once again, Paco was commanded to restore order. This war became very personal for Paco because the opposition broke into his Miami home, killed two of his men, and sexually abused his wife.

Echevarría's account of this second war, as recorded in a police intelligence report, is only really comprehensible to those who understand the argot of the drug business, who know the background, and who can identify the allegiances of the "akas"—the "also known as", the aliases traffickers invariably use. Nevertheless, even to the uninitiated, the awfulness of what happened comes through:

> Subsequent to these killings, "Cumbamba" went in search of "Gamín" and caught up with him residing in an apartment in Miami. "Gamín" was present in the apartment with two other Colombian nationals. He was handcuffed and removed from the apartment and taken into an awaiting van after the two in the apartment were slain and left there. . . . "Gamín" was then taken into the *caleta,* which was located in the vicinity of the Tamiami Gun Shop. He was tortured in the *caleta* in an attempt to obtain the names of the perpetrators in the aforementioned homicides. "Cumbamba" then shot "Gamín" in the head, drained the body of its blood, and packed the body in a box. The box was dumped in an unknown location.

Dadeland

It may sound far-fetched, but by November 1982, when Echevarría's statement was written down, every homicide detective in Dade County was used to finding worse.

Extract from Metro-Dade Police Case Summary, Case Number 7229-B, dated January 7, 1981:
Further investigation revealed that the victim had been severely beaten about the face, strangled by an unknown ligature, shot in the left side of the face just below the eye, and shot through and through just below the lower jaw. Post mortem abrasions of the chest cavity and right shoulder indicated that the victim had been dragged on unknown surface. It is also to be noted that the victim had four to five broken ribs.

Extract from Case Summary Number 8353-B, dated January 8, 1981:
The two victims were found dumped on a dirt roadway . . . The victims had been tied up and taped (hog tied) and gagged with socks and masking tape. Both victims' heads had been covered with green plastic garbage bags and they were then shot through the bags.

Extract from Case Summary Number 144851-B, dated May 1, 1981:
The victim was found hog tied, wrapped in plastic garbage bags and stuffed into a brown cardboard box. The exterior of the box was wrapped with silver duct tape . . .

Extract from Case Summary Number 371778-A, dated November 8, 1980:
The victims had been deceased for approximately two days. The [woman] victim's right ear had been cut off, and said ear has not been found to date. Both victims had been shot numerous times in the back of the head at the base of the skull.

Extract from Case Summary Number 337215-Y, not dated:
The victim's legs were cut off at the knees. His arms were severed at the shoulders. An attempt to cut off the victim's head was unsuccessful. . . .

Still, at least those ghastly acts were committed in private, in people's homes or on the side of deserted roads, where the public was not in harm's way. Echevarria's explanation for the reckless disregard of the public's safety at Dadeland was that it was caused by confusion: Griselda Blanco had so much wanted the particular target dead that she gave a contract on his life to *two* gangs. Members of both gangs caught up with him at Dadeland and, according to Echevarría, at least some of the shooting was at each other, "not realizing they were both on the same side."

Their target was a thirty-two-year-old Colombian trafficker named Germán Panesso. Echevarría did not say what Panesso had done to earn Blanco's extreme displeasure, and US officials who have since endorsed the claim that Blanco was to blame have given two conflicting explanations: that Panesso had ripped off forty kilos of cocaine from the Blanco organization, and to the contrary, that Blanco owed Panesso money and having him killed was one way to take care of the debt.

Whatever the real reason, the first victim of the dispute was not Panesso, but his live-in maid, a forty-nine-year-old Colombian woman with a history of arrests for shoplifting. On April 17, 1979, her decomposing body was found in a field in a remote corner of Dade County. She had been stabbed three times in the chest, though these wounds would not have killed her. More likely she was asphyxiated by the adhesive tape across her mouth or the rope around her neck. She was handcuffed, and her feet were tightly bound.

The subsequent events suggest that Panesso did not take the death of his maid lightly—and was determined to repay in kind those he held responsible. Six days after her body was found at about high noon, travelers on the Florida Turnpike were startled to see an Audi chased by a Grand Prix racing down the highway with the occupants of both cars firing machine guns at one another. The running battle continued for several miles along residential streets and onto US Route 1, until the police intervened by assembling a road block. The Grand Prix broke off from the chase and turned tail. Then a new chase began through much of South Dade, this time with police cars in pursuit of the Audi, whose occupants continued to fire their guns.

Eventually the Audi was abandoned, and the driver and his two or three passengers fled on foot. There was one occupant who could not flee: in the Audi's trunk was the body of a man who had been handcuffed and bound, who had a rope around his neck and adhesive tape across his mouth—just like Panesso's maid. Like her, he had been asphyxiated.

The Audi was Panesso's. The victim, one Jaime Suescún, belonged to a rival gang of Colombian traffickers. "Word on the street," which was all the police had to go on, said that Suescún had died because of "a narcotics deal gone bad between the occupants of the Audi and the Grand Prix," in the words of the case summary. Perhaps. But the manner of Suescún's murder, with its striking similarities to the death of the maid, suggests that Panesso was also intent on delivering a message to his enemies: whatever was done to him would be repaid.

And in a way it was, even after Panesso was killed, along with his bodyguard, at Dadeland some three months later.

Dadeland marked the start of a series of wars in Miami that were fought in public without care or concern for who might get hurt. People were gunned down at shopping centers, in restaurants, and at busy intersections during rush hour. José Castro Osuna, a bodyguard for Paco, was driving to a McDonald's for lunch when he was machine-gunned from a passing van. The bullets only grazed his neck, but two of them hit his three-year-old son in the head, killing him instantly.

Raúl Díaz, in his new job in Homicide, concluded that for the rival Colombian gangs, Dade County had become a war zone in which there were no civilians or innocents; the "fucking Colombian dopers" would kill anybody who happened to be in their way.

Joe Díaz, no relation but one of Raúl's most highly prized detectives, reached the same conclusion when he responded to a reported homicide at a luxury house in Kendall, the community Dadeland serves. As he drove there from Miami, other officers reported over the radio what they had found at the scene: one body, then two, then three, then four. By the time Díaz arrived at the house, the final count was six; four men who had been bound and strangled, and two women who had been shot. The "Kendall Six" massacre was never officially solved, but one certainty about the victims is that at least two of them were utterly innocent: the gardener and the maid just happened to be in the way.

5

The Birth of Centac 26

Raúl Díaz's brief on joining Homicide in 1980 was twofold. First, he was to rebuild the department's morale, which had been shattered by the revelation that at least three Metro-Dade Homicide detectives had been dealing in cocaine. Second, he was to "do something" about the Cocaine Wars, which had been escalated by the arrival in Miami of yet another wave of Cuban immigrants—125,000 people from the port of Mariel. By Castro's design, those refugees had included a significant number of the most hardened inmates of Cuba's jails. ("It's easy to be tough in a democracy," said Díaz. "It's not so easy in places where you have the right to remain silent only so long as you can stand the pain. Some of these people were *bad.*")

To some extent, the two problems were interrelated. High morale in the homicide department required self-respect, and there could be precious little of that when—thanks to the Cocaine Wars—the number of murders in Dade County went from 320 to 515, an increase of 62 percent in one year, while the "clear-up" rate fell through the floor; in fully two-thirds of drug-related homicides in Dade County in 1980, the case files were marked "offender unknown."

The city of Miami had fared even worse: in 1980, what was then merely the forty-first largest city in America became its murder capital, with 70 homicides per 100,000 residents—3.5 times the national average for large cities, and more than twice the rate of New York. And, since the jurisdictional boundaries between the city of Miami and unincorporated Dade County

68

were only arbitrary lines on a map—a man could kill in Miami one moment and in Dade County the next simply by crossing a road—the city's problems were the county's problems and vice versa, and they had the same common root. Díaz believed that the only way to improve the morale of the Metro-Dade Homicide department was by first accomplishing the second half of his brief—"to do something" about the Cocaine Wars. In December 1980 he submitted to his superiors a written proposal as to how that might be achieved: through the formation of a new and highly specialized squad.

Díaz believed that "drug-related homicides" involving Latin Americans—either as the perpetrators or victims—were particularly difficult to solve because the cases usually lacked one or more of the three elements necessary to detection: physical evidence, confessions, and the evidence of witnesses.

More often than not, the killers and their victims were difficult if not impossible to properly identify. Most were illegal immigrants who used aliases and had no records or fingerprints on file in the United States. And sending fingerprints to, say, Colombia in the hope they might be identified there was an exercise in complete frustration; if the Colombian Police replied at all, it could take up to a year.

Another extraordinary factor was the abundance of weapons available to the traffickers, few of which were registered. And police had seized so many weapons in Dade County that by 1980 it was no longer feasible to run routine ballistic checks on them to establish if they had been used in earlier homicides.

Witness statements were usually impossible to obtain because, assuming there were any witnesses, they were usually involved in trafficking themselves—and feared their colleagues more greatly than they did the police. Confessions by Latin American murder suspects were practically unheard of.

Finally, the overworked homicide departments of Miami and Metro-Dade simply did not know enough about the drug traffickers' milieu, nor did they have the time to learn.

So Díaz believed that Metro-Dade and the DEA should establish a special force that would concentrate only on investigating drug-related homicides, and only those where the victim or the suspect was Latin American.

The concept of a joint state and federal task force to tackle

particular problems of crime, or particular criminal enterprises, was not new. By 1980 the Justice Department had sanctioned twenty-five Central Tactical Units or "Centacs" as they
were called for short, in various parts of the United States, each
one designed to combine the local knowledge of state or city
police with the formidable resources of one or more of the
federal government's law enforcement agencies. Centacs had
an impressive track record because they were given the luxury
of concentrating on specific targets, and were thus not easily
sidetracked, and because they were designed to cut through the
red tape, the jealousies and the mutual suspicions that normally hampered more loosely constructed "joint investigations." Bluntly, federal agents investigating the drug world do
not trust local police officers who have been exposed for any
length of time to the massive temptations of the narcotics trade.
"There's not a sheriff in Dade County who can't be bought,"
said a senior official of the DEA, echoing a prejudice that is
widely held in Washington. But formal marriages under the
Centac system, in which hand-picked local police officers team
up with hand-picked federal agents, had sometimes overcome
the mistrust and provided highly motivated and effective units.
Hence, in December 1980, Raúl Díaz proposed the formation of
America's twenty-sixth Centac, to "do something" about the
Cocaine Wars.

The language of his written proposal was dry and bureaucratic, and remarkably unspecific. For example, in the final
version of the Operational Plan for Centac 26, which Díaz took
to Washington for approval in May 1981, the section headed
"Method" consisted of eight brief paragraphs, none of them
more forthcoming than this: "Establish a multi-agency operational force capable of identifying and successfully prosecuting the drug trafficking groups responsible for the homicides."
How that miracle might be accomplished was never addressed
in the operational plan, but, in Díaz's words, "there were a lot
of other typewriters clicking away in the background"—and a
lot of closed-door meetings where "method" was very specifically addressed.

"Centac 26 was created to kick ass," said Díaz. "We were to
target particular people and make their lives a misery, and

continue to do that until we caught them doing something illegal, and put their ass in jail, or until we killed them. We weren't going to violate their constitutional rights, but they were either going to die, go to jail or leave Florida."

Ideas have their moment, and early 1981, when the proposal for Centac 26 reached Washington, was a very good moment to propose "kicking ass." President Reagan had taken office in January, promising to "do something" about drugs and the violent crime associated with them. Among those who saw the need for more radical action was Peter Bensinger, administrator of the DEA, and a man determined to keep his job. Bensinger, appointed by President Carter, had honored the convention of offering his resignation to the new administration at the White House, although he was bent on staying where he was. "I'm with you," said Bensinger when Raúl Díaz arrived in his office with the proposal for Centac 26. Within two days that proposal had been examined, argued, polished, and in principle, approved.

Which is not to say that Centac 26 existed. By 1981 Metro-Dade had become the biggest police force in the southeastern United States, with a complex hierarchy to match, and whatever Washington thought or wanted, Raúl Díaz had not yet won the political battle that counted.

In the past, when other Centacs had been created, the local officers hand-picked to join them were invariably narcotics detectives. For Centac 26, however, Díaz had proposed that the local recruits should be *homicide* detectives—a logical suggestion given the nature of the problem, but one that reckoned without the internal clout of the Organized Crime Bureau (OCB) of Metro-Dade, which regarded narcotics investigations as its exclusive turf. In the Metro-Dade hierarchy in 1981, the commander of OCB outranked the commander of Homicide and eclipsed Raúl Díaz in terms of influence, and so, when Centac 26 formally, and very quietly, began operations in July 1981, it did so with narcotics detectives attempting to conduct murder investigations for which they had neither the experience nor the aptitude. Raúl Díaz, who lacked clout, not political acumen, bided his time.

In its November 23, 1981 issue, *Time* magazine devoted its

cover story to South Florida, under the title "Paradise Lost?" The query mark was redundant, for *Time*'s view of "America's favorite winter playground" was little short of apocalyptic: "South Florida . . . is a region in trouble. An epidemic of violent crime, a plague of illicit drugs and a tidal wave of refugees have slammed into South Florida with the destructive power of a hurricane."

For a region so dependent on tourism and sales of real estate it was devastating "propaganda" (and, more than five years later, still certain to provoke near-apoplexy at the Miami Chamber of Commerce). Within days of its publication, by co-incidence or not, Raúl Díaz was appointed head of Centac 26 and given permission to hand-pick his own team of narcotics *and* homicide detectives. He was told to "be seen to be kicking ass" before the end of the year.

One fashionable explanation of the savage nature of the in-creased violence in Miami was to blame it almost exclusively on Colombians, on some national characteristic that allowed Colombians to kill without any compunction or concern for the age, sex, or innocence of their victims. A senior intelligence analyst at the DEA, who knew Colombia well, developed a the-ory that what Miami was witnessing in the early 1980s was an imported version of *La Violencia,* the bloody civil war in Co-lombia that claimed more than 300,000 lives. Colombians, he said, would make a point of killing their victims' wives and children; he compared them, very unfavorably, with the Mafia who, he said, managed their murders with civility, never harmed the victim's family, and sent flowers to the funeral.

But while Colombians started the Cocaine Wars and set the tone at Dadeland, they certainly did not hold the monopoly on extreme violence.

The man selected by Raúl Díaz as Centac 26's first quarry, the number one target on their most-wanted list, was a thirty-eight-year-old Venezuelan: Rafael León Rodríguez, better known to his friends and to the police as "Amílcar." He was small, and his mannerisms bordered on the effeminate. Most people found Amílcar unfailingly courteous—what Detective Joe Díaz calls "a charmer." Raúl Díaz, though, says his eyes gave him away:

"They were empty, like a shark's eyes." What distinguished Amílcar, and what singled him out as Centac's first priority, was that he liked killing people; not having them killed by associates or hit-men, but committing the act personally. Perhaps as a result one of his fourteen different aliases was "El Loco."

By Amílcar's own account, he began to kill while a teenager, as a left-wing terrorist in Venezuela, where he shot a police officer. He fled to Colombia and killed again, this time for profit, and impressed himself on some of Medellín's major trafficking families.

In the late 1970s, with the aid of his own "lieutenants," Amílcar established cocaine distributorships in both Miami and New York. He dealt severely with dissidence. In New York, a married couple named Toro fell into dispute with Amílcar and did not heed his warnings. One night the couple returned home to find their baby-sitter, their twelve-year-old daughter, and their ten-year-old son missing. Their bodies were eventually found in the basement of an abandoned post office. The females had been raped, the boy had been sodomized, and all three had frozen to death. The description of a man seen leaving their apartment building that night fitted Amílcar, at least to the satisfaction of Raúl Díaz.

By late 1981 when Díaz was assembling his Centac team, Amílcar was caught up in a full-scale war. He had fallen out with one of his lieutenants, another Venezuelan known as Winston; the two men and their respective armies had become engaged in a grim struggle to see who could eliminate the other. Amílcar was not necessarily getting the best of it. He had been shot once, outside an apartment building in New York, and a second time at his home in Fort Lauderdale.

On the second occasion, the shooting had been done with submachine guns while Amílcar was swimming in his pool, and Raúl Díaz, who did not like Amílcar, hoped that might be the end of it. After five days in a hospital, however, "the sonofabitch" discharged himself, which is when Díaz decided that Amílcar's name would be placed on the top of his list.

And though Amílcar did not know it, Díaz had an edge. For the first time, the police had solid evidence of Amílcar's homicidal nature: a living witness who was prepared to give evidence in court. Raúl Díaz had obtained that evidence and, in the process, proved once more, at least to himself, that the expert use of informants was the best way to prosecute the war on drugs.

Informants are at their most valuable when they need something and in March 1981 a young Cuban "hit-man"—a subcontractor to the drug trade who killed people for money—needed help very badly. Hipólito Visuña had been caught red-handed in an act of attempted murder in Miami Beach, a municipality with its own police force within whose ranks Hipólito had no friends. But he had been an occasional informant for Raúl Díaz for seven years, and languishing in jail, facing the prospect of a life sentence, Hipólito sent word through his wife to Díaz that he had valuable information about Amílcar. Raúl Díaz and Joe Díaz, both then with Homicide, went to see him in jail.

In 1979, Hipólito told them, he had been offered a contract by Amílcar's personal bodyguard. For $100,000 or two kilos of cocaine, whichever he preferred, Hipólito was to lure two Cuban drug dealers to an isolated house on the western outskirts of Miami, where they would be killed. Hipólito did not accept the contract, but he knew who had: Armando González, a fellow Cuban, and, at the time, a fellow inmate of the jail. González was a huge square-shaped man, known as "Maleta" or "suitcase"—because, said Díaz, "he was built like one."

As Hipólito told it, Maleta had baited the trap by offering the two luckless Cubans the opportunity to buy ten kilos of cocaine for $220,000, an exceptional price at the time. He had led them to the isolated house, where they were supposed to collect the merchandise, and to calm any fears they may have had about being set up, Maleta had taken along his wife. At the house, Amílcar and his long-time bodyguard were waiting, hidden. As the two Cubans walked through the front door, they were both shot in the face. Maleta made sure to describe Amílcar's trademark, a .357 nickel-plated Magnum to which he owed his epithet as "the man with the silver gun."

Maleta was not yet a member of the club made up of Raúl Díaz's informants, although he was about to join because he, too, needed help. He and his wife were no longer partners in crime or in marriage, and were engaged in a bitter custody battle over their children. So far Maleta had custody, but if his wife, who was in New York, discovered he was in prison, she could use that information in court to get the decision reversed. Could Díaz help? asked Armando. That depends, said Díaz.

But of course Díaz could help. His remarkable effectiveness as a police officer was due in no small measure to providing informants, and potential informants, with favors, which he had the power to do. So for the next few months, while Díaz waited for Centac to be given the go-ahead, and while he patiently built his case against Amílcar, Armando "Maleta" González was taken from his prison cell once a week and escorted to his mother's house in Miami, where his children were living. They would have lunch together while the children waited for the weekly telephone call from their mother in New York. Is your father there? she would ask when she called, perhaps hoping he was not, and for evidence of his unreliability. Of course, said the children, in all truthfulness. Mrs. González was never made aware of this arrangement even when, in due course, she was approached by Raúl Díaz and offered immunity from prosecution in return for her corroborating testimony against Amílcar, an offer she accepted.

Sometimes, it seemed, Díaz could be too clever for his own good. He persuaded the state attorney to grant immunity to Armando González; it was only *after* the deal was signed that González was asked to submit to a polygraph test—which he flunked. His description of Amílcar's participation in the double murder was not the problem, but the answers he gave about his own participation were.

"Did you play any active part in the homicides of Angel Acosta and Raimundo Martínez?" the examiner asked.

"No," Maleta said—an answer the polygraph machine instantly damned as a lie. No matter how often he attempted the test, he always failed at that point.

"Tell the truth," said Díaz.

"Does the deal still stand?" asked Maleta.

"Only if you tell the truth."

The truth was that after Amílcar and his bodyguard had fired the opening volleys, Maleta had also shot both the victims, in what remained of their faces, as they lay on the ground. Whether they were already dead, or whether it was his bullets that killed them, nobody could possibly say.

Neither could they say with certainty that Raúl Díaz had been made a fool of. If the state attorney had known *before* the deal was signed that Armando González was a participant in murder, not just an accessory, would he have granted immunity?

The question was academic, of course. Raúl Díaz had what he needed to get Amílcar.

Through bureaucratic nicety, Raúl Díaz's Centac 26 came into formal existence on December 11, 1981, a Friday, and Raúl Díaz decided to delay the start of the hunt for Amílcar until after the weekend. The unit did not yet have its own office, and its five detectives, one sergeant, and three analysts spent part of the first day colonizing a corner of the Metro-Dade Homicide squad room. Díaz had his own cubbyhole, which was just large enough to accommodate team meetings, so long as everybody remained standing. In another corner of the Metro-Dade building, computer programmers from the DEA began the task of putting into a data-base details of every drug-related homicide that had occurred in Dade County in which the victims had been Latins.

On Monday morning the hunt began and by late afternoon Centac had found Amílcar. An astonishing feat, given that he no longer lived at home, or, indeed, spent more than one night in the same bed, and given that he owned nothing that could be traced to him and that he employed fourteen different aliases. Díaz shrugged it off: "We were well prepared."

On Monday, December 14, Centac's first operational day, an informant told Díaz that Amílcar was at the Mutiny Hotel in the district of Miami called Coconut Grove. The Mutiny was then a favorite gathering place for drug dealers; indeed, it was where Raúl Díaz sometimes met his better-heeled informants, and he knew the area well.

He called the Metro-Dade Police Department and the DEA for extra men, and then hurriedly sketched a map of the Mutiny and its surroundings. On the map he placed the positions of seven surveillance cars, each of which would have two officers. He assigned two men to watch from the lobby of the hotel, and chose for himself a vantage point by a pay phone. After three hours of watching from that vantage point, Díaz saw Amílcar and his bodyguard walk out of the Mutiny and drive away in a two-door Pontiac. Díaz followed in his own car at a discreet distance, assembling his forces by radio and waiting for an appropriate moment to spring the trap. And then, in the evening rush-hour traffic, the team lost Amílcar.

By then they had left Miami for the more genteel city of Coral Gables, which adjoins it. Díaz began systematically searching the area, forcing his car through traffic, and eventually turning onto the main shopping street, Miracle Mile, which has a raised concrete median in the center, dividing the traffic into two opposite flows. As Díaz went in one direction, he suddenly saw the Pontiac going in the other; as they passed each other he thought he saw Amílcar smile and wave his hand in mocking farewell.

As luck would have it, one of the other cars scouring the area saw the Pontiac and gave chase. Amílcar, however, had survived the attentions of the police, and of his rivals, for so long only because he had a keen sense for trouble, and, when he smelled it, the reactions of a cat. Heading north towards the airport, on a major thoroughfare in the middle of the evening rush-hour, the Pontiac made a dead stop in the middle of its lane. Despite the protests of other motorists, it stayed there.

The car in pursuit contained a Centac detective and a DEA agent. They gingerly maneuvered their car to the head of the rapidly growing line of vehicles, and parked it as they had been trained, so as to block the road. And, as they had been trained, they approached the stalled Pontiac with their hands on their guns ready to draw and begin firing the instant a door or a window should open.

But the training manual as then compiled took no account of the Pontiac's tinted windows, which prevented them from seeing inside the car, nor did the manual foresee that Amílcar and his companion would fire *through* the windshield. Without warning, it exploded, showering the detective and the agent with splinters of glass, sending them diving to the roadway for their lives.

What outraged Díaz, who was three blocks away and stuck in

a now-monumental traffic jam but able to listen over his radio, was that the DEA agent Amílcar and his companion had just attempted to kill was a woman. Díaz expected to be shot at in Miami, and even took pleasure in the danger. (Knowing that, his wife had threatened to divorce him unless he took a safer job.) But shooting at women, even those who packed guns and were trained to use them, was to Díaz beyond the pale, "god-dammit." When he heard over the radio that the detective and the agent, in a car, were now in pursuit of Amílcar's companion, who was on foot, he gave an angry order: "Don't take chances. Run the sonofabitch over," which is precisely what they did.

Meanwhile, Amílcar fled into the parking lot of an adjacent Burger King, climbed into the front passenger seat of a gray Toyota, and put his gun to the startled owner's temple while ordering him to drive. When they were a few blocks away, Amílcar freed the owner and calmly made his escape.

Díaz was furious but he consoled himself and his team with the thought that even a cat has only nine lives and, surely, Amílcar had used up his ration. Two days later Centac found Amílcar again, and this time Díaz's rapidly assembled trap was impossible to escape.

Amílcar's downfall was the telephone. He was as aware as any trafficker of its dangers and, like most other traffickers, he received all of his messages through an electronic beeper (a device so ubiquitous in Miami that a Martian might believe he had landed on a planet populated by two races—one of them tiny and parasitic, its members attached like chattering leeches to the waistband of every human). To make calls, Amílcar would use only pay phones, never making more than one call from each phone.

But to defeat such ingenuity, Centac had at its disposal a device known as a "trap and trace," which when placed on any telephone line, traces the number from which *incoming* calls are made. (Since a "trap and trace" does not record conversations, it does not require a warrant, only the cooperation of the telephone company.) So, all Centac had to do was guess where Amílcar might call *to,* get a "trap and trace" installed on those lines, and wait.

On December 16, 1981, Amílcar called one of the monitored telephones from a pay phone near Miami International Airport. This time Díaz built a "perimeter" around the area, a ring of police officers and agents that slowly contracted as the search narrowed. Amílcar and his longtime bodyguard, also wanted for a double-homicide, were eventually caught in an alleyway. When two Centac detectives, Joe Díaz and Bobby Fiallo, attempted to arrest them, Amílcar and his bodyguard opened fire and then fled to the communal laundry room of an apartment complex, where they took cover behind a row of washing machines. When Raúl Díaz learned that over his car radio, he ordered Joe Díaz and Fiallo to "shoot through the washers." He said that because the members of Centac were not restricted to regulation five-shot revolvers and regulation ammunition. He knew that Joe Díaz was carrying an automatic equipped with steel-tipped bullets that would slice through washing machines as if they were butter. Raúl Díaz wanted Amílcar dead.

But Amílcar and his bodyguard also heard the order over the radio, and before Joe Díaz could carry it out, they surrendered.

Once in custody, Amílcar was unfailingly courteous. He shook Joe Díaz by the hand and congratulated him on a fine piece of police work. He said he had always known that telephones would be the death of him. He apologized for opening fire, saying he was sure Joe Díaz would understand, it was business: "Your job was to catch me. My job was to get away." He had no regrets because his family had all the money they would ever need. Amílcar said he did not mind going to jail.

That last claim turned out to be untrue: For the next three years, Amílcar and his bodyguard did their level best not to go to jail, each of them hiring one of the best criminal defense attorneys that money can buy in Miami. Partly as a result, Raúl Díaz found himself caught up in a series of events that would lead to his resignation from the police force.

It is arguable, therefore, that America's "War on Drugs" would not have lost one of its most effective exponents if only there had been time for Joe Díaz to obey the order and open fire. Certainly, it is to Raúl Díaz's eternal regret that his detective did not.

6

Decline and Fall

During his spectacular career as a police officer—rising from rookie to lieutenant in nine years—Raúl Díaz inspired fierce loyalty and lasting respect—among some. The belief that he was one of the most effective weapons in the war on drugs is held by officers and agents in the police departments of Metro-Dade and Miami, the DEA, the Coast Guard, and US Customs, the Internal Revenue Service, the CIA, the Florida Department of Law Enforcement, and by local government officials. When in July 1987 Díaz married for the second time, the wedding and reception resembled the reunion of a fan club. The ceremony was performed by the mayor of Hialeah, a satellite city of Miami with the greatest concentration of Cuban Americans in the country (and where there are signs in only some of the shop windows saying "English spoken.") The manager of Dade County—at $114,500, one of the highest-paid local bureaucrats in the country—was there, and so were senior police officers, federal agents, former CIA operatives, former US prosecutors, and luminaries from Miami's Cuban community.

So too, in all probability, were agents of the FBI—perched, perhaps, on some convenient rooftop, taking surveillance photographs. For in his career as a police officer, Raúl Díaz also fostered great resentments and enormous suspicions. There are officers of almost every local, state, and federal law enforcement agency in Miami, and prosecutors in the US attorney's office, and investigators for Congress, who believe Díaz was a thoroughly corrupt and corrupting cop. They believe he sat at the center of a web of corruption; that he made up his own laws and selectively enforced them, not necessarily for personal profit—though that allegation hangs in the air—but to pursue his own idea of justice, and to further his career. Since leaving the police force he has been accused of fashioning an unholy alliance between drug traffickers and the CIA in order to supply the Contra rebels in Nicaragua with funds.

Díaz has been subpoenaed by a federal grand jury, and by the US Senate, to answer questions about his alleged relationships with drug traffickers, including the Ochoas of Medellín—for whom he has, indeed, indirectly worked.

The walls of his office are covered with plaques of commendation and tribute from federal agencies, of which this one, dated July 1981, is typical:

DRUG ENFORCEMENT ADMINISTRATION

UNITED STATES
DEPARTMENT OF JUSTICE

PRESENTS THIS

CERTIFICATE OF

APPRECIATION

TO

RAUL DIAZ

For Outstanding Contributions in the Field of Drug Law Enforcement

Yet in the Narcotics and Dangerous Drugs Information System (NADDIS), the federal government's computerized summary of all knowledge about trafficking, Raúl Díaz was, and is, listed as a suspect.

Nothing criminal has been proved against Díaz, nor is their any evidence that he stole or corruptly received any money. Even so, US prosecutors are still trying to put him in jail. One of them described him as "the most dangerous man in Miami."

Centac's spectacular debut brought immediate dividends. The police departments of both Miami and Hialeah volunteered extra personnel; Hialeah sent a detective, Miami sent three, and an expanded Centac began kicking ass all over Dade County.

Suddenly, killers and those who had ordered killings found themselves in jail or under severe threat of going to jail. Centac's methodology was remarkably direct. Those suspected of involvement in homicides, or of having knowledge about them, were "targeted" and placed under "aggressive surveillance." They were followed and watched, sometimes quite openly, making it difficult for them to pursue their normal trade. Those who tried and were caught in possession of drugs were given a hard choice: they could either cooperate with Centac, or face state charges under a racketeering statute that mandated a minimum of fifteen years in prison, without prospect of parole.

It would be an exaggeration to say that the traditional walls of silence crumbled, but Centac's ability to concentrate on just a handful of targets, and to tap the knowledge and resources of the DEA, produced remarkable results. In 1982, its first full year of operation, Centac had a "clear-up" rate of more than 100 percent because, in solving new cases, it managed to close the book on many old ones as well.

Likewise, by the end of 1982, the ever-rising tide of murder in Dade County had turned: in 1982 there were 68 fewer homicides than there had been in 1981; in 1983 the body count would drop by a further 118. Miami, too, necessarily benefited from this program of "garbage removal," resuming its rightful place as merely *one* of the most dangerous cities in America.

The morale of the Centac team was correspondingly high. There had been some teething problems: one of the original recruits was suspected of corruption, and the squad's sergeant—Raúl Díaz's deputy—carelessly confided that he did not really trust "Latins," by which he meant Cubans; since most of the team—including, of course, the boss—happened to be Cuban, he was rapidly sent on his way. To replace him Diaz recruited a new sergeant from Homicide, Alan ("Al") Singleton, and what had been a good team became a great one.

Singleton is impossibly thin, and once, when he asked what

costume he should wear to a police Halloween party, he was told "paint yourself green and go as a blade of grass." The name stuck; from then on Al Singleton was "The Blade." But his physique is deceiving. In his hometown of Cincinnati, Ohio, he volunteered for the Marine Corps, going to Vietnam "because it seemed a good idea at the time." He became a platoon leader and, for a year, was stationed in a Vietnamese village in Thua Thien province from where he and his men ambushed the passing Vietcong. Returned to civilian life, he would have become a cop in Cincinnati but was rejected by his hometown because of poor eyesight. He moved to Miami when he discovered that Metro-Dade's standards were, in that respect, less demanding, and he became an obvious leader in Homicide. Raúl Díaz had to fight to get Singleton for Centac because he was far from being the only lieutenant in Metro-Dade who thought that Cincinnati must be mad.

Singleton, like Díaz, was not enamored of office work, and both of them would find any excuse to be on the streets with the rest of the team. Centac became an elite, to themselves and in the perception of others in the Metro-Dade police department, some of whom came to resent it.

Regular Homicide detectives might find themselves working on ten or even twenty different cases at the same time because there was then an average of more than 2,000 "unattended deaths" in Dade County every year. While three-quarters of those would turn out to be from natural causes, each still required investigation by Homicide and created their ration of paperwork. Centac detectives, on the other hand, could pick and choose their cases, and work them for weeks. They could target anybody, and go wherever their leads took them. They could turn up at a murder scene, after Homicide had done the spadework, and say, "We'll take this one."

One of Centac's major strengths was its affiliation with the DEA. Federal drug agents have no jurisdiction in homicides and the DEA's role in Centac 26 was limited to providing logistical support and, occasionally, extra manpower for surveillance operations and backup for arrests. But what also counted was the access to powerful forces which the relationship gave Raúl Díaz: through the DEA, he could talk to other federal agencies and, indirectly, to Washington. Through the network of contacts he built, Díaz could—with a telephone call—get things done that few other police officers could hope to achieve, whatever their rank. Díaz could also find out things he was not supposed to know: for example, that by the summer of 1982, he was under secret investigation by the FBI.

To achieve significant victories in the drug war and make real dents in the trade, law enforcement agencies depend primarily on intelligence. It may, occasionally, come from painstaking analysis: from studying the thousands of names of known and suspected traffickers and their associates that are stored in the DEA's sophisticated computers, from trends and patterns, from piecing together tidbits of information gleaned from around the world, from travel plans and wiretaps and the movement of money, and from good old-fashioned surveillance. But overwhelmingly, the intelligence that matters comes from informants.

Informants are to detectives what "confidential sources" are to reporters: lifeblood. Since detectives, like journalists, are rarely present at the events they attempt to reconstruct, they depend, when they can, on those who were.

In police work this is especially true of narcotics detectives because they face the peculiar difficulty that the crimes they investigate are, in one very real sense, victimless. If a consignment of cocaine, or any other drug, is successfully imported into the United States, and then sold and resold along the distribution chain until it reaches the streets, no one involved is going to complain: there is no "scene of the crime," no photographs, no fingerprints—no physical evidence to provide the clues. So narcotics detectives depend on knowledge for their convictions; preferably *prior* knowledge. To build their cases against organizers of drug trafficking—who may never go within a mile of the "merchandise"—what investigators need is knowledge and evidence of the conspiracy to import drugs. Barring a miracle, there is only one way to get it: through informants.

They come in a variety of disguises, but there are essentially two breeds: "confidential informants" (CIs), who are usually caught red-handed and who, in return for leniency or immunity, agree to provide information and even testimony against their principals; and "confidential sources" some of whom live in the nether world between lawlessness and law enforcement, who are seldom required to testify, and who earn a degree of immunity by keeping an ear to the ground.

It is axiomatic that the best confidential sources are those who are closest to "the action." But that necessarily implies that they are involved in "the action," or have intimate, advanced knowledge of it. Therein lies the danger: that the best sources are those most involved in drug trafficking, and that they will misinterpret their secret relationship with the police as a license to operate.

There are other dangers—for one, of utter confusion: given the number of law enforcement agencies operating in South Florida and given their heavy dependence on intelligence, it is inevitable that there are informants who inform on other informants, who probably are informing on them. A consequence of that is selective prosecution: arbitrary decisions made by police officers and agents as to who will go to jail and who will be allowed to remain on the street. Given the vast amounts of money at stake in the drug business, selective prosecution raises the specter of corruption, or at least the appearance of it. Successfully managing a stable of informants in Miami's unique criminal environment is like crossing a minefield on a tightrope. For ten years, Raúl Díaz was a master of that art, of maintaining the delicate balance. Or so it seemed.

If he had a weakness it was that he sometimes became too close to his sources and too protective of them. Certainly, he overprotected his most legendary informant, Ricardo "the Monkey" Morales. And as events were about to prove, Díaz had become much too close for his own good to a woman named Nancy Lamazares.

There was no one Monkey Morales would not betray, and no one he would not betray them to. His known occasional employers included Castro's secret police, the CIA, the FBI, and Venezuela's secret police, the DISIP. He was at various times a drugs trafficker, a Cuban terrorist and, conversely, head of airport security in Caracas. He made bombs in Miami and signed arrest warrants for others who did the same elsewhere. As a trafficker or a terrorist, he might inform on an associate—and then advise the associate to leave town; if the police complained that their quarry had been tipped off, Morales would likely blame *them* for the leak. Monkey Morales was, in short, a consummate liar and a constant dissimulator. Yet Raúl Díaz liked "the sonofabitch."

Díaz also liked Nancy Lamazares, whom he met when she became the widow of his first important informant. Díaz was a rookie detective in Metro-Dade's Organized Crime Bureau, and Nancy's husband was a mid-level trafficker in Little Havana, when Díaz caught him in 1972 and, in the jargon, "flipped" him. To save himself from jail, Germán Lamazares began informing on his associates; unfortunately, with too little care. Though Díaz warned him not to, he wrote down his reports, which he kept in the glove compartment of his car. One day he loaned the car to an associate, forgetting that he had not yet handed over his latest report, and the next time Díaz saw Nancy's husband, he was lying in a shallow grave.

Nancy discovered who had killed her husband, and why, but the Monkey provided the corroborating evidence. The information was passed on to Homicide, which arrested one Eladio Armando Ruiz, and put him in jail. That might have been the end of it, had Ruiz not made bond—and had Raúl Díaz and Nancy not become lovers.

Eladio Ruiz discovered from court documents who had "fingered" him, and on May 25, 1973, he ambushed the Monkey in his car, shooting him in the head. The Monkey was nothing if not resourceful. The bullet merely wounded him, and he removed it from his skull. He then removed the bulb from the interior light of his car, enabling him to open the passenger door without giving warning, and pursued his would-be assassin down the street. As Ruiz waited at a stop sign for a break in the traffic, the Monkey sprayed his car with submachine-gun fire.

Ruiz, too, survived but Raúl Díaz was certain that it was only a matter of time before one of them killed the other. He was right. On August 2, 1973, Eladio Ruiz turned up dead on the Monkey's doorstep, and Raúl Díaz was called upon by the Miami police to find the Monkey and persuade him to surrender. Again, that might have been the end of it, but the Monkey was acquitted of murder when a witness failed to identify him, and he continued to be Díaz's friend and occasional informant. And on and off, Nancy and Díaz continued their affair.

Throughout the early 1970s, the violence that most troubled Miami was caused not by traffickers, but by anti-Castro zealots who shot and bombed anybody who had or had proposed dealings with Cuba, and frequently, they shot each other. Díaz switched from narcotics to the antiterrorism squad, and the Monkey switched from informing on drug dealers to informing on terrorists. In December 1975, after bombs had gone off at the state attorney's office, the FBI building, and Miami police headquarters, it was the Monkey who identified the bomber—after inviting both him and Díaz to his Christmas party.

But his most spectacular act of double-dealing came two years later, in 1977, when Díaz had returned to investigating drug traffickers. It concerned a series of events that took place in and around a stucco house surrounded by a high wall, on Miami's SW 16th Street; events which would come to haunt Raúl Díaz and which demonstrate all too well how selective justice in Miami can be.

The cast of characters in this saga of the Monkey's duplicity is vast: police officers from Metro-Dade and Miami, federal agents, prosecutors who suddenly become defense lawyers, and drug traffickers who are, sometimes, also informants and who switch roles with bewildering frequency. The only two that matter to its comprehension are Carlos Quesada, a flashy Cuban trafficker who favored silk shirts and lizard-skin shoes and, of course, the Monkey.

Carlos Quesada owned the house on SW 16th Street, which by early 1977 was the base for a number of cocaine and marijuana traffickers, including the Monkey. A number of them—like the Monkey—were informants for different agencies and police departments, and at least two of them—but *not* the Monkey—informed the authorities of what was going on. In the spring of 1977, detectives from Miami and Metro-Dade put a tap on Quesada's telephone and began recording hundreds of hours of conversation. In November 1977 they put the house under surveillance and photographed anybody who entered or left it;

reviewing the results, said Díaz, was like looking at the delegates to an informants' convention. In March 1978, as a result of what they learned from their surveillance, Metro-Dade and Miami staged joint raids on a "stash" house owned by one of Quesada's associates, and seized fifty-six pounds of cocaine and more than $900,000—which, at the time, as a jubilant police spokesman said, was a bit like winning the Super Bowl. Quesada and eight other people were arrested.

The Monkey was not arrested, or even implicated, because during the crucial period when the police were collecting their evidence, he stayed away from SW 16th Street. However, as soon as he was free on bond, Quesada resumed his trafficking activities and police, who were still listening in to his phone calls, heard him make the arrangements for a pick up of 20,000 pounds of marijuana: when police intercepted the convoy on its way to collect that marijuana, the Monkey was driving the lead car.

In jail on charges of conspiring to import marijuana, unable to come up with the $350,000 required for his bond, the Monkey once again displayed his remarkable resourcefulness. He leaked word to the streets that he had "deduced" what nobody except the police then knew: the identity of the two informants who had originally supplied the evidence leading to the court-approved tapping of Quesada's telephone. When this news reached the streets, the two informants were "scared shitless," according to Díaz; they forgot everything they had previously remembered and changed their stories. Suddenly the validity of the warrant for the telephone tap was in doubt, as was the admissibility of the recorded conversations.

While the prosecutors struggled to rescue their case against Quesada and his associates, the Monkey was acquitted of the charges against him. He immediately recommenced trafficking, though this time of cocaine. He also resumed his work for the government: having done his best to sabotage the case against Quesada, he now rescued it. "What would you do if Quesada flipped?" the Monkey asked a startled prosecutor. Give heaven and earth, was the effective answer and, thanks to the Monkey, Quesada duly agreed to testify against his associates; he got immunity, they went to jail.

Back home on SW 16th Street, Quesada formed a new trafficking group that included the Monkey. Quesada should have known better. As John Rothchild, a journalist who knew the Monkey, wrote in 1982 for *Harper's* magazine: "One of [his] abiding talents is to arrange things so that nobody ever feels completely defeated on his account." Having got Quesada off the hook by forcing the government to do a deal with him, the Monkey now gave the government—who else, but Quesada. In December 1980 the Monkey revealed to Miami police that the SW 16th Street house was back in the cocaine business, had never really been out of business, and that Quesada and his new partners were thinking of trafficking in heroin.

The undercover operation that resulted from the Monkey's latest indiscretion was elaborate, even for Miami. The caretaker of the SW 16th Street house was briefly detained for a traffic violation so the police could make a copy of his frontdoor key. The police then planted a listening device behind a wall clock in Quesada's living room and, for the next few months, tape-recorded every conversation. (Since every conversation was punctuated by the ticking clock, the operation was inevitably labeled "Tick-Talks.")

It did not end well for the police. Their bug was discovered when the clock fell off the wall, and they were forced to move in much earlier than they had intended. Quesada and forty-seven other people were arrested, but there was no cocaine to seize and the only significant evidence of the conspiracy was the taped conversations, and the word of the Monkey. The latter ceased to have much value when the Monkey admitted to a defense attorney during pre-trial proceedings that he had indeed murdered Eladio Ruiz in 1973, and had lied about it under oath. When a judge ruled that the tapes were inadmissible as evidence, all of the Tick-Talks charges were dropped.

There is a significant postscript to the saga of the Monkey and the house on SW 16th Street. Perhaps the only real loser in this extraordinary affair was one of Quesada's original trafficking partners, a Cuban named Rodríguez-Gallo, who became the principal defendant after Quesada "flipped." The $900,000 police seized in their raid on the stash house belonged to him, and he drew the longest sentence: fifteen years.

Rodríguez-Gallo appealed, but he was obliged to remain in prison because he could not raise the $1 million bond the government insisted upon. Then, abruptly, the government moderated its demand, and Rodríguez-Gallo won temporary freedom.

Reviewing that development for his article in *Harper's,* John Rothchild wrote: "Naturally, there is a rumor around Miami about why the government let him out: Rodríguez has been flipped, and now he's an informant, too. The rumor doesn't say who is left to inform on."

The answer, we now know, was Raúl Díaz. Rodríguez-Gallo claimed that the money Díaz and his men had seized was not $900,000 but $2.7 million—and that they had stolen the balance. As 1982 progressed, and Centac cut its swathe through the drug world, there were an increasing number of people willing to believe it.

Díaz's relationship with Nancy had ended in the mid-1970s when she married Juan Cid, a young Cuban medical student. The affair resumed briefly in 1981 when Nancy announced that she and Juan Cid had split up. Later she told Díaz that her husband would not pay her alimony which she thought unreasonable because, whereas he claimed to be a private detective earning about $16,000 a year, in fact he trafficked in marijuana and made millions. She asked Díaz to make a case against him.

Díaz refused. Homicide was now his beat and, anyway, it would hardly look good in court if Juan Cid was arrested because of an investigation by his wife's lover, or even ex-lover. Díaz did agree, however, to pass on the information to a Miami PD narcotics detective, and to a friendly agent at the IRS.

Unfortunately for Díaz, the police investigation proceeded very slowly, and, worse, the IRS *informed* Juan Cid that it was investigating his financial affairs. Cid was sufficiently astute to realize that Nancy had informed on him. When she admitted it, he offered her a deal. They would get back together, and he would buy her a new car, on one condition: she would help him fix "fucking Raúl Díaz."

In January 1982 Nancy called Díaz at the Centac office and told him she had been subpoenaed to appear before the grand jury investigating the Tick-Talks case. What should she say, she asked Díaz, if questioned by the grand jury about her relationship with him. "Lie," said Díaz.

That, he says, was an instinctive reaction. His wife had finally carried out her threat to begin divorce proceedings, and he did not want those negotiations complicated by news of his adultery. Anyway, he immediately thought better of his reaction and told Nancy on the telephone that she must not commit perjury. He also told her, however, that nobody could make her take a polygraph test, just as nobody could force her to testify to the grand jury: unless she was granted immunity she could plead the Fifth Amendment. It never occurred to him that Nancy was tape-recording the telephone call.

Transcripts of that conversation were given to agents of the Florida Department of Law Enforcement (FDLE), the state police, by Juan Cid. Their immediate reaction was to arrest Nancy—on eight-year-old warrants against her for writing bad checks. Once she was in their custody, however, they began to ask questions about Díaz, and received in reply some startling allegations: that she had given him expensive gifts, including a $1,000 watch; that she and Díaz had smoked marijuana together; and, best of all, that Díaz had plotted the murder of Eladio Ruiz, the killer of her first husband.

In due course, and with her second husband by her side, Nancy repeated, and elaborated, that last charge to the FBI. In her presence Monkey Morales had told Díaz that he was going to "take care" of Ruiz, she said. After the murder, she continued, Díaz had helped the Monkey fabricate an alibi, and they had even discussed swapping guns. She also claimed that on the night the Monkey was bonded out of jail, the three of them had gone out to celebrate the well-deserved death of Eladio Ruiz.

It was sensational stuff, though immensely difficult to prove. On the other hand, the FBI could have easily disproved Nancy's claims by submitting her to a polygraph test, which she would have failed on every count.

But by then there was a small army of police officers and federal and state agents in Miami who intensely disliked the high-flying and sometimes cocky young lieutenant in charge of

Centac. Díaz had a reputation as a womanizer, and an extremely successful one at that. He flouted tradition: for example, his squad's "choir practice"—the ritual after-work drink—was never held on a parking lot or in some modest bar; Diaz insisted on holding his gatherings in Ronnie's, a popular nightclub where, as often as not, he would sing in the cabaret. He had too many powerful friends for most people's liking, too many friends in other police agencies, and far too many informants for whom he would do "favors." As Díaz himself admitted, in a system that depended on favors because there was no money to buy information, there was sometimes "what looks like corruption."

As if the claims of Nancy were not enough, the jails were suddenly full of people arrested by or because of Raúl Díaz who accused him of corruption. There was Rodríguez-Gallo, the Cuban who claimed that Díaz and his men had stolen $1.8 million from the stash house. A temporary victim of the Tick-Talks operation claimed that he, too, had been "ripped off" by Díaz.

And in the fall of 1982, a federal parole officer complained to the Internal Review section of the Metro-Dade Police Department that Díaz and two members of his Centac team had behaved "improperly" in their handling of two informants who also happened to be charges of his.

The two men concerned were extremely important to Centac, since they had provided the unit's spectacular debut: it was their information that had enabled Centac to target "Amílcar" León, the Venezuelan, as its first priority, and their testimony was crucial at his pending trial. Meanwhile, supposedly, the two of them had gained parole, and operated as though they had a license to commit crime—a license they said had been granted by Raúl Díaz. Whenever they had been arrested or got into trouble, or the parole officer had tried to put them back in jail, Centac had intervened.

To his cost, Díaz did not take any of this very seriously as he learned of it on the grapevine. He joked about it to his men and told them it was a compliment, a signal to Centac's success: they were making waves, and putting a lot of drug dealers in jail, and they had to expect a hostile reaction.

But as Díaz continued to receive whispers that there were now two separate investigations, one by the FBI and one by Internal Review, he became less cavalier. Díaz expected that the FBI or Metro-Dade's investigators would question him; as the weeks passed and they did not, he grew nervous, then impatient, and then angry. In October Díaz went to his immediate superior, the captain who commanded Homicide, and demanded to know what was going on. The captain said: "If they want to talk to you they will." Díaz said he had been asked to kick ass and create waves, which is what he had done, and now that the waves were rushing towards him he was entitled to support. The captain instructed him to get on with his job.

Díaz felt increasingly isolated. His men were unfailingly loyal, and his network of contacts never failed him, but he felt he was being manipulated, that some unseen hand was orchestrating a campaign against him. In November he lost his temper and telephoned the FBI in Miami and told the agent he knew was in charge of the investigation: "If you've got questions, come on over and ask them." The agent said Díaz's call was "inappropriate" and threatened to report him to his superiors.

On December 15, 1982, almost a year to the day since Centac began operations, news of the two investigations and some of the allegations against Díaz were published in *The Miami Herald* under the headline, "FBI Probes Homicide Supervisor: Metro Officer Denies Corruption Allegations." The following day, Díaz was relieved of his command of Centac but was told he could pick his next assignment; he chose to go to Miami International Airport as commander of the afternoon watch— the equivalent of going to Siberia, which he thought appropriate.

At the airport, Diaz took two jobs because he needed the extra money to help pay for his divorce. From 10 A.M. until 3 P.M., he worked for Eastern Airlines, watching the baggage carousels to ensure that nobody stole the luggage. At three he put on his squad commander's uniform and tackled the daily paperwork, which took, on average, forty-five minutes. For the rest of his shift, until 11 P.M., he would stalk the airport, greeting arriving passengers: "Welcome to Miami."

There were two separate boards of inquiry into the allegations against Díaz. Nancy testified and admitted that she had invented her allegations against Díaz, in the hope, she said, of helping her husband. The polygraph examination she submitted to indicated that this time, she was telling the truth.

Monkey Morales also testified that Díaz was not involved in any way in the murder of Eladio Ruiz—or in anything else illegal or improper, so far as the Monkey knew. That was his last contribution to the drama: three days after he gave his formal statement to the inquiry, the Monkey went drinking with Nancy and was shot dead in a sordid bar fight.

Both inquiries exonerated Díaz. All of the charges against him were held to be "not sustained" or "unsubstantiated," save for the allegation that he attempted to influence Nancy not to testify to a grand jury by advising her of her constitutional rights. He was also held to have violated a Metro-Dade Police Department rule by "associating with criminal elements"—namely, Nancy and the Monkey—but no punishment was prescribed.

In September 1983 Raúl Díaz resigned from the police department.

It took Díaz a long time to establish who had orchestrated the campaign against him. Eventually he decided, to his own satisfaction, that the culprit was a Miami attorney named Douglas Williams.

Williams is a tiny man whose courtroom technique depends on a persistence excruciating to watch. He wears away at resistance like a dripping tap, provoking audible groans from judges, and even juries, every time he stands up. "What is it *now,* Mr. Williams?" a judge will say, or, "Will this take much longer?" Williams ignores the provocations and drills away like some manic dentist, oblivious to the pain he is causing, determined to get to the root.

He is the butt of many jokes among his colleagues, jokes that tend to concentrate on his lack of height. Conversely, he is highly respected by his peers as a brilliant attorney, a formidable one who will never give up; they liken him to a terrier who takes hold of a case and shakes it and shakes it until it is dead.

When Raúl Díaz was a rookie detective in Narcotics, Doug Williams was a young prosecutor, an assistant state attorney. It was Williams who unsuccessfully prosecuted the Monkey for the murder of Eladio Ruiz, the man who killed Nancy's husband and, in the process, developed suspicions that Díaz was much too close to his sources. In the course of that prosecution, Williams telephoned Internal Review to say he had "pertinent information" about Díaz, but he never called back to say what it was.

When Williams switched sides, and became a criminal defense attorney, he inevitably came to represent people Díaz arrested—often on the basis of information supplied by informants who, often enough, included Monkey Morales. Inevitably, as part of his defense strategy, Williams would attack the "tainted" evidence, and those who provided it, and never more successfully than in the Tick-Talks case where he was responsible for destroying the Monkey's credibility.

Attacking the prosecution's "tainted" witnesses is a standard defense ploy in Miami, one that nobody takes very personally. With Williams, though, it was different. He seemed to genuinely believe that his clients were the victims of selective prosecution and that there was a conspiracy between some law officers and favored drug traffickers which Raúl Díaz was at the heart of.

In 1982 Williams gained two clients who served to cement his conviction: Amílcar's bodyguard, and Nancy's husband, Juan Cid. As a result, Williams leaked the information that Díaz was under investigation, by planting in court documents the allegation that Díaz had "counselled . . . witnesses to be evasive or dishonest."

Having pinned the blame on Williams, Díaz did not make threats, but he did remark that he had a long memory. He also told friends that when he was fifty-five, and entitled to his police pension, he would donate it all to "The Doug Williams Memorial Fund." A friend pointed out that by then, $12,000 a year would not be worth very much. "No," said Díaz. "It's going to be a very small memorial."

7

Enter the Task Force

Centac 26 was not destroyed, but the enthusiasm for it visibly diminished. Miami and Hialeah eventually withdrew their reinforcements for "budgetary reasons" and even Metro-Dade reduced its financial support. Raúl Díaz was replaced by a lieutenant who *was* enamored of desk work. Sergeant Al Singleton, "The Blade," found himself the effective supervisor of a squad that, bit by bit, shrank to two intelligence analysts and three detectives. The detectives and their sergeant became more like a family than a police unit: they worked impossible hours, socialized together when work was finally over, and commiserated with each other on their divorces.

In Washington, too, the Centac concept lost its appeal. The nominal resignation of the DEA administrator, Peter Bensinger, was accepted by the Reagan administration, despite his best efforts to be seen as doing something. He was replaced by Francis Mullen, Jr., a former FBI agent, whose appointment symbolized the mood of the Reagan White House: in January 1982 the FBI was given "concurrent jurisdictional powers" with the DEA to conduct drug investigations and, henceforth, the director of the FBI, and not the administrator of the DEA, had "general supervision" of the war on drugs.

On January 30, 1982, the war on drugs became The War on Drugs, formally declared, when Reagan established the South Florida Task Force to coordinate the activities of the federal agencies engaged in that fight, under the authority of Vice-

President George Bush. "To those who commit crime, who engage in violence, we say, the American people have great patience, but that patience has been sapped," Bush told a gathering of Miami Citizens Against Crime in February. A month later, Bush was back in Miami to announce "several major steps" that had been taken to "stop the surge storm of cocaine, marijuana and counterfeit pills that has been drowning the citizens of Florida in a sea of murders, violence, fear and blood-drenched narcodollars."

Stirring stuff and, on the face of it, credible, because the forces the vice-president sought to marshal to the front line were formidable: the US Attorney's Office, newly headed in Miami by Stanley Marcus, "a brilliant young prosecutor with a proven record of accomplishment in the area of organized crime," said Bush; the DEA, which was given the money for 20 new agents for its Miami office and which transferred from other areas 40 more agents, 10 supervisors and 3 intelligence analysts; the FBI, similarly reinforced with 43 new agents; the Customs Service, which was given novel authority to investigate drug-related crimes, 145 more investigators, and the use of US Army Cobra helicopters to intercept suspected drug-carrying aircraft; the Bureau of Alcohol, Tobacco and Firearms, which transferred 45 agents to Miami, providing an overnight increase in manpower of 167 percent; the Internal Revenue Service, which appointed an assistant commissioner for criminal investigations to lead the pursuit of those in South Florida who did not declare their incomes from drug trafficking for tax purposes; the Coast Guard, which got more cutters, and support from US Navy warships; the US Border Patrol, which was ordered to reduce the flow of illegal immigrants from Colombia; the US Marshals, which transferred 11 more deputies to Miami; and the Treasury Department, which recruited for its Financial Law Enforcement Center 20 new analysts to focus exclusively on money laundering in South Florida.

There was more help from the navy, which—after some nudging from the Senate Armed Services Committee—agreed that its E2C surveillance aircraft on routine training missions over Florida and the adjacent oceans would, henceforth, track suspected drug planes and ships. Lastly, Chief Justice Warren

Burger promised to provide as many federal judges as necessary to cope with the flood of prosecutions that would inevitably follow.

Within six months the results were sufficiently impressive to allow President Reagan to appear in South Florida and stand before tons of seized marijuana, kilos of cocaine, and an armory of assorted weapons while proclaiming the task force "a brilliant example of working federalism." And what did it matter if one of the raids that produced the booty was deliberately delayed until it could coincide with the president's visit?

In the task force's first year, the US Attorney's Office prosecuted 664 drug-related cases, an increase of 64 percent over the previous year. In 1983 six tons of cocaine were seized in South Florida. In 1985 the figure was twenty-five tons: in other words in 1985, in South Florida alone, the authorities seized almost twice as much cocaine as the DEA's Miguel Walsh had estimated to be Colombia's entire cocaine production just six years before. In 1986 cocaine seizures in south Florida topped thirty tons.

This might seem to be a stunning endorsement of the task force's success, but there are other, equally dramatic statistics that deny it.

In 1982, when the task force was established, the purity of cocaine sold on America's streets averaged 12.5 percent, meaning it was diluted, or "cut," eight times. In 1987 the average purity, at least in Miami, was 33 percent, meaning it had been cut three times. So, seen from a trafficker's viewpoint, whereas one kilo of smuggled "merchandise" once provided eight kilos of "retail cocaine," it now provided only three kilos. Yet, despite that and despite the record seizures and despite the fact that more people in America used cocaine than ever before, there was a glut on the market in 1987.

Just how large a glut is best illustrated by the price. When the task force began work in 1982, one kilo of cocaine of *any* purity cost $47,000 to $60,000 in Miami. In late 1987 one kilo cost between $9,000 and $14,000 in Miami, and there were places in the city where at night cocaine was more easily and openly available than cigarettes.

What went wrong? "We win battles while they win the war,"

said special agent William Yout, a blunt Boston Irishman who until mid-1987 was the DEA's exceptionally forthright spokesman in Miami. In Yout's view—a view widely shared in law enforcement *and* by the other side—the task force failed, and continues to fail, because its strategy is flawed, because it fights on the wrong front, and because for all the hoopla and all the political rhetoric, there is in Washington neither the understanding nor the political will to win.

There is a particular fondness in Washington for the flashier weapons of the War on Drugs, exemplified by the attention and money the government has showered on what it calls Blue Lightning. It is a "strike force" within the task force, established in 1986, and run from an elaborate marine surveillance center in Miami. Linked to the Blue Lightning center by radio network are twenty-seven federal, state, and local agencies that, among them, operate more than one hundred boats. Pride of the fleet are super-fast catamarans operated by US Customs that the vice-president traveled to Florida to launch, and which he invariably named *Blue Thunder I, Blue Thunder II,* and so on.

The rationale behind these boats was curious and indicative. According to its own publicity, the task force's great success was in disrupting smugglers by denying them "their preferred routes of entry": before the task force began operations, most of the cocaine and marijuana that reached Florida did so, supposedly, on small aircraft landed on unattended strips. But the dramatically improved surveillance with which the task force policed the skies supposedly forced the smugglers to switch to fast boats; hence Blue Lightning, and the fleet of *Blue Thunders.*

In fact, as we shall see, what makes the traffickers so effective is the variety of smuggling methods available to them, and their willingness to switch between them. Cocaine is as likely to land at Miami International Airport in a Boeing 747 airliner as it is to land on some hidden airstrip in a light plane. Cocaine has been hidden behind panels and in the nose cones of commercial jets and in cargoes of orchids. It has been packed in false panels in heavy wooden furniture, brought in by freighter, and dissolved in bottles of imported wine. It has been smuggled over the border from Mexico in trucks and cars and similarly brought in from Canada. It has been unloaded from ships off Long Island, New England, California, and Oregon, and flown in on aircraft hidden among the planes and helicopters serving the oil rigs in the Gulf of Mexico, and that then head directly for Texas or Louisiana.

True, most cocaine still arrives in Florida, and always has— 70 to 80 percent of it, by separate estimates of the DEA and Customs. But it is also true that much of that—probably most of it—has always arrived on small boats and continues to do so.

The crews of those boats do not take the threat posed by Blue Lightning very seriously. For one thing, there are more than 124,000 pleasure craft registered in South Florida; there are Sunday afternoons and warm summer nights when it seems most of them are at sea. For all of the high-tech wizardry available to them, the operators at the Blue Lightning surveillance center cannot possibly focus on more than a handful of boats, which they must choose almost at random. As Luis García, a veteran smuggler who will figure much in this story, said: "They haven't invented radar yet that can tell the difference between a boat that is carrying dope, and one that isn't; they're all blips on a screen."

Some are not even that, for radar-jamming equipment is readily available. So, too, is paint which, when applied to fiberglass hulls, makes them virtually undetectable.

There are other reasons why smugglers are not overworried by Blue Lightning or other attempts at what the government calls "border interdiction." As an investigation by the General Accounting Office (GAO) found in September 1986, the Customs Service in Miami and the Coast Guard are plagued by staff shortages and equipment breakdowns. According to the GAO report, the fifteen Coast Guard patrol vessels covering South Florida are out of commission 45 percent of the time. And, Customs does not have anything like enough crews to keep its super-fast boats at sea for twenty-four hours a day, seven days a week; GAO said that some of the smugglers had obtained Customs' work schedules, and knew when they could operate with impunity.

Finally, in this unequal battle between smugglers and those who try to catch them, there is the question of psychology. Thanks to the much-publicized *Blue Thunder* fleet, Customs now has boats that are every bit as fast as the smugglers'. What they do not have is the same incentive to take the considerable risks that can accompany the boats' use.

Luis García put it this way: "It's all very well doing sixty miles an hour on Biscayne Bay with some congressman on board, to show him how well the government's spending its money. Its another thing to try that at night, in a six-foot swell in the Gulf Stream, or heading across the bay towards sand-banks you can't see. There are places in the bay where the water is two feet deep and less, and the channels that you have to use are unmarked. Now, a good doper knows those channels because he studies them. He's also making ten, twelve, fifteen thousand dollars—it depends on the load—for four hours' work, and for that kind of money he is expected to take the risk of getting it wrong. The guy chasing him is making maybe a hundred bucks for a shift, on which he's going to pay tax, and if he hits that sandbank at sixty miles an hour he isn't going to collect his pension because he's going to be dead. Now, you're in the Customs' boat heading for that sandbank: Which way do you want to push the throttle?"

One of Luis García's most proficient "boatmen" was a Cuban who was known within the trade as "Black Carlos." In the summer of 1987 Black Carlos, then "in retirement," agreed to talk informally to a DEA agent in Miami who wanted a professional's opinion of the effectiveness of the government's interdiction efforts. Asked if the threat posed by Blue Lightning was the reason why he had retired, Black Carlos laughed, saying "no," his reasons were personal. He then offered the agent a deal. To prove how easy it was, he would take the agent, there and then, on his boat to the Bahamas to collect a consignment of cocaine that he knew was awaiting transportation. If on their way back to Miami they came anywhere near to being caught, Black Carlos would surrender and go to jail. If, on the other hand, they made the run undetected, Black Carlos would be allowed to keep the cocaine, as a sort of consultant's fee. The agent declined the offer, but he had no doubt it was serious.

What professional smugglers and the traffickers who employ them *do* fear is informants and, worse, the penetration of their operation by undercover detectives. They guard against infiltration as best they can by being extremely careful of whom they deal with and whom they employ. But as we have seen, there is always the risk that some associate or employee has been "flipped" by the authorities or that the latest customer will carry a badge. Colombian traffickers have a distinct edge in this area since, where possible, they employ and deal only with their fellow countrymen: Colombians are more difficult to "flip" because of the consequences for their families, and they have not yet been recruited into American law enforcement in any great numbers. Still, even major Colombian trafficking families, including the Ochoas and Pablo Escobar, have been infiltrated on occasion and "burned."

That ever-present danger induces a state of constant paranoia in the trafficking industry because inside information is one of law enforcement's most potent weapons. Fortunately for the traffickers, it is the weapon the task force has most neglected.

The foot soldiers of Reagan's war in Miami are the undercover narcotics detectives of the Miami and Metro-Dade police departments who, day after day, fight their battles on the streets. They are typified by two detectives from Metro-Dade's Vice and Intelligence Narcotics Unit of the Organized Crime Bureau, South Section, which covers southern Dade County. The detectives are part of a team of about twenty, who work out of an undistinguished pink building in suburban west Miami. Outside is parked an eclectic collection of cars, most of which have been confiscated from "dopers" and are used by the detectives for transportation. Although this policy spares the budget, it is risky because any dealer worth his salt can have a license tag checked in the state's computer: if the computer says the license number is "no longer in service," the dealer can safely assume he is under surveillance. Undercover detectives, like drug dealers, prefer the anonymity provided by rental cars; unlike drug dealers, they cannot always afford them.

Preston Lucas and Luis Fernández are, in some respects, the real-life models for Crockett and Tubbs, the fictional detectives of the television series "Miami Vice," which in more than sixty countries around the world, is a popular and stylish exponent of what the war on drugs is supposed to be like. Indeed, there are striking similarities between Ricardo Tubbs of "Miami Vice" and Metro-Dade's Preston Lucas, a thin, thoughtful black from North Carolina who, in the opinion of his supervisor, Sergeant Ed Howett, "could buy dope from the Pope." Luis Fernández, like his television counterpart Sonny Crockett, is much the flashier of the partnership: a young, fast-talking Cuban who, like Crockett, frequently poses as a dealer. Sergeant Howett considers him "the most aggressive I've got" and says, "he can smell a drug deal a mile away." At the age of twenty-five, Fernández already has the reputation of being one of the best undercover agents in Dade County.

But there the similarities between "Miami Vice" and the real world end. In the real war on drugs, the constants are mind-numbing routine and enormous frustrations caused by bureaucracy and lack of money and resources. There are moments of real and terrifying danger, but they are usually resolved somewhat differently than on television. According to *The Miami Herald,* which keeps a count, fifty-three people were killed in the 1986 series of "Miami Vice." Lucas and Fernández, who disdain police-issue revolvers and carry personal weapons which they have had "customized"—and who argue passionately with each other about the merits of muzzle velocity versus stopping power—have never shot at anybody. "Listen," said Fernández, "if I shoot somebody with this, they will take it away for ballistics and evidence, and I won't get it back for months; and I spent $300 customizing the sucker."

Lucas's normal beat is Perrine, a black ghetto to the south of Miami distinguished by block after block of grim and depressing public housing and drug peddlers on almost every street corner. He roams the area on foot in a variety of disguises: as a shuffling addict in search of supplies; as a street-wise "jitterbug" looking to deal; as a white-robed priest of Santería, an Afro-Caribbean religion popular in Miami.

His main assignment is to locate "crack" houses, the latest and most alarming manifestation of the cocaine explosion. A derivative of cocaine, crack is produced by literally cooking—

in a pan in an oven or microwave—cocaine hydrochloride, baking soda, and water or ammonia and allowing the resulting mixture to cool and crystallize. The end product is cut up into small squares or "rocks" of almost pure cocaine: they are heated until they melt and vaporize, and the vapor is inhaled, producing a "rush" that reaches the brain in two to three seconds. "Freebasing" crack, as this method is called, is the most addictive way of using the drug, and perhaps the most deadly. It is also the most affordable, and crack is spreading through poor communities in America like the plague.

Lucas has to succeed in getting inside the crack houses and buying drugs if he is to obtain the search warrant that will allow him to raid them. He describes the risks involved quite calmly: "You walk into a base house, and you don't know what to expect. Someone might grab you at the door and throw you up against the wall, which has happened to me. They'll pat you down. They'll pull guns on you, just to see what you'll do." The potential for danger is always there, but because he is essentially an actor playing a role, he goes unarmed, his only defense a fake driver's license.

Crack houses operate like any business, with their own rules and regulations. He raided one bearing the notice: "No cursing." Some offer customers sophisticated services, such as a safe place to park their car, and a free ride to and from the crack house, "like a limousine service." Most contain caches of arms: "We find guns, grenades, machine guns," said Lucas. "In one house we found fourteen and one-half kilos, and seven guns—one a MAC-10 machine gun. We lost the cocaine charge, based on a technicality, but we won the weapons charge."

But Lucas is bitterly aware of the inadequacies of the job he is doing: "It's just a big fat game, and we're losing." And he despairs at the way that drugs are taking over the black community. "You go into stores, service stations and there's jitterbugs selling stuff over the counter, behind the counter. It's always there. [In some black ghettos] I don't think there's a corner where you can't buy dope. It's bad, and it's amazing." When he goes home, he tries to stop thinking about his work, "but then I'll go to the 7-Eleven on my way home, and somebody will come up to me and ask if I want crack. I just say, 'No, I've got mine,' just to make them go away." He does not bother to arrest them, because he does not see the point.

He keeps doing the job out of anger, furious anger that there are small children on the streets of Miami who, for fifty cents or one dollar, will act as touts for the dealers. Lucas has been asked by a seven-year-old boy: "Do you want crack?" The children also act as paid lookouts and "they can spot our undercover cars ten miles away."

Lucas understands why they do it: "Let's say you're ten years old. There's this guy you know who's sixteen, who all of a sudden has this brand-new car and all this gold, and you're ten years old. And you want this. And obviously your mother and father can't give it to you. And the government's not going to give it to you. They tell you to go to school, to do right and everything. But then there's peer pressure, and all this kind of stuff. You don't want it ten years from now. You want it now. And so you go out, whether you want to do it or not, and you start doing it."

He has little sympathy for the users and pushers but he reserves his real anger for the dealers who supply the ghettos with cocaine. He recalls a raid he took part in on a Colombian dealer in Kendall where, he claims, there are houses, office blocks, and shopping centers "built with drug money": they recovered nearly $1 million in cash from a house with a Ferrari parked in the front driveway and $12,000 go-carts for the children. The house was so heavily fortified they had to use a tow truck to rip the bars off the windows. "Here I am, an average tax-paying citizen. I earn $37,000 a year, on average. I don't want to be rich, but what upsets me is that they make money from misery."

Lucas has been too close to the misery. He has seen an eight-year-old child hooked on crack and a six-year-old child "with his momma on the pipe." He once stopped a small child, who was carrying a loaf of bread, in the street and asked why he was not at school. The child said his mother was on crack and that he had to look after her; Lucas could only shrug his shoulders in despair. Lucas's own sister "burnt out" on drugs. A friend of his wife's was married to a world-class track athlete who spent nearly $10,000 of their savings on cocaine in less than year.

Lucas last saw him selling watermelon on the street, and he begged Lucas for a dollar.

Lucas continues to do the job because, now and again, he achieves small victories, like persuading witnesses to testify despite great risk to themselves. He also has the satisfaction of removing drugs from the street, even though he seizes only a fraction of what is available: "That's the part that turns me on." What terrifies him is the prospect of his own children—aged two and five—being offered drugs. "I pity the person I find trying to sell dope to any of my kids," he says. But he knows that in present-day Miami, they will inevitably be offered it in high school.

Luis Fernández, the Sonny Crockett of the real Miami, prowls the streets of West Kendall, strutting the shopping malls like a fighting cock, heading for the pay telephones dealers use like offices and from which their calls cannot easily be traced. Fernández has made his reputation through his ability to spot traffickers on the pay phones of suburban Kendall, and persuading them he is the market to deal. If he sees a Cuban and a Colombian together, then "you've got cocaine," and he will follow them because, "usually I get something." He identifies his targets by their "uniform" of designer clothes, a roll of quarters, and the ubiquitous telephone beeper. To evade the likes of Luis Fernández, the more sophisticated dealers have taken to removing the clip, enabling them to hide their beepers inside cigarette packets. It has not worked: to Fernández, the sight of a Marlboro packet in a top shirt pocket is *prima facie* evidence that he is looking at a dealer.

Fernández comes from a wealthy, aristocratic Cuban family and, according to his colleagues, he does not need the job; he does it "for kicks" and because he hates narcotics. When he was eighteen, he worked temporarily as a prison guard and got talking to an inmate who seemed totally out of place. Fernández asked him what he had done: "He told me he had got hooked on coke. He was vice-president of a company and making $75,000 a year. He had a brand-new Corvette and a condominium, fully furnished. Then a friend hooked him on *basuco* [a mixture of marijuana and crack or cocaine sulphate] and he started getting addicted. He sold his Corvette, took all the money out of his account, lost his house, everything. He sold his stereo set for ten dollars to get some coke. The last time he tried to score he went to a bakery. It was a Sunday afternoon. He went into the place and asked if they would give him ten dollars for a hit. The lady looked at him as if she didn't believe him, and he pulled out a gun and he shot her. He took the money from the register. There was seven dollars in there."

So Fernández is on a mission. He goes out of his way to cultivate CIs and protects them assiduously. He has had cases thrown out of court because he refuses to produce his informants, so their identities are not revealed. He is exceptionally protective of what is a rare breed in Miami, or anywhere else: two Colombian informants who have enabled him to penetrate deep into that mafia. Because of the risks they take, he calls them Walking Death One and Walking Death Two.

It was information from Walking Death One that allowed Fernández to infiltrate an Ochoa family trafficking operation in Miami and to arrest a nephew of Jorge Ochoa. The nephew was moving five hundred kilos of cocaine a week until Fernández "got him" with six kilos and $15,000 in his apartment. He obtained bond and fled, but at least Fernández was able to seize a further $171,000 hidden in a stash house.

For that, the Ochoas put out a contract on Fernández's life and, until the threat receded, he and his wife had to leave their home and spend each night in a different motel. She was scared; he loved it. "I think it's a thrill. It's the only satisfaction I get." For Fernández's superiors, it was a startling new development: that Colombians would attempt to kill a police officer. Fernández found it easy to understand: "It was to show they're powerful. If you get to the level where you're really big, you can't let people make a fool of you. You have a name to keep up." He later had to rescue Walking Death One from an attempted kidnapping in a shopping mall. In a scene he thought reminiscent of the Keystone Cops, Fernández scooped Walking Death One into his car, and then made a split-second decision as to whether he should save his informant by fleeing, or attempt to arrest the would-be kidnapper. He saved the informant.

But he is rarely given the time to develop those kinds of cases. As Fernández describes his work, "everything is frustrating. You might have a perfect case, and they'll start putting down restrictions and restrictions and restrictions. Before you know it, what could have been a hundred keys [kilos] of coke, is down to one key. And you don't even have the money for that."

He needs to have money in order to successfully pose as a drug buyer. But if he needs to "flash" $50,000 to make a buy, he has to give his supervisors at least two days' notice, before he can have the money. He believes such limitations are ludicrous: how can he pretend to be a dealer when he doesn't have the money to deal?

He likes to keep watch on stash houses, but if his vigils last for more than a day, he gets called off by his superiors. If he attempts to "brainwash" his superiors, tries to persuade them this is his biggest case so far, they will tell him to give it to the DEA. "And, the DEA will say, 'No, we can't handle it because we're too busy.'"

He spends far more time than he likes helping to bust crack houses because, thanks to the work of Lucas, such busts guarantee arrests, and arrest statistics are important propaganda in the war on drugs. Fernández hates being taken away from his Colombians and put on the "crack force." Given the choice, he deals with his paperwork as fast as possible so he can "go out and play." Dressed in tight gray jeans, a striped T-shirt, and a lot of gold jewelry, he takes a gray Chevrolet from the parking lot. He sometimes also wears a gold earring, though winning permission to do so was a "first." When he joined the department, "I came in and I put on an earring and they told me to take it off." He patiently explained to his superiors: "You have to go to parties and hang out, and you get the best clothing and everything that is in style. . . . You can't work narcotics looking like a cop. You've got to relax a little." His superiors relented.

He usually works West Kendall, beyond 132nd Avenue, which is practically in the Everglades, an area of seemingly endless "communities" and the endless shopping malls that serve them. Fernández says he can "almost smell a doper's house." He identifies them by the extraordinary security displayed: bars on every door, window, and balcony. He also looks for a satellite dish. Some houses have two or three: "They use them to communicate with Colombia."

He spends long and tedious hours on surveillance, sitting in his car with the seats lowered, peering out of the back window through a pair of binoculars. If he sees a likely target, he follows them, hoping they might be on their way to a rendezvous or, even better, to a stash house. He hopes, too, that he can find some legal excuse to stop and search them.

If his gut tells him that there are drugs or money inside a house, he will call for backup, knock on the door, and ask if he can make a search. He is obliged to point out that he does not have a warrant, hence no right to search without permission. It is a gamble worth taking because, in his experience, Colombians will often consent to a search even when they have drugs hidden in the house; a consequence, perhaps, of their recent immigration to the United States and their unfamiliarity with laws and conventions allowing obstruction of the police. Cubans, on the other hand, invariably call for their lawyer. Fernández once stopped a Cuban in his car and before he could ask him so much as one question, the man's attorney arrived in a $65,000 Porsche, summoned by cellular telephone. There are times when Fernández thinks his fellow Cubans have been living in America for too long.

Fernández believes he and the other front-line troops are not doing much more than fighting a guerrilla war in which they stage ambushes, because they do not have the means to do otherwise. His unit is better staffed than it was, but if he gets into trouble, he has to call on the uniformed branch of Metro-Dade for help: it could take one of the other undercover detectives up to twenty minutes to respond and, like Lucas, Fernández does not carry a gun when he's working undercover.

Also like Lucas, Fernández fully recognizes the futility of his job. Perhaps like all soldiers at the front, he sees no winning strategy nor any real evidence of a will to win from the top. He believes the government, if it is sincere, must provide the resources, and he points out that a young FBI agent, supposedly part of the elite, makes $23,000 a year. Fernández compares that to the earnings of a twelve-year-old boy who sold cocaine for his godfather. At thirteen, the boy had a chauffeur to whom he paid $200 a week. At eighteen, he was making $10,000 a day. When he was arrested, he had just bought his family a one-million-dollar house, and had hidden away $758,000 in cash.

Nevertheless, like Lucas and the other members of the undercover unit, Fernández keeps a constant vigil, except after midnights and on weekends—in this war, there is not enough money for overtime.

The task force offered another illusory promise: to work with foreign governments "to cut the flow of illegal drugs into the United States."

In March 1982 when the vice-president returned to Miami to report his first month's progress to Miami Citizens Against Crime, he was extremely encouraging about the response of those foreign governments which, he said, had given "enthusiastic support" for the task force.

Vice-President Bush reported the president of Bolivia's commitment to reduce his country's enormous coca crop "to levels needed for legal production." The establishment of the task force had motivated the leadership of Peru, Bush said, "to expand efforts to control their own illicit drug trade." And the government of Colombia "welcomed" the task force, predicting great things for its efforts to reduce the flow of drugs.

There was one other foreign government to which the vice-president referred with optimism: that of the Bahamas. He said that he was sending a senior US government official to Nassau, the capital, that very week, and he implied that the Bahamian government was anxious to cooperate with the task force.

Bush may have meant it. If so, he was a victim of his own enthusiasm; guilty of no more than whistling in the wind.

PART TWO

A NATION FOR SALE

The traffickers needed a transshipment point and a safe refuge. Less than fifty miles from the Florida coast, they bought paradise.

8

Kojak

In the summer of 1978, some three months after his forty-sixth birthday, Luis García shaved from his head what little hair still remained, thereby increasing his already remarkable resemblance to the actor Telly Savalas and to Kojak, the bald-headed New York cop Savalas had made popular on television. It was a menopausal act of a middle-aged man who was deeply bored with every facet of his life and it did seem to change his luck. A bank loan that had been stalled for months finally came through, allowing García to buy a new press for his small printing business. Business picked up and with the improved profits García was able to buy, for $1,600, the derelict hull of a Formula-24 speedboat, which over the next six months he totally rebuilt and equipped with a powerful Chrysler engine. At his print shop in Miami he painted the deck white and the hull jet black and along each side, in luminous yellow letters, the name *Mister Kojak.* The boat and its owner became a familiar sight on Biscayne Bay, drawing the attention of *The Miami Herald,* which reported on the "good Samaritan" who looked like Kojak and who was known for helping fellow boatmen in distress. His obvious mechanical ability and his seamanship also drew the attention of a foul-mouthed Cuban named Víctor Segura, who in early May 1979, bluntly proposed to Kojak that he become a drug trafficker.

Segura had been a fisherman in Cuba until 1963 when he fled Castro's revolution in a small dinghy and, after twelve days adrift at sea, was rescued by the US Coast Guard. Given asylum in the United States, he became a lobster fisherman based in Miami until the Bahamian government barred foreign lobster boats from its waters. Segura, and many like him, turned easily to running drugs, in his case marijuana and with considerable success.

"How much are you making as a printer?" Segura asked Kojak.

"Four hundred dollars, five hundred a week."

"In my business that's chickenshit to tip goddamn doormen," said Segura. That may have been an exaggeration but, as Kojak was to discover, Segura was in the habit of keeping on hand $250,000 in cash, in the trunk of his car.

Kojak asked for time to consider the proposition that he become Segura's "right-hand man." On May 13, 1979, his forty-seventh birthday, Kojak reflected on a life he still found unsatisfactory—a hand-to-mouth business and a marriage firmly stuck in the doldrums—and decided that whatever risks the drug trade might pose, they were preferable to death from boredom.

On May 18, Segura and Kojak formally shook hands. Kojak liquidated his printing business and visited his friends to warn them, ambiguously, that he would not be around for a while. Then, he sat down his wife and his three children and told them of the course he had decided to embark upon and the risks that it entailed. They preferred to hear about the potential rewards: the prospect of the money he might make delighted them.

Luis García had not led a blameless life. He admitted that his youth, which was divided between the United States and Cuba, was "wild": as a teenager in Havana, he had been part of a strong-arm gang that protected a politician, and he'd carried a gun; in New York he had done odd jobs for the Mafia and, still a teenager, he had found employment as a pimp. Still, after moving to Miami and for most of his adult life, he had held regular jobs, paid his taxes, nurtured his family, and stayed within the law. His mid-life decision to step outside it and become a drug trafficker was not a casual one, nor were his motivations simple.

Certainly, he was seeking excitement and money. He, like so many people, was ambivalent about marijuana, the drug he intended to smuggle; he did not use it, preferring tobacco and alcohol, but he did not see it as a great social evil. And, perhaps above all, he saw trafficking as an opportunity to excel at something, to finally make his mark: if the likes of Víctor Segura could run rings around the law-enforcement efforts of the United States government, and boast about it, Luis García could become "the best goddamned trafficker in America."

Perhaps he did. Kojak's career as a trafficker lasted for almost four years. In that time he imported drugs into the United States with the regularity of a scheduled carrier. By his estimate, 98 percent of his shipments got through. None of the people who worked for him were killed in that process, nor did he cause anybody else to be killed. Though by the end he was known to just about every local, state, and federal agency engaged in the war on drugs, he was never seriously investigated, nor questioned, nor indicted, nor prosecuted. His "retirement" was voluntary, and he took the trouble to go to the DEA and announce it. As a result, he was required to inform on his associates. Though they knew that, because *he* told them, there was only one serious threat on his life, and there remained a small army of men who would have smuggled drugs for Kojak any day, if only he had agreed to resume his career.

There were times when he was tempted. As part and parcel of his "retirement" scheme, Kojak agreed to go to Washington to testify to the President's Commission on Organized Crime on the techniques and technicalities of drug trafficking. He was asked five questions, of which the most potent was how had he taught himself to fly an airplane? (The answer, paraphrased: With the controls in one hand and a bottle of rum in the other.) Neither then, in 1984, nor later did any federal agency pay serious regard to the fundamental lessons that Kojak could teach them.

Frustrated by the empty rhetoric of the war on drugs and the blatant inadequacies of its pursuit, Kojak would sit at the wheel of his boat, a twenty-eight-foot cruiser, and propose: "Let's go south." By which he meant that two hours after leaving his house in Miami, he could be in the Bahamian island of Bimini;

he could acquire without difficulty up to 600 pounds of cocaine, and take it on board; in a further two hours he could be back in Miami with a cargo worth $3 million. Given the number of boats among which Kojak's might hide, given the resources and the lack of resolve of US Customs, the Coast Guard, and the rest of "the opposition," and given his knowledge of the waters, the chances of detection would be negligible.

When he said "Let's go south," he was joking, of course.

Kojak's entry into the drug-smuggling business coincided with some fundamental changes in the way in which that business was generally conducted. Until the late 1970s, most of the marijuana that reached Florida from Colombia did so on board "mother ships"—bulk carriers that would transport the drug across the ocean to within spitting distance of the Florida coast, from where small, fast speedboats would make the final dash. Víctor Segura, for example, would sail down to Colombia is his forty-two-foot lobster boat, *Yvette,* and collect anywhere between 14,000 and 17,000 pounds of marijuana. Then, moored in international waters somewhere between the Bahamas and Florida, he would be met by a flotilla of small craft that, depending on the state of the seas and the seamanship of the crew, might carry up to 1,500 pounds each.

As for cocaine, the amounts then being consumed in the United States were sufficiently small that the market could easily be supplied by "body packers" or "mules" who would import the drug into the United States strapped to their bodies or hidden inside false compartments in their suitcases. (There were the foolhardy who carried cocaine *inside* their bodies, contained in condoms they had swallowed. If all went well, the condom, in the natural course of things, would pass through the body and be retrievable in Miami. If not, and the condom became trapped in the upper gut, the rubber would eventually disintegrate, releasing lethal quantities of cocaine into the bloodstream. There are documented cases of couriers who, awaiting this fate, preferred to kill themselves.)

But in the late 1970s, the dramatic expansion of the cocaine industry, and, for marijuana smugglers such as Segura, the need to remain one step ahead of law enforcement, demanded new techniques. Kojak's first assignment was to take $24,000 from the trunk of Segura's car and open a bank account, something Segura had been unable to do for himself because he could neither read nor write in any language. Kojak's second job was to accompany his new employer on what turned out to be for them a voyage of amazing discovery.

Draw a straight line on the map between northern Colombia and Florida—which is what Kojak did in a public library—and it will pass inevitably between the 700 islands and more than 2,000 islets or "cays" (pronounced keys) of the Bahamas, most of them uninhabited. One of those islands, Bimini, is just forty-eight miles from Miami, about one hour by fast speedboat. In fact, there are two Biminis: North Bimini, which is where the inhabitants live and where thousands of tourists go to enjoy the fishing; and South Bimini, where the airstrip is, and where, after dark, the world might end, and nobody would notice.

In June 1979 Víctor Segura, Kojak, and two of Segura's associates, Cuban traffickers Segura referred to as "pollution," made the short voyage from Miami to North Bimini on *Yvette*. Even though their mission was entirely pacific, and the *Yvette* carried nothing of value, Segura's associates insisted on toting AR15 assault rifles, which they kept handy. As a result, when they arrived in Bimini, Edward, the young Bahamian customs officer who went on board to clear them, threatened to file a report. Despite Segura's belligerent objections, Kojak took $100 of Segura's money, and taking Edward aside, apologized for the "mistake." He promised that if Edward were to return in ten minutes, there would be no sign of any illegal weapons on the boat. The readiness with which Edward agreed to the compromise and took the $100 bill were Kojak's first indication that the Bahamas were for sale.

Just when the Bahamas first became a significant transshipment point for drugs is not clear. As early as 1968, when the islands were still under British rule, an American pilot named Jack Devoe flew 250 pounds of marijuana from Jamaica to Bimini and hid the bales at the end of the airstrip, ready for collection by a boatman who took them to Florida. Certainly by 1974 the Royal Bahamian Police Force had sufficient evidence of drug trafficking to consider it a "serious problem" and in response, increased aerial surveillance of the islands from 60 to 100 flying hours per month. In 1976 the Police Marine Division was expanded and renamed the Bahamas Defence Force, and its priority was changed from the prevention of illegal fishing to the pursuit of traffickers.

Then in early 1979, Lawrence Major, an assistant commissioner of police, made a surprise visit to the island of Great Exuma—some 150 miles from the Bahamian capital, Nassau—and decided on impulse to search the light aircraft that had landed at George Town airport immediately before his plane. On board the aircraft he found 247 pounds of almost pure cocaine—at that time, worth some $2 billion on the streets of America and also the biggest drugs seizure ever made. Assistant Commissioner Major was a remarkably persistent pursuer of traffickers, a virtual one-man task force who would go alone, armed with only a revolver, to any island or cay that aroused his suspicions. Shortly after his record-breaking seizure on Great Exuma, Major went to Black Rock, a deserted outcrop off the island of Grand Bahama, where he discovered a cache of marijuana so enormous he had to pace it out to estimate its measurements: it was six feet high and more than two miles long.

On March 12, 1979, Major and two other senior officers submitted a report to the police commissioner that eloquently described the importance the Bahamas was rapidly assuming in the international narcotics trade. The report identified fourteen islands and chains of islands from which drugs were being transshipped: in order of importance, the Exumas, Andros, Grand Bahama, Bimini, Abaco, the Berry Islands, Cat Island, Crooked Island and Acklins, Ragged Island and its surrounding cays, Mayaguana, Eleuthera, Long Island, San Salvador, and Inagua; in short, from just about everywhere in the Bahamas.

Major reported that one island in the Exumas, Norman's Cay, had been literally taken over by armed traffickers who had closed the hotel, declared the airstrip off-limits, and hoisted the Colombian flag. On Pigeon Cay, also in the Exumas, two helicopters were engaged on a permanent basis to ferry cocaine from island to island, and a local resident kept a 55-gallon fuel drum on his truck so that the helicopters might be refueled. Elsewhere, other locals had become involved, at first by retrieving bales of marijuana they had found floating in the sea, later by working for the traffickers as loaders, or occasionally, by hijacking their drugs. At least four men had been murdered in the Bahamas, and there had been gun battles with the police: on Bimini, police officers had been machine-gunned by traffickers and a sergeant left for dead.

With understandable urgency, the commissioner of police passed on these observations to the Bahamian government in his own report that was little short of apocalyptic: "The security of this country is being threatened by the incursion of armed foreign criminals," the commissioner wrote on March 16, 1979. "The Bahamas is being deluged with drugs. It is an extraordinary situation."

The commissioner "strongly recommended" to the government equally extraordinary measures to "make an impression on those persons engaged in this wicked type of business." His shopping list included: more men and paramilitary training for the Internal Security Division, the establishment of a "strike force" trained and equipped to carry out lightning raids on the traffickers' bases, and tough new laws that would give the police powers to confiscate the traffickers' equipment and their profits.

Nothing happened for three years. Or, more accurately, during the next three years the Bahamas became to traffickers what Panama is to money launderers: a safe haven, a place where they could conduct their business with almost total impunity, so long as they paid. If in 1979 the Bahamas was deluged with drugs, by 1980 it was sodden with them. If in 1979 Assistant Commissioner Major was merely remarkable for his diligence, by 1980 he was practically unique, one of the few cops on the force not tainted by corruption. If in 1979 there was an incursion of armed criminals, by 1980 it had become an invasion.

Much of the blame for what happened rests with Kojak. He did not invent bribery, of course, nor was he the first and only one to pay bribes in the Bahamas. But it was Kojak who introduced to those islands what he calls, in all seriousness, "true communism": a philosophy of "if I make a buck, everybody makes a buck."

Kojak paid police officers, customs officials, and immigration men. He paid lawyers, judges, and politicians. On Great Harbor Cay he paid the local doctor to maintain a tap on the island's telephone exchange, and he gave money to the town drunk. Almost no one was too unimportant or too mighty to benefit from Kojak's largesse: he treated lowly constables and officers up to the rank of assistant commissioner alike. Kojak paid the chairman of the ruling political party in the Bahamas, and was led to believe he also paid the prime minister.

Nine months after Kojak "retired" from the drug trade, a Commission of Inquiry was established in the Bahamas to investigate the mess of corruption he and others had created. The commission secured the services of one senior detective from each of three Commonwealth countries—Britain, Canada, and Australia—and of those three it fell to Detective Superintendent David Stockley of Scotland Yard to examine Kojak's activities. In the course of his investigation Stockley could not help develop a grudging respect for Kojak as "a very charming, very likeable, brave and efficient man." Nevertheless, Stockley also came to regard Kojak as a man who had done something "truly evil"; almost single-handedly, he had corrupted an entire nation.

In early December 1979 Kojak watched a Fairchild 27 turbo-prop aircraft land on the airstrip at South Bimini. It taxied to a halt and was immediately surrounded by trucks and vans from which emerged a small army of Bahamian "loaders." While the pilot kept one engine running, and while a small group of police constables stood guard, the Bahamians retrieved the plane's cargo, 150 bales of marijuana, each weighing some forty pounds. It took less than six minutes and only a few minutes more for the plane's fuselage to be swept clean of any traces of the marijuana. Within ten minutes at the most, the Fairchild had taken off and resumed what the US authorities had no reason to believe was anything other than the uninterrupted flight of an empty plane from Colombia.

The vans and trucks took the marijuana two miles across South Bimini to a private dock at Buccaneer Point where the boatmen were waiting. Each one was a private subcontractor, part of what is a major cottage industry in Miami. They are known as *peces*—fish—and their strength lies in their detailed knowledge of the shallow waters along the Florida coast and their secret *huequitos*—little holes—where they land. There are hundreds if not thousands of "little holes" in South Florida—inlets, coves, bays, canals, causeways, swamps, and estuaries—and every boatman has his own, unknown not only to law enforcement agencies, but to his colleagues as well. On that December night in 1979, all of the "fish" made it safely to Florida, and within one week all of the marijuana had been sold to wholesalers. After paying their Colombian supplier and all of the expenses, Víctor Segura and his two associates made $400,000 between them.

Kojak's cut was a mere $30,000 but the practical knowledge he gained from this, his first "trip," was simply priceless. Since his recruitment by Segura in May he had been diligently researching his new trade, from books and magazines at the public library and in the Santa Barbara, an unsavory bar beside the Miami River that was a hangout for smugglers who, with enormous profanity, would boast and argue about their exploits. The arguments often led to fights, and occasionally to homicide; more than once Kojak and *Mister Kojak* would have to speed to Bimini, taking the winner of such fights beyond the reach of the law. Sometimes Kojak would be asked to smuggle people in the opposite direction, from Bimini to Miami: the "Cocaine Wars" were then in progress in Miami, and he had little doubt that some of the sullen young men who were his passengers on *Mister Kojak* were on their way to carry out deadly assignments.

It was, on Kojak's part, deliberate strategy, designed to gain knowledge of the drug industry, as well as an array of contacts within it, and a reputation for guts and resourcefulness. It was never his intention to remain Víctor Segura's right-hand man for very long; just long enough to learn what he needed to know and to establish his credentials. After his first "trip" in December 1979, all that he lacked was experience of the Colombian end of the business, and a supplier there who would agree to deal with him. An unexpected opportunity to complete his education came very quickly.

Segura was a heavy cocaine user, an addiction that had taken its physical toll, and by December he was in no condition to play an active part in any further "trips." And although few people—including Kojak—knew it he had been indicted for trafficking and was awaiting trial. (Segura was eventually convicted and sentenced to fifteen years.) With the Fairchild due to make a second run that month to Colombia to pick up a further 6,000 pounds of marijuana, Segura announced to his two associates that he intended to take a vacation and that, while he would provide his share of the financing, Kojak would take his place as a full partner, in name if not in fact. Kojak took immediate advantage of his new status to declare that he would accompany the crew of the Fairchild to Colombia, "to take care of security."

When the plane landed at Santa Marta airport in northern Colombia on the morning of December 17, Kojak found waiting a black Mercedes and, inside it, a stocky well-tanned Colombian in his early forties, Juan Noguera.

The Noguera family and Santa Marta were to marijuana what the Ochoa family and Medellín are to cocaine. Santa Marta was the first town founded in Colombia by the conquistadores, in 1525, and it is now the country's most popular seaside resort, though not for foreigners. It is essentially a sprawling, dangerous shantytown surrounded by luxurious resorts and golden, unsafe beaches: "It is extremely dangerous to wander off the beaten track," warns *The South American Handbook,* the bible of travelers to that continent. "[Our] correspondents have been robbed at gunpoint." But to connoisseurs of marijuana around the world, the city means only one thing: Santa Marta Gold—perhaps the palest, strongest, and finest "grass" that money can buy. Through an empire of legal and illegal businesses the Noguera family—and one other—dominated the marijuana trade in Santa Marta and, although he was the youngest son, Juan Noguera ran the show.

Noguera drove Kojak to the resort of Puerto Galleón where a private villa had been reserved for his comfort. Noguera remained with Kojak throughout the rest of that day, personally ensuring that all of the arrangements for the Fairchild's return flight were in order. He was also at the airport that night when the Fairchild was taxied to the end of the runway, to an inlet from the ocean that was filled with small canoes. An army of Indians scurried over the dunes, carrying bulging gray garbage-disposal bags that they completed loading onto the plane in less than six minutes. That night, as the Fairchild made uneventful passage towards Bimini, Kojak slept on a warm and pungent bed of the finest marijuana, confident that he now had a willing supplier and all the knowledge he needed to go into business for himself.

Just before Christmas, after all of the marijuana had been safely delivered and sold, Kojak went to a Holiday Inn close to Miami International Airport to meet Rafael Noguera, the eldest of the Noguera brothers, and to hand over the first installment of the $420,000 he owed the family. While underlings counted the money, contained in brown grocery bags, Noguera took Kojak to the hotel bar and told him the family was ready and willing to deal with him directly. He could have unlimited credit; if he needed money to set himself up as an independent operator, he could have an interest-free loan. Finally, Noguera invited Kojak to revisit Colombia as the family's guest, so that he might see for himself the extent and sophistication of the Noguera organization.

When Kojak duly landed at Barranquilla airport, three hours by road from Santa Marta, on January 10, 1980, he was met by Juan Noguera, who made sure he passed through customs and immigration without any formalities. For the next three weeks, Noguera took personal pains to ensure that Kojak received a tour fit for royalty.

On most mornings a young pilot would take Kojak in one of Noguera's planes on aerial tours of the banana-growing country southeast of Ciénaga to inspect the literally hundreds of private airstrips, most of them clandestine and perfectly camouflaged by the surrounding jungle. For almost one week he toured the arid Guajira Peninsula, the home of primitive nomadic Indians, where there are yet more clandestine strips, and on the rugged coast, countless coves and inlets where marijuana could be safely stored and loaded onto boats. On mule-back he climbed up the foothills of the Sierra Nevada to the high valleys where marijuana is grown in well-maintained plantations stretching as far as the eye can see. A few days later, with Juan Noguera at the wheel of a Land Rover, he rode at the head of a convoy of trucks transporting the harvested crop from the plantations to the Nogueras' various warehouses. Noguera carried a *carriel* (a leather pouch worn as a sling), from which he would take stacks of fresh bank notes to pay a toll at each and every checkpoint maintained along the road by the police and the army. Only when the bribes had been accepted would Noguera use the Land Rover's sophisticated radios to tell the convoy it was safe to proceed.

Kojak was taken to see facilities where the marijuana was dried, sorted, and stored and, on the edges of downtown Santa Marta, to two warehouses where samples of different grades of the finished product were displayed in air-conditioned rooms for inspection by prospective buyers. In Ciénaga, the Dangond family—distant relatives of the Nogueras and their greatest rivals—showed Kojak a communications center that would have done credit to NASA. Kojak's visit to Colombia was made the more extraordinary by the fact that Julio Dangond, the head of the rival family, set out to compete for his attention, even going to the extent of taking over the villa next door to the one where Kojak was housed. Night after night, the Nogueras and the Dangonds would compete to provide Kojak with the most lavish hospitality, "two devils vying for my soul." Kojak played one against the other, endeavoring to offend neither of them. He apparently succeeded because both the Nogueras and the Dangonds were to become his suppliers.

By the time he had returned to Miami in early February 1980, Kojak probably knew as much about the techniques and technicalities of drug smuggling as any man alive. Aided by a $100,-000 interest-free loan from the Nogueras, he acquired on lease a DC-3, a venerable airplane but a doggedly reliable one, and capable of carrying a payload of up to 8,000 pounds. By the end of February he had "crowned" his first trip as an independent operator. By the end of March, he was firmly installed in temporary headquarters at the Complete Angler Hotel on North

Raúl Díaz, founder of Centac 26. Now, supposedly, "the most dangerous man in Miami."

Raúl Díaz rose from police rookie to Homicide lieutenant in nine years. Relieved of his command of Centac, he chose banishment to the "Siberia" of Miami International Airport.

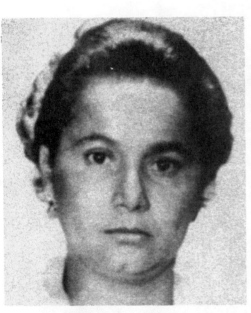

Griselda Blanco, the "Ma Barker" of Medellín cocaine traffickers.

There was no one Ricardo "The Monkey" Morales would not betray.

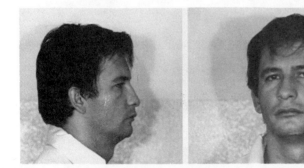

Rafael Leon Rodriguez's fondness for killing people made "Amilcar" Centac's first target.

This "Blue Thunder" is one of the fleet of fast boats that are the pride of the Blue Lightning Strike Force in Florida. They can catch anything afloat—*if* their crews are prepared to take the risks.

Luis Fernández and Preston Lucas, the real-life counterparts of the heroes of "Miami Vice." They argue passionately with each other about the merits of muzzle velocity versus stopping power but they have never shot at anybody.

Money, of course, is at the root of cocaine trafficking—sums of money so vast as to be almost meaningless. Above, $5.4 million in cash seized by the US Customs Service from a private jet at Fort Lauderdale, Florida.

In the summer of 1978, some three months after his forty-sixth birthday, Luis García shaved from his head what little hair still remained. It was a menopausal act of a middle-aged man who vowed to become "the best goddamned trafficker in America." *Left*, Kojak with his mother in Cuba. *Below right*, with Neysa, who would become his third wife; *below left*, with the Cessna he taught himself to fly; *bottom*, at the wheel of his 27-foot cruiser.

The Tribune

The Tribune

"Crooks and liars" was Kojak's description for Sir Lynden Pindling (*left*), prime minister of the Bahamas, and Everette Bannister (*above*). Bannister's son Gorman (*below*) says Pindling always got his share of bribes and kickbacks. "Tommy" Maillis (*below left,* with his daughter) gave the CIA photographic evidence linking Pindling to Norman's Cay.

Paul Eddy/Reporters International

Carlos Lehder, Colombia's most prodigious smuggler of cocaine, who used Norman's Cay as a transshipment point to flood the United States with drugs.

Bimini, directing by radio what had rapidly become a fleet of five aircraft.

The money poured in. But, unusually for his trade, Kojak reinvested most of the profits back into the business. One of his priorities was to devise and build a communications system that might rival the one he had seen in Ciénaga, and that would make detection of his boats and planes by the US authorities as difficult as possible. Another was to find some method of overcoming the acute logistical problem posed by the inability of drug-carrying aircraft making clandestine flights to readily obtain fuel. It was the ingenuity that Kojak applied to these and other problems that contributed much to his success.

The range of his first DC-3 was about 850 miles or more than six hours of flying time—about as long as it took to fly from Bimini to Santa Marta. That left no margin for contingencies, and no fuel for the return flight; although in theory the Nogueras and the Dangonds were supposed to supply fuel at their clandestine strips, that was easier said than done. Since the strips had no electricity, they had no pumps, and the fuel had to be siphoned into a plane's tanks from five-gallon drums. Besides being tedious, such a refueling operation carried with it grave risks of the fuel becoming contaminated; an explanation, Kojak believed, for many of the fatal crashes other traffickers were experiencing. Kojak's first solution to the problem, achieved with a $20,000 bribe, was to arrange for his planes to be refueled on both legs of their journey at Great Inagua, which lies at the extreme southeast end of the Bahama chain. Infested by fearsome mosquitoes, it is one of the least charming of the islands, but it lies approximately half-way between Bimini and Santa Marta, thus giving Kojak's planes all of the range they needed to avoid refueling in Colombia—in theory.

But as "Rocky" Powers, one of the most experienced pilots Kojak employed, was to discover, the theory collapsed if anything significant went wrong: after flying all the way down to Santa Marta and wasting fuel while waiting for landing clearance, Powers was told he could not land, presumably because of some temporary dispute between the suppliers and whichever Colombian officials they had neglected to bribe. Powers made it back to Great Inagua by the skin of his teeth, and only by operating the engines at minimum power, barely enough to keep the plane above its stalling speed; he landed with no more than ten gallons of fuel left in the tanks.

The much more effective solution Kojak eventually adopted was to equip his planes with rubber bladders filled with fuel which occupied the otherwise empty cargo hold on the way down to Colombia. The bladders contained 800 gallons of extra fuel and were "plumbed" directly into the plane's regular fuel tanks contained in the wings. As the engines fed off the wing tanks, the bladders automatically replenished those tanks so that they remained full. Simultaneously, of course, as the bladders gave up their fuel they deflated, making room in the cargo hold for the drugs. Through this ingenious solution Kojak's DC-3s, of which he had three, were given a nonstop flying range of twenty-two hours. There was one catch: rubber bladders filled with high-octane fuel effectively converted the planes into flying bombs. Still, the pilots were paid up to $60,000 for a single round-trip flight which, in Kojak's view, was adequate compensation for the risk.

Another risk facing the pilots—and more so, the boatmen who transported the drugs on the last dash from the Bahamas to Florida—was that of interception by any of the agencies charged with interdiction or, for that matter, by rival traffickers and would-be hijackers. An essential element of every successful drug run was Kojak's ability to talk by radio to the pilots, the boatmen, the loaders waiting in the Bahamas and in Florida, and to the suppliers in Colombia. But if they could hear him, so could anyone else monitoring the same wavelengths— *if* they knew which channels to listen in on.

The standard equipment for small boats operating in offshore waters is VHF (Very High Frequency) radio, which, on the marine band, has seventy-two separate channels. Switching between those channels at frequent intervals in any conversation was one way in which Kojak's people thwarted eavesdropping, and by using a simple code to announce each change in channel, they made it all but impossible for any monitor to keep up with them. (The code was based on *bolita,* an illegal numbers game that is highly popular in Miami, especially among Cubans. Each of the one hundred numbers in the game has special significance: for example, the number sixty-eight means death. So instead of saying "Switch to channel sixty-eight," the elliptical instruction to change to that channel might be "I'll see you at the funeral." Judging from the scraps of bizarre conversation that can be heard on the marine band in South Florida, the code is still widely used.)

Not satisfied with that, Kojak also equipped his boatmen and many of his ground personnel with powerful hand-held VHF radios that broadcast on the aviation band, which has no fewer than 720 channels with which to confuse potential listeners. Then he supplied yet more radios that operated on the two-meter waveband—the one commonly used in America by cab companies and radio-dispatched vehicles—and, finally, high frequency sets, like those used by ham operators to talk across vast distances. Given the multiplicity of the choices of communication Kojak provided, it is not surprising that none of his planes and boats was ever intercepted.

The crowning glory of his communications network was a high frequency set that Kojak had built for himself. It was eventually installed in the bedroom of his house in Miami and equipped with an aerial concealed under the eaves of the roof. Already sufficiently powerful to broadcast and receive signals from almost anywhere in the world, it could, if necessary, be boosted by an amplifier, though only with the penalty that the lights in his house, and every house in the neighborhood, would dim. The radio was always on, tuned to an emergency frequency on which Kojak could always be contacted. It became such an integral part of his life that when he retired and finally turned it off, both he and his new wife experienced enormous difficulty in sleeping.

But all of the sophisticated equipment, all of the precautions and clever tricks, were mere accessories to Kojak's success, not the cause of it. What he depended upon above all else was the greed of other people, and the fact that his profits were fabulous enough to allow him to feed it.

Kojak paid the Nogueras and the Dangonds an average of $70 for each pound of marijuana he collected in Colombia. In Miami he was able to sell it to a wholesaler for an average of

$240 per pound (and, in New York, for $325 per pound and more). So, on an average load of 5,000 pounds, his gross return was a minimum of $850,000. Of that, the pilot and the copilot of the plane would receive $100,000 between them, and the boatmen would receive $30 for every pound they brought in. There would be other workers, such as ground personnel, who might receive anywhere between $5,000 and $15,000, and Kojak would have to meet all of the fuel costs for the plane, and supplies and provisions for his Bahamas base. Even so, he could expect to easily clear half a million dollars from each trip—and there were times when Kojak was "crowning" *up to four trips a week.*

In Bimini, where Kojak operated until May 1980, he paid a minimum of $110,000 per trip to locals who acted as loaders, and to police officers and local officials who, metaphorically at least, looked the other way. (Metaphorically because they were usually on hand to make sure things went smoothly; some would even help with the unloading.) When Bimini became overrun with other traffickers, and in Kojak's terms "too hot," he moved to Great Harbor Cay in the Berry Islands where he paid $100,000 per trip for the cooperation of the local people and the three-man constabulary; in addition he paid $10,000 to the sole customs official on the island, who insisted on receiving the money from Kojak in person. Lionel Glinton, a young constable who moonlighted as Kojak's assistant in the Bahamas, received payments of more than $800,000 for services which included recruiting onto Kojak's payroll Chief Superintendent (later Assistant Commissioner) Howard Smith. When, under intense pressure from US authorities, the Bahamian government could no longer resist establishing a "strike force" to combat trafficking, Smith was made the head of it. In return for an Oldsmobile Cutlass imported from Miami and $10,000 a month, Smith warned Kojak in advance of every raid the strike force intended to make: according to telephone records, he called Kojak in Miami thirty-five times from his home, and four more times on the direct line in his office.

It was not only the active participants in Kojak's schemes who took his money. At the Graveyard Inn at Bullocks Harbor, the only settlement on Great Harbor Cay, the drinks were always on Kojak, and his bar bill averaged $600 a week. In the Bahamas and in Florida, people who were "sympathetic" would receive $100 tips, bracelets, Rolex watches, and even cars; asked to estimate the value of the cars he had given away as gifts, Kojak could remember only some of them, and they were worth more than $250,000. Deciding it prudent to maintain a lower profile, he gave away his Formula-24 racing boat, the only condition being that the recipient remove the flamboyant lettering, *Mister Kojak,* from its sides. Deciding that his original DC-3 might have become "too hot," Kojak gave it away, too.

In Kojak's view these casual gifts were worth inestimably more than they cost because they created for him a network of "friends" who would "watch my back." In 1981, for example, when the FBI became curious about Kojak's planes and began to make discreet inquiries at Opa-Locka airport, north of Miami, where most of them were based, Kojak knew within minutes: a modest bracelet he had once given to a female employee at the airport brought as its reward the all-important warning telephone call that allowed him ample time to cover his traces. Similarly, when DEA agents made inquiries about Kojak at Opa-Locka, they were told by airport employees that he ran a legitimate operation importing lobsters from Belize, which was his cover story but, as the employees well knew, utter nonsense.

Kojak said that after his "retirement" as a trafficker he came to regret much of what he did, especially the fact that, in the end, he broke a promise he had made to himself and smuggled cocaine, indeed, what was probably the largest single load of cocaine brought into the United States at the time. He also regretted that he exposed some members of his family to trafficking, some of whom could not resist using "the merchandise," and some of whom refused to quit. A son-in-law has since died of a cocaine overdose and a cousin was brutally murdered in Miami. At the time of writing, a brother-in-law with lethal associates and insane drug habits stands as the next most likely victim.

But Kojak was unrepentant about the people he bribed with money and coerced with gifts, insisting that he did not corrupt anybody who was not willing to be corrupted: "I have also made love to a lot of women in my life," he said, "and I haven't raped one yet."

To an extent, though, he did excuse his "willing partners in crime" by saying that most of them, those in the outer islands of the Bahamas, were poor, or poorly paid officials who simply grabbed at the opportunity to share, for once, in sudden prosperity. He also pointed out that most of them were relatively honest, in that they delivered what he paid them for.

All of which is vastly more than could be said for the "crooks and liars" who led the Bahamian government.

9

The Men Who Stole Paradise

"**T**he Chief is a Thief" is a slogan much used in the Bahamas to describe Sir Lynden Oscar Pindling, prime minister of that country since before independence, Knight Commander Order of St. Michael and St. George, member for life of the British sovereign's Privy Council, and the longest-serving elected leader in the Commonwealth. It was first applied to him by his political opponents in 1984 when a Commission of Inquiry established that in the previous six years Pindling had received $2.8 million in what he claimed were "gifts" and "loans," and a further $240,000 for which he had no explanation at all. That inquiry was into drug-related corruption in the Bahamas and, since the commission found no evidence that any of the payments to Pindling came from drug traffickers, it effectively exonerated him. But there were witnesses, privy to secrets about Pindling and the nature of his government, from whom the inquiry did not hear. Had they testified, and been believed, the commission's verdict might have been very different.

There are two such witnesses who have since broken their silence. The first, Gorman Bannister, arrived at Miami International Airport on a flight from Nassau, on April 12, 1987, with a battered red suitcase that contained virtually all of his possessions, and a head full of extraordinary stories of corruption in the Bahamas that went way beyond anything the Commission of Inquiry had heard. He arrived in Miami with the notion that he could sell his story to the newspapers "for a few dollars," and disappear. "Few" is not a word that Bannister was brought up to comprehend, and had he succeeded in his plan, and however much money he got, he would, without doubt, have spent every cent of it on drugs. As it was, he ended up telling his story to agents of the DEA, and then to US prosecutors in Florida who promptly placed him in the Federal Witness Protection Program, and moved him to an undisclosed location. In their view, the fact that Gorman Bannister had been more or less addicted to cocaine for fourteen years did not make him an unreliable witness; he was one who needed to be protected, not least from himself.

Bannister's defection to the United States was crucially important because his father, Everette, was, for fifteen years, the "Mr. Fixit" of the Bahamas: the man to whom organized crime figures, international fugitives, deposed dictators, drug traffickers, and legitimate businessmen needing favors all paid millions of dollars. Gorman said Bannister, in turn, had paid government officials, leading members of the ruling Progressive Liberal Party, cabinet ministers, the prime minister, and the prime minister's wife. Gorman Bannister was, for part of that time, his father's "financial advisor," the keeper of the checkbook. The bribes and kickbacks received by Everette Bannister were far too prolific, and handled far too casually, for anybody to keep accurate records, but Gorman knew more than most about where the money came from, and where it went.

His motives for talking were complex and not entirely admirable. After living off his father for thirty-one years, the money had run out and, "I am no longer able to live in the style to which he made me accustomed." Gorman also wanted to get back at his father for refusing to break off a long-standing affair with a woman Gorman detested.

But, paradoxically, Gorman wanted to avenge his father. If it did nothing else, the Commission of Inquiry effectively destroyed Everette Bannister's usefulness as a "bagman" because it overexposed him. Having lost his usefulness he had, in Gorman's view, been "abandoned" by the prime minister and just about everybody else—which is why the money had run out. Most positively, Gorman defected because he wanted to break his own addiction to cocaine and to expose, through his first-hand knowledge, the appalling effect that cocaine and cocaine trafficking have had on the Bahamas.

So, Gorman talked: about a society in which, at almost every level, cocaine use has reached epidemic proportions, where "there is a crack house on every corner"; about the increasing direct involvement of Bahamians in trafficking and, thus, the shanty houses in Nassau where there is no electricity but "a Mercedes at the door, and twenty keys [kilos of cocaine] under the bed"; about trips to Colombia, and threats by Colombian traffickers to "remove people from the population count"; about blackmail and extortion and deportations of the uncooperative, achieved with a single telephone call; about the interception of secret US diplomatic cables, and the removal from Nassau of a State Department official who was proving "difficult"; above all about money, incalculable millions of dollars taken and received by every corrupt official and politician in Everette Bannister's pocket—and by "The Man," the prime minister, who *always* got his share."

The second witness, Athanasios "Tommy" Maillis, did not volunteer to talk. Indeed, when he was first traced to a small Greek island in May 1987, he prevaricated and hedged with all the skill of somebody trained in dissimulation by the CIA, which he was. Eventually, however, Maillis did tell at least some of what he knows. If his testimony is true, and there is evidence to support it, it damns the prime minister because it links him directly to the most notorious trafficking ring to operate in the Bahamas.

Maillis's testimony also raises a disturbing question about the role and the objectives of the CIA: If, as Maillis claims, the agency went to considerable lengths to obtain direct evidence against Pindling, evidence that would surely have sunk him, why was it not used?

Other than mutual greed for money, and a mutual propensity for womanizing, it is difficult to discern the reason why Lynden Pindling and Everette Bannister should have become so closely linked to each other. Bannister may respect the prime minister, but he does not much like him: "He's a greedy motherfucker," he told his son. And, for his part, Pindling has kept Bannister at a distance, rarely socializing with him. Their relationship is, for the most part, strictly business.

Their backgrounds are dissimilar, too. Bannister's education was perfunctory, as it was for most Bahamian blacks of his generation because the ruling whites would allow them only twenty high school places a year. Pindling won one of those places, at the Nassau Government High School, under the stern supervision of a father who was absolutely determined that his only child was going to succeed. Pindling senior had been trained as a teacher in his native Jamaica before moving to the Bahamas in 1925 to join the colony's police force. (Under white rule, many of Nassau's black policemen were imported from Caribbean islands, presumably to prevent the locals from getting ideas above their station.) Though he left the police force in 1934 to open a small grocery store, Lynden's father continued to be a strict authoritarian at home. "Only his mother tempered the discipline with a little mercy," said one of Lynden's few childhood friends. His mother was a warm, religious woman who hoped that he might become a preacher. "Preacher!" said his father. "Sometimes when the plate goes round there is only one penny in it." So in 1948, while Everette Bannister at the age of twenty-one found himself a wife on Bimini and emigrated to the United States to seek his fortune, Pindling, as a very frightened eighteen-year-old, took the same route as many future Commonwealth leaders: to London and the law.

In 1948, the year he arrived, blacks were an uncommon sight in England, as Pindling discovered when a young child approached him and began rubbing his skin to see if the color would come off. Racism was widespread. Pindling would arrive at a house to rent a room and, in his words, "you could see the shocked expression on their face and the place that was available ten minutes before suddenly became unavailable." When, through a friend, he eventually found a small flat in London, he was charged almost twice the rent it was worth. Pindling tolerated the discrimination until the passage of the Rent Act when he went before a tribunal and got his rent reduced from £4 to under £3, his first victory as a lawyer.

It was in London that Pindling developed an interest in politics and skill as an orator. On Sundays he would stroll to Speaker's Corner in Hyde Park and mount a soapbox to rail at the evils of colonialism. He was never a fire-breathing revolutionary; indeed, in 1952, having obtained his law degree from the University of London, he stayed on in England so he could see the coronation of Queen Elizabeth II. And when, much later, he committed his one violent act of defiance against the British Crown by hurling the ceremonial gold mace through a window of the parliament in Nassau, he first ensured that the window was open, to avoid causing damage. "We shall win with a mighty meekness," he would say, always cautioning black Bahamians against violence.

Still, on his return to the Bahamas from London, he became sufficiently troublesome to the ruling whites to have his name included on a list of lawyers that all major Bahamian companies boycotted. In 1953 he was one of the first blacks to join the new Progressive Liberal Party (PLP), formed by fair-skinned Bahamians of mixed race. In 1956, when the PLP fought its first election, Pindling was one of six members to win a seat in parliament. Two years after that, as general counsel to the taxi drivers' union, he helped organize a seventeen-day strike that paralyzed the economy and forced the British Colonial Office to begin political reform.

But the Bay Street Boys, so called because they controlled all of the businesses on Nassau's Bay Street, had no intention of surrendering the power they had held for three hundred years, and their cynically named United Bahamian Party was as rich as the PLP was poor. Pindling and his colleagues also faced the rigid bigotry of the British governor, Sir Ralph Grey, who could not countenance power in the hands of what he called "this bunch of baboons." Britain, though increasingly weary of its colonial burden, was not yet willing to shed it. So, as time passed and the Bay Street Boys continued to cook the books, restrict the electorate, and rig the constituencies, Pindling and his colleagues turned increasingly to the United States for help, in terms of both money and support. In New York City Everette Bannister was among those glad and able to lend a hand.

Bannister had done well for himself, though the route had been unlikely. Having begun work in New York as a doorman at a steak house, he had, by 1954—when Gorman was born—found employment as a butler. In due course, he obtained a new position as butler *and* chauffeur to Dick Howard, owner of the Peter Pan Foundation Company, manufacturers of ladies' undergarments and lingerie. Howard was not much interested in the company, which he had inherited, preferring to spend his time gambling, and Bannister therefore found himself virtually running Peter Pan. The rewards were sufficient to allow the Bannisters to live in a comfortable house in a middle-class neighborhood of East Elmhurst, and for Gorman and his elder brother to receive the education their father had been denied.

Unfortunately, Howard's gambling eventually proved ruinous, and there were times when he failed to pay Bannister's wages. (Gorman still regards Howard as "one of the greatest human beings who ever lived," but, to his father, nonpayment of monies due Everette Bannister is a felony; Bannister rarely spoke to Howard again.) Bannister tried his hand at running a travel agency. When that did not succeed he threw in his lot with a group of Jewish businessmen from the garment district of New York, whom he had met through Dick Howard, whose interests included The Anchorage, a small hotel on West Bay Street in Nassau.

It was in this period, during the run-up to the 1967 election in the Bahamas, that Pindling and his colleagues spent a lot of time in New York, seeking financial help. Gorman remembers his father taking Pindling around the garment district to meet his "influential friends." He also remembers being given a photograph, autographed with the inscription, "To Gorman: The sky's the limit, Lynden Oscar Pindling."

"At that time we would have accepted help from the devil," said one of the men who helped Pindling in his US fund-raising efforts. Michael McLaney was not exactly the devil but he was an apparatchik of Meyer Lansky, who rose further in the ranks of organized crime than any other hoodlum of non-Italian descent. McLaney—or more likely, Meyer Lansky—bankrolled the PLP's 1967 election campaign to the tune of $65,000. According to McLaney, the incentive was that if the PLP won, McLaney would organize gambling in the Bahamas in conjunction with the new government.

The election ended in deadlock with the PLP and the United Bahamians winning eighteen seats each, but Pindling persuaded two independent members to support him and, on January 16, 1967 he took the oath of office as prime minister. Almost his first act was to ask Queen Elizabeth to appoint a Royal Commission of Inquiry, which eventually decided that Michael McLaney was "a thoroughly dangerous person who is likely to do nothing but harm to the Bahamas." McLaney was run out of the country, becoming the first—but, by no means, the last— crook to learn that bribes paid in the Bahamas are nonrefundable, and not necessarily honored.

Pindling's election victory earned for Bannister vague status as a "consultant" on tourism to the new government, and he began commuting to the islands from his home in New York. His journeys to Nassau were so frequent, he eventually attracted the attention of the FBI, which sent agents to question him about what on earth he was doing over there. In part the answer was, running The Anchorage hotel, which Bannister somehow acquired as his own and which he renamed The Atlantic.

But Bannister had much larger aspirations than hotel keeping. Within months, if not weeks, of the PLP's narrow victory at the polls, Bannister and Pindling were devising schemes to take advantage of the prime minister's power to enrich themselves. It is fair to assume that they both felt they were owed something by the Bahamas because, when the time was right, they pursued those schemes with the rapaciousness of creditors out to collect a debt long overdue.

On July 10, 1973, the Bahamas finally became an independent nation and Pindling gained his indelible reputation as "Moses," the man who led his people to freedom. Shortly thereafter, the Bahamas also became the home and sanctuary of Robert Vesco, an engineering school drop-out turned financial wheeler-dealer who was once well described by *Fortune* magazine as America's most famous rascal. Vesco had fled the United States in 1972 with whatever was left of the $224 million he had bilked from investors of International Overseas Services (IOS). Having established through bribery one refuge in Costa Rica, Vesco moved to the newly independent Bahamas with the overwhelming confidence of a man who *knew* he was not going to be extradited.

Vesco already owned the Bahamas Commonwealth Bank in Nassau. It was a small institution but, under Vesco's proprietorship, it gave away money as if it were printing it. In March 1974, much less than a year after Vesco had moved to the Bahamas, *Business Week* magazine estimated that his bank had advanced $50 million in loans, most of them unsecured and almost none of them repaid. "Who does he think he's talking to?" said one debtor whom Vesco supposedly asked for repayment. "If he doesn't like it here, he can always leave."

The money flowed out of the Commonwealth Bank like water from a leaking tap, with Everette Bannister collecting most of it, though not all for himself. David Probinsky, at the time a public relations consultant to the prime minister, later described to American investigators how it worked: "I've had members of the government in my office call Everette and say, 'Everette, I need to borrow $50,000.' He would say, 'No problem. Go down Thursday and see somebody'—some teller or something—'and you'll get it.' The guy would go down and sign for $50,000. Probably millions of dollars went out to government people through the Vesco bank. Millions."

But in Everette Bannister's world, charity *always* begins at home. Before doling out Vesco's money to other people, Bannister grabbed a lion's share. The vehicles used to extract that money were two companies of which Bannister was part owner: Bahamas World Airlines (BWA), created in 1968 as a paper airline, and Airport Caterers, purchased in 1972 for $3.6 million, all of it borrowed from Vesco's bank. Both of those companies depended for their very existence on government favor—the airline for its charter licenses, and the catering company for the exclusive franchises which it held at the two main airports in the Bahamas, Nassau and Freeport. It was Pindling's government that bestowed those lucrative favors. What Pindling never revealed until he was forced to was that he had been given large amounts of stock, held in trust, in both companies.

Airport Caterers, to be fair, was not a bad banking proposition because the company was well run; Bannister had little to do with its administration. Bannister did administer BWA, however, which was probably the worst-run airline that ever flew, albeit seldom. Nevertheless, Vesco's bank advanced BWA $3.1 million to buy two aircraft and granted an overdraft which, in the words of the bank's eventual liquidator, David Jones, was "a continuous tap that somebody forgot to turn off." The airline repaid not one cent of the money it borrowed and precious little interest. By April 1974, when Vesco's bank collapsed, the airline owed $10.5 million, secured by nothing more than its two aircraft. The liquidator managed to sell those for a total of $450,000.

In the wake of his bank's collapse, Vesco left the Bahamas temporarily for his original refuge in Costa Rica. Undaunted, Bannister renamed BWA as Bahamas World Airlines (1974) Limited, and looked around for fresh "investors." Gorman Bannister, by then at college in the United States, abandoned his original academic discipline, psychology, in favor of business studies at the behest of his father, who bribed him with a $200 increase in his already generous monthly allowance. Everette promised Gorman that BWA would rise from the ashes and that, upon his graduation from college, there would be a lucrative job awaiting him in the Bahamas. Knowing his father's capacity for acquiring other people's money, Gorman never doubted it.

The roll call of those who were to "invest" in BWA (1974) reveals a collection of disparate people with one thing in common: the need for favors from Pindling's government.

First and foremost was Resorts International, formerly the Mary Carter Paint Company, which in 1969 had obtained the right to operate gambling casinos in Nassau and in Freeport. Since it held legal tenure, and operated its casinos with great propriety, Resorts International was not an obvious target for extortion. But James Crosby, then the chairman of the company, well understood the founding creed of Pindling's Bahamas: "What the government has given to foreigners, the government can take away."

It was all too easy. Foreigners, even prominent ones, needed permits to live and work in the Bahamas, and permits could be denied, or withdrawn, or not renewed. And, according to Gorman, among the legions of people who got money from Bannister whenever he needed it was a senior official in the immigration department, "a very intricate piece on the chessboard" who could "send four immigration men down to a person's house, put them in a bus, take them to the airport, and put them out of the country"; Bannister could cause that to happen, his son says, "at the drop of a dime."

To preclude any such possibility, Resorts International paid Bannister a "consultant's fee" of $50,000 a year, and one of Gorman's jobs, as his father's "financial advisor," was to stroll over to Resorts' casino on Paradise Island every two weeks to pick up the check. Gorman insists that his father did provide Crosby with advice on all sorts of matters, usually over dinner at Resorts' casino. From the results, that advice seems to have invariably included, "Pay Me."

Bannister owned the Las Palmas Hotel, and 200 acres of land surrounding it, at Kemp's Bay on the island of South Andros, which is Pindling's constituency. Bannister had "bought" the hotel from one of Vesco's companies for $320,000—every cent of it "borrowed," of course, from Vesco—and more than once he used it as security to "borrow" money from Crosby. He would then take it back, telling Crosby that some "investor" wished to buy it—then repledge it to Crosby for yet a further "loan." As described by Gorman, the deals were dizzying but had one certain result: Everette Bannister made money.

In 1976 he finessed the Las Palmas into a truly spectacular deal, persuading Crosby to put up the money to renovate the twenty-room hotel and provide its operating capital. Supposedly, Bannister was to manage the hotel, and split any profits fifty-fifty with Resorts. Profits were extremely unlikely, however, for South Andros, though it offers superb scuba diving, has no scheduled air service and is well off the tourist track. And any intrepid tourists who did make the journey were liable to find themselves turned away from the Las Palmas, even if they held reservations, because the prime minister was in residence. To the envy of his male friends, Pindling had an arrangement with his wife that allowed him to spend his weekends with friends at the Las Palmas while she remained at home in Nassau. He also had an arrangement with the Las Palmas that provided him and his guests with rent-free accommodation, and food and drink at cost.

Resorts International's "investment" in the Las Palmas

Hotel, which was eventually written off in the books as a loss, totaled $1.3 million. Asked after his defection to the United States to explain this remarkable deal, Gorman Bannister said it was "a sophisticated way of paying off the prime minister and my father."

QUESTION: And why did Resorts need to pay your father and Pindling?
BANNISTER: Because Resorts needed to stay in the Bahamas.
QUESTION: And if they had not paid?
BANNISTER: Who knows? They did.

They continued to do so. Resorts inevitably "invested" in Bahamas World Airlines, though modestly compared to Vesco. And Crosby paid Bannister a "finder's fee" of $580,000 in connection with the sale of the toll bridge linking Nassau to Paradise Island, a bridge that Crosby personally owned. Finding a buyer for the bridge was not too difficult; the trick was in securing government permission for the sale. Pindling was the chairman of the committee that vetted such transactions. Permission was forthcoming.

Perhaps the most generous gesture made by Resorts International, which directly benefited Bannister, was its agreement to sell its casino in Freeport for the bargain price of $5.5 million, which represented less than one year's operating profit. The new owners were to have been a group of Americans: Victor Sayyah, a wealthy insurance magnate; Lester Steiner, who was in the slot machine business; and, Sorkis Webbe, who claimed to be the group's general counsel. In applying for the necessary license to run a casino, the Sayyah group came highly recommended by Resorts International, which claimed to have carried out "background investigations" and to have found the would-be owners "upright corporate citizens" and "sound businessmen."

They were nothing of the sort. As even a perfunctory investigation would have established, Sorkis Webbe was a mobster from St. Louis, Missouri, who had been thrown out of Las Vegas because of his direct connections with organized crime. And, according to investigators for the Bahamas Gaming Board, when Sayyah and Steiner were asked for information about themselves, they submitted answers that were "inconsistent, incomplete and inaccurate to an extent that implies either complete incompetence or a wish to frustrate proper inquiry." In rejecting their application for a license, the Gaming Board, for the first time in its history, refunded the "nonrefundable" fee that applicants for a casino license have to pay: "The money was so hot we didn't want a cent of it polluting the treasury," said one member of the board.

This rejection by the Gaming Board did not matter to Bannister for, long before then, he had obtained for his airline a "loan" from the Sayyah group of $500,000 and a line of credit up to $2.6 million. Under the terms of the deal, Bannister did not have to repay the $2.6 million, or one cent of interest, for twenty years.

Gorman Bannister estimates that his father, as "the man who gets things done in the Bahamas," extracted between $70 and $100 million from "investors" in his various schemes, the largest single contributor being Robert Vesco. A great deal of that money was indeed spent on the airline because "my father had dreams of having an international airline on the lines of a Sabena, a Lufthansa, a British Airways." But the airline's payroll was always thoroughly padded with the salaries and expenses of leading members of the PLP and the prime minister's cronies, who demanded and got their share of the loot, doing nothing in return.

Others took their cut without even the pretense of working for it, turning up at Bannister's office in Nassau and demanding loans, in Gorman's words, "as if by right." To Gorman's chagrin, some of the money went to his father's mistress: Bannister provided the capital for two of her husband's businesses, and he bought a BMW for her eldest daughter's eighteenth birthday.

Some of the money went to the prime minister's wife. Bannister treated Lady Marguerite Pindling as though she were the Queen of the Bahamas, which is how she regarded herself. He bought her clothes, paid for vacations, and indulged her taste for Dom Perignon champagne imported, at her insistence, from Harrods in London; once, when Harrods cut off her credit for nonpayment, Bannister personally flew to London with $7,000 to settle the bill. According to Gorman: "There was nothing my father would not do for her."

And much of the money went to the prime minister. How much is anybody's guess because there is no income tax in the Bahamas and no requirement to keep personal financial records. From bank records, the Commission of Inquiry established that, between September 1978 and the end of 1983, Bannister gave Pindling $674,979, but there were other transactions to which the Commission was not privy. One of them, witnessed by Gorman, stands out simply because it illustrates Bannister's innate opportunism, and his willingness to promise anybody anything—so long as they could pay. It also illustrates the extent, and the limits, of the license under which Bannister operated.

In July 1980, General Anastasio Somoza, the deposed president of Nicaragua, having worn out his welcome in the United States, sought a new refuge in the Bahamas. When his emissaries arrived in Nassau to negotiate the details, Pindling was out of the country on official business. They therefore negotiated with Bannister, who instructed them to have Somoza sail his yacht to George Town on Great Exuma where he, Bannister, would meet him.

"Don't leave the office until I return," Bannister told his son as he left to take the short flight to George Town. "Don't move. No matter what time, don't leave."

Bannister returned about 5:45 P.M. the same day. According to Gorman, he was in exceptional spirits: "My father has a way. . . . You can always tell when something's going right for him because he walks stiff-backed and very fast. You can always tell. 'How are you doing?' I say, 'Okay, okay.' He says to me, 'Gorman, I am looking for a piece of paper.' "

Bannister searched the bag he had brought with him, pretending to look for the piece of paper, instead finding bundle after bundle of $100 bills he placed on the desk. "I wonder if I put it in my socks," said Bannister, searching them but finding only more $100 bills. He continued the pantomime until the desk was covered with money. "Count it," he said.

Gorman counted $320,000. "Count it again," said Bannister. When Gorman had confirmed the count, he was told to divide the money into two piles: one of $280,000 and one of $40,000. Meanwhile Bannister made a telephone call and Gorman heard him say: "Let me speak to the lady." After a pause: "I'm bringing the money round in a few minutes."

Gorman was—and remains—in no doubt that his father had spoken to the prime minister's wife. And as his father began to put the pile of $280,000 back into the bag, he had no doubt as to who was to get the lion's share of the money. Gorman protested: "I said, 'Hey Dad, this breakdown here, this doesn't look right. I mean, I can understand it's not fifty–fifty, I can understand sixty–forty, but you're going to break it down now to just about ninety-three–seven.' He said, 'Well you know Gorman, if it wasn't for The Man, I wouldn't be able to do the things I do, you know.' I said, 'Yeah, but if it wasn't for you, he wouldn't be able to do the things he does either.' He said, 'Yeah, but you know he's also a greedy motherfucker, too, so. . . .' " A few moments later, Bannister left his office with the $280,000 to drive, so far as Gorman knew, to the prime minister's house.

Bannister told his son that Somoza had displayed six trunks full of money on board his yacht and had said: "Everette, take what you want. Take as much as you want. I just want to stay in Nassau. I just want to stay alive."

Gorman complained to his father that, in that case, he should have taken more because "you know he's a dead man." "No," said his father, explaining a cardinal rule of the successful confidence trickster, "when you take too much from people you end up owing them too much." Bannister's theory, as he explained it, was that if a man had $20 million and you took only $1 million, "he isn't going to be that pissed if things don't work out." Somoza did not receive sanctuary in the Bahamas. Instead he fled to Paraguay where, two months later, he was assassinated.

Bannister's theory of not over-exploiting his victims (with the exception of Vesco, who was in no position to complain) stood up very well in the Bahamas until it was applied to drug traffickers. Some of them—in particular, Kojak—believed they were entitled to what they had paid for, and not giving Kojak his due was to be the start of Bannister's downfall. But for a while, Bannister and others like him, and members and officials of Pindling's government, took drug money from traffickers as readily as they had taken it from businessmen, mobsters, and criminals on the run.

That process began in 1978, coinciding with the start of the "cocaine explosion." It also coincided with the return to the Bahamas of Robert Vesco, who was forced to leave his sanctuary in Costa Rica when Rodrigo Carazo Odio campaigned for the presidency of that country on a specific platform of expelling Vesco, and won. (The economy of Costa Rica promptly went into disastrous decline.)

On his return to the Bahamas, Vesco became involved in drug trafficking. It seems remarkable that a man who had stolen $224 million and got away with it, should expose himself to the risks of the narcotics trade. After knowing Everette Bannister for at least four years, however, perhaps he felt he needed the money.

Bannister's trademark is a huge cigar that he holds in his mouth, but rarely lights. He does not drink alcohol and he despises those who use illegal drugs. Gorman's abiding memory of his years in Nassau is sitting on the veranda of the house his father had bought for him, "doing drugs" with his friends, watching and waiting for the inevitable approach of his father's car. Bannister would find any excuse to visit the house and every opportunity to slyly search it. Once, when he found Gorman's stash of cocaine hidden in a pile of *Playboy* magazines, he flushed it down the toilet. Pindling, too, has every reason to hate and fear cocaine, because his youngest son is addicted to it.

Yet both men became actively involved with a Colombian trafficker named Carlos Enrique Lehder Rivas: "Joe" Lehder to his friends, "Carlos the Terrible" by popular reputation, and, to the DEA, one of the most prolific transporters of cocaine into the United States.

Lehder took over the island of Norman's Cay by force majeure in late 1978, and was allowed to ship drugs from it by the ton until late 1982, when *he chose* to leave. Use of the word "allowed" implies, of course, that Lehder had the consent or at least the acquiescence of the Bahamian authorities. Pindling has always emphatically denied that charge, but it is the only reasonable conclusion that can be drawn from the evidence.

10

Devil's Island

Norman's Cay is the most westerly of the Exuma Islands, some fifty miles from Nassau. From the air it still looks to be the paradise it once was: a hook-shaped coral island set in a turquoise sea, fringed by a white sand beach four miles long. It is only on closer inspection that it becomes apparent that Norman's Cay is no longer a place of enchantment.

Before Carlos Lehder arrived there, it was a civilized retreat for wealthy people. The island store sold excellent wine, and the restaurant at the Norman's Cay Yacht Club and Hotel served an elegant dinner, insisting that gentlemen wear jackets. Every evening a cistern truck would rumble up and down the island's only road spraying pesticides to keep the mosquitoes at bay.

The island used to be a favorite anchorage for yachtsmen because its natural harbor, sheltered on three sides by land, was ideal for sitting out the storms that sometimes race through the Bahamas. But in April 1980, the yacht *Kalia III* was found adrift at Norman's Cay stained with blood, its owner dead in the dinghy, which was riddled with bullet holes. In all six families were rumored to have disappeared from their boats near Norman's Cay, giving the island a menacing reputation among yachtsmen that lingered long after Lehder had left.

By then the island was eerily deserted, as though its inhabitants had been suddenly evacuated because of a hurricane warning. Long stone driveways wound up to empty $150,000 homes with sweeping views of the Caribbean, occupied only by lizards and bats. Along the road were scattered new Buicks, Jeeps, and mini-vans, all abandoned. Five crashed planes littered the water, the largest, a Convair, sitting half-submerged in the harbor. And on the highest hill, rising to 300 feet, sat a houseboat, tilted to an absurd angle, which Lehder's Colombian guards dragged to the top, perhaps to break the monotony of the fathomless blue sky.

At the long-abandoned yacht club somebody had written a prayer on the menu blackboard, deepening the impression that something evil had visited Norman's Cay, and might still be there:

> Banish hence all the wickedness of the Devil.
> Let angels of peace draw near to keep such discord
> As destroys the souls of men
> From finding any place on this island.

Carlos Lehder was born on September 7, 1949, in the city of Armenia, capital of Colombia's western province of Quindío. His mother was of humble origins, but strict moral upbringing. His father was an engineer who had emigrated to Colombia from Germany in the 1930s. When Carlos was still a young child his parents separated, and, when he was fourteen, his mother took him to the United States, where she lodged him with relatives in Detroit. While there, he was homosexually abused—an experience that profoundly affected him and left scars on his adult life. By the age of twenty, he was in trouble, running with a band of car thieves in Detroit, and in 1973, he was arrested and charged with interstate transportation of stolen automobiles. He skipped bail, only to be arrested three months later in Miami for possession of 237 pounds of marijuana. This time he went to jail, in Danbury, Connecticut, where he shared a cell with George Jung, a part-time marijuana dealer.

Together, according to Jung, they spent their time in jail plotting to flood the United States with cocaine. Lehder boasted that he had access to unlimited amounts of cocaine in Colombia. Jung had access to a distribution network in Los Angeles, supplying drug users in the film and record industries. Lehder was not interested only in making money: he told Jung he was a Marxist who saw America as a decadent society that he wanted to tear down. Jung, a former member of Students for a Democratic Society, was not unsympathetic.

In 1975 Lehder was released from prison and deported from the United States. He was back in the country within two years, however, having married Jemel Nacel, a Cuban-American, whom he met in Montreal, Canada. She provided him with a New York driver's license stolen from Joe León, one of her former schoolmates. Lehder used the license to cross the United States border (and, thereafter, became known to his American friends as "Joe") and he and Jemel rented an apartment in Miami Beach. Shortly afterwards they were joined by George Jung, who had been best man at the couple's wedding, and Lehder and Jung began to turn their jailhouse dreams into reality.

Lehder obtained the drugs from Colombia and Jung sold them in California, becoming a virtual commuter on the "red-eye" special as he shuttled between Miami and Los Angeles. Their first consignments of cocaine were smuggled into the United States in suitcases carried by "mules"—on one occasion, by Lehder's mother. Jung said she arrived at his hotel room with a bellboy and two suitcases containing eight kilos of cocaine, so nervous she needed a drink. He was, he said, outraged. Lehder explained: "Everybody has to work, and she wanted a free trip to L.A. to see Disneyland."

Business was so good—Jung said he once sold fifty kilos in two weeks, at a profit of $2.2 million—that in August 1977 Lehder and Jung brought in their first plane-load of cocaine— 250 kilos supplied by Pablo Escobar. The plane was flown from Medellín to Fort Lauderdale by Barry Kane, a Massachusetts lawyer. Kane received $2.5 million; Lehder and Jung got $1 million each.

But none of this was sufficient to satisfy Lehder, who had much grander plans. In early 1978 he told Jung their partnership was over, that Jung was "finished."

Lehder and Jemel left the United States for the Bahamas where Lehder became the president of an aircraft company that was in a position to make generous donations to worthy causes. Lehder announced that fact in a letter to the governor of his home state, Quindío, written on the stationery of Air Montes, which gave its address as Nassau, the Bahamas. Lehder told the governor that his "board of directors" had decided to bestow upon Quindio a Piper Navajo aircraft for its official use.

Shortly afterwards, the governor received a telephone call telling him that the plane was on its way. He ordered a member of his cabinet to go to the airport and welcome Mr. Lehder's representative and to invite him to the governor's office for a drink. But the young and ill-dressed American pilot who landed the Navajo at Armenia's El Edén Airport wanted none of it: he handed over the keys to the governor's man and disappeared.

For the next three years the Navajo sat at the airport while the governor pondered what on earth to do with it. It was of precious little use as official transport, since the entire province of Quindío has only one airport. And Quindío could not sell the plane, since Lehder had neglected to send the title papers. It was not until 1981 that Quindío was able to realize any benefit from Lehder's generous gift by selling the plane—to Lehder. By then, he had returned to his home town, with money to burn.

Robert Vesco returned to the Bahamas to live, hotfoot from Costa Rica, on April 30, 1978. This time he was determined to make money out of the Bahamas, rather than the other way round, and there was no faster way of doing that in 1978 than by investing in the explosively expanding cocaine business.

According to Gorman Bannister, who regarded Vesco as "an uncle," the entrée was provided by K. C. "Kenny" Cartwright, a white Bahamian who was the owner of an auto dealership in Nassau. Cartwright was such an energetic wheeler-dealer that he was known around town as "the white Everette Bannister," though it is doubtful that he had Bannister's contacts. Still, he had got to know Vesco well during the financier's earlier stay in the Bahamas. And Cartwright certainly had contacts in the drugs trade.

Those contacts may have included Carlos Lehder, for by mid-1978 Vesco and Lehder were frequent companions in the Bahamas—and possibly more than that.

Beginning in September 1978, Lehder incurred capital and

operating costs in the Bahamas that, in a little over a year, totaled $8.9 million—not including his generous gift to the governor of Quindío. Lehder's first expense was the purchase of the largest house on Norman's Cay, which belonged to Charles Beckwith, the owner of a Florida amusement park. Lehder turned up at Beckwith's door unannounced with a briefcase containing $100,000 in cash. Beckwith took the cash and left Norman's Cay the same day.

Next, and more judiciously, Lehder had incorporated in the Bahamas a company called International Dutch Resources, which purchased two large lots of land at either end of Norman's Cay. At the south end of the island his purchase included a marina, a yacht club and hotel, and, of most particular interest to Lehder, a well-paved airstrip 3,500 feet long. By the end of the year, Lehder had taken up residence on Norman's Cay, along with forty Colombian and German "employees," and his German mistress. (Jemel occasionally visited the island but spent most of her time in the United States and Colombia.)

Meanwhile, Vesco was also acquiring an island retreat. On October 9, 1978, Cartwright, acting, he says, for Vesco, purchased for $180,000 a deserted Exuma island called Cistern Cay, which lies some ten miles south of Norman's Cay.

Cistern Cay had no obvious attractions and no airstrip. The only practical way to get there from Nassau was to fly to Norman's Cay and continue on by boat. That may be why Vesco became such a frequent visitor to Norman's Cay—and why the DEA and the US Justice Department became convinced that Lehder and Vesco were partners.

Lehder was not the first trafficker to be attracted by the strategic position of Norman's Cay, its remoteness, and, above all, its fine airstrip. Since 1976, Edward Hayes Ward, his wife Emilie Lassie, and their partner, Charles Von Eberstein had been quietly smuggling planeloads of Colombian marijuana through the island, paying pilots to fly it directly to small airports in northern Florida. They had invested some of their profits in building and buying houses on Norman's Cay, and were gradually laying the foundations of a small but impressive organization. On a monthly basis, and sometimes more often, their twin-engined Beechcraft Bonanza would carry 1,400 pounds of marijuana from the island to Florida and, a few days later, return with cash, most of which was laundered through an off-shore corporation aptly named Caribbean Ventures Limited. And on Norman's Cay, their wealthy neighbors were none the wiser.

But it did not take Lehder very long to work out what the Wards and Von Eberstein were up to. By his standard, they were rank amateurs (and, indeed, Ward and Von Eberstein had previously earned their livings as sales clerks at the Sears Roebuck store in Orange Park, Florida.) They were certainly stuck in the small time: each planeload of marijuana they were smuggling was worth, perhaps, $300,000 at wholesale prices. The same weight of cocaine was worth at least $26 million, wholesale. In June 1978, even before he acquired any property on Norman's Cay, Lehder delivered an ultimatum to Ward: he and his organization could stay on the island and continue smuggling marijuana, but only if he made ten trips smuggling cocaine for Lehder. On September 6 Ward called a meeting at his house on Norman's Cay to tell his partner and some of his pilots of the new arrangement. Lehder, who was at that meeting, gave them $604,000 to buy a new Merlin III and packed them all off to flying school in Texas to learn how to handle it. In their absence, he got on with the business of transforming Norman's Cay into what he regarded as a "secure base."

The changes Lehder wrought were drastic and, for the residents, highly traumatic. Philip Kniskern, a retired property developer, had bought a vacation home on Norman's Cay in 1975, and subsequently invested $300,000 in developing a tourist business: he leased the yacht club and hotel, built three villas for rent, and established a diving school to exploit a "wall" of coral that, not far off-shore, plunges 100 feet into a sea of deepening blue. The business was building nicely until Lehder announced peremptorily that he intended to lease the villas for one year, to house his "employees." A month later, Lehder declared that the airstrip was to be closed for extension work and that bookings for the hotel "will no longer be recognized." It was made very clear to Kniskern, and to other residents, that they were no longer welcome on Norman's Cay.

Charles Kehm, who managed property on the island, met

Robert Vesco by chance on the yacht club dock and complained about the harassment. According to Kehm: "He told me the best advice he could give me was to get off the island and keep my nose out of other people's business." Kehm and most of the other residents left.

Professor Richard Novak, however, was made of sterner stuff. Though by profession a lecturer in oceanography at a small university in New York state, his hobby and his passion is deep-sea diving. He had leased the diving concession from Kniskern and, having invested considerable amounts of his own time and money in building it up, he had no intention of quitting. At first Lehder attempted to bribe Novak, offering him $50,000 to "amuse my friends" by teaching them to dive. But the blunt, powerfully built professor is by nature an acutely suspicious man, marked with a streak of Old Testament morality. He told Lehder he wanted nothing to do with him or his friends. Instead of amusing them he began spying on them, keeping meticulous records of their frequent comings and goings.

They had begun in January 1979 when Edward Ward and one of his pilots flew Lehder to Colombia in the new Merlin to collect 500 kilos of cocaine. They returned with the cargo to Norman's Cay, where smaller planes waited to fly it on to Florida—a pattern that was to be repeated at an increasingly hectic pace. Meanwhile, Lehder began shipping in more and more equipment: fast boats, Jeeps, helicopters, and sophisticated radio and navigation aids for the airstrip.

Lehder's activities were much too blatant to go unnoticed. As early as November 1978 the DEA had got wind of what was happening on Norman's Cay and had requested and got permission from the Bahamian Ministry of Foreign Affairs to conduct a thirty-day undercover operation on the island. ("That," said one of the DEA agents involved, "was when we were on the same side.") As a result, much of the detail of the take-over was spelled out in the report to the police commissioner, coauthored by Assistant Commissioner Lawrence Major in March 1979; Major, the virtual one-man task force, recommended that Norman's Cay be raided. There were also the alarms sounded by the evicted property owners, most of whom were American citizens who complained loudly to the embassy in Nassau or to their congressmen at home.

And in June 1979, having been placed under virtual house arrest by Lehder's men, Professor Novak finally agreed to leave Norman's Cay. He went directly to Nassau and to the US Embassy there, taking with him his meticulous records, photographs, and even movie film of Lehder's airlift. Novak told his story to the American chargé d'affaires, Andrew Antipes, and, a few days later, to two agents of the DEA. That meeting was confidential and, supposedly, secret, and Novak had no qualms about returning to Norman's Cay to collect his diving equipment; he had no way of knowing that somebody had photographed the meeting, or that the resulting evidence had been sent to Lehder. He obtained a letter from Antipes, asserting in the boldest terms that Professor Novak was an American citizen on legitimate business who should not be molested. Armed only with that and accompanied by his son, Novak chartered a small plane and flew to the island.

When the plane landed just before dusk it was immediately surrounded by Lehder's men. They refused to allow Novak to enter the building where his diving equipment was stored. When he returned to the plane, he found that the radio equipment had been smashed and the tanks drained of almost all of their fuel.

Flying at night under any circumstances is prohibited in the Outer Islands of the Bahamas for the sound reason that there are no navigational aids and no lighted airstrips—or, at least, none that operate legitimately. The wrecks littering the waters around Norman's Cay, and most other islands that traffickers have used, are testimony to the hazards of "flying blind" in those conditions.

Flying at night with no radios and almost no fuel was tantamount to suicide, but Novak was given little choice. At gunpoint, he and his son were ordered to take off. "I took the plane straight up as high as I could," Novak said later, "until we'd used our last drop of fuel." In a powerless glide, he then headed due north, across twenty miles of open water, hoping to reach Cape Eleuthera, where there was a 6,500-foot asphalt runway in excellent condition. They did not make it. The plane crash-landed on a beach at South Eleuthera, and that Novak and his son were not seriously injured or killed was sheer luck.

Attempted murder—for that is what it amounted to—was

now added to the list of complaints against Lehder and his men at Norman's Cay. Still the Bahamian government did nothing.

It was the then leader of the opposition, one of the last two remaining white Bahamians in parliament, who finally brought matters to a head. Like almost everybody in Nassau, Norman Solomon had heard of the "strange" goings-on at Norman's Cay, and on July 19, 1979, he deliberately sailed his boat as close as he dared to the shore paralleling the island's airstrip. He was followed on shore by two pick-up trucks containing men who watched his progress through binoculars. They continued to watch him until he had passed the southern tip of the island and, indeed, until he disappeared over the horizon. Solomon thought their behavior distinctly odd.

So, on July 21, on his return trip to Nassau, Solomon anchored his boat off Norman's Cay, swam ashore, and began walking along the beach to see what would happen. Before long he was accosted by a "large blond man" who told him he was trespassing on private property. Not so, said Solomon with the certainty of a legislator: the Bahamas had laws that nobody could own land below the high-water mark. Three more men arrived, apparently armed, to press the argument but Solomon refused to leave. Finally an American, describing himself as the manager of Norman's Cay, joined the group and told Solomon that if he strayed beyond the high-water mark, "I will not be responsible for your safety."

Solomon remained on the beach for a further ten to fifteen minutes, watching a blond woman photograph his boat through a telephoto lens. He then returned to Nassau to report his considerable suspicions about Norman's Cay to the police commissioner, and to begin what would become a campaign to have Carlos Lehder removed from the island. That campaign nearly cost him his life. On March 31, 1981, Solomon's house in Nassau and his car were bombed and, as we shall see, there is now little doubt that Lehder was responsible.

There was one other important visitor to Norman's Cay in the summer of 1979: Sir Lynden Pindling.

The fact that the prime minister made such a visit did not emerge publicly until 1984, when the Commission of Inquiry into drug-related corruption in the Bahamas attempted to establish why Lehder remained apparently immune for so long. Timothy Minnig, one of several convicted traffickers who testified to the commission, mentioned, almost in passing, that "in the early months of 1979" he was visiting Norman's Cay and saw a helicopter landing. The passengers, he said, were Lehder and the prime minister.

In his testimony Pindling denied Minnig's claim: "The incident Minnig described never happened," he said. But he did volunteer that, in June 1979, he had visited Norman's Cay and his suspicions had been aroused by the sophisticated nature of the radio equipment installed there. Pindling said that on his return to Nassau he reported his suspicions to the police commissioner.

It was a ludicrous story. By June 1979 the police commissioner hardly needed telling that there were suspicious signs at Norman's Cay: after all, it was the police commissioner who, *three months before,* had warned the cabinet in his apocalyptic report that the Bahamas, including Norman's Cay, was under invasion from "armed foreign criminals."

The commission, however, accepted Pindling's explanation, as it accepted other far-fetched aspects of his evidence. Indeed, the commission even credited Pindling's "concern" as one reason why Norman's Cay was eventually raided by police. The raid was a fiasco.

Code-named "Operation Racoon," the official assault on Norman's Cay was to have taken place on September 1, 1979, and should have been led by Assistant Commissioner Major, who had been pressing for it since March. At the last moment the raid was postponed for reasons that have never been explained. It was only after Major had gone on vacation that the raid was rescheduled for September 14. By then, according to Edward Ward, it was "common knowledge" on Norman's Cay that the police were about to descend.

The commanding officer of the raid who substituted for Major was Howard Smith, at the time a chief superintendent, later the head of the strike force—and one of Kojak's more valuable informants. Smith had at his disposal ninety police officers, including twelve detectives; three boats from the Bahamas Defence Force; and a chartered DC-3. The invasion began at 7 A.M., and quickly degenerated into farce.

Lehder was on the beach when the defence force boats arrived. He ignored commands to "Halt" and the warning shots that were fired at him, and repaired to his house, which was not the most impressive on the island but which had steps leading down to a small dock where his powerboat, *Fire Ball,* was waiting. The defence force next caught sight of Lehder as the *Fire Ball* headed out past the yacht club towards open water. Again, Lehder ignored the warning shots that were fired at him, this time by two marines in a rubber dinghy and by police officers on the shore. He steered the *Fire Ball* into shallow water, where the defence force boats could not follow, and emptied into the sea what the police described as the "white powdery" contents of four plastic packages. Having disposed of such evidence as remained, Lehder accepted a tow from a defence force boat and was taken ashore, where he was arrested and handcuffed.

But not for long. By lunchtime at the latest, and having been interviewed by Smith, Lehder was free, and wandering the island as though he owned it. Smith's eventual explanation for that fact, given to the Commission of Inquiry, was that he did not know Carlos Lehder was the main target of the raid he led. He also claimed he knew of no evidence that would have justified Lehder's arrest.

Others were not so lucky. Though Norman's Cay had, surely, been sanitized before the raid, the police still found eight handguns, two automatic rifles, one shotgun, two tear-gas launchers, thirty-five sticks of dynamite, 618 rounds of ammunition, and two spears. Thirty people were arrested and taken to the airstrip for transportation to Nassau on board the police's chartered DC-3. They included Edward and Emilie Ward, and Lehder's German mistress, Margit Meie-Linnekogel.

Emilie Ward says she overheard Lehder talking to Margit: "Don't worry," he said. "I've paid off the police." As the DC-3 took off, Lehder stood by the airstrip waving good-bye.

When in 1984 the Commission of Inquiry investigated these events, it came to the conclusion that Smith, and other senior officers who took part in the raid, had been bribed by Lehder.

A constable testified that he had found $80,000 hidden in a garbage bin that he had handed over to Smith. That lucrative discovery did not appear on Smith's official account of the raid and the money was never traced. A further $40,000 was found in a briefcase in Margit Meie-Linnekogel's bedroom and handed over to Smith. He claimed he gave it back to Lehder, who said it was the payroll for his Norman's Cay staff, but the commission clearly disbelieved him.

Thus, the commission accepted a wholly simplistic explanation for the failure to dislodge Carlos Lehder from Norman's Cay in September 1979: that it resulted from the casual corruption of a handful of senior police officers. The question the commission did not address was how on earth did they get away with it?

The raid on Norman's Cay was the largest operation of its kind ever mounted by the Bahamian authorities, and was predicated on enormous pressure: information gained by the DEA during its undercover operation in late 1978, reinforced by a similar operation mounted in June 1979; Lawrence Major's assertions of "an armed incursion" of the island that were included in the police commissioner's report to the cabinet of March 1979; complaints from the island's property owners, delivered via the US embassy; Professor Novak's detailed evidence of the airlift, and his account of the attempt to kill him; Norman Solomon's description of his hostile reception and his campaign to have Lehder evicted; the first-hand suspicions of the prime minister.

Yet Chief Superintendent Smith was able to limit the damage to the token arrest of Lehder's helpers—token in that most of them were released without charge the next day—without anybody questioning his actions.

The only real victims of the raid were Edward and Emilie Ward who, before being released, were charged with the illegal possession of weapons and drugs, the latter being a small quantity of marijuana found in their son's bedroom. This was a severe blow to the Wards because it was the second sign in two months that their smuggling operation was in trouble. In July one of their marijuana planes en route to Florida had been forced to turn back when the pilot realized he was being followed by another aircraft. When the plane was examined at Norman's Cay, the mechanics discovered that somebody—in fact, the DEA—had secretly installed a transponder, a radio transmitter that sends a constant signal to reveal an aircraft's exact whereabouts.

And, worse was to come. In January 1980 Ward learned that the Bahamian immigration department had placed him on the "Restricted List," a list of foreigners who are regarded "undesirable" and who require special and written permission to enter the Bahamas. That effectively made Ward an illegal immigrant, and removed the last modicum of his "cover" as a wealthy but respectable businessman.

On Norman's Cay, the Wards sought advice from one of Lehder's Bahamian employees as to what to do. The answer was "pay." The Wards were told that Lehder was paying $40,-000 a month for "protection" and was manifestly receiving it. "Pay whom?" asked the Wards. "The prime minister's right-hand man."

In February 1980 Emilie Ward, who had not been placed on the Restricted List, flew to Nassau and, by arrangement, went to Eddy Smith's restaurant on John F. Kennedy Drive. There, she was taken into a back room by the proprietor and introduced to a distinguished-looking man. He put out his hand and said: "I'm happy to meet you. I'm Everette."

Everette Bannister can be personable, charming, and articulate, or evasive and utterly profane. He will tell lies so audacious as to be breathtaking: as Gorman Bannister puts it, "he can look you in the eye and deny his own existence." Gorman, who does a very credible impersonation of his father's voice, says his *first* instinct is to lie, and that he expects to be believed: "I could have a conversation with him on the phone and five minutes later, if it suited him, he would say, 'Gorman, you *know* that was not me you were talking to.' "

Recognizing that trait, a parliamentary select committee that looked into political influence peddling in 1982 described Bannister as a man who was "likely to bring nothing but shame, scandal and disgrace upon the Bahamas." He sees himself somewhat differently. He would boast to Gorman that there were two prime ministers in the Bahamas: one for politics and one for business, and that he, as the latter, was the more important. Similarly, in the back room of Eddy Smith's restaurant in February 1980, he told Emilie Ward: "Our prime minister and other people are just figureheads and it's actually people like us who run the government. We have all the say-so. We are the ones who do all the work."

Bannister also told her that he was anxious to help her husband. "We feel badly that he's in the situation he's in," he said, "but, believe me, its only temporary. We can take care of everything."

"How?" she asked.

"Well, we have our ways."

Bannister said that he could not be seen on Norman's Cay and therefore Ward should come to Nassau with her to make the arrangements. Emilie pointed out that her husband was on the Restricted List and dare not show his face in Nassau. No problem, said Bannister. They should just make sure that they arrived at the airport after 4:30 P.M. when, in the section reserved for private aircraft, the customs post closed. Almost as an afterthought Bannister told her that they should bring with them $100,000.

Back on Norman's Cay, the Wards discussed the proposal with Charles Von Eberstein, their partner, and decided they had no choice but to go along with it. Emilie counted out $100,000 from their stash of hidden money and put it in a briefcase. The Wards then went to Nassau where their passage through the airport was as trouble-free as Bannister had predicted. They checked into the Ambassador Hotel where, sometime after 8 P.M., Edward Ward received a telephone call telling him to go alone to Eddy Smith's restaurant.

What transpired in the next few hours was crucial to the Commission of Inquiry because, if the Wards were telling the truth, it demonstrated emphatically that corruption in the Bahamas had reached the highest levels of government. Ward claimed that at the restaurant he met Everette Bannister, who asked only one question: Did he have the money? Bannister then took Ward in a car to Paradise Island and on to a houseboat that Ward thought was called *Yellow Tail.* Waiting there was a man who Bannister introduced as George Smith, no relation to the restaurant proprietor but Minister for Agriculture in Pindling's cabinet and one of the prime minister's closest friends.

Smith's first question was also: "Have you got the money?" Ward opened his briefcase to show the $100,000. Smith and Bannister then explained that this would be only an initial payment, to have Ward's name removed from the Restricted List and to have the charges against him and his wife dropped. To provide "an umbrella of protection," they said, they would require $300,000 a year. Ward says he asked where the money was going. "When I leave here," Smith replied, "I'm taking it directly to the prime minister."

Despite outright denials from Bannister and Smith, the commission believed the Wards' testimony, though it was careful to add there was not a shred of evidence that the prime minister was in any way involved. The commission also believed that, in June 1979, Smith had accepted the gift of a BMW car, worth $25,700, paid for by Lehder. In its final report, it recommended "with regret" that the attorney general "review the evidence." Smith resigned his cabinet post.

In November 1985 Smith was duly prosecuted, on charges of accepting a bribe from Ward—and acquitted. Some six years after the meeting on the houseboat, Ward was unable to identify Smith in court. (Instead, he picked out Smith's brother, who was a spectator.)

That singular turn of events allowed the Bahamian government, and its apologists, to denigrate the Commission of Inquiry for naively taking the word of "a self-confessed drug smuggler" against that of a government minister. In July 1987, when the Bahamas held elections and Pindling ran for his sixth consecutive term in office, George Smith was invited to run on the PLP ticket. He was re-elected—as was Pindling. It was widely rumored that Smith would soon be in the running for a new cabinet position.

From his hiding place in the United States, Gorman Bannister watched the public resurrection of George Smith with amused cynicism. He said that Smith had long been his father's lackey, the tame cabinet minister he took around the world to add luster to his never-ending schemes to find "investors." Gorman ridiculed his father's claim that he barely knew Edward Ward and had met him only twice: throughout most of 1980, Gorman said, Ward was a frequent visitor to Bannister's office in Nassau, attempting to secure the help he had been promised.

That leaves the main plank of the Bannister-Smith defense: that they did not have access to a houseboat on Paradise Island, and therefore, the pay-off meeting that Ward described could not possibly have taken place. "Lies," said Gorman. He said that among the favors provided to his father by Resorts International was the exclusive use of a houseboat "called *Red Snapper* or *Yellow Snapper,* some kind of fish." It was moored behind the Britannia Hotel on Paradise Island and was used by Bannister and selected friends to hold the kind of parties requiring some discretion. Gorman said there were only two keyholders to the houseboat. One was his father. The other was George Smith.

The wretched Wards never did get what they had paid for. Each time Edward Ward went to see Bannister in his office, he received a more elaborate excuse to explain the delay in solving his problems. The message was usually encouraging, however; the Wards just needed to be patient. Once, after interrupting a meeting to take a telephone call, Bannister claimed that he had just spoken to the prime minister to make him fully aware of the Wards' continuing difficulties.

Bannister charged for these services, of course. He "borrowed" $6,000 from Ward to pay for a prostate operation in Miami and a further $14,000 for other expenses. And in June 1980, Bannister told Ward that it would cost another $25,000 to have the criminal charges dropped because there was a new magistrate on the bench who needed to be squared. Ward paid up. The next day Bannister told him that the new magistrate's price was $50,000.

At that point Ward finally came to his senses and said no. He retreated to Norman's Cay, only to be told by Lehder that their arrangement was over: Ward and his people were to leave the island immediately. "Why don't you take a vacation," said Bannister when he learned of their new predicament. He said it would take him a maximum of six months to resolve their problems; meanwhile, he recommended Haiti. The Wards and their partner, Von Eberstein, moved to Haiti, where they were arrested. They were unceremoniously deported to the United States, where the DEA was waiting. All three are now serving long prison terms.

In the summer of 1985 the Wards' eldest son, Kurt, was to be found on Norman's Cay protecting the long-abandoned houses that were all that was left of his father's empire. He had grandiose plans for "renovating the place" and reopening Norman's Cay as a yacht haven, but no possible means of achieving them. Reflecting on his father's career, and his downfall, he said he should never have got mixed up with the likes of Carlos Lehder and Everette Bannister: "I guess you could say he was way out of his depth."

If Carlos Lehder was in any way intimidated by the raid on Norman's Cay, he did not show it. On the contrary, he complained loudly to the Bahamian press about "police harassment." "In retaliation" he expelled from the island a gang of Bahamian workers he had imported from Nassau to help build a 1,000-foot extension to the airstrip. (In his planning application for that extension, Lehder said he wanted to be able to fly in jets from Colombia.) His smuggling operation continued unabated. Without bothering to obtain planning consent, he had built two imposing hangars inside which his planes could be loaded and unloaded away from prying eyes. He imported a dozen more Jeeps and cars, which were parked along the airstrip to light it at night. He also imported twenty-three Doberman pinscher dogs, which were tethered along the strip on long leashes to deter any unwelcome visitors foolish enough to land.

There were two more raids on Norman's Cay: "Operation David" in November 1980 and "Operation Hope" in January 1981. Both were lost causes because Lehder was tipped off well in advance, and temporarily suspended his operation. Gorman Bannister claims that those tip-offs were delivered by his father, who obtained the information from the police commissioner; according to Gorman, they would have breakfast together every Saturday morning at Eddy Smith's restaurant.

In October 1981, by which time Lehder was spending most of

his time in Colombia, a police detail was permanently stationed on Norman's Cay. That news encouraged the dogged Professor Novak to return to the island with a companion on board his boat, *Reef Witch.* He realized that was a mistake when he found Lehder's Colombian guards still in residence, and when he saw uniformed police officers helping to push aircraft into the hangars. The Colombians terrorized Novak. They cut off water and power supplies to his villa, and circled it at night in Jeeps, blowing the horns and shouting threats. Novak and his companion took it in turns to stay awake, armed with a loaded .357 Magnum and a cutlass, until they could take it no more; in fear of their lives, they fled.

Perhaps the height of audacity came on July 10, 1982, when the crowds gathered at Clifford Park in Nassau to celebrate the ninth anniversary of Bahamian independence from Britain. The highlight of Independence Day is always a marching display by the police band, an inspection of the ranks by the governor general, and, finally, a ringing speech from Prime Minister Pindling. In 1982, as that climax neared, one of Lehder's light aircraft made several passes over Clifford Park while two men aboard it tossed leaflets down on to the crowd. The message was "DEA GO HOME." To make it more compelling, many of the leaflets had $100 bills attached to them.

On September 5, 1983, the NBC "Nightly News" broadcast the stark allegation that, for more than four years, Norman's Cay had been the base for "one of the biggest drug smuggling operations in the world." NBC quoted as one of its sources a classified US Justice Department report which stated that Vesco and Lehder were behind the operation, and that they were paying Bahamian ministers, including Pindling, $100,000 a month.

The response was extraordinary. Pindling, his foreign minister, and his attorney general all put their names to a counteraccusation of "a conspiracy by certain government agencies and departments in the USA to attack the present Government of The Bahamas and bring it into disrepute." And Pindling sued NBC for libel—though in Canada, rather than America, where few people could have seen the broadcast but where the libel laws favor the plaintiff.

Under pressure from some members of his cabinet, Pindling

also agreed to establish an independent Commission of Inquiry to investigate drug-related corruption. Those ministers were furious at being included, by implication, in the general allegation and wanted their names cleared. However, it is also the case that at least two of them, Hubert Ingraham and Christie Perry, suspected there was some truth in NBC's accusation—and wanted the matter aired. Indeed, they argued in cabinet that the commission should be free to investigate *all* corruption from *any* source, but on that point, Pindling would not be moved.

Having sat for 146 days, heard 360 witnesses, and examined more than 1,000 documents, the commission decided there was no evidence that Pindling had taken money from drug traffickers. Conversely, it decided that Everette Bannister most certainly had. That raises an interesting conundrum: Since Bannister gave almost $700,000 to the prime minister, and, since by his own admission Pindling rarely asked where the money had come from, how could he know whether the funds were "drug-related" or not? One of the three members of the commission, the Right Reverend Drexel Gómez, Bishop of Barbados, was sufficiently concerned by that question to insist on writing a minority report. "It is certainly feasible that all of [Bannister's] payments could have been made from non-drug related sources," the bishop wrote. "But in my opinion, the circumstances raise great suspicion and I find it impossible to say that the payments were all non-drug related. Some could have been but, however that may be, it certainly cannot be contested that the Prime Minister did not exercise sufficient care to preclude the possibility of drug-related funds reaching his bank account. . . ."

But suspicion of Pindling goes much further than that.

By the end of 1979, there can scarcely have been a soul in any authority in Nassau who did not suspect that Carlos Lehder was running a major drug-smuggling operation out of Norman's Cay. Lehder's cover story—that he was a wealthy Colombian money changer who was developing the island into a "resort complex"—might have survived so long as there was any development work going on. But after the abortive police raid in September 1979, the pretence was dropped when Lehder abandoned his plans to extend the runway. From then on Norman's Cay looked increasingly to be what it was: an island occupied by armed gunmen who were up to no good.

It was, surely, the last place that the prime minister of the Bahamas would wish to spend weekends, enjoying Carlos Lehder's extravagant parties. Yet, in 1980 and 1981, that is what Pindling did—at least according to Athanasios "Tommy the Greek" Maillis, a paid informant for the DEA and, he says, a trained and trusted operative for the CIA. Maillis claims that in 1980 he learned through his contacts in the drug business that the prime minister was spending occasional weekends "partying" on Norman's Cay. He claims that he informed his CIA "controller" of that allegation in one of his routine reports, and that he was instructed to attempt to obtain evidence. Maillis suborned one of Lehder's Bahamian employees on Norman's Cay. In due course, he says, he was handed black-and-white copies of three highly compromising photographs of Pindling, taken in Lehder's house. One showed him with a group of young women whose company he was clearly enjoying. The second photograph showed him on a bed with some of those women, who were no longer dressed. The third showed him seated at a table with the women around him; on the table was what looked to be about one pound of white powder.

To his great regret, Maillis did not make copies of the photographs. He showed them to a DEA agent in Miami named Peter Saron, who did not make copies either. ("You want to see a DEA agent kick himself?" said one of Saron's colleagues. "Ask Pete about those photographs.") The photographs then went to the CIA, and nothing except rumor has been heard of them since.

So Maillis cannot prove his story—though Agent Saron does confirm that Maillis showed him the photographs. What can be proved, remarkably, is that Maillis *did* work for the CIA in the Bahamas. And whatever it was he did for the agency, it was sufficiently important to earn him great gratitude.

Tommy Maillis comes from Kalymnos, a rugged Greek island set near the Turkish mainland, where most of the population seems to have relatives living in the United States. The early Maillis emigrés, however, preferred the Bahamas, where they married locals and became part of a thriving and industrious Greek community under British rule. In 1965, at the age of seventeen, Tommy obtained passage on a cargo ship from Greece to join his extended family. He got a job with Airport Caterers, then in Greek hands, and worked his way up to the position of a supervisor. When, in 1972, Airport Caterers was taken out of Greek hands by the prime minister and his friends, Maillis went into business for himself and eventually became the owner of a nightclub called the Connection Room, in Freeport, on the island of Grand Bahama.

Freeport is an anachronism, a throwback to the days of white rule, in that it is run as a state within a state by the Grand Bahama Port Authority. (The Port Authority operates under government licence, which expires in 1990. Its British owners have a history of being exceedingly generous to the prime minister: between 1981 and 1983, for example, the authority gave him over $1 million in "election expenses" and "loans".) As much if not more than Nassau, Freeport is the entertainment capital of the Bahamas. And in the late 1970s, Tommy Maillis's Connection Room was one of Freeport's most fashionable rendezvous. In the fall of 1978, Maillis walked into the Miami offices of the FBI to volunteer the information that among those trying to make connections in his club were major drug traffickers.

In those days the FBI was not concerned with drug investigations—a legacy of the era of J. Edgar Hoover, who feared his agents would become corrupted. Maillis was, therefore, referred to the Miami offices of the DEA, where he readily agreed to help the agency mount what was to become a spectacular undercover assault on the Colombian marijuana trade.

It was codenamed "Operation Grouper" (a DEA witticism: since bales of marijuana are sometimes air-dropped into the sea for collection by fishing boats, they are known as "square grouper.") Thanks in no small measure to Maillis, in March 1981 it netted 156 people and led to the seizure of 1.3 million pounds of marijuana. Maillis's role was to help the DEA infiltrate a dozen different trafficking groups by introducing two undercover agents who posed as smugglers and as his cousins. One of those agents, Pete Saron, later described Maillis in almost heroic terms: "[He] did one heck of a good job for us. All the smugglers knew his home, knew his address, knew his phone number. He was flying back and forth from the Bahamas to Miami to arrange meetings. He personally was on a couple of boats that we used to offload mother ships. He really put his life on the line and he gave us the best effort he possibly could. . . . We looked on him as being a real asset."

By early 1980 Maillis had completed his part in Operation Grouper, but the federal government was not yet through with him. Again, according to Saron of the DEA: "The FBI took a renewed interest in Mr. Maillis and there was a large meeting that took place between him and a bunch of FBI people at Howard Johnson's Motel on 36th Street [in Miami], and it seemed the information that Mr. Maillis had developed over the past year or two was of vital interest to the FBI." Saron said he was told by Charles "Chuck" Archer, then the FBI supervisor in Miami, that Maillis "was being forwarded to the CIA and that they were going to do a large-scale money-laundering type investigation, and they thought Mr. Maillis would be a great asset to them." Saron said that for the next eighteen months he kept in touch with Archer, who reported that Maillis "was doing a fantastic job."

According to Maillis, the CIA submitted him to extensive vetting that included lie-detector tests, and then trained him in arts he will not describe. Having qualified, he was given "a handler," (an agency supervisor), a salary of $3,000 a month, and an expense account that was never questioned. His first assignment in the Bahamas for the CIA was to penetrate the strict banking secrecy laws that make Nassau so attractive to a variety of people: despots building their retirement funds; US corporations and individuals seeking to avoid taxes; swindlers like Vesco; and, of course, drug traffickers. Maillis said he was able to establish a network of bank employees, and somebody at the central bank who kept him informed on a regular basis of who was moving how much money in and out of the Bahamas. Maillis, in turn, reported the transactions to the CIA when he met with his handler, usually in hotel rooms in Miami. Why the CIA wanted that information, and what it did with it, was, said Maillis, "your guess."

Meanwhile, Maillis continued to run the Connection Room in Freeport, which continued to be a rendezvous for traffickers who had no notion of Maillis's involvement in Operation Grouper, even after the trap was sprung in March 1981. That was partly because, at his insistence, nobody in the Bahamas was arrested or implicated in that operation, though many people could have been. So, people who had drugs to sell would go to the Connection Room in search of a buyer, and, on occasions, Maillis would act as the middleman. Among those he helped was a Bahamian employee of Carlos Lehder who had developed a profitable if risky sideline on Norman's Cay: pilfering small quantities of Lehder's cocaine and selling it through Maillis.

The risk lay in Lehder finding out that cocaine was missing, but perhaps that was minimized by the enormous quantities of cocaine being consumed on Norman's Cay. Lehder himself was a constant user of *basuco,* as was his mistress, most if not all of his Colombian and German guards, and even some of his pilots. (The Convair that sits half-submerged in Norman's Cay harbor was landed there by a pilot who was so addled by cocaine he did not realize he had missed the runway.) To keep his workers and his guests amused, Lehder would give spectacular parties, flying in prostitutes from Colombia. According to Professor Novak, they would often end riotously with Lehder and his bodyguards cruising the island in cars, spraying submachine-gun fire at the wild peacocks that inhabit the underbush.

It was Lehder's Bahamian employee who told Maillis that the prime minister was an occasional guest at these parties. Maillis claims he made several clandestine visits to the island in order to verify the allegation. Having done so, he says, he informed the CIA: he was instructed to obtain "hard evidence"; "three to four months later," he handed over the photographs which, had they been published, might easily have wrecked the prime minister's career.

There was one other covert operation launched against Pindling. According to Maillis, he was also instructed to arrange for the transportation of sophisticated electronic listening devices and receiving equipment to Freeport from Miami. He says he had them smuggled in to Freeport on board a yacht and, on instruction, handed them over to a senior Bahamian police officer whom he knew to be "the FBI's man." Maillis claims that, as a result, the prime minister's office and his home were successfully "bugged" for six months.

In late 1981 Maillis was informed by the Bahamian immigration department that he had been placed on the "Stop List"— the department's ultimate sanction, making him persona non grata. Despite the fact that he had lived in the Bahamas for seventeen years, that he had a home and a business, a Bahamian wife and three Bahamian children, he was required to quit the country almost immediately.

That effectively ended Maillis's CIA career. But the agency clearly felt that it owed him a debt, which it repaid generously. First, Maillis and his family were given permanent-resident status in the United States under Public Law 110, a statute passed by Congress to provide refuge for "persons who have given service of great interest and value to the national security." Maillis settled in Tarpon Springs, Florida, which has a large Greek community and a local industry of sponge fishing, where he opened a restaurant. He also continued associating with drug traffickers and informing on them to the DEA. Unfortunately for him, the sheriff's department in Tarpon Springs came to believe that Maillis himself was trafficking in cocaine and, in October 1983, he was arrested and charged with an offence that, upon conviction, carried a *mandatory* minimum sentence of fifteen years imprisonment. In 1985, Maillis was convicted; reenter the CIA.

It is not unusual for drug traffickers convicted in Florida to claim some affiliation with the CIA, and it is not unusual for their defense attorneys to serve subpoenas on the agency demanding its records. The CIA routinely resists such subpoenas and the courts routinely quash them. Maillis's case was no exception.

But in Maillis's case the CIA then *volunteered* to provide the court, in camera, with information certain to assist him. In a sworn affidavit dated May 24, 1985, Robert E. Fronczek, who described himself as deputy chief of the Directorate of Operations of the CIA, confirmed that Maillis had worked for the agency until the summer of 1982 "with great vigor and initiative." The affidavit continued: "He followed his instructions and successfully completed the primary assignment he was given, way, way ahead of what we had planned would be the schedule."

Just what that "primary assignment" was or what else Maillis had done for the CIA were not described in the affidavit, nor did Maillis reveal any details to the court. Nevertheless, the judge was sufficiently impressed to show great leniency: he had no choice other than to sentence Maillis to fifteen years' imprisonment, but he suspended all but three of them. What is more, Maillis was permitted to serve the bulk of his term in a "halfway house," a hostel that required his presence only at night.

Maillis had been prosecuted by the state of Florida, rather than the federal government, and the state prosecutors were infuriated by the "interference" of the CIA and outraged by the leniency that had resulted. They protested to Florida's Court of Appeals, and won: Maillis was ordered to serve all of his fifteen-year sentence in prison and to pay a fine of $250,000.

But four days before that decision was due to be announced, Maillis walked out of the halfway house and bought an airplane ticket to Greece. Though his passport was in the custody of the court, he somehow acquired it. Though his name was on the "watch list" at every major airport in Florida, he had no difficulty in boarding a flight to New York, where he changed planes for Athens. Safely in Greece, he telephoned the prison authorities in Florida and said, "I'm sorry, but I won't be back."

Maillis resettled his Bahamian family in Kalymnos, from where he regularly telephoned the DEA in Miami to keep abreast of developments in the Bahamas. He refused to reveal how he knew that the appeals court was about to rule against him: "I had a feeling," was all he would say. He also refused to reveal how he obtained his passport.

He said he would reveal "everything I know" for an unspecified but very large sum of money, and he claimed to be in negotiation with a "major American television company" to do just that. On the other hand, he was also writing letters to the prime minister of the Bahamas, attempting to negotiate terms under which he might be allowed to return to the country.

In the fall of 1987, Maillis was growing cool on the idea of "telling all." He said the negotiations with the prime minister were "going well."

"If You Play, You Pay"

Not much more than a year after his acquisition of Norman's Cay, Carlos Lehder was able to leave its day-to-day running to others, and return to his hometown in Colombia with extravagant plans. He had enough money, he bragged, to transform Armenia into an international city: "I'm going to make this a real capital, so that the entire world can visit it, and the fucking Yankees can finally appreciate what we have here."

Assisted by a small group of local professionals—some of them members of the most aristocratic families in the province—Lehder set up a parent corporation, *Cebú Quindío.* Its first project was the planning of an "Alpine" resort, some ten miles from Armenia, which Lehder said would cater to "the world traveler." During his rebellious childhood, his father had owned a German inn in Armenia, *Pensión Alemana,* and, perhaps in filial rebuke, Lehder announced that his much grander establishment would be called *La Posada Alemana:* costing $3 million, it was to have a gourmet restaurant and a sophisticated wine bar, thirty well-equipped villas, several swimming pools, and an assortment of other amenities, including a small zoo and a discotheque named after John Lennon. The murdered former Beatle was the second of Lehder's idols, next to Hitler. As the centerpiece to his resort, Lehder commissioned a renowned Colombian sculptor, Rodrigo Arenas Betancourt, to render a statue of a naked Lennon, with a gaping bullet hole in his back.

With construction of the resort underway, Lehder and the executives of *Cebú Quindío* criss-crossed the province looking for other "investment opportunities." They traveled in a ten-car caravan led by a silver Mercedes and a gray Porsche that were equipped with the latest cellular telephone equipment—a strange sight in a region where horse-drawn carts and tractors are the norm. The immediate effect of Lehder's millions on Quindío's economy was a sudden increase in property values throughout the province. Nobody knew how much he had available to invest, but estimates ranged from $30 million to $270 million—an amount so vast that it could have had no meaning in such an impoverished and almost forgotten part of Colombia.

Evidence of Lehder's millions was everywhere. At the local airport, he kept three aircraft and two helicopters on permanent standby. He bought large cattle ranches, including the 700-acre *Hacienda Pisamal,* where he would have built an airstrip had a detachment of the Colombian army not moved in to stop him.

In downtown Armenia the bustling headquarters of *Cebú Quindío* was equipped with a complex and highly sophisticated communications system that gave it instant access to the outside world. In its heyday, the company employed 268 people, twice the number of Bavaria, brewers of beer, which, before Lehder, had been Armenia's major private employer.

As head of this empire, Lehder became a celebrity. Local newscasts kept daily track of his schedule, running detailed accounts of what the "Colombian-German investor" or the "Colombian-German industrialist" had done or was about to do.

It was news when Lehder announced he was so appalled at the decrepit state of the fire engines in Armenia, that *Cebú Quindío* would donate a new truck. Encouraged by the televised cheers of the firemen, he promised to start "a series of studies" to determine whether other municipalities in the province needed his financial help.

At the dilapidated headquarters of the association of local journalists in Armenia, Lehder said: "It is not fair that journalists, who represent the voice of reason and the flame of freedom in our democracy, have to conduct their affairs in a place like this." At a ceremony held before a battery of cameras, Lehder presented a check for $3,000 to the association's president, to pay for a facelift to the building. When it was completed, the grateful reporters named one of their refurbished rooms *El Salón Bahammas* [sic], in tribute to their benefactor.

By the beginning of 1982, Gorman Bannister's drug use was so heavy his father told him that his only future was "working in a cocaine laboratory for Joe Lehder." To escape his father's chiding, Gorman would sometimes fly to Miami and take a room at the Holiday Inn on NW 79th Street where he could snort cocaine to his heart's content, at least until the money ran out. In September 1982, at the end of one such sojourn, Gorman telephoned his father in Nassau to ask as always for an air ticket home. "No," said his father for once. "I'm coming over tomorrow and I want you to go south with me."

The next day Gorman met his father outside Eastern Airline's Ionosphere Club at Miami International Airport. Bannister said that Carlos Lehder—or "Joe," as he called him—had sent an emissary to Nassau to request that Bannister fly to Colombia for a meeting. Bannister had insisted on taking Gorman along, perhaps as protection; in Gorman's words: "It would be two of us they would have to kill, instead of one." The two Bannisters joined up with Lehder's emissary, a Colombian named Guillermo Gómez, and the three men, pretending not to be together, boarded an Eastern Airlines flight to Bogotá. They were supposed to be met at the airport on arrival, but the driver failed to show up. Instead they took a taxi to the terminal reserved for private aircraft, where one of Lehder's planes and two of his pilots were waiting.

The plan was to fly directly from Bogotá to Armenia. En route, however, the weather deteriorated and the plane was buffeted by turbulence so severe that even Bannister, a veteran traveller, was heard to mutter "Oh, Jesus." After what Gorman describes as "forty minutes of terror," the pilots diverted to Cali where the party spent the night at the Intercontinental Hotel. Gorman and his father shared a room and became involved in an argument—inevitable whenever the two of them were alone together—over Bannister's affair with his secretary. Gorman says: "I told him, 'You've seen those Hollywood movies with the young girl and the old man; he always loses. Just keep that in mind.'" Early the next morning, after too little sleep, the squabbling Bannisters resumed their journey to Armenia, and Carlos Lehder's extraordinary kingdom.

The entrance to the *La Posada Alemana* was marked by a gate and guarded by two men armed with machine guns, "the kind 'The Untouchables' used," says Gorman. He and his father were driven through the resort complex, which was still under construction, to a two-storey villa where, inside, Lehder was waiting for them. According to Gorman, the man whom Bannister insists he does not know, has not met, has never spoken to, held out his hand and said: "Everette, how are you?"

And then, after a few more formalities, Lehder said: "Everette, you know you guys have closed down the Cay and put me out of business."

"Well," said Bannister, "that doesn't seem to have made much difference to you because now you're running your drugs through the Berry Islands." Both men laughed.

Lehder complained that he had paid a considerable sum— "$60,000 or $600,000, something like that," says Gorman—to a Nassau attorney named Nigel Bowe to facilitate the reopening of Norman's Cay, but nothing had happened. Bannister said that since Nigel was not the one who had closed down the island, he did not see how Nigel could reopen it; "He's ripping you off."

"I know Nigel is ripping me off," replied Lehder. "And, when I get proof, I'm going to have him removed from the population count."

What happened next remains a secret between Bannister and Lehder because Gorman was excluded from their detailed discussions, which lasted for most of the rest of the day. He heard only snatches: when, for example, they sat down to a gargantuan lunch at the resort's restaurant, where a cow had been slaughtered in the Bannister' honor; and later when, accompanied by two Jeep-loads of bodyguards, they drove to Lehder's substantial *finca* in a bullet-proof Mercedes that Lehder said had previously belonged to Helmut Schmidt when he was

chancellor of West Germany. One of the things Gorman overheard was Lehder's admission that he had been responsible for
the bomb attacks on Norman Solomon, then the leader of the
opposition party in the Bahamas, who had campaigned vigor-
ously against Lehder's presence on Norman's Cay. Lehder said
he resented the way in which Solomon had "depicted my people as animals." Bannister said: "You should have killed him."

Another resentment Lehder harbored concerned the disappearance of a $250,000 necklace he had sent to George Smith,
the minister of agriculture, to be given to Lady Pindling as a
gift. Gorman gathered from the conversation that the prime
minister's wife had rejected the necklace, but Lehder had been
unable to get it back. "It wasn't the dollar amount that bothered
him, but the principle," said Gorman. His father promised
Lehder, "I'll deal with that when I get back." (That was one
promise that Bannister did try to keep, according to Gorman.
Spurred on by the fear that Lehder might "have George killed
for something like this," Bannister spent weeks attempting to
retrieve the necklace, shuttling between George Smith and
Nigel Bowe, both of whom claimed that the other had it. Matters came to a climax when three Colombians arrived in Bannister's office in Nassau insisting they were not going to leave
until they had the necklace; it took a frantic telephone call to
Lehder, and all of Bannister's persuasive powers, to have the
Colombians recalled. So far as Gorman knows, the necklace
was never recovered.)

All in all, by the end of their day-long visit, it was clear to
Gorman that his father and Lehder had resolved whatever past
differences existed between them. Bannister had rejoined
Lehder's payroll—and, being Everette Bannister, he was to receive a substantial sum up front. Lehder told Bannister that he
could have the money in Armenia, but that it would take a
couple of days to get it. Bannister rejected that offer because, in
Gorman's words, "two black men arriving at Miami International from Bogotá with a bag full of cash was not a good idea."
Lehder then proposed that Bannister collect the money in
Miami on the way back to Nassau, which, according to Gorman, is what happened.

Before they left Armenia for Bogotá and their flight home,

the Bannisters were taken by Lehder to a downtown jewelry store, flanked by the machine gun-toting bodyguards. As they inspected the expensive merchandise, Bannister nudged his son as if to say, Choose something. Gorman asked to see a gold bracelet. "You like that?" said Lehder. "Okay, take it." For himself, Bannister picked out a gold watchband and a pair of emerald earrings, and Lehder had one of his bodyguards write out the check.

It was when they were on their way home, re-embarked on their endless debate about Bannister's adultery, that Gorman realized the emerald earrings were not intended as a present for his mother. "I've got to get something for her," said Bannister as they changed planes at Miami. At an airport bookstall he bought his wife a gift: a copy of *The National Enquirer.*

There are times when it seems that all roads in the Bahamas led to Everette Bannister: that whenever there was a chance of a deal to be made, or a whiff of money in the air, sooner or later Bannister would be there, wheeling and dealing, promising the earth. Luis "Kojak" García smuggled drugs by the ton through the Bahamas for more than two years without Bannister's assistance, and without paying him a penny; he was, however, merely delaying the inevitable.

The man who brought Kojak and Bannister together was "Tommy the Greek" Maillis, still at that time a resident of the Bahamas and a valuable asset of the CIA. Which master Maillis was serving in doing that is difficult to say because, by then, he had several allegiances. The best guess, perhaps, is that on this occasion Maillis was first and foremost looking after himself.

Maillis's extended family in the Bahamas included an uncle, Alexander, and a cousin, Pericles, who ran a prominent law firm in Nassau, Maillis & Maillis. In 1979, at Tommy's behest, Maillis & Maillis acquired for $600,000 the ownership of Gorda Cay, an idyllic retreat in the Abaco chain, a boomerang shaped arc of islands just 200 miles from the Florida coast, as the drug plane flies. The purchaser was Frank Barber, who claimed to be a wealthy, retired businessman worth $50 million, and who claimed, inevitably, that he intended to develop Gorda Cay into a tourist resort. Having obtained the island, Barber joined the rush to import drugs, usually marijuana, into the United States. Barber's one distinction is that he did not trouble with boatmen or other people's airstrips; he had his own, in Delray Beach, Florida, attached to a sumptuous home.

Barber's set up was almost perfect. There were no curious neighbors on Gorda Cay, indeed, no neighbors at all. And since Barber's planes merely refueled on the island en route from Colombia, there was no need to keep a large workforce that might attract the attention of the authorities; just two or three men who could claim to be the caretakers of the only house on the island. But these same qualities also made Gorda Cay extremely vulnerable to takeover, and in early 1982 one of the corrupt police officers on Kojak's payroll proposed exactly that.

Kojak had by then obtained a pilot's licence and was addicted to flying. On a clear February morning, he took off from Opa-Locka airport, north of Miami, in a Piper Aztec, supposedly to practice Visual Flight Rules; five miles from the airport he turned due east, and in not much more than one hour he had Gorda Cay in sight. As he made his approach to the landing strip he could see a Jeep carrying two "caretakers" armed with rifles, racing to meet him. Kojak landed, ostentatiously shoved a Colt-45 into his waistband, and prepared to give his best impression of how he imagined a DEA agent might behave.

"Who the fuck are you guys, and what are you doing here?" he said. "Waiting for a load of dope?" When the two "caretakers" hesitated, Kojak demanded to see their papers. He demanded to know who else was on the island, how they got their supplies, even what frequency their radio was tuned to. He wrote it all down, admonished them to "keep your noses clean," warned them he might return, and took off. As soon as the Aztec was airborne, he tuned his radio to their frequency and heard them broadcast the urgent warning that "the heat" was on. Kojak said he laughed all the way back to Miami.

The next day the Aztec returned to Gorda Cay, this time flown by one of Kojak's pilots and containing three Bahamian police officers, all in uniform. Meanwhile, three more of Kojak's men arrived by boat, heavily armed, and having been surprised and overwhelmed, the two caretakers were given a simple choice: they could either spend the next seventy-two hours tied to a tree or they could "cooperate" and earn themselves some extra money. They chose to cooperate. Within one hour of the take-over, the first of Kojak's planes was on its way to Colombia to collect the first consignment of marijuana. By the time the invaders left Gorda Cay three days later, 3,600 pounds of marijuana had passed through the island en route to Florida.

The celebrations were still going on at Kojak's apartment in Miami when he received a message from one of the caretakers: Frank Barber, the rightful owner of Gorda Cay, wanted to meet him, "to shake you by the hand." As it turned out, Barber also wanted to negotiate "a little business." When the two men met at Barber's Florida home in mid-February, Barber proposed that they work together: Kojak's planes would fly drugs from Colombia to Gorda Cay, and Barber's planes would fly them from Gorda Cay to his airstrip in Delray Beach; each would pay his own expenses, and they would split the profits fifty–fifty. Kojak was initially wary at the notion of flying drugs into Florida because of the risks of radar detection; he had always preferred to use boats. But Barber reassured him, saying he knew of an aerial "corridor" along which his planes could fly undetected. He also told Kojak, "I've got a federal agent on my payroll."

That was not the whole truth. On the contrary, it was *Barber* who was supposed to be working for the federal government. In late 1980, a court-approved wiretap had caught Barber offering to sell drugs and, to avoid prosecution, he had agreed to cooperate with the DEA to build "a major case" against some unsuspecting trafficker. In early 1981 Barber had been given as his "controller" Jeffrey Scharlatt, one of the most senior DEA agents in Miami, who had been the overseer of Operation Grouper. Scharlatt was corrupt. In late 1981 Barber listed two pieces of property with Scharlatt's wife, who was a real estate broker; they were worth $2.3 million, and she stood to make $138,000 in commission. Then, in return for further bribes, Scharlatt allowed Barber to continue smuggling marijuana, supposedly in order to build his "major case."

Blissfully unaware of all of this, Kojak entered into the new partnership with great energy. During March 1982 his DC-3s transported into Gorda Cay five and one-half million Quaaludes, Colombian-made tablets of methaqualone, a nonbarbiturate sedative that was then highly popular on the illicit drug market in the United States. Kojak bought them in Colombia and flew them to Gorda Cay for a total cost of thirty-five cents each; Barber said he could sell them, in Philadelphia and Cincinnati, for ninety-five cents apiece. On Gorda Cay, Kojak ordered the digging of underground tunnels where the cases of Quaaludes were stored until they could be smuggled into the United States.

There were simply too many of them for Barber's small planes to cope with alone. So Kojak's boatmen joined the effort, smuggling into Miami some two million Quaaludes without losing so much as a single one. Meanwhile, the DEA agents who had Barber's Delray Beach airstrip under surveillance reported that two planes had landed. "Dry runs," said Scharlatt, ordering the agents to do nothing; they were to wait until he gave the order to move.

There is little doubt that Kojak was being set up: that he was to be the "major case" that Scharlatt and Barber had promised. Presumably the plan was that Kojak would be arrested, while Scharlatt and Barber would take the credit—and the profits from the Quaaludes that, after the supposed "dry runs," now sat inside Barber's house.

It was Barber's greed that saved Kojak. To help cover the cost of the bribes he was paying Scharlatt, Barber dunned his pilots for contributions. The pilots complained to Maillis who, as always, was in the market for any rumor. Maillis told his main DEA contact, Pete Saron. According to Saron: "He called me up one day and said, 'Pete, I don't know if you know what's going on but Jeff's on the juice.' I said, 'I don't understand that. What do you mean, on the juice?' He said, 'Frank and Jeff are smuggling drugs.' And I told him, 'Thomas, don't say that unless you know for sure it's happening. I don't want to hear that kind of talk if it's only gossip.' He said, 'It's not gossip . . . I don't like to see this kind of thing happen.' "

Saron, faced with evidence that his own supervisor was a crook, did not know whom to trust, and so he told the FBI in Washington. On March 25, 1982, after a third plane had landed at the Delray Beach airstrip and Scharlatt had described it as yet another "dry run," FBI agents and DEA inspectors raided Barber's home and found one and one-half million Quaaludes.

Barber refused to talk, at first. But Maillis volunteered his services, and after spending thirty minutes or so alone with Barber in his prison cell, he emerged to tell waiting agents, "Gentlemen, he'll talk to you now." In return for a promise of considerable leniency, Barber betrayed Scharlatt and agreed to help gather evidence against him. In due course, Scharlatt pled guilty to charges of obstruction of justice and receiving an unlawful gratuity, and was sentenced to five years imprisonment. Barber received similar treatment. (Federal Judge Norman C. Roettger, who sentenced Barber, was infuriated at the deal Barber had struck with the government, which allowed him to get away with one charge of tax evasion. The prosecutors described the deal as "a necessary price that ultimately serves the public interest." "Take a message back for me," said Roettger. "Don't bring me any more cases where [the government] works out a deal with somebody they should not be in bed with in the first place.")

For Kojak, the arrest of Barber created a considerable scare. He ordered Gorda Cay closed down, and the remaining Quaaludes dumped in the ocean, while he took the first flight he could get, from Miami to New York, and went into hiding at the Hilton Hotel. From there he kept in touch with his Miami milieu by telephone, waiting for the first indications that he was a wanted man. He was assured by Barber's wife that "Frank hasn't talked," but he knew enough about Barber's character not to believe it. In the end he assumed—correctly—that the DEA was more concerned with nailing a "dirty agent" than it was with building a case against him.

After two weeks Kojak returned to Miami, reopened Gorda Cay, and put his people back to work. But though he continued to smuggle drugs with the same intensity as before, he was beginning to lose his appetite for it. He was depressed by the company he was obliged to keep and by the greed of his associates, some of whom had begun to steal from him. So too had his son, Richard, who had become accustomed to seeing Kojak's living room rug covered in its entirety by knee-high piles of dollar bills. Richard began helping himself, thousand of dollars at a time, to buy jewelry; he was, at the time, just thirteen years old.

There was also the nagging fact that, since Christmas of 1980, Kojak had been on the Bahamas' Restricted List, and subsequently elevated to the Stop List. Being persona non grata had not made much difference to him, because so many immigration officials were on his payroll, and he continued to travel about the Bahamas almost at will. But from his initial researches into the drug business, Kojak had decided that all smuggling enterprises had a "natural life" of three or four years at the most. The presence of his name on the Stop List, and the scare provided by Frank Barber's arrest, planted in his mind the first thoughts of retirement.

But at the end of April 1982, Tommy Maillis telephoned Kojak to say "there is somebody I want you to meet." Maillis said he knew a man who was "real powerful" in the Bahamas, who could have Kojak's name removed from the Stop List.

Kojak was instantly suspicious. He did not know Maillis was a DEA informer but he distrusted him because, in Frank Barber's absence, Maillis had tried to stake a claim to the ownership of Gorda Cay, and thus a share of Kojak's "action." And some months before, Kojak had paid $50,000 to a stalwart of the ruling PLP party who said he could rewrite the Stop List; nothing had happened.

"All I ask is that you meet him," said Maillis, and in the end Kojak agreed because he had it in the back of his mind that when he did retire it should be to the Bahamas: he thought he might open a bar in Nassau, and call it Smuggler's Cove.

Meanwhile, Everette Bannister waited in Miami with ill-tempered impatience. Gorman was by then living in the city, sent there by his father to learn the insurance business, and he recalls Bannister staying at his apartment, growing increasingly angry as the meeting he had come for failed to materialize. Bannister was constantly on the telephone, complaining about the delay: "What the hell kind of guy is this we're dealing with?" he said.

Eventually Kojak and Everette Bannister did meet, at a hotel near Miami International Airport, where Maillis introduced them. They skirmished with each other for a while and then agreed to meet again the next day at the office that Kojak maintained as a "front" for his activities. At the second meeting Bannister came straight to the point: Kojak's name could be removed from the Stop List for $200,000; "I guarantee it," said Bannister. Alternatively, Kojak could encounter severe problems. "I deal directly with the prime minister and some other power people," he continued. "Shit, if I want to I could pick up that phone and have you arrested in five minutes."

"And I," said Kojak, "can have you killed in one minute, or I can do it myself."

Having established the ground rules, they did a deal. Kojak agreed to pay Bannister a "deposit" of $20,000, the balance to be paid when he was no longer persona non grata. Bannister returned to his son's apartment in a much better mood than when he had left and even gave Gorman "a couple of hundred dollars spending money."

What Kojak got from Bannister for his $20,000 was a forged "transire," an official permit issued to yachtsmen who wish to cruise the islands. When he attempted to use it to enter the Bahamas, legally for a change, he was arrested and thrown into jail. He spent the night in a cell, listening to his arresting officer arguing furiously with Bannister on the telephone over a $4,000 bribe that Bannister had promised the officer to "let Kojak in," but that he had failed to deliver.

Kojak was released the next day, but the consequences of his arrest were to be felt for a considerable time. From that point on, his smuggling enterprise took on a distinctly more sinister aspect. After Bannister's deception Kojak's attitude, he said, was "fuck them." Barber sold Gorda Cay, but when the new owners insisted on taking possession of the island, Kojak ordered it to be retaken, by force if necessary, and a Haitian worker who attempted resistance was badly beaten up. In the fall of 1982, two headless corpses washed ashore near Gorda Cay. Kojak had little doubt that the victims were former workers of his who had been caught stealing marijuana. "I did not ask for details," he said.

And in November 1982, Kojak broke the promise he had made to himself that he would not smuggle cocaine. Approached by a representative of the Ochoa family, he agreed to import into the United States 500 kilos of cocaine. In the event, the Ochoas could only come up with 360 kilos; it was still the biggest single consignment of cocaine Miami had yet received.

Kojak spent Christmas of 1982 in New York with Neysa, the woman who was to become his third wife. Though she had played an active and enthusiastic part in his enterprise for more than two years, she had grown increasingly nervous about the risks, and urged him that the time had come to quit. On their flight back to Miami in January 1983, Kojak decided she was right.

Gene Francar was a biologist by training who became a DEA agent on the strength of a whim. Having graduated from the University of Wisconsin, he accepted recruitment by the US Food and Drug Administration as an inspector. He quickly discovered that his job consisted mostly of pulling tubers from the ground, and examining them for traces of disease. He quit, and joined what was then called the Bureau of Narcotics and Dangerous Drugs, intending to stay there as long as it took to fix on a new career. Seventeen years later, he was one of the longest-serving DEA agents in Miami, and the one who received the news that the legendary Kojak wished to retire.

Francar, who looks much more like a biologist than he does a drug agent, telephoned for an appointment and then dropped by Kojak's office. His visit was premature in that Kojak *intended* to retire; as he acknowledged to Francar, he still had "some shit going" but "I'm going to retire. I am going to do it, and soon." Francar told him that if he got caught he was on his own. Still, he gave him his business card and suggested that Kojak call him once a week. "Do me a favor," said Kojak. "Call me Lou."

For the next few weeks the two men met regularly while Kojak "tidied up the loose ends." Francar always claimed he was "not on duty" at these meetings, and he never pressed for information. Finally Kojak called to say that he and his wife were planning to take a prolonged vacation in Spain. Francar asked if he might drop round for a last chat, and "do you mind if I bring my partner?"

When Francar and his partner, Hank Spencer, arrived at

Kojak's office there was no pretense about being "off duty." Kojak told them that they had no need to worry about him any more; he had retired for good. He said he was not willing to "squeal" on anybody, but if he could help the DEA with "intelligence information" without incriminating anybody, "I'm at your service."

"Nice try," said Francar. "Let me explain the facts of life."

They were harsh. While Kojak might have retired, and while the DEA had no evidence with which to prosecute him, it would be six more years before the Statute of Limitations made prosecution impossible. In that time it was probably inevitable that one of Kojak's pilots, or a boatman, a supplier, or a customer would be caught and, to save themselves, would agree to testify against Kojak. There was also the question of income tax: the IRS had not yet inquired into Kojak's means, but it could. Francar and Spencer suggested that while Kojak enjoyed his vacation in Spain, he should give his "situation" some thought.

Eight months later, in January 1984, the United States government and Luis "Kojak" García entered into a written agreement. It gave Kojak immunity from prosecution for his past crimes, but on draconian terms.

To begin with: "Luis García agrees that he will truthfully and without reservation disclose to government investigators, agents and prosecutors . . . all information concerning the activities of himself and others, and will truthfully and without reservation testify in any civil or criminal trial or other proceeding with respect to the criminal or civil liability of defendants in any indictment or investigation in which he has information. . . ." So much for not "squealing."

"It is understood that Luis García must at all times give complete, truthful and accurate information and testimony. Should it be determined that Luis García has intentionally given materially false, incomplete, or misleading testimony or information . . . he shall be subject to prosecution." The agreement went on to say that if he was prosecuted, his own testimony could be used against him; he was specifically required to waive every right against self-incrimination granted by the Federal Rules of Evidence, and the Constitution.

And further: "Luis García agrees that he will cooperate, in

any manner requested, with government agents and prosecutors . . . in the conduct of their investigations of others." The government said it would not jeopardize his safety "unreasonably"; he would not be put in any greater danger than "that to which an undercover law enforcement officer would be exposed in the normal course of his duties."

The agreement was tempered by a "gentlemen's understanding" that Kojak's former associates would not be prosecuted for their past crimes that he revealed; and, he insisted on telling them what he had done, and that they should quit while they were ahead.

But the agreement had no time limit. Any day it wanted, the government could have put Kojak on any witness stand or into any undercover investigation and, had he refused, his own testimony would have sent him to jail. He regarded his "job for life" and the risks it entailed philosophically: "If you want to play," he said "you have to be willing to pay."

The FBI sent Kojak to the Dominican Republic to persuade an errant accountant to return to Miami, and reveal what he knew about money laundering.

The DEA used Kojak to wiretap two prominent Bahamians who offered to allow him to smuggle 1,000 kilos of cocaine through the islands for $300,000. They were arrested by the DEA when they went to Miami to collect the down payment; the tapes, and Kojak's testimony, sent them to jail.

And somebody in the federal government told NBC "Nightly News" of the catalog of corruption in the Bahamas which Kojak had given the DEA. He agreed to talk to NBC and, though he had no direct evidence against Pindling, it was his revelations that encouraged the network to broadcast its sensational accusation. When, as a result, the Commission of Inquiry was established, Kojak agreed to testify. He did so at the Bahamian consulate in Miami, providing devastating evidence against, among others, the former head of the strike force, Assistant Commissioner Howard Smith, and Everette Bannister.

The commission recommended that both Smith and Bannister be indicted and, when they were, Kojak agreed to go to Nassau to testify. He did not do so, however, because when he arrived in Nassau the Bahamian government refused to sign a cast-iron guarantee of immunity from prosecution. Kojak flew back to Miami, and the charges against Smith and Bannister were dropped.

Still, he had already done enough damage. According to Gorman, in the aftermath of his exposure by the commission hearings, Bannister's lifestyle went into sharp decline. He had by then parted from his wife and was living with Gorman in a rented house on Paradise Island. They could not pay the rent, and there were constant attempts to evict them. They could rarely pay other bills either, and more than once their electric power or their telephone were cut off. Bannister no longer received his "consultant's fee" from Resorts International, and neither could he any longer use the kitchen of Resorts' hotel as his personal commissary. He was forced to sell the Las Palmas Hotel, this time for real, but Gorman says he was cheated and did not get paid.

When Gorman tired of this very reduced life-style and "defected" to the United States in April 1987, he eventually agreed to meet Kojak—though with some trepidation, fearing that the sins of the father might be visited on the son. Kojak persuaded Gorman to talk to the DEA about his father and Carlos Lehder.

Gorman insisted on telephoning his father in Nassau to tell him of that decision. He also told him that "Kojak sends his regards."

"Kojak?" said Bannister. "Never heard of him."

Six months after Everette and Gorman Bannister had visited Lehder at *La Posada Alemana,* the resort was formally opened with a grand party. It was attended by representatives of the provincial government, local politicians, church leaders, and military officers and, of course, reporters. It was a huge public relations success for Lehder.

But very rapidly the reputation of *La Posada Alemana* soured, and with it, Lehder's. The discotheque became notorious because of the wholesale use of drugs, and guests at the resort complained frequently about naked young men and women chasing each other through the grounds. There were complaints, too, about Lehder's appetite for young women. "It is well known in Armenia," said the private secretary to the governor of Quindío, "that a number of young girls of good family are believed to have run away to stay with Lehder, perhaps as many as twenty."

Local charities, headed by members of influential families, began turning down his donations. And Armenia's prominent social clubs, such as *El Campestre, El América,* and *Corporación Bolo Club,* which had never accepted him as a member, now denied him even admission.

Lehder angrily told friends that he was being rejected for political reasons. "The Armenian aristocracy doesn't want me here," he said, "because I came to serve the people and not to serve them."

His attacks against Armenia's *clase dirigente* (the ruling class) became more frequent and bitter. His improvised political speeches were celebrated by his friends, and, early in 1983, sixteen of them—mostly liberals and professionals—encouraged him to form his own political party.

The hastily organized *Movimiento Latino Nacional* adopted as its platform the right of people to possess small amounts of marijuana and implacable opposition to the extradition of drug traffickers from Colombia to the United States. "Marijuana is for the people," said Lehder. "Cocaine is for milking the rich."

Reflecting his admiration for the Nazis, the party was modeled upon Hitler's National Socialists, and had its equivalent of the Hitler Youth, *Los Leñadores* (The Woodcutters), who were equipped with khaki uniforms, white hard hats, and four-foot wooden staves to be used for crowd control. At the resort, Lehder established a school where followers were taught that the *nacionalistas latinos* were a master race which in time would dominate the Yankees of North America; Europeans, they were told, were already "finished." He urged his *Leñadores* to form an army to "defend the fatherland against the imperialists and the Communists." He declared *Sábado Patriótico* (Patriotic Saturday) a day of political prayer. In halls and warehouses around Quindío, he attracted crowds of up to 10,000, using as bait cardboard boxes containing food and $5 bills.

As his movement grew in apparent popularity, so did Lehder's delusions. "Yes, I want to become a Congressman," he said in an interview. "I want to speak for those threatened with extradition, those threatened with kidnapping, those noble trade unionists, and those who are the poorest of the poor."

He also began publishing a weekly newspaper, *Quindío Libre,* which was distributed nationally by his fleet of aircraft. *Quindío Libre* opposed anything American. "We do not accept advertisements from any multinational; we are only interested in promoting Colombian enterprises," the paper warned in the first issue.

The editor, Luis Fernando Mejía—who earlier had worked at the Colombian Embassy in Spain—wrote laudatory pieces about his publisher-in-chief: "Lehder, a man of a new era, captain of the seas and of the skies, landed in Quindío, home of Indian chiefs, warriors, poets and idealists, at a time when dark clouds hang over the Republic." Long feature articles that looked at Medellín were lavish in their praise of such "business leaders" and "civic benefactors" as Pablo Escobar and Jorge Ochoa.

Above all else, *Quindío Libre* concerned itself with the extradition treaty between Colombia and the United States, signed in 1979 by the administration of President Julio César Turbay Ayala. "Damned be the treaty that Julio César Turbay Ayala and [Colombia's ambassador to Washington] Virgilio Barco Vargas signed," wrote Lehder in a signed editorial. "These two gentleman will have to bear the burden of having sold out the Colombian people. Damned be the puppets of the imperialist machinery."

The madness reached its height in June 1983 when Lehder was interviewed by an influential radio network and boasted of his involvement in drug trafficking from Norman's Cay. He described marijuana and cocaine as "the great Colombian bonanza" and said he smuggled them for the love of his country.

The furor this created was made the more intense by Lehder's next revelation that, in 1982, he had given $325,000 of drug money to the election coffers of the ruling Liberal Party. In July he insisted on giving more interviews in which he described cocaine as Colombia's "natural resource." He made headlines again when he attempted to walk onto the floor of the national legislature in Bogotá for a debate in which Justice Minister Rodrigo Lara Bonilla was accused of accepting money from a drug trafficker. Unable to gain access, he demanded entry to the press gallery, and sat there surrounded by his bodyguards.

It was, therefore, no surprise when, on September 2, 1983, the US government formally requested his extradition, and the Colombian authorities ordered his arrest. "Over my dead body," said Lehder at his last press conference before going "underground."

In Armenia he left behind his latest lover and their daughter, his adoring well-bred girl friends, his aircraft, his newspaper, and a pile of unpaid bills. His company collapsed and *Movimiento Latino,* the party that promised a master race, fell into disarray. *La Posada Alemana* was left unattended, and the animals in its zoo left to starve. The resort remained abandoned for a year, until somebody burned most of it to the ground.

Carlos Lehder was not yet finished as a drug trafficker but his reign as the self-styled "king of cocaine" was over. Nevertheless he could claim he had achieved what he set out to do: flood the United States with cocaine.

Lehder revolutionized cocaine-smuggling methods. By adopting and refining the techniques of Kojak and other marijuana smugglers, and by seizing Norman's Cay as his transshipment base, Lehder helped transform the cocaine industry from one that dealt in kilos to one that dealt in tons. In due course, and with only a hint of exaggeration, an American prosecutor—US Attorney Robert Merkle—would describe Lehder as the "father" of modern cocaine smuggling. "He was to cocaine transportation as Henry Ford was to automobiles," said Merkle.

Merkle also portrayed Lehder as a bitter man, motivated by hatred for the United States, which he regarded as a "police state." In Merkle's view, Lehder was a revolutionary who regarded cocaine as a weapon that could seduce and destroy a "decadent society" already reeling from the consequences of the Vietnam War and Watergate.

That scenario may seem farfetched. But if Merkle is right, if Lehder really did see the mass availability of cocaine in America as a means of seducing and destroying society, there is evidence to support Lehder's theory.

No city in the United States has felt the impact of "Carlos Lehder's revolution" more than Miami. And, in modern times, no city has been more corrupted.

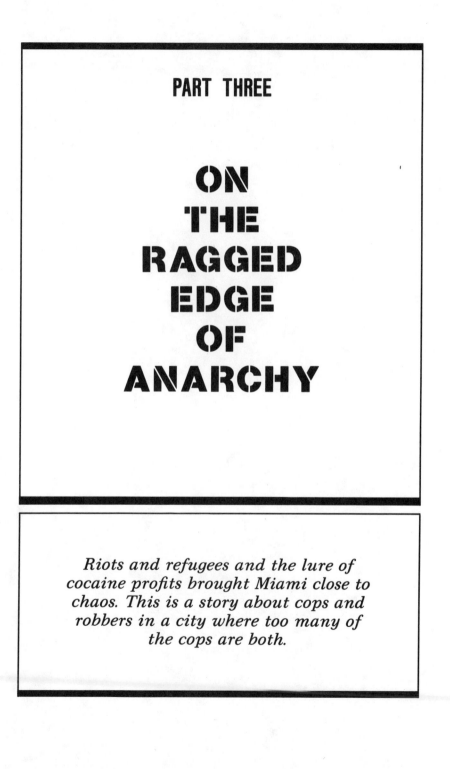

PART THREE

ON THE RAGGED EDGE OF ANARCHY

Riots and refugees and the lure of cocaine profits brought Miami close to chaos. This is a story about cops and robbers in a city where too many of the cops are both.

·12·

The Fraternal Order

Unlike the city it serves, the Miami River is short on distance, long on history. At least 3,000 years before the first Europeans "discovered" America, it served as a freeway for the Indians, and an important source of their drinking water (hence "Miami," which supposedly derives from one tribe's word for "sweet water"). Equally, the river served invaders from Spain, and England, and the US Army—and the latter, having finally vanquished the Indians (though with far more difficulty than they had imagined), paved the way for the pioneers, who settled on the banks of the Miami River, and used its water to power their mills. In time Henry Flagler arrived, bringing with him the railroad, and on the riverside site of what had been an Indian burial ground he built the Royal Palm Hotel, thus founding Miami's tourist industry, which he promoted by giving away Indian skulls as souvenirs.

When the Royal Palm opened its doors in 1896, Miami was no more than a settlement, with just 348 registered voters. Nevertheless, they elected their first mayor and voted to incorporate Miami as a city, and looked around for some way of extending the habitable land which then consisted of a coastal ridge just four miles wide. The Miami River provided the answer. In 1909, engineers began digging a canal to extend the river into the Everglades swamp, thereby releasing a flood-tide that lasted for weeks. When it finally subsided, the water table had dropped dramatically, many of the Everglades springs had dried up, and a strip of swampland twenty miles wide and thirty miles long became available to fuel the future land booms. As a side benefit, the canal gave Miami deep-water moorings that would attract large ships: today, rusting freighters from Panama and the Cayman Islands, and container ships from most of South America; dirty Haitian coasters collecting their piled-high cargoes of second-hand bicycles and mattresses; and luxury yachts with drafts as deep as their owners' pockets.

At night the canal extension is an eerie place, bullet-straight after the twists and turns of the river, narrow and black. The ships lining the container yards on the northern bank hum with the sound of generators and bilge pumps, but it is rare to see a soul on board; it is as though they had all been abandoned. Cruising up these dark waters, dwarfed by their huge hulls, it is easy to imagine that evil events could take place on the river at night, and few people would notice.

In the late afternoon of July 27, 1985, a small borrowed motorboat set off on a voyage up the Miami River, heading for the canal. On board were four men, one of them an experienced cocaine trafficker, three of them serving officers of the Miami Police Department. They had no business together, no legitimate business, and one of the officers, named Román Rodríguez, wondered aloud what they could possibly say if they were stopped.

The purpose of their voyage was to locate and keep watch on a forty-foot fishing boat named *Mary C.* Had everything gone according to plan, she should have journeyed up the river under her own power and be safely berthed at Jones Boat Yard, one of the oldest and largest establishments on the river. But on her approach to Miami, the *Mary C* had been boarded by US Customs and searched, seriously delaying her arrival. Then her engine had broken down and her crew had been obliged to call by radio for a tow; by late Saturday afternoon, nobody ashore knew for certain where the *Mary C* was, or when she might arrive.

So, police officers Román Rodríguez, Armando García, and Armando Estrada had elected to borrow a motorboat and cruise the river in the hope of finding her. Over the nervous objections of Rodríguez, they had taken along Pedro Ramos because he could easily identify the *Mary C* and find where her cargo was hidden. The tension created by Rodríguez's anxiety was made worse by an argument between him and García as to who should share in the spoils they had yet to seize from the *Mary C*. Estrada, the natural leader of the group, was nervous, too: he had promised himself that, after the *Mary C,* he would retire from crime, and with that goal in sight he worried that their luck might not hold.

There was no sign of the *Mary C* on the river, or at any of the yards and marinas on either bank. Whether she had reached the safety of Jones Boat Yard was impossible to tell because a large yacht was moored at the yard's entrance, blocking the view.

Miami sits farther south than the southernmost tip of California and on the same latitude as Calcutta, and on summer evenings subtropical thunderstorms are liable to come rolling in from the Everglades, draping the sky with huge black cumulus clouds. As evening approached, the three police officers and the cocaine trafficker decided to head back downriver, and find a more comfortable way of maintaining their vigil for the *Mary C*. They had gone no more than a mile when Rodríguez, still unhappy to be in the company of Pedro Ramos, claimed they were passing the spot where his car was parked, and demanded to be put ashore.

The *Mary C* had in fact reached the sanctuary of the Jones yard, and was now berthed in one of the repair basins, protected from the elements by a roof. The best place to watch her was not from the river, but from the junction of NW 33rd Avenue and South River Drive, where she was easily visible through a chain-link fence. This was desolate terrain, and a no-man's land at night, so the watchers—now numbering about a dozen—had little fear of being seen. In any event, since they were police officers, and in uniform, no passer-by was going to question their presence. And while they could see the *Mary C,* bathed in the yard's spotlights, those on board the *Mary C* could not see them, hidden by the darkness of the street. All the watchers required was patience.

There were six men aboard the boat: the crew of three who had brought her from the Bahamas; two "offloaders" to help with the cargo; and Pedro Martínez, a forty-eight-year-old Cuban-American whose special expertise had made him a wealthy man.

In pre-Castro Cuba, Martínez was a police officer; indeed, he was assistant and right-hand man to Rafael Salas Cañizares, chief of police and one of the more notorious officials of President Batista's regime—a fact that caused Martínez to become one of the first Cuban refugees when Castro came to power. In America, he married twice, fathered four children, started two businesses that specialized in applying a "popcorn" finish of glistening stippled paint to people's ceilings, and smuggled drugs.

He had begun with two boats, and marijuana. He had prospered sufficiently that by 1985 he owned or operated six steel-hulled boats, all unremarkable fishing craft, yet all of them capable of safe passage to and from Little Abaco Island in the Bahamas. The cocaine that the boats collected from there was carried to a marina in Key Largo or, more usually, to one of two yards on the Miami River, Tamiami Marine and Jones Boat Yard.

Martínez's success as a smuggler was based in large part on his ingenuity in devising hidden compartments for his boats. They cost as much as $80,000 to build and install, but they could easily contain 700 pounds of cocaine, and they were virtually undetectable. When Customs officers had boarded the *Mary C* as she approached Miami, they had found nothing to justify their suspicions. And later, when Customs had time and cause to take the *Mary C* apart, they still could not find the hiding place. It was not until long after the night of July 27 that they were told the compartment was sandwiched between two rear bulkheads, its entry masked by a fiberglass panel indistinguishable from the rest of the deck. They were unable to confirm it for, by then, the *Mary C* had vanished.

Martínez had been the transporter for a loose-knit trafficking organization for at least four years. His helpers were a mix: casuals recruited from a labor pool that sat and waited in a courtyard behind Izquierdo's supermarket in Miami's Little

Havana; and regulars, like his good friends Pedro Báez and Oscar Molinet, who were with him that July night on the *Mary C,* and who, as usual when a big load was coming in, had gone to the elaborate lengths of telling their neighbors they were off on vacation, and of moving their entire families to a motel on Miami Beach.

Martínez, too, was a cautious man, and he waited a long time before giving the order to unload the *Mary C*'s hidden cargo. Had he waited longer he might still be alive for, at about 1 A.M., Officer Estrada telephoned Pedro Ramos and complained that "nothing is happening," and that he and his colleagues were thinking of calling it a night. But shortly after Estrada made that call, Pedro Martínez removed the seven screws that secured the panel leading to the hiding place. He and his helpers began to transfer plastic garbage bags, filled with what looked like shoe boxes, from the *Mary C* to the back of a light brown Ford van. The boxes contained four hundred kilos of almost pure cocaine, with a wholesale value of more than $13 million.

Robert Downs had been the night watchman at Jones Boat Yard for six years, working the midnight shift seven nights a week. His main task was to patrol the yard once an hour, and to punch a time clock to confirm that he had done so. He was not armed—a minor miracle for Miami—and he had standing instructions not to resist any attempted robbery. If people wanted to work on their boats in the dead of night, well, that was not his affair.

When he was not on patrol, Downs sat at the reception desk in the front office where he could keep an eye on the main entrance door. In the early hours of July 28, 1985, at about 2 A.M., Downs heard pounding on the door and, through the glass, saw a man in uniform standing outside. The man said: "I hear you've got a boat loaded with dope out there. Open up."

The night watchman did as he was told, and a group of men pushed past him. There were about a dozen of them, dressed in dark uniforms. They charged through the office and out of a side door which led to the repair basin, about forty or so feet away.

Standing on board a yacht moored next to the *Mary C,* Oscar Molinet heard a commotion and looked up to see five men coming towards him brandishing guns. He heard them shout: "Police, police!" When they got nearer, he heard one of them yell *"¡ Mátenlos!"*—"Kill them!" Pedro Báez also heard the chilling command. He was standing next to the brown van with Pedro Martínez, who said: "Hang on, it could be a rip-off." Then Martínez abruptly changed his mind and shouted: "Boys, make a run for it. It's the cops." Báez and Martínez ran to the river and jumped in. Báez felt something or someone pulling him down. He broke free, and came to the surface to see one of the other loaders who was begging for help. But Báez could do nothing for him—he was half-drowned himself. He made it to the bank where he clung to a wooden stanchion.

Ten minutes later, or so it seemed to Downs, one of the uniformed men returned and ordered him to unlock the main gate; once he had done so the raiders left, taking with them the brown van. In his watchman's log Downs made this laconic entry:

> Police raided the *Mary C* at 2am. Crew went for a swim. Police confiscated a brown van.

But there was no police activity on the Miami River that night—or none that the police reported. And some crew members of the *Mary C* could not swim. In less than eight feet of black oily water, three of them drowned.

On Sunday July 28, 1985, a dozen hours after the raid on the *Mary C,* Pedro Báez decided he should tell somebody what had happened.

Báez and another loader, Rubén Ortiz, had survived their involuntary swim by clinging to stanchions for four hours until they were sure the coast was clear. Then they had hauled themselves out of the river and returned to Jones Boat Yard where the ever-obliging night watchman had allowed them to retrieve their car. Meanwhile, Oscar Molinet, the third survivor, had swum to the opposite bank, found a telephone, and summoned his wife to collect him.

But Pedro Martínez and the remaining two members of the

crew had disappeared. Martínez could swim, and the best guess was that he had died trying to keep the two others afloat. The last Báez had heard from them was their cries for help—a grim detail he did not include when, on that Sunday, he gave his account of the raid to Martínez's nineteen-year-old son, Faustino.

Faustino is not an innocent. He is part of a whole generation in Miami that has grown up knowing nothing other than the risks and rewards of cocaine trafficking—much like a whole generation of Belfast children has been bred on political and sectarian violence. He has been a part of the fast scene that allows young men to earn in a day more than most people make in a year; to buy $57,000 cars for cash, with no questions asked; to spend in a few hours enough money at restaurants such as Sundays on the Bay to send the waiters home with $600 in tips. He has also seen the downside: like many of his generation in Miami, Faustino uses cocaine, and on bad days he becomes furtive and paranoid, and talks about guns and "blowing people away."

His first reaction to Báez's account of the raid on the *Mary C* was to do nothing. His father had a violent temper, and Faustino had felt the weight of his hand more than once for "fucking up"; if his father had survived, and was simply hiding out somewhere, he would not want Faustino "making waves." But by Monday there was still no sign of him, and no word either, and Faustino decided to go to Jones Boat Yard to make inquiries. When he arrived there were "cops everywhere," so he sought the safety of the opposite bank. From there, he watched the grotesque scene as police divers worked to recover three bloated bodies that had been spotted floating in the river; they were temporarily secured with boat hooks to prevent them from drifting away.

For someone addicted to cocaine, Faustino reacted with remarkable calm. First, he telephoned his mother, instructing her to pack and leave the house before the police—or anybody else—might arrive and confiscate the considerable amount of money his father kept there. Next he found and returned the rental car that his father had, as always, taken the precaution of using.

Then, late that same afternoon, Faustino went in search of

help to get even with "the suckers" who had killed his father. He turned automatically to Luis "Kojak" García. Faustino went to school with Kojak's son, Richard, and knew that García kept a loaded AR-15 automatic rifle in his bedroom.

It was the loan of that, or any other gun, that Faustino had in mind when he arrived at Kojak's house on July 29, in a considerable state of agitation. Having heard the young man's story, Kojak called Gene Francar of the DEA who, in turn, called Centac 26. That night, less than forty-eight hours after the crew of the *Mary C* "went for a swim," a detective from Centac sat in Kojak's house and received the first indication that the Miami Police Department was riddled with corruption.

The same day as the raid on the *Mary C,* three men posing as police officers abducted a woman in the street, took her home, and robbed her of $50,000. They may or may not have been genuine cops. By then, it was difficult to tell, for Miami had experienced so many "home invasion" robberies carried out by men in police uniform, or men claiming to be police, that the public was officially advised not to open the door to any officer without checking with the local precinct that, first, he was genuine, and, second, that he was there on official business.

In August, José Clausell—who was without doubt a Miami PD officer—was arrested after allegedly offering to sell three police badges, a police radio, and a MAC-10 submachine gun to a man he did not know was a police informer. In October, $150,000 went missing from the safe of Miami PD's elite Special Investigations Section, while two officers were arrested for possession of cocaine; six others had already quit or been fired for suspected drug use, and two more who died in car crashes had cocaine in their bloodstreams.

Meanwhile, internal security detectives were investigating the suspected police involvement in the murder of a wealthy widower—bringing to four the number of homicides in which police were the main suspects. By the end of 1985, five more officers of the department, and one former officer, had been arrested for their part in the deaths in the Miami River and the rip-off of cocaine from the *Mary C,* and Centac suspected—rightly—that at least another dozen were involved. Those arrests put a cap on a year in which morale and public confidence in Miami PD sank to an all-time low. "What's the matter?" said a woman motorist stopped for speeding. "Quiet day on the river?"

Miami's police chief, Clarence Dickson, tried to make the best of it. "The last two days have been a total positive," he said. "I'm not shocked. I'm not depressed. There's nothing negative in what we're doing. We've made tremendous progress."

But then, in early 1986, a twenty-one-year-old Cuban woman named Jacqueline Quintana began to tell government investigators about her affairs with two Miami police officers. One of them, Aldo Suero, had let Jackie ride around in his police car, smoking marijuana, and loaned her his police cap and gunbelt that she wore, in absence of anything else, around her apartment. He also stole a police radio over which Jackie transmitted music from "Miami Vice" to bemused dispatchers and made fake emergency calls. Eventually, Suero asked Jackie—who had some strange friends—to get him a bazooka so he could blow the doors off the US Customs building in Miami and steal its haul of seized cocaine.

Instead, Jackie moved on, to a new police lover, Ricardo Alemán, who confided in Jackie that he had been paid $100,000 to "babysit" cocaine ripped-off by his fellow officers from the *Mary C.* She told investigators that Alemán had paid credit card bills, given cash to his relatives, opened several bank accounts, traveled to Argentina and the Bahamas, made a $10,000 down-payment on a Corvette, and "spent about $15,000 on clothes, shoes, stuff like that."

After five months, only $5,000 remained, so Alemán allegedly ripped-off a drug dealer who was supposedly a friend, and then plotted to murder him. He was arrested in March 1986 after police found a bag containing a machine gun, cocaine, and cash left near his car.

Later, when he had to explain his actions, he steadfastly denied any involvement in drugs or murder plots, but was disarmingly frank about the on-duty sex lives of some Miami police officers. Jacqueline Quintana, it transpired, was only one of a group of young women who were known to the police as "quickies," to be taken between calls while out on patrol, though she, he said, was "awesome." When he first saw her, he said, his eyes popped out. She wore a tube top, "no bra," a miniskirt, and white stockings: "Very sexy . . . the way she looked. Why say no? I enjoyed it." Alemán produced photographs of Jackie, taken by another officer, showing that she did indeed pose wearing a police belt, holster, and gun—and nothing else. Alemán also revealed that in Miami the police badge was known as "Master Badge," in that, like a Master Card, it could get an officer anything he wanted. For example, when Alemán tired of having sex with Jackie in the back seat of his patrol car, he would get them a free room at a motel simply by flashing his badge.

Then, on May 7, 1986, special agents from the FBI arrived at the headquarters of Miami PD bearing a subpoena entitling them to remove boxloads of files. The subpoena had been issued by a federal grand jury that, in light of the Miami River case, had begun a secret investigation into unsolved murders, the possible suppression of evidence, and the disappearance of seized narcotics. The focus of the grand jury's investigation was the Special Investigations Section (SIS), manned by handpicked officers to handle everything from probes into major narcotics trafficking and organized crime to anti-terrorism and VIP protection.

The subpoena not only demanded records but the appearance before the grand jury of the assistant chief of police, the highest-ranking Hispanic in Miami PD; the head of Internal Security; the head of the Patrol Section; the former head of the antiterrorist section of SIS; the commander of the burglary, auto thefts, and fraud units; and the recently retired commander of the SIS. At least twenty-one of the twenty-five officers named in the subpoena had worked at some time in SIS.

"We are literally on the ragged edge of anarchy," a federal judge told a private audience in Miami, and it did not seem an exaggeration. The city had seen police corruption before, and it had seen utter lawlessness in the streets, for instance during the cocaine wars. But what it was now experiencing was the double jeopardy of rampant, violent crime *by* police, and on an extraordinary scale. In time, one of those Miami officers who abused his uniform, his badge, and his authority to make more than $1 million, would sit down to compile for the authors of this book a list of fellow officers, past and present, whom he personally knew had also "gone bad." It contained sixty-seven names.

The immediate cause of the state of anarchy within the Miami police department is easy to describe: "God, the temptations," said Geoffrey Alpert, director of the University of Miami's criminal justice program. "If you are a police officer here, someone can offer you $20,000 just to turn your head."

As Alpert also said, police corruption stems from opportunity and greed, and both existed in a great abundance in Miami. An internal report by Metro-Dade police once eloquently described the kind of society the police are required to guard: a society where "local merchants cater to drug dealers in subtle ways"; where "real estate brokers continually rent or sell homes to individuals who pay with cash carried in large grocery bags"; where "automobile dealers frequently sell fleets of cars to corporations and private parties for export to South and Central America"; and where "local banks likewise profit by accepting enormous amounts of cash deposits in bogus-name accounts."

Most Miami police officers get a close-up view of those sections of society that enjoy the lavish rewards of drug trafficking. In the hope of reducing the temptations they face, it is official policy in the city of Miami that officers be allowed to earn extra money by "moonlighting," in uniform. By some estimates, up to 80 percent of officers have second jobs, many of them as security guards at the private clubs and discotheques and restaurants of Coconut Grove, an area of Miami favored for entertainment by drug dealers and by the bankers, lawyers, accountants, auto dealers, real estate brokers, and others who benefit, directly and indirectly, from their trade. And Coconut Grove is also heavily policed by on-duty officers at night, and especially on weekends, to ensure that it is a safe and pleasant place to be.

So they see, indeed they are required to guard, the flashy young men who drive Porsches and Ferraris and customized Thunderbirds, and who sport gold jewelry and Rolex watches and the other trappings of easy wealth. And they see, and guard, the lawyers and the bankers and the other "respectable" members of society whose displays of wealth may be more subdued but who derive it, indirectly through their fees, from the same source: drugs, and principally cocaine. As Professor Alpert says, it is of little wonder that some police officers are tempted to grab their share.

But corruption on any real scale—certainly on the scale that Miami has experienced—cannot exist without opportunity, opportunity that comes from a lack of official vigilance and strong control. Given the cocaine explosion, and the twin floodtides of drugs and money that poured into Miami, there can hardly have been a city in America that could less afford an ill-selected, ill-trained, and ill-led police force. It is an American tragedy of great proportion that that is precisely what Miami got.

In late 1968, at a time when Miami was already experiencing great stresses, the city fathers launched an exhaustive nationwide search for a new chief of police. The requirement was urgent. That summer, the Miami Police Department had barely coped with the riots that had accompanied the Republican party convention held on Miami Beach, and that had erupted in an atmosphere of simmering resentment among blacks over their treatment by local police. In addition the city was now playing host to the new waves of exiled Cubans, yet there was hardly a Spanish-speaking officer on the force; in short, Miami PD had become the last bastion of white, Southern bigots, who were disinclined to deal with the needs of an increasingly cosmopolitan city.

For almost twenty years, the department had been run as the personal fiefdom of Walter Headley, a chief of police who did not easily take orders from men he often and publicly described as "the pip-squeaks" of city hall. It was cancer, and not city hall, that finally deposed The Chief. Nature having taken its course, city hall was determined to fill the vacuum with a new chief who would be more responsive to its needs, and one who would be willing and able to drag the police department into the twentieth century.

The city commissioned the International Association of Chiefs of Police to conduct the nationwide search and present a list of suitable candidates. All of them, bar one, were rejected by the city—and the one who was approved turned the job down. Six local candidates, all of them majors and above in the Miami PD, were interviewed but there was never any serious prospect of their advancement. In great secrecy, Melvin Reese, Miami's city manager, went to Tucson, Arizona, to make a direct pitch to one of the most respected police chiefs in the land.

Bernard Garmire had been Tucson's police chief since 1957, when he was chosen from a field of one hundred candidates. In his first two years of office that city grew, through annexation, from twenty square miles to fifty-four, and the population from 80,000 to 257,000. Garmire had to increase the department from 157 to 450 officers in just four years, and the success with which he did it partly accounted for his national reputation.

But he was also recognized for his radical and progressive style of police management, and a scholarly approach which led him to be known as "the dean of American police." In Tucson he "forced" his men into college programs, with the full support of the University of Arizona and the GI Bill; no fewer than thirty of them went on to be chiefs of police in various cities and one became deputy director of US Customs.

In 1968, there was no earthly reason why he should want to leave Tucson for Miami, but Mel Reese offered two powerful incentives: an executive retirement plan, which he did not have in Tucson, and a 50 percent increase in salary.

Garmire had been active in the International Association of Chiefs of Police, and had been its treasurer for six years. He knew every chief of police in the United States, in any department of any size, many on a first-name basis. When they heard the news, the reaction was almost unanimous: don't take the job. They warned Garmire that Miami PD was a hotbed of intrigue and racism and corruption. He was told, too, that the Miami chapter of the Fraternal Order of Police had spent up to $10,000 investigating his background, in the hope, Garmire assumed, of finding some "skeletons in my closet." His FBI contacts talked darkly about the department's "tunnel vision."

Garmire discounted the warnings and became chief of the Miami police department on June 15, 1969. It was the biggest mistake of his life.

The police department that Garmire inherited included, in the detective bureau, a sergeant called Marion Murrow who was very much part of the old guard, an experienced officer but a hard-drinking one, and an inveterate prankster.

Murrow resented the new regime under Garmire, and challenged it in the way he was most adept, by inventing and spreading scurrilous stories. One of his most outrageous was the accusation that Garmire was not really a man; indeed, that beneath his well-pressed pants he wore pantyhose. Nobody took it seriously—until the story took on a life of its own.

It was then the practice of the police department, when ordering stenographer's pads, to sell the first page of the pad as an advertisement to defray expenses. At the time Murrow's story was going around the department, the advertisers taking advantage of that opportunity happened to be pantyhose manufacturers. The first page of all thousand notebooks was removed and destroyed. Murrow said: "Garmire's pissed because they're not his brand."

The story may have become exaggerated with time, and Garmire says it was certainly not on any orders from him that the pantyhose advertisements were removed. But it neatly illustrates the atmosphere that prevailed when Garmire tried to gain control of what he described as a juggernaut without a driver. Determined to "make haste slowly," he found himself faced with a department in chaos and a force resistant to change of any kind.

For at least the last year of Chief Headley's tenure, the various departments had been allowed to operate independently, with no central management that Garmire could see. The only cohesive forces that operated were the Fraternal Order of Police and the Police Benevolent Association; tight-knit organizations, both dominated by a white male majority that seemed to have been recruited en masse from the "cracker" population of south Georgia. ("Crackers" are ultra-conservative southern whites who, in the immortal words of Miami's first Hispanic mayor, "don't like Jews, they don't like foreigners, and they don't like blacks"; the name supposedly derives from the crack of the bullwhips that they once used to drive cattle, and negro slaves.)

They were an anathema to Garmire, as were some of their conventions. For example, it had become custom and practice to profit from police work: one officer in the Investigations Bureau, who handled auto theft, sold information about the recovery of stolen vehicles to car rental agencies that paid a reward for such information; a colleague reported the names of the writers of bad checks to the state attorney's office, which paid $15 a head. More seriously, Garmire became convinced that senior officers in those departments respectively responsible for gambling, prostitution, and narcotics in Miami were recipients of a share of the proceeds from those three enterprises.

There was also an attitude within the department of extreme laissez-faire: there was an officer who doubled as a traffic reporter for a local radio station, and another who had a second job as a navigator for Pan American Airways and who would take off for days, on round-the-world trips.

But these peccadilloes were overshadowed by what Garmire saw as his first priority: the immediate need to build bridges over the chasms that existed between the department and much of the community it served. The department had a reputation, and not only among the blacks, of being brutal. One local journalist recalls the Miami police as being "headknockers," who would equip their patrol cars with racks that prominently displayed their weaponry. The blacks, Garmire says, were regarded by his department as third- or even fourth-rate citizens.

Garmire secured generous funding from the federal government to develop a comprehensive community relations program, which would, if nothing else, serve as a means to keep lines of communications open and "keep the pot from boiling over." The resistance he met from his own men was typified by their reaction to a program of "conflict management," which Garmire set up with US government money and the aid of a Washington psychologist. A group of blacks and a group of his officers were brought together, over a period of two days, as a means of establishing a dialogue. In spite of the support of a popular police union chief, and an unusually aggressive speech from Garmire in which he ordered his men to participate, the program was met with indifference bordering on insubordination. Calling it "King Kong U" and "holding hands with the niggers," some of his men sat through the entire two days of the program with their arms folded, staring straight ahead. Angry and resentful at this foreign concept of "community relations," they arrived and remained flagrantly armed with weapons.

The resistance Garmire met was not confined to matters of race. He found himself faced, time and again, by the rigidity of the Civil Service Commission that controlled appointments within the police department and which was fiercely protective of the Fraternal Order. When Garmire attempted to remove officers he thought were corrupt, he faced an uphill struggle with the commission, which would not concur, short of a criminal conviction. And if Garmire launched a prosecution of one of his men, the Fraternal Order would invariably provide funds for the officer's defense.

Any attempts Garmire made at "personnel development" were rejected. The Fraternal Order took particular exception to a program that would have put the best and the brightest through doctoral programs at college and develop them into police managers whose motivation was not the number of arrests, but a more modern philosophy of community policing. Garmire was by then cynical enough to realize that his success in taking policewomen from desk jobs and putting them on the street—and under Garmire, Miami had the first woman in the United States to be promoted to the rank of sergeant—was because women were more acceptable to the rank and file than blacks.

The resentment against Garmire was enormous. A local journalist was invited to hear the department's grievances and turned up at the Fraternal Order's local headquarters expecting to meet four or five officers. He was astonished to find that almost the entire afternoon shift, from lieutenant down, had left their posts to talk to him. He recalls sitting in a smoke-filled room, listening to complaints about logistical changes and different requirements for filing reports. It was petty stuff, but there was no mistaking the contempt for Garmire: his ideas, they said, came from "Micky Mouse"—and "Garmouse," as they called him, was destroying the department.

Confused and demoralized, the men frequently misunderstood Garmire's management style, finding him cold and aloof.

He chose not to fraternize, to "glad-hand" as he put it, until he felt sure he was in control of the department. Even those working closely with him became convinced that he considered the department to be an "inferior race," an assumption that was only strengthened by the tragedy of a rookie officer named Roland Lane.

Lane had been a Miami police cadet since the age of 16, he was known to everybody on the force and universally liked. Soon after he graduated from the police academy, he responded with his young partner to a burglary call at a rundown hotel in one of Miami's black ghettos, and was shot down. It happened in the early hours of the morning, and Garmire, awakened from a deep sleep, only registered that one of the men had been shot—a not uncommon occurrence—and he was assured that everything was under control. He went back to sleep. It was not until near dawn that he learned that Roland Lane was dead. Once he realized what had happened, he went to Lane's parents and offered his condolences, but it was not soon enough: Major Newell Horne, who had originally called Garmire with the news of the shooting, was among those who thought "the sonofabitch didn't care enough about Roland to come in."

Relations between Garmire and most of his men continued to deteriorate. The bottom line was he did not trust them. Indeed, he would not hold sensitive conversations in his office until he secured a federal grant allowing it to be swept for listening devices every morning.

This atmosphere of mutual distrust between the chief and his men had a chilling effect on morale, and Dick Witt, who was an aide to Garmire as well as a senior official of the police union, suggested that the chief should attend roll call, to show the men his support in what were dangerous times on the streets of Miami. Garmire admits he hated the idea of "playing God." Witt suspects he refused to do it because he feared the men would take it as a signal that they should "go out and kick ass."

Above all else was a profound difference in attitudes. Dick Witt remembers writing a speech for Garmire in which the chief would have talked about "my police officers"; Garmire struck out the phrase and substituted "officers of the Miami police department." Witt, in despair, asked Garmire how he could ever hope to provide leadership when he would not even acknowledge the forces he commanded as "my men." The truth was, of course, they were not.

Melvin Reese, the city manager of Miami who hired Bernard Garmire, was a difficult and embittered man, thoroughly disliked by almost everybody who met him. He was, nevertheless, a strong and powerful manager, who controlled Miami more effectively than any politician. Having eventually won his battle with Chief Headley, albeit by default, Reese gave Garmire, the successor he chose, his absolute support, even though Garmire disappointed him by not "cutting a broad swathe" through the police department. So long as Reese remained at city hall, Garmire had the protection he needed. But, in 1974, Reese resigned as city manager to take a highly paid job as a consultant, and to allow himself more time for golf, his great passion. When he called Garmire in to break the news, he predicted that the chief might soon begin to encounter "some problems" at city hall. He was not exaggerating.

It is a fundamental criterion of modern police management that in order to survive and succeed, a police chief must have the substantial support of his department, or the community, or the political establishment. Given time Garmire might have won over the community: after all, his essential concern was for the ethnic minorities, blacks and Hispanics, who in Miami make up the vast majority. (The "Anglo" population of the city is now under 10 percent, and falling.) Given a miracle, he might even have converted the police department which, though it kicked and screamed, was obliged by Garmire to accept at least the trappings of modernization: a new police headquarters, computer systems, and state-of-the-art communications. But once Reese had departed, city hall became enemy territory for Garmire, and his loss of political support was fatal.

Perhaps there was good reason for city hall's animosity. In 1972, in the course of a corruption investigation of one of his own officers, Garmire had inadvertently sparked off a massive political scandal in Miami. It concerned alleged bribery of public officials, and by the time it had run its course, more than twenty judges, magistrates, and state and local officials had been implicated. A member of the state senate had been charged with corruption, and so, too, had the mayor of Miami; although the mayor was eventually acquitted, his political career was ruined.

As a result, by 1974 Miami had a new mayor, the first Hispanic to hold that office, whose priority appeared to be "Get Garmire." Maurice Ferré was only thirty-eight, but he had managed Hubert Humphrey's presidential campaign in Florida in 1968, he had served in Florida's House of Representatives, and, according to both his friends and his enemies, he was a keen student of the works of Niccoló Machiavelli, which he read not for pleasure but for instruction.

No sooner was Ferré in place at city hall than he took to calling Garmire down to commission meetings to interrogate him. "Bring the chief before me," he would say, and behave towards him in such a way that Garmire complained that, at the least, "I deserve to be treated like a gentleman." The Fraternal Order of Police and the Police Benevolent Association began gathering ammunition against Garmire, and he found himself called before a grand jury to answer questions about departmental administration and his plans for addressing the crime rate.

The grand jury's scathing report, based on the testimony of less than a dozen dissidents within the police department, allowed Mayor Ferré to announce a series of day-long hearings into the morale of the Miami police and Garmire's alleged "misfeasance." Garmire sat through two of those sessions in which members of his staff presented a litany of petty complaints: for example, that police radios did not work in certain downtown areas and that there was an officer who had not been issued a raincoat. In the circus-like atmosphere that city hall encouraged, such grievances received much more weight than the testimony of one of Garmire's assistants—who was, ironically, a paid-up member of the Old Guard—who declared that the mayor and the commission were destroying what remained of the effectiveness of the police department.

When Ferré scheduled a third hearing, Garmire decided that

enough was enough. His wife, Elizabeth, had already suffered a stroke that he blamed on the stress of his job, and, to some extent, on his men. "You bastards," he told them when he stormed into a meeting of his top staff to announce his resignation, and accused them of making his wife ill.

"Chief, if you tell us when you're leaving," said one of those present, "we'll buy your airline ticket."

Garmire imposed one condition on his resignation: that he and Elizabeth be allowed to leave town before it was announced. When reporters went looking for an explanation for his sudden departure, it was an aide who provided it: "He's just taken more than one man, and one man's wife, can stand."

13

Fruits of Rage

In the early hours of a Monday morning in December 1979, just a few blocks from the heart of downtown Miami, Arthur McDuffie, a black insurance agent and former US marine, was beaten senseless by a group of white police officers. At least six of them, and perhaps as many as a dozen, pummeled McDuffie to the ground. While he lay there, handcuffed, one of them straddled him, took a heavy Kel-Lite flashlight in both hands and rained blows on McDuffie's head, as though he were chopping wood with an ax. When McDuffie died four days later, and the medical examiner attempted to assess the force that had been used to split his skull wide open, he likened it to a fall from a four-storey building, head first, onto concrete.

The police officers who beat McDuffie to death then attempted a cover-up. They pretended he had fallen from his motorcycle while negotiating a corner and, to give credence to their story, they kicked the bike, smashed the gauges with their nightsticks, and then drove over the machine with one of their patrol cars. They broke his glasses, and discussed the best way to break his legs. Out of sheer vandalism, one of them put McDuffie's watch on the ground and fired at it with a second revolver he was carrying, one that could not be traced.

Their deception failed because the damage they inflicted on McDuffie and his motorcycle was far too severe to be accounted for by any accident. And, anyway, on December 26, one of those involved turned himself in to police headquarters. He said he had spent Christmas Eve thinking of McDuffie's two young children spending their first Christmas without their father, and he confessed.

There was a time, within living memory, when the beating of blacks by white police in Dade County was routine, and even officially encouraged. It kept "the coons" in line and gave Miami what one admiring judge described as "the most respectful and law-abiding class of Negroes of any city in the south." The sheriff's department ran with pack dogs it called "nigger hounds," and the Miami Police Department had a novel way of ridding the city of blacks it regarded as troublemakers. In the words of one of its officers, speaking in 1928: "We stripped them and beat them and ran them off. We took them outside the city limits in a . . . car and fired once or twice to see how fast they could run." The police chief of that era, Howard Leslie Quigg, was himself indicted for the beating death of a black, and though a grand jury found him "wholly unfit" for office and he was dismissed, it was only a temporary setback; Quigg was reinstated and, under him, the police department terrorized blacks in Miami for nearly thirty years. His successor, Walter Headley, was supposedly more enlightened, and claimed the credit for hiring the first black police officer in the south. By the mid-1950s, he had sixty blacks on the force, albeit they were called "patrolmen" to differentiate them from white "policemen," and their beat was confined to "Colored Town." But in 1967 Headley concluded that he had been too soft on "negroes," and he called a press conference to announce that, henceforth, Miami's black ghettos of Liberty City and Overtown would be patrolled by officers armed with shotguns and accompanied by dogs. "We don't mind being accused of police brutality; they haven't seen anything yet," he said. "They'll learn that they can't get bailed out of the morgue."

All of that was supposed to change when Bernard Garmire took over Miami PD, and when the Sheriff's Department was disbanded and replaced by what became the Metro-Dade Police Department. But for all of Garmire's efforts to civilize his department, and for all of Metro-Dade's determination to create a modern force that reflected and served the community, Miami's blacks—who make up almost one third of the city's population—did not readily recognize the difference. What did change was their willingness to tolerate it.

The Miami riots of 1968, which occurred during the Republican party convention in Miami Beach, were part of a national black uprising that came during that long, hot summer, and were much less serious than those in, say, Watts. Between 1970 and 1979, however, there were thirteen violent confrontations between blacks and whites in Dade County, all of which resulted from or involved real or perceived "police brutality."

In that context, Arthur McDuffie's truly brutal death in December 1979 at the hands of officers from Metro-Dade, was simply intolerable, and the wonder is that Miami did not immediately erupt into violence. Perhaps that was because there was an illusion that justice would be served: four Metro-Dade officers were charged with McDuffie's murder, and tension in Miami's black communities subsided, though barely.

It still ran sufficiently high that, in March 1980, a judge in Miami ordered the trial of the four officers moved to Tampa, Florida, saying the case was "a time bomb" and "I don't want to see it go off in my courtroom or in this community." The judge did not know, or did not think it relevant, that an all-white Tampa jury had recently acquitted a white police officer of beating to death a young black motorcyclist.

Two months later, while Miami's blacks waited for the promise of justice to be fulfilled, Miami's Cuban community celebrated something that would turn out to be just as illusory: an apparent, momentous defeat for the man who is referred to in Miami, even by some sections of the English-language press, as "The Dictator Castro."

The Mariel boatlift, which would produce the single biggest influx of Cuban refugees into Miami and lurch the city into crisis, was born of classic miscalculations on both sides.

In Havana in early April 1980, Castro seriously underestimated the number of people who wanted to quit his revolution. When, on April 1, a small group of would-be refugees crashed the gates of the Peruvian embassy in Havana, seeking asylum, and a policeman was accidentally killed in the process, an enraged Castro withdrew guards from the embassy compound, and those that wished to go there could do so. Indeed, Castro said, they could, if they wished, leave the country. Cuban officials gambled that a few dozen "malcontents" would take advantage of the opportunity, certainly no more than a few hundred. By April 6, 10,000 filled the compound, and thousands more were trying to get inside, and an embarrassed Cuban government had little choice other than to accept an offer from Costa Rica to organize an emergency airlift.

It was, to that point, an unmitigated public relations disaster for Cuba, and threatened to continue to be so. For the United States it was, to that point, a triumph: it could enjoy the television pictures of freedom-loving Cubans arriving in Costa Rica to denounce the Castro regime, without having to shoulder the burden of taking care of them.

But Fidel Castro had never lacked survival skills, nor the ability to turn the most awkward situation to his own advantage. Barely had the airlift begun than it was canceled—because, the Cuban government said, there was no need for it. In the words of an editorial in *Granma,* the official Communist party newspaper, published on April 18: "To travel to the US, there is no need to make a stop in Costa Rica. It costs less and is quicker to travel directly to Key West, [Florida] some 90 miles away."

And in Miami, word rapidly spread that the Cuban port of Mariel was "open": anybody who had relatives in Cuba who wished to leave, could collect them.

On April 20, Sergio Pereira, then the assistant manager for Metro-Dade, was attempting to raise money to improve Miami's desperately overstretched airport (today, second only to New York's Kennedy Airport in terms of international air passenger and cargo traffic). Pereira had a group of Wall Street bankers corralled in his office when he was interrupted by an urgent telephone call from the District Director of the Immigration and Naturalization Service (the INS). As Pereira later recalled it, the conversation went like this:

"Sergio?"

"What is it?"

"We have two hundred Cubans."

"Two hundred Cubans? We've got half-a-million Cubans in Dade County. What are you talking about?"

"Sergio, there are more coming."

Indeed there were. In the next three weeks or so, Pereira found himself in the midst of a struggle to cope with an influx of 30,000 refugees, and that was merely the start of it.

It seemed as if everybody in Miami with access to a boat was on their way to Mariel. Rudy Arias, who was then the owner of a gas station in Miami Beach, found himself instinctively loading his boat onto a trailer with the idea of setting off to Cuba to rescue his father's family. It was only as he headed for the ocean that he realized his boat was far too small for such a voyage—and that he had no idea of how to get to Mariel. Luis "Kojak" García had no relatives in Cuba, but most of his boat people did. Drug trafficking in Miami came to a virtual stop as they opted to transport human cargoes, and Kojak, caught up in the mood of things, spent $100,000 acquiring boats for people who wanted to go.

Whether the boatlift should have been permitted was a question that thoroughly confused and divided the Carter administration. While the Coast Guard escorted the armada of boats headed for Cuba, the State Department warned that such trips were illegal. And while President Carter said the refugees would be welcomed with "open arms," some of the administration's spokesmen said the opposite.

One reason for the confusion was that the White House received contradictory advice. Sergio Pereira, who was asked by Carter to head a "national relocation effort" and who wanted the boatlift halted, was told it could not be, because there would be riots in the streets of Miami.

"Where do you get your intelligence?" Pereira said. "Who's giving you that bullshit? There is absolutely nothing going to happen down here."

He was told that Omega Seven, a right-wing anti-Castro group in Miami, would blow up the town.

"Omega, my ass," said Pereira. "Omega Seven is nothing."

But it was all to no avail. Untold thousands of boats arrived in Mariel where they had to wait in the harbor for days, and then weeks, while Cuban officials attempted to manage the exodus; manage *and* manipulate. For as Wayne Smith, head of the US Interests Section in Havana at that time, noted, the character of the human cargo suddenly changed. Whereas the first boats to arrive had been allowed to take back refugees from the Peruvian compound and families who had registered their desire to leave with Immigration, later arrivals were obliged to take on board a mixed bag of passengers. Typically, according to Smith, three-quarters of them were not the family members for whom the boats had been sent, but passengers chosen by the Cuban government.

At the receiving stations in Key West and Miami it rapidly became clear that the new influx—which eventually totaled more than 118,000 people—was markedly different from the earlier waves of Cuban refugees. The new arrivals were much younger, with an average age of only thirty-four; almost half of them were unmarried; and 70 percent of them were men. There was a higher percentage of blacks than had been seen before, and many of them had an unusual skin pigmentation, an indication that they had suffered from malnutrition.

It also became clear that thousands of them had come directly from Cuban jails. They included dissidents, homosexuals, prostitutes, and what Castro described as "chicken thieves"—people who would hardly be classified as criminals in the United States. But they included, too, some of the most hardened prison inmates, people who were criminals by anybody's definition.

Major Larry Boemler of the much-troubled Miami Police Department recalls being at an old Customs shed in Miami that was used as an emergency clearing-house, and watching some of those who passed the hasty and peremptory checks that were used in some attempt to screen out undesirables. He saw them saunter up the road to Coconut Grove, and immediately begin hustling, attempting to deal in women, drugs, "you name it."

"My God," said Boemler out loud. "What has Castro done to us?"

As the human floodtide continued, an all-white jury in Tampa, Florida, retired to consider the fate of the four white police officers accused of the brutal murder of Arthur McDuffie.

Fruits of Rage

In the early afternoon of Saturday, May 17, after only two and three-quarter hours of deliberation, the jury returned. It took a further thirteen minutes for the court clerk to read the verdicts, but only because of the number of counts in the indictment. The jury's answer to every one of them was the same: Not Guilty.

The news reached Miami at 2:42 P.M. when it was broadcast by WEDR, a radio station with a mainly black audience. The station manager went on the air to appeal for calm, and to suggest that black leaders should meet with the state attorney on Monday to "get some answers," but it soon became clear that Monday would be too late.

Crowds began to gather around the radio station and on the street corners of Liberty City, Overtown, and the black section of Coconut Grove, and the first volleys of rocks were thrown. At the Metro Justice Building, an impromptu protest rally attended by some 3,000 blacks of all ages, and even some whites, spontaneously erupted into a full-scale riot. A police car was overturned and set on fire, and black youths smashed the glass doors of the justice building and set fires in the marble lobby. They moved on to the headquarters of the Metro-Dade Police Department, and, while the policemen trapped inside called desperately for help, they set fire to the front of the building. And Liberty City, too, soon began to burn.

By the time it was all over, eighteen people were dead, there was $80 million worth of property damage, and 1,100 people had been arrested. But what marked the riot, what made it so shocking, was the intensity of the rage of blacks against whites; whites of any description, men, women, and children.

There were any number of truly appalling scenes as black mobs hunted white people, and attempted to kill them.

Eighteen-year-old Michael Kulp, his brother Jeffrey, 22, and a young friend, Debra Getman, had spent the afternoon on the beach and were unaware of the McDuffie verdict, and its consequences. At about 6:30 P.M., Michael Kulp was driving the three of them home when his car was hit by a shower of rocks and bottles. Michael was struck on the head by a chunk of concrete hurled through the windscreen. He lost control of the car, which swerved across the center median, across the lanes of oncoming traffic, and mounted the sidewalk where it struck a ten-year-old black girl, Shanreka Perry, pinning her against a wall, crushing her pelvis, and severing her right leg.

An enraged mob dragged the Kulp brothers from their car and beat them with rocks, bricks, and pieces of concrete. A newspaper vending machine was brought crashing down on Jeffrey Kulp's head. Both brothers were shot several times and a green Cadillac was driven over them; the driver then stabbed both of them with a screwdriver. The beating went on for fifteen or twenty minutes. When it was over, a local derelict placed a red rose in Jeffrey Kulp's bleeding mouth.

Debra Getman managed to escape with the help of other blacks, who put her into a taxi. Michael survived, although he was left severely handicapped. Jeffrey died two weeks after the riot. Shanreka Perry was hospitalized for seven months, and now walks with crutches.

At about 10:15 the same evening, Emilio Muñoz, a sixty-three-year-old Cuban-born butcher, had his car stoned and overturned. As he lay trapped in the wreckage, the crowd beat him and jabbed him with sticks. Then gasoline was poured on to the car and it was set ablaze. By then, according to the medical examiner, Muñoz was dead: choked on blood that trickled into his lungs as a result of the beating.

Muñoz was not removed from the car until the following day. In the Cuban port of Mariel, at about that moment, unaware of what had happened, his wife and son boarded the fishing boat that would bring them to their new life in the United States.

·14·

Panic at City Hall

Miami was a city under siege. As the fires in Liberty City still smoldered, the city and Dade County began to experience an extraordinary curve in their homicide statistics. In part, that was because of the Cocaine Wars; in part, because of the criminal element among the new arrivals from Cuba, who were called, with scorn, *Marielitos.* Many of them attempted to muscle in on the drug business, which intensified the war, and many of them became its casualties.

Among the citizenry of Miami, particularly the small but powerful "Anglo" establishment, there was a feeling of total outrage that eventually manifested itself in the formation of Miami Citizens Against Crime, a "concerned group" that included the chairman of *The Miami Herald,* the chairman of Eastern Airlines (Miami's biggest private employer), prominent attorneys, and a local archbishop. In their propaganda they described Miami as a city of "organized crime, warring drug gangs, slaying in the streets and citizens afraid to leave their homes." They pointed out that Mariel, the black riots, and the fact that the city was *the* major entry point for drugs into the United States had penetrated the national consciousness, and all of that had enormous financial ramifications for Miami: for example, Burger King, the closest rival to the McDonald's hamburger chain, which not only had its headquarters in Miami but its "Burger University" as well, had threatened to relocate.

At city hall, Miami's Machiavellian mayor, Maurice Ferré, and the other four members of the city commission found themselves taking the blame. Because of their budgetary restraints, the Miami Police Department was at its lowest strength in five years. Large-scale desertions by senior officers and a three-year hiring freeze had left Miami with just 654 "sworn" officers, which was 60 less than there were supposed to be, on paper—and a good 300 less than the recommended norm for a city of Miami's size. At public meetings at city hall the commissioners were sternly lectured by concerned citizens on the need to restore law and order. In an atmosphere that resembled panic, the commissioners authorized a program of mass hiring.

In one year, between October 1980 and September 1981, the police department filled all of its "paper vacancies" and recruited a further 270 new officers, making 330 in all. In the following year, the department's strength was increased by another 186 "sworn positions," which were filled with new recruits, and 140 more were hired to replace members of the "old guard" who quit, making 326 in all. So, in just two years, the size of the Miami police force almost doubled—and by the end of that remarkable expansion more than half of the men and women in uniform, 56 percent, were new recruits; by the end of the third year, the proportion of new recruits was nearer to 70 percent.

If inexperience had been the only flaw to mark this new, hastily assembled force, it might not have mattered; after all, experience comes with time. However, the mass hiring program in Miami was conducted under a peculiar set of rules that influenced the quality of the force: they were well-intended, and more than justified by past events, but in the circumstances in which they were applied, the consequences were bound to be disastrous.

By 1980, the city of Miami was the subject of two Consent Decrees—legally binding promises the city had made in order to avoid severe financial penalties, which dictated who could be hired as new recruits for the police department. The first resulted from a lawsuit filed by black officers within the department who claimed that blacks had been discriminated against

in terms of recruitment, pay, promotion, and work assign-
ments. The city, with no possible defense, "consented" to hire
more blacks and other minorities, and to treat them equally.
Towards that end, the Industrial Relations Center of the University of Chicago was hired, at a cost of $600,000, to devise and
administer unbiased tests that would decide both entry into the
force, and promotion within it. So far, so good.

But not much happened. In the year following the signing of
that decree, only two blacks and thirteen Hispanics were hired,
and the police department remained what it had always been:
predominantly Anglo, white, male, and fiercely resistant to
change.

So in late 1975, no less than the US Department of Justice
filed suit against Miami, alleging blatant discrimination
against minorities *and* women, and threatening to remove $8.7
million of federal "revenue sharing" funds unless the city
agreed to change its ways. In time the city did agree, though in
the face of enormous resistance from the Fraternal Order of
Police, and the courts approved a Consent Decree that had two
crucial provisions: that 56 percent of new recruits would come
from the minorities, and, that all new recruits must live within
the boundaries of the city of Miami. It seemed to make perfect
sense because it envisaged a gradual and orderly change: as
Anglo officers retired or resigned, the majority of their places
would be taken by people who better reflected the makeup of
the community they served.

The fact that there was precious little change as a result was
largely the fault of the hiring freeze. Most of the Anglo officers
who quit during that period were not replaced by anybody. But
to all appearances, it seemed that the police department was
still stalling, still determined to retain one of the last bastions
of Anglo power. And so in 1979, when Hispanics first gained a
three-to-two majority on the city commission, a new and
draconian requirement was introduced: that, henceforth, 80
percent of all new recruits must come from minority groups
within the city boundaries of Miami. That rule was still in force
when the city commissioners decreed that the size of the police
force would be practically doubled, and virtually overnight.

Police recruiters dutifully went out to visit the high schools of Miami, and they set up employment booths at Sears Roebuck department stores. But they faced a fact of life that while the city's boundaries contained ample communities of blacks and Hispanics, those communities tended to be dominated by the least-educated, the least-motivated, and the least well-off; the "achievers" tended to move out of the ghettos, to more affluent communities *outside* the city limits. Yet under the hiring rules the department was supposed to find, from within the city, hundreds of blacks and Hispanics—a fair proportion of them women—who wanted to be police officers and who the rules also insisted must be: no younger than twenty-one, but no older than thirty; physically fit and possessed of good eyesight; sufficiently educated; fluent in spoken and written English; holders of a driver's license; not convicted felons and not associated with criminals; and non-users of drugs. Colonel Dick Witt, a former aide to Chief Garmire who in 1980 was in charge of training, went to Mayor Ferré and told him it was impossible to implement city hall's writ within the hiring rules. Then, said the mayor, bend the rules.

The residency requirement was circumvented by requiring potential recruits to have a Miami address only on the day of application—and if it belonged to an aunt or a friend, or it did not exist at all, so be it. In any case, said Witt, in a sprawling metropolis like Dade County, who knew where Miami's exact boundaries began and ended? To get around the requirement that police recruits be able to read and write—and some of them could not, beyond sixth-grade level—the city hired them anyway, and enrolled them in remedial English classes (which, seven years later, are still being held). When, even so, their written reports proved to be lacking, their supervisors were ordered to "tidy up the paperwork."

The saving grace of this gerrymandered recruiting program was the entry test, devised and administered by the University of Chicago. It measured the academic ability of candidates and also their suitability to be police officers, on the basis of a psychological test that was then very much the rage among recruitment professionals. It consisted of a series of written questions, each one accompanied by "multiple choice" answers, for example:

Question If someone insults me, I:
Answer Sulk.
   Walk away.
   Punch him on the nose.

This was not a test that one passed or failed: rather, from the responses it was, supposedly, possible to draw a psychological profile that might raise a warning flag indicating that a candidate was perhaps too reckless, or too timid, to be entrusted with a badge and a gun.

But such tests were imperfect, at least in the context in which they were used in Miami, because they were largely devised by white Anglo males who had no cultural empathy with the candidates who took them. In the opinion of Colonel Witt, the test was as likely to "weed in" bad candidates as weed them out. As the University of Chicago eventually conceded, the business of preparing intimate psychological profiles carried with it enormous ethical burdens. For example, a candidate's profile might reveal, as it did in the case of one female recruit to Miami PD, that they had "problems of sexual adjustment"—a subjective judgment that was scarcely germane to her suitability as a police officer, but a piece of information that could cause misery if it fell into the hands of her colleagues. With good reason, therefore, the university stopped handing over its profiles to laymen. Instead, it gave Miami's Department of Human Resources, the city's personnel experts, what was merely a summary of test results, and the personnel people in turn passed on to the police department a list of supposedly "qualified" candidates.

Miami's current Chief of Police, Clarence Dickson, who inherited the department created by such practices, says it was "a miracle" that the mass hiring did not lead to "total catastrophe," and his view is shared by many who witnessed it. According to Geoffrey Alpert, the criminal justice expert from the University of Miami: "The police department opened the floodgates. They took them like cattle, putting a badge on the chest and a gun on the hip." Colonel Witt described too many of those hired as "badly trained underachievers."

And Kenneth Harms, who was chief of police at the time,

said: "I'm convinced that we got some folks with their rubber bands strung too tight who shouldn't be carrying a gun and a badge"; men who, "on their best day should never have been police officers."

The deficiencies of the "Class of '80"—and for that matter, of '81 and '82—soon became apparent. As early as the middle of 1981, senior officers at the police department received reports that supervisors were being harassed and intimidated by some of the new recruits. One supervisor had his car tires slashed; another found the front seats of his car covered with shaving cream; yet another had the emergency light bar stolen from her patrol car. A shift captain proposed to Chief Harms that he be assigned the toughest lieutenants and sergeants in the force, and be allowed to "sort things out," but nothing was done.

Far more alarming was the news that Joaquín Miranda, one of the Hispanic officers in the department assigned to carry out background investigation of Hispanic recruits, was associated with drug dealers—and that in at least six cases he had left out of his reports potentially damaging information about recruits, including their use of illegal drugs. Procedures were changed, so that in future both the police department and the Department of Human Resources carried out separate background checks, but there was no practical way of re-screening recruits who had joined since 1979. Colonel Witt estimated that the number of those whose clearance had to be regarded as suspect ran into "hundreds." The training staff began to refer to the new intake as "a whole lot of ticking time bombs." As Witt recalls: "We decided the only thing we could do was pray."

It was perhaps fortunate that the police department had, during this turbulent period, a strong and solid police chief. Kenneth Harms had joined the force in the late 1950s and by the time he became chief, at the age of forty, he had completed two college degrees and risen steadily through the ranks. Liked and respected by his men as "someone you could relate to," he had the support of the largely Anglo officers whose career path had closely followed his, and although some members of the black community grumbled that he paid only lip service to minority recruitment and advancement, he nevertheless managed to juggle the demands of the often-warring factions within the department. Mayor Ferré, who had put Harms in place, appeared, at first, to have every confidence in the new chief.

But good cop though he was, having obtained the seat of power, Harms began to acquire what others saw as delusions of grandeur about his role in the community. Not long after he was appointed chief in March 1978, Harms was invited to attend a Congressional subcommittee hearing held in Miami to investigate crimes against the elderly, and chaired by Florida's longest-serving and indomitable representative, Claude Pepper. Five minutes before the hearings were due to start, there was no sign of Harms, and Colonel Witt, then in charge of Homicide, went in search of him. Harms was waiting down the street; waiting, he explained, until he could make "an appropriate entrance." Sure enough, a few minutes after Congressman Pepper had rapped the gavel to start the proceedings, Harms pushed his way through the crowds until Pepper, noticing the commotion, stopped in mid-sentence and got up to "greet the chief"—all of it in full view of the television cameras.

With his talent for self-promotion, Harms started to become a powerful political entity in his own right. In 1981 he put together a comprehensive legislative package on law enforcement which he addressed not to city hall but to the governor of Florida, and his cabinet in Tallahassee. It was the unfortunate Witt who was summoned by Mayor Ferré and instructed to remind Harms that he was chief of police "only within the city limits," and to remind him precisely whom he worked for.

Harms found himself increasingly at odds with the mayor, and with other members of the city commission, not least because he would use *The Miami Herald* as a public forum for his disputes with city hall. But in much the same way that Chief Garmire had been protected and supported by a strong city manager, so, too, was Harms—for a while. His patron was Howard Gary, who was Miami's first black city manager, and whose strengths at city hall included the fact that his uncle was an influential community leader, widely reckoned to be able to deliver the black vote. Harms and Gary were personal friends who "worked out" together to keep fit. Gary felt that Harms "had a good team" and "kept things afloat real well." He also thought that, given time, Harms's relationships with city hall would improve.

But for reasons that are not clear, the relationship soured. Gary, at the request of the mayor, commissioned a study from a nationally known consulting firm—Booz, Allen & Hamilton—to determine ways in which the police department's operations might be streamlined and improved. The focus was on "civilianization" of administration, as a means of saving money and getting more uniformed officers onto the streets.

Gary was under no illusions as to what the mayor's strategy was: "Ferré wanted it to embarrass Harms, to be a hatchet job." Predictably, when Harms saw the results of the study, he exploded. He telephoned Gary and told him the consultant's report was "ludicrous," and he promptly wrote a 150-page rebuttal. But Gary had already gone on record to the press, saying that Harms was essentially in agreement with the report. Harms became "absolutely incensed." He told the mayor and the other commissioners precisely what he thought, and when a *Miami Herald* reporter telephoned, with a deadline to meet and hopes of a colorful quote, Harms did not disappoint him: "The Booz, Allen, Hamilton report," he said, "is 90 percent bullshit." When that remark was published, Gary accused Harms of "insubordination at its highest."

What was now a war between the two men intensified when Harms was tipped off that federal agents were investigating the Sunshine State Bank in Miami, of which Gary was a director. The premise of the investigation was that the bank was laundering drug money, and Harms was privately warned that a federal indictment was imminent and that Gary's name might be included on it.

Harms began his own investigation, not only into Gary but Mayor Ferré as well. He inquired into rumors that both men were occasional guests at parties at the Venetia Hotel, where cocaine was consumed and where prostitutes were available, and he began to compile files that he locked in his office safe and which were, supposedly, a closely guarded secret.

But there were members of Harms's senior staff, men with access to his inner sanctum, whose loyalties were not to the chief but to city hall. On January 26, 1984, when Harms came to realize that, and to suspect that his secret investigations were no longer secret, he staged a minor coup, removing from his staff the people he believed were leaking to city hall, and changing the locks on his safe. In so doing, he understandably failed to consult with city hall, thereby laying himself open to the accusation that he had acted intemperately and without the necessary authority. By then, Howard Gary was convinced that Harms had authorized a surveillance operation against him.

At 2:47 A.M., on the morning of January 27, when he was at home asleep in bed, Harms received a telephone call from Gary announcing that he was fired. Gary told him to turn in his gun and his badge, and to stay at home until further notice. Instead, Harms roused his wife, and together they drove to Gary's house where they found the cars of the city commissioners and two of Harms's most trusted assistants parked in the driveway. At police headquarters, where they drove next, they found the parking lot filled with staff cars, and late-night oil burning in most of the offices, including his own. In the course of that night, Harms's office was thoroughly searched and, to his great chagrin, his two pet fish—named Maurice and Howard, of course— were "murdered" when their tank was broken. More important, Harms's files on the supposed indiscretions of Gary and Mayor Ferré were removed from the safe. *The Miami Herald* later claimed that "The Harms Papers" were no more than memos that the chief had dictated to himself, in which he revealed frank conversations between himself and city officials. The notes reported that Ferré had called Gary "the worst city manager in recent history," and that he had described one of his fellow city commissioners as "crazy . . . devious and unstable." *The Herald* went on: "The revelations included all manner of delicious tidbits, but not much of solid nutritional value."

On February 9, 1984, Harms wrote a twenty-three-page typed, single-spaced memo to Gary in which he disputed the stated reasons for his dismissal—the unauthorized reassignment of his staff. In it he said: "Your claim that such transfers left the department 'out of control' actually reflected only your fear that you would no longer be in a position to gain confidential police information."

The city chose not to confront Harms's numerous allegations. Instead, he was given a generous settlement, on one condition: that he should remain mute, and not attack the city, its employees, or his successor; if he did, he would be subject to financial penalties imposed by an arbitrator that might amount to fines of up to $15,000. Howard Gary received death threats in the aftermath, and for months afterwards he had bodyguards assigned to him by the Miami Police Department.

Gary was never accused of any wrongdoing in connection with the operation of the Sunshine Bank, though it was closed down by state authorities in May 1986, after the discovery that it was $23 million in the red. And though the authorities charged that much of the bank's revenue came from drug deals, Gary's embarrassing association appeared to be limited to his membership of the board and his acceptance of a $95,000 loan.

But there were whispers of other alleged improprieties, some of them contained in Harms's files, that doomed him. For instance, the state attorney's office looked into allegations that Gary had run up a bill of over $8,000 for repairs to his personal cars at the city motor pool. Gary insisted he had the right to such a perk; the city attorney ruled, the following day, that he did not.

And Gary made the profound mistake of alienating much of the Cuban community in Miami by launching a strident public attack on President Reagan, accusing him of racism and saying the only difference between the president and the Ku Klux Klan was "he doesn't wear a white sheet and doesn't terrorize black folks at night." Gary later apologized, but his honeymoon with the commission—during which he became the highest paid city manager in the United States—was clearly over. In October 1984, during a city commission hearing on police matters, he was once more accused of having "a relationship" with drug dealers, and the meeting became so heated that police had to be called to restore order.

Gary was fired as city manager later the same month. The circumstances of his dismissal will never be fully explained because Mayor Ferré destroyed his notes describing the events that led to that decision. *The Miami Herald* filed suit against

Ferré for willfully destroying public records, and a circuit judge forbade him from destroying any more, but it was, by then, too late to matter.

The reaction within the black community was one of outrage, and Ferré eventually paid the price: in the next mayoral election his share of the black vote fell from 98 percent to 5 percent, and he was removed from office.

But before that could happen, the city commission made a placatory gesture to Miami's blacks that was to have considerable significance. In January 1985 Chief Harms's replacement was himself replaced by Miami's first black police chief, Clarence Dickson—a twenty-seven-year veteran of the force who had never managed to pass the captain's exam. A personable figure, with a quiet manner but with a penchant for cowboy hats, he was widely acknowledged to be a nice guy. As Dick Witt described him: "A super guy . . . You like him so damn much you'll do anything not to let him get into trouble. Gentle man is a literal description."

But Dickson was also widely regarded as being hopelessly naive. As Geoffrey Alpert of the University of Miami put it: "A nice individual, but as a major city police chief he lacks some qualities." Kenneth Harms, while acknowledging his fondness for Dickson, went further: "They needed a black, and Clarence was available. Clarence wasn't quite bright enough to say no." It was Harms who had promoted Dickson to his first staff position but, "he was very carefully monitored. Clarence by accident could screw up more things than most people could on purpose."

In late 1985 the grim results of the city's panic hiring policies became alarmingly obvious. As crime flourished and drugs continued to flow unchecked, Miami's police force of too many ill-trained, undisciplined, anarchic, and corrupt officers was led by a man who, in Kenneth Harms's words, "just doesn't have it."

·15·

The Little Havana Midnight Shift

Rodolfo "Rudy" Arias was one of the "class of '81," though he was almost rejected out of hand by police recruiters when they read on his application form that he weighed 258 pounds. They changed their minds when they saw for themselves that most of his bulk was muscle.

Arias could have been a professional football player, and indeed he tried out for the Miami Dolphins but did not survive the cut. Earlier, after high school, he was offered a football scholarship at the University of Wisconsin, River Falls, but after enduring one week of racist insults—on arrival at the university he was instantly nicknamed "Spic"—he returned to Miami. He got a job at a gas station, and then as a driver for Gulf Oil, delivering parts and accessories. He worked sufficiently hard that, at the age of twenty, he was able to put down a deposit on a gas station of his own in Miami Beach, where he and his wife worked long hours and prospered. Soon there was enough money to rent a waterfront home, and to have a small boat moored behind it.

But Arias wanted to be a cop. He first applied in 1976 but was not even considered because of the hiring freeze. In 1980 when he applied again, in the midst of the hiring panic, he was enthusiastically received by the Miami Police Department, even though his grades in the written tests were no better than "C"; at that stage literacy was not the department's overriding priority.

Arias had been born in Santiago, Cuba, and was raised there until the age of twelve, when he traveled to Miami on one of the so-called freedom flights in 1968. He was, therefore, bilingual and Americanized, but not entirely; he was what Mayor Ferré once described as an "American-Cuban," a hybrid with a foot in both societies, but he really belonged to neither of them.

The worst of the hard-core criminals from the Mariel boatlift had tended to concentrate in the Little Havana section of Miami—known in police jargon as 60 Sector—where they hung around the bars and the streets, particularly at night, hustling, dealing in drugs and using them, and getting into fights. It was no coincidence that the police department put some of its largest, most aggressive American-Cuban recruits like Arias on the midnight shift in 60 Sector to deal with the *Marielitos*. It was not only Castro who regarded them as "scum." So, too, did Arias and his colleagues. And in that, they were encouraged by their superiors.

Arias learned very quickly that everything he had been taught in police academy was, as he put it, "a joke." In Little Havana at night, "you couldn't go by the book. If you did, you might as well consider yourself dead." In his first few months on the streets, he had the support of FTOs, Field Training Officers, with whom he shared a patrol car and, in theory, their experience. But every FTO he rode with had himself been on the force for less than one year; in the frenetically expanding Miami PD, rookies trained rookies, because there was nobody else to do the job. The example set by the inexperienced FTOs was often extremely brutal.

Signed off as being competent to ride solo, Arias would face situations where, alone, at five o'clock in the morning, he would go into a bar to check it, and be faced with up to half a dozen *Marielitos* for whom there were arrest warrants. In those circumstances, Arias said, he would call for backup, hoping for a tough officer who would help him to "beat the shit out of the *Marielitos.*" In Little Havana in the early hours "your only friend was your backup."

Arias and his colleagues would stop *Marielitos* constantly. They would demand to see their victim's driving license, rip it up and drop the pieces in the sewer, ask for the license again, and then arrest them for not having one. Arias claims it was a surefire bet that, once they had created a "legal" excuse to search the car, they would find an illegal weapon or drugs. It was a strategy that was not without risk. Early one morning, Arias stopped a brand-new El Dorado that "you just knew was stolen." The driver said his license was under his seat, and reached down to get it, but he produced instead a sawn-off shotgun. It took all of Arias's wits and cunning to talk him out of using it, and to persuade the other passengers in the car, all *Marielitos,* to surrender their weapons, all of which were stolen. By then, Arias's backup had arrived to help "beat them up real good."

Almost without exception, his fellow officers were American-Cubans and, if they were not aggressive when they joined the Little Havana midnight shift, they soon learned to be. Many of them worked out at gyms and prided themselves on their physical strength and fitness. And Arias and a fellow officer, Osvaldo Coello, played tackle football for the police department. The highlight of the season was the annual Pig Bowl tournament against Metro-Dade. In 1985, when Miami was being thrashed 41 to 0, Arias and Coello—"one of the most aggressive human beings ever found in a bar, mean as could be"—took turns to jump the opposing quarterback in the two final plays and hurt him so badly, they were thrown out of the game.

Arias, Coello, and the rest of the midnight shift saw themselves as having to retake the streets, every night. The truth was, after midnight, Little Havana was a place without any semblance of law and no vestige of civil rights. They learned that, in the absence of any proper supervision, they could do what they liked to get "the scum" off the streets, and nobody would either know or care. On a nightly basis they would "fudge the paperwork" to cover every eventuality. An unauthorized meal break would be described in their reports as "meeting with a contact at Burger King." And the serious abuses they committed against *Marielitos* were always sanitized and toned down on the "A-forms," the arrest documentation. Arias called it "creative writing."

Sometimes things got out of hand and were not so easy to cover up. The worst thing a midnight shift officer could appear to be to his colleagues was a *penco*—someone who "had no balls." So if, as sometimes happened, they tracked down a *Marielito* who had given them a particularly hard time, or who had led them on a chase, he might be shot at even if he was unarmed, or beaten so badly that his skull was split open and his ribs were broken. Arias and his colleagues were called before Internal Security on several occasions to answer brutality complaints, usually filed by *Marielitos'* lawyers, but "we always denied everything. And we always got away with it."

Arias estimated that what he saw and learned on the streets of 60 Sector in one year would have taken most other patrolmen, in other parts of the city, the best part of a career to experience. There cannot have been many officers who handled, as Arias did, up to forty cases a month, and his personnel docket rapidly filled with commendations for "good arrests" and exceptional bravery.

But the atmosphere that the midnight shift worked in was thoroughly poisonous. Arias recalls with some bitterness his feelings at that time: with almost no supervision, he and the others felt alone and beleaguered, risking their lives every night for what they believed was Washington's error of judgment. They were exposed constantly to the worst kind of criminals, who had no moral restraints and who would not hesitate to kill anyone who got in their way: "They dragged us down to their level," Arias said. In this atmosphere of stress, of high danger and of disillusionment and cynicism, it was of no surprise, certainly to Rudy Arias, that before too long, he and his partners "went bad."

In late 1982, Rudy Arias and two other members of the midnight shift raided an illegal gaming house in Miami and seized the loot. They turned most of the money in to the property room but kept $300 for themselves. They told each other they deserved it. In 1983, Arias and Arturo De La Vega, having seized $66,000 from two drug traffickers during a routine traffic stop in Little Havana, kept $4,000. And then, on September 3, 1984, Arias stole $14,000 from Celestino Peñalver and Osvaldo Rivera, who had traveled from Massachussetts to Miami looking for drugs. It was all so easy.

Peñalver and Rivera were eating a meal on the patio of a Little Havana bar when they were approached by Arias, who asked for their identification and demanded to search them. He found a small amount of cocaine in Peñalver's pocket and, using that as the legal excuse, searched their car, where he found $14,000 in a paper bag in the trunk, and a further $3,000 in the glove compartment. When Peñalver and Rivera were arrested and taken to the police station by other officers who had arrived on the scene—and who were not part of the conspiracy—Arias handed in to the property department only $3,000, claiming it was all he had found. Peñalver was angry enough to protest that the rest of his money had been stolen but nobody believed him.

As Arias knew, some other members of the midnight shift were committing similar acts of occasional and opportunistic larceny. And in late 1984 or early 1985, Arias and seven or eight of his fellow officers joined together in a criminal conspiracy that was much better organized.

Raúl Rojas was a stocky, forty-year-old *Marielito* and small-time trafficker whom Arias had constantly harrassed and once arrested for possession of a .45 pistol and a small amount of cocaine. To save himself from further grief and to make money, Rojas agreed to tip off Arias and his colleagues when his drug transactions were about to take place. He would give them information about some of his buyers, their vehicles, and the time of the rendezvous. The officers would intercept the buyers and stop them for some invented traffic violation, or raid the rendezvous, and simply confiscate their drugs or their money.

For example, in early 1985 Rojas told Arias that a large quantity of Quaaludes were stored at a Miami auto-body shop. On the pretext of investigating a hit-and-run accident, Arias, De La Vega, and two other officers raided the shop and searched a green Mercedes-Benz owned by "a fat Colombian," in which they found 97,000 Quaaludes in seven or eight plastic containers that were "two feet tall." As part of the scheme, Raúl Rojas' brother claimed the drugs belonged to him and the Colombian—by now extremely nervous—was allowed to go, grateful, no doubt, for his "lucky escape." The officers "confiscated" the

Quaaludes and pretended to arrest Rojas' brother. They let him go *outside* Dade County Jail.

But disposing of the Quaaludes proved to be difficult, partly because cocaine had become so plentiful and cheap in Miami, and the officers made only $5,500 each. It was petty crime, hardly worth the risks.

What Arias and his colleagues needed was information from a more significant trafficker than Rojas who could tip them off about bigger deals. They found the man they needed in March 1985 when Arias was approached by another crooked cop operating independently in Little Havana. That officer had formed an alliance with a dealer named Luis Rodríguez—and, as Arias well knew, Rodríguez and his "lieutenant" were in a position to facilitate spectacular robberies.

Rudy Arias's favorite movie is *Scarface,* and to him Luis Rodríguez was the epitome of the violent anti-hero of that film, portrayed by Al Pacino, albeit in miniature. Like Scarface, Rodríguez had been imprisoned in Cuba, and not for political crimes. According to one of his fellow prisoners, his jail nickname was *miador*—the one who urinates—because, to gain favor, he leaked everything he knew to the authorities. Once in Miami, he, like Scarface, became an inhabitant of "Tent City," one of the more notorious holding camps for Mariel refugees who were housed under canvas, beneath an overpass of the city's main traffic artery, I-95. His companions in that squalid camp were largely hustlers, pimps, and homosexuals.

Out on the streets, he quickly began to accumulate a string of arrests: for possession of burglary tools, concealed weapons, and small amounts of cocaine—petty stuff for which he usually got probation. But within four years of arriving in America from Mariel, Rodríguez had somehow become the owner of a bar in Little Havana, the *Molino Rojo.* It described itself, in flashing neon lights, as a place of *ambiente familiar,* "family entertainment." Actually it was a dive, a place where drugs were openly sold and used. There were frequent fights at the *Molino Rojo* and, once, a double homicide.

Rodríguez, a slight, dapper man who dressed in white and festooned himself with gold jewelry, employed as his "lieutenant" Armando Un, a fifty-year-old Cuban of Chinese extraction. Un was also a *Marielito* and also a former inmate of the same Castro jail, though his crimes *were* "political." During the final years of the regime of President Batista, Un had lived in exile in Mexico, where he joined Castro's revolution. After it succeeded, he returned to Cuba in 1963 and served in Castro's secret police. But he soon became disillusioned with communism, and after not much more than one year he was arrested and sentenced to death for his part in a plot to overthrow Castro, and though that was commuted—thanks to the influence of an uncle—he was forced to watch his own brother's execution, and to serve sixteen years in jail.

Un arrived in Miami from Mariel a fervent anti-Communist, but a wise one. Though he joined one of the rag-tag groups in Miami dedicated to the violent overthrow of Castro, his experiences had taught him "not to be crazy." He limited his involvement in the campaigns to sitting a safe twenty miles off the Cuban coast, releasing raft-loads of anti-Castro literature into favorable currents, in the hope that they might be washed ashore. Meanwhile, to pay the rent, he became a construction worker and then a uniformed security guard at Luis Rodríguez's *Molino Rojo.* He eventually became the bar's manager, working the 6:00 P.M. to 1:00 A.M. shift. He also assisted Rodríguez in his primary trade, for which the bar provided a convenient cover.

Rodríguez, with Un's assistance, was a distributor of cocaine and marijuana who used the *Molino Rojo* as a convenience store to sell drugs to small-time dealers. He was making, by Un's estimates, up to $200,000 every fifteen days, and Un was responsible for hiding the proceeds. The methods he used were not very sophisticated: he would stuff up to $50,000 in cash into socks, and hang them from wire coat hangers which were then hidden in wall cavities in Rodríguez's small apartment.

As a result of drug sales and drug use, the *Molino Rojo* became increasingly well-known to the officers who patrolled 60 Sector, and Luis Rodríguez and Armando Un had become Arias's favorite targets. Rodríguez did not have a driving license because Arias and his colleagues deliberately picked on him until he had so many infractions, real or imagined, that he lost it. The police also picked on the *Molino Rojo.* Rodríguez would attempt to be placatory, saying: "Come on guys, give me a break." But Armando Un, his manager, took great exception to the harassment and on one occasion, when Arias went to arrest Rodríguez for cocaine possession, Un attempted to block his path. Arias punched Un so hard "he bounced off the table."

Rodríguez had countered this problem in what was for Miami classic fashion—by offering himself to the Miami Police Department as an informant. He approached one patrolman who was markedly different from the rest: Armando Estrada was modestly built, and only 5 feet, 6 inches tall, and he never attempted to be physically threatening; a "quiet little guy" as Arias described him, and one who, dressed in civilian clothes, looked more like a banker than a cop. Using Un as his conduit, Rodríguez approached Estrada and offered him a deal: "Stop harassing my customers, and I'll give you information on drug dealing."

Estrada had accepted the offer, and thus Luis Rodríguez became a confidential informant who informed on others in order to secure a measure of protection for himself. The relationship worked well enough that, in the summer of 1984, Rodríguez allegedly gave Estrada a "gift" of a few hundred dollars. A short while later, he "loaned" him $8,000, to enable Estrada to bring his family out of Cuba. From there, it was only a short step to wholesale corruption.

Just as Raúl Rojas had told Rudy Arias about his drug deals to enable Arias and his group of corrupt officers to rip them off, so Rodríguez collaborated with Estrada and two other midnight shift officers. The conspiracies were more or less identical except that Rodríguez equipped "his" officers with beepers to alert them when transactions were about to take place. Un took the precaution of renting the gadgets through a "beeper broker"; a trade that flourishes in Miami because it offers drug traffickers anonymity.

Between them the two groups of officers carried out some twenty or so rip-offs. None of their victims complained; how could they? Most were simply grateful that, having been relieved of their property, they were allowed to go on their way. It was almost the perfect crime.

But in March 1985, Rodríguez proposed to Estrada a much bolder enterprise: ripping-off boatloads of cocaine that were being imported into Miami on behalf of a Colombian known to Rodríguez only by his nickname, *El Mono,* "The Monkey." Estrada was willing, but not without assistance from some of the tougher members of the midnight shift. He therefore approached Rudy Arias and invited him and his group to join the enterprise. Arias agreed.

For the scheme to be feasible, it was obviously necessary to know when and where the boats would arrive, information that was not normally available to the likes of Luis Rodríguez. But Rodríguez and Un both knew somebody who did know or, at least, who was in a position to find out.

Pedro Ramos was yet another soldier in that vast army of subcontractors to the drugs trade in Miami. His particular expertise was as a marine mechanic, and when called on to do so, he would leave the radiator repair shop which he ran as a cover and fly to the Bahamas to carry out engine repairs. Among the smuggling boats he worked on in the Bahamas were those owned or operated by Pedro Martínez, such as the *Mary C,* and Ramos knew a great deal about Martínez's business. In particular, he knew the secrets of the exquisitely concealed compartments which Martínez installed on his boats, which even the Customs men could not find.

For a while Ramos had also been the owner of a Little Havana bar, the *Quisqueya,* which is how he had first met Rodríguez and Un, and he had listened to Rodríguez brag that he had "cops on the payroll." Now, in the spring of 1985, he listened again when Rodríguez proposed a cynical deal: if Ramos would provide information about incoming loads of cocaine, he would provide the police officers to steal them. Ramos agreed: Why not? In the world he occupied, scruple and allegiance were not common currency.

Ramos, in turn, recruited others to this enterprise, and the corrupt Miami police officers found themselves in allegiance with an unsavory collection of men who committed violent robberies; traffickers; and even contract killers—the very "scum" whom the midnight shift had been harassing for so long (though, for the record, Ramos was not a *Marielito* nor even Cuban, but a native of the Dominican Republic).

The first two joint ventures of this motley crew were not a success. In early April 1985, Arias and Estrada, working together for the first time, staked out a waterfront house where they had been told a boat loaded with marijuana was due to dock. It never arrived, because it was seized by the authorities en route. Next, they were told by Rodríguez of a freighter moored on the Miami River, which, he said, had cocaine hidden on board and only two men to guard it. But the freighter turned out to be deserted, and Rudy Arias—who had become the effective leader of the corrupt officers—said he was "not about to spend a week looking for the dope." The operation was called off.

However, in mid-July 1985, Ramos came up with more solid information about the imminent arrival on the Miami River of one of Pedro Martínez's boats, a converted coast guard cutter called *Mitzi Ann.*

On July 12, at 9 A.M., Rodríguez hosted a planning meeting at his small apartment in Coral Gables. Present were Pedro Ramos and Armando Un, and, for the police, Armando Estrada and his regular partner on the midnight shift, Román Rodríguez (no relation to Luis), who was not thought by his colleagues to have very big balls and who was known derisively as "Estrada's wife"; it was generally held that Román Rodríguez would do whatever Estrada told him. The plan they jointly devised was simple. According to Ramos, the *Mitzi Ann* would berth at the Tamiami Marine, which sits at the end of a small tributary off the Miami River, and her cargo of cocaine was due to be unloaded at nine o'clock that night and transferred to a van. Tamiami Marine is not an isolated spot: indeed, the boatyard is faced by a row of houses, some of which have porches on which the residents are liable to sit. So, it was agreed, the police would wait until the van had left the boatyard, and intercept it at some more remote location. Román Rodríguez was not anxious to take part in the rip-off itself, but since he lived "real close" to the marina, he said he would act as the look-out.

It did not work out quite as envisaged. Nine o'clock came and went without any sign of activity on the *Mitzi Ann,* and at 10 P.M. Ramos—who had the insider's knowledge—telephoned Un to tell him that the plan had changed, and the cocaine was not going to be unloaded from the boat that night.

That might have been the end of it, but an hour later

Ramos called Un again, to say he had talked to Estrada, who told him that the midnight shift had decided to carry out the rip-off "the ballsy way." Ramos called once more, at midnight, to tell Un to be at the 7-Eleven convenience store situated next door to the boatyard, and to bring with him a hammer and a screwdriver.

When Un duly arrived at the rendezvous he found two Miami PD patrol cars and ten officers, all in uniform, who had already clambered over the boatyard's chain-link fence. Un joined them and gave Ramos the tools he had brought, and Ramos began searching the deck towards the stern of the *Mitzi Ann,* chipping away at the fiberglass until he found the panel that led to her secret compartment. The panel was secured by eighteen screws. When they were removed, and the panel was lifted to reveal the cocaine, according to Un, the police "all started screaming." Un lowered himself into the compartment, with the intention of beginning the unloading, but he was neither big enough nor strong enough to be able to satisfy Rudy Arias, who said he was going to throw Un in the water. Osvaldo Coello—Arias's brutal accomplice on the football field—came to Un's rescue: "One of the big guys that weighs about a thousand pounds helped to pull me out. He pulled me out like a balloon. He lifted me up like nothing . . . , Coello then started pulling out these bags, as if they were stuffed dogs. They were black nylon bags. Bags this big [he said, fully stretching his arms]. They were heavy."

The officers formed a human chain to transfer what was 400 kilograms of cocaine across the boatyard, over the fence and into their patrol cars. But their cars could not contain it all, and so they also loaded Un's car until it was filled to the roof.

The operation took no more than thirty minutes, and it was only when it was complete that they discovered the *Mitzi Ann* had guards aboard, in the cabin, who were hiding. The police discussed killing them but, in the end, merely beat them up with a piece of wood they found nearby, and threw them into the river. Fortunately for the guards, they could swim.

There was momentary panic when Arturo De La Vega realized he had left his police flashlight—engraved with his name and police identification number—on board the boat, and he,

Arias, and Coello went back to find it. Then, all that remained was getting the cocaine to a safe place.

But as the convoy of police and civilian cars, loaded with cocaine, headed for an empty house on NE 30th Avenue, Un and Estrada—who was following behind Un—got lost. As they drove around in circles, Un became increasingly fractious: barely able to see out of his overloaded car, he finally stopped and told Estrada that he was going to dump the cocaine in the middle of the street, and go home.

Instead, the two men went to a modest house on SW 5th Street in Little Havana, owned by an elderly woman whose children were habitués of the *Molino Rojo*. In return for the promise of one kilo of cocaine, she agreed to store the booty, and it was unceremoniously dumped in her front yard. Having counted the bags, Estrada departed, leaving Un to transfer it to the woman's bathroom.

Un was paid $100,000 in cash for his efforts that night by Luis Rodríguez, and Pedro Ramos should have received more than $350,000 for supplying the all-important information, though he claims he did not receive all of it. Everybody else was paid in cocaine.

The timid Román Rodríguez received one kilo for his efforts as the look-out. Four officers who took part in the raid but who were considered junior partners, each received between four and ten kilos. The six senior partners—Rudy Arias, the hulking Osvaldo Coello, Armando Estrada, and three others—each received an average of thirty kilos of cocaine. Luis Rodríguez got 126 kilos.

Arias kept careful records, and when he had sold his share of the cocaine, and added the proceeds to his previous earnings from rip-offs, he calculated that he was a millionaire; to be precise, that he had made $1,080,000. And that, he thought, was enough. Through crime he had been able to buy a new lakeside house in a western suburb of Miami for $172,-000, complete with a swimming pool and a Jacuzzi. Unbeknownst to his wife, he also gave his mistress the down payment on a condominium and helped furnish it. He gave friends and colleagues over $60,000 in cash and gifts. And all of that in a year when his official take-home pay as a police officer was $22,754.45.

Many of the others had done equally well. Osvaldo Coello had bought a $55,000 candy-apple red Lotus for himself, expensive cars for two girl friends, and the services of high-class prostitutes who charged $2,000 a night.

Armando Estrada had bought a new house for $83,000, and spent over $4,000 on interior decorations. He bought his small son a toy motorcycle that cost $682, and, for himself, a $15,000 Pontiac Trans Am.

Even Román Rodríguez, Estrada's timid partner, was in a position to sign a contract for a $100,000 house, and he was negotiating to buy the home next door for members of his family. When his house was ready, he would spend $6,000 for a television satellite dish, $4,500 for an interior decorator, $3,000 on mirrors for the house, $5,500 for furniture bought at a baby store and $7,000 for a dining room table.

So when, just two weeks after the raid on the *Mitzi Ann,* Luis Rodríguez proposed another rip-off, this time of Pedro Martínez's boat, *Mary C,* at Jones Boat Yard, Arias said no, and he attempted to persuade his colleagues to say likewise. He knew that, sooner or later, something would go wrong, and he believed that they had pushed their luck as far as it might reasonably stretch.

When most of them insisted on going through with the raid on the *Mary C,* Arias left town. To give himself a cast-iron alibi for the weekend the rip-off was due to take place, he invited his wife's sister, her husband, and their children, and his wife's brother and his girlfriend to accompany his family on a trip to Disney World, some two hundred safe miles away from Miami, in Orlando, Florida. His choice of companions for that weekend was calculated: if things did go wrong, Arias knew that his unwitting brother-in-law would make a solid alibi witness; he happened to be a US Marshal.

The three drownings in the Miami River that resulted from the raid on the *Mary C* left a lot of very nervous policemen in Miami—though, after it, four of them could count themselves multimillionaires, in that their share of the total take rose to $2 million each. Collectively, officers of the Miami police department made $18 million from the rip-offs they carried out for Luis Rodríguez.

For his part, Rodríguez had made at least $10 million from the rip-offs, according to Armando Un. But in the aftermath of the *Mary C* debacle he, too, was extremely nervous—and with good reason.

Rodríguez had a considerable appetite for women and, in his attempts to impress them, a tendency to boast: he had told girl friends—some of whom were as young as fourteen—of his plans to enrich himself through rip-offs, and one of them had tape-recorded his claims and subsequently played the tape to a criminal associate of Rodríguez, one who was not a beneficiary of those schemes and who resented the fact. Meanwhile, Rodríguez had become a positive liability to members of the midnight shift, because of his bragging—and not just to Pedro Ramos—that he had "cops on the payroll." Perhaps most worrying of all, *El Mono,* the Colombian whose cocaine Rodríguez had arranged to have stolen, not once but twice, was rumored to have become highly suspicious of Luis Rodríguez.

Rodríguez had become a chronic cocaine user and, under its influence, paranoid. Even before the raid on the *Mary C,* he refused to spend the night in his own apartment, where he was having trouble sleeping, and took to checking into expensive hotels, for one night at a time, always on the move.

He spent the last day of his life, July 29—the day after the raid on the *Mary C*—trying to find a hiding place for $200,000 in cash. At about 9 P.M. that night, Armando Un was supposed to meet Rodríguez at a Miami nightclub called the Dynasty Lounge, but by the time Un arrived his employer had left; "nervous," "visibly worried," according to witnesses, and anxious to obtain a car that could not be traced to him. The last person known to have seen Luis Rodríguez alive was Officer Armando Estrada, the least intimidating of the midnight shift, who met him at 11 P.M. on July 29 in the deserted car park of a Little Havana shopping center. Estrada admits to the meeting. He says that they talked and that Rodríguez then went on his way.

The next afternoon at 5:30 P.M., a brown pick-up truck reversed onto waste ground near to Our Lady of Mercy cemetery, at NW 109th Avenue, near the Dolphin Expressway, and deposited a pine-wood crate, three feet high and three feet wide. When the crate was opened by police it was found to contain Rodríguez's body, neatly folded inside, packed in lime. He had been executed: shot several times in the head and neck from close range.

Armando Un seems to have been the only genuine mourner. "He was a good friend of mine," he said, "with all his faults." *The Miami Herald* published a fitting obituary: "Luis Rodríguez was a small man with big ideas who got shot one day and wound up in a box."

16

"Clintino"

By the summer of 1985, Centac, a shadow of its former self, consisted of: a lieutenant who kept largely to his desk; Sergeant Al Singleton, "The Blade," who supervised the squad; two analysts; and just three detectives—Joe Díaz and George Plasencia, who were founding members, and Alex Alvarez, a new recruit. Alvarez was the youngest of the team, and the least experienced homicide investigator; after an insensitive visiting reporter from Washington had likened him in appearance to Clint Eastwood, the actor, he was immediately dubbed "Clintino"—baby Clint—by the others, and obliged to endure a good deal of ribbing. Still, Centac is a revolving democracy in that the detectives take turns as lead investigator, and on July 29, 1985, when Kojak persuaded Faustino Martínez to tell the police what had happened on the Miami River, it was Alvarez's turn to take the lead. He interviewed Faustino at Kojak's house and then, at the age of twenty-six and after only six months with Centac, found himself calling the shots on what would become Centac's most important case by far.

There was precious little to go on: Faustino's account of what had happened at Jones Boat Yard was dramatic but entirely second-hand—depending on what Pedro Báez had told him—and neither he nor Alvarez had any possible way of knowing if the men who had staged the raid on the *Mary C* were real policemen; Alvarez thought, in all probability, that they were not.

247

Faustino gave Centac the names of all three survivors of the raid, and they were picked up one by one (Pedro Báez when he turned up at the funeral home to pay his last respects to Faustino's father). But none of them would admit to any involvement or any knowledge of the events on the Miami River. Nor was there any physical evidence. Alvarez asked Customs officials to search the *Mary C,* and "take it apart" if necessary, but they were unable to find the hidden compartment or any traces of cocaine. And too much time had passed since the raid for there to be any hope that the boat, and the miscellaneous items found on board—an empty wine bottle, a packet of Marlboro cigarettes, a paper bag, and a fire extinguisher—would yield any identifiable fingerprints.

All Centac had to support Faustino's story was the account of the night watchman, who insisted that he would not be able to recognize any of the men in uniform, and three bodies, none of which bore any marks of violence. Alvarez decided it was not even worth impounding the boat. He later changed his mind, but by then the *Mary C* had been taken from her berth and had vanished.

In the absence of evidence or leads, Centac resorted to its tried and tested formula for invigorating a stalled investigation: it hit the streets. Dealers and informants and the riff-raff who inhabit the fringes of their world were visited in their homes and hang-outs and pushed for any sliver of knowledge, or gossip, or rumor that they might have about the Miami River deaths. Centac's detectives also approached their contacts in every other law enforcement agency in Miami, calling in past favors and asking them to push their informants for the slightest clue.

As a result, in less than a week Centac had two promising leads: first, that the little-lamented Luis Rodríguez had had some connection with the raid on the *Mary C,* and his murder may have resulted from it; second, that Luis Rodríguez had been an informant for one of the officers on Miami PD's Little Havana midnight shift. On August 6, 1985, Centac therefore asked Miami PD to arrange for an informal interview with Officer Armando Estrada, and at 11 P.M. that night, when Estrada checked in for his shift, Sergeant Singleton and Alvarez—"The Blade" and "Clintino"—were waiting for him.

Singleton and Alvarez both find it difficult to describe what it was about Estrada's demeanor at that interview that made them so suspicious. On the face of it he was friendly, apparently cooperative, and informative, offering detailed explanations for the deaths of Luis Rodríguez and the three men in the river. His tale of internecine rip-offs and murderous retaliation were credible enough given the background of the Cocaine Wars, and he even volunteered to produce the "street source" from whom, he said, his information had come. But his story did not quite gel with the word on the streets and, for Alvarez, there was something about the look in Estrada's eyes that deeply disturbed him. At one point in the interview, Alvarez and Singleton excused themselves from the Homicide office where it was being held, and went out into the corridor.

"He's lying," said Alvarez.

"I know," said Singleton. "He's our man. But how do we prove it?"

Neither of them could think of an immediate answer, so they settled for telling Estrada that they wanted to meet his "source" as soon as possible. Four days later, Alvarez was summoned to the parking lot of a deserted shopping center in Little Havana, where Estrada and the source were waiting to give what Alvarez found to be a wholly unimpressive performance: the source, a *Marielito,* was curiously unsure of the details of his account, and Estrada found it necessary to prompt him continually. For no good reason that Alvarez could see, Estrada's partner, the timid Román Rodríguez, hovered in the background like some nervous midwife concerned about a difficult birth.

When Alvarez drove home, a little before dawn, he was absolutely convinced that the source had been "coached," and that Estrada and Rodriguez were therefore somehow involved in the raid on the *Mary C.* And if two officers of the Miami Police Department were involved in that raid, then so, in all probability, were ten more. It was, he says, a chilling realization.

Later the same day, Centac discreetly approached the Internal Review section of Miami PD, and asked for the personnel files, the worksheets, the logs, the arrest reports, and the "dispatch tapes"—tape recordings of every radio conversation between patrolmen and dispatchers, which totaled four thousand hours—of the entire midnight shift. While Centac's detectives returned to the streets and resumed their search for inside information, Centac's analysts began to probe several years' worth of the midnight shift's "creative writing."

As a recent recruit to the War on Drugs, the FBI is not highly regarded by other law enforcement agencies in Miami. Like some regiment newly arrived at the front, it keeps to itself— aloof, uncertain, and distrustful—and there is a standing joke that what its acronym really stands for is Fumbling Bumbling Idiots. Nevertheless, it was to an FBI special agent that Centac owed its second major breakthrough: Roberto Díaz, who worked for the foreign counterintelligence section of the agency in Miami, told Alvarez that he had an informant who might know something about the murder of Luis Rodríguez. Díaz said that two days before the Jones Boat Yard incident, he had driven past his informant's house and seen a Mercedes-Benz parked in the driveway. As a matter of routine, he had run a check on the license number: the owner was Luis Rodríguez.

So it was that Alvarez asked detectives George Plasencia and Joe Díaz to pay an informal call on fifty-year-old Armando Un. The two detectives and Un stood as classic examples of the two extremes of the Cuban diaspora. Plasencia and Díaz left Cuba as children, and were raised in Miami by parents with the foresight to ensure they became thoroughly bilingual and thoroughly assimilated; they are Americans, of Cuban descent. Un, in contrast, a product of Castro's jails and a *Marielito,* had not assimilated at all. Un spoke barely a word of English; he is a Cuban, living in a foreign land.

When Díaz and Plasencia arrived at Un's apartment, the sight that greeted them on the coffee table in the living room was that of a loaded M-16 rifle. It was there for a purpose, a test designed by Un to establish if these two young detectives had guts.

"Nice gun," said Plasencia. "Is it yours?"

"Yes, it's mine," said Un. "Aren't you going to try to take it away?"

"No," said Díaz. "If you reach for it, I think we can get there first. It doesn't bother us."

Un laughed. Later he told Centac that the reaction of FBI agents to a similar test had been close to panic; Díaz and Plasencia, on the other hand, had established their credentials as "men" and not "chickenshit." Such theatrics began the elaborate courtship of perhaps the most crucial witness in the Miami River case.

Un did not reveal at that first meeting what he knew about Luis Rodríguez or the Miami River murders; indeed he did not admit that he knew anything at all. But he did not resist the detectives' proposition to "talk again," and, for the next six weeks, Díaz, Plasencia, and Alvarez made a habit of "dropping by" on Un once or twice a week. As the painstaking analysis of the records of the midnight shift produced more and more names, and more and more clues, they would drop them into the conversation, guesswork disguised as certain knowledge, while constantly offering the bait of immunity for Un in return for his cooperation. On a Sunday in October, Alvarez telephoned Al Singleton in a state of great excitement: "Un's going to flip," said Alvarez.

He was, but not quite yet. Little by little, Un allowed that he did know about Luis Rodríguez, and about the Miami River case, and about massive police corruption, but he hesitated to take the final step that would turn him into a government witness. Then, in the last week of October 1985, the gentle persuasion and the weeks of patience finally paid off: Un volunteered to go to Centac's office and, in a debriefing that lasted for sixteen hours, he described in immaculate detail the inner workings of the Luis Rodríguez organization, and its terrible affinity with the midnight shift.

"We were very, very excited," said Singleton, "but we were also very realistic." Un had described a whole series of corrupt acts, he had given names, places, and approximate dates, and he had managed to identify six culpable members of the midnight shift from a selection of photographs he was shown. But Un's unsupported word fell far short of proof, or at least it would in a courtroom, and for Centac the name of the game became "corroboration."

There was nobody in a better position to supply supporting evidence than Pedro Ramos, the marine mechanic from the

Dominican Republic who had supplied Luis Rodríguez with the vital information about the when and wherefores of incoming boatloads of cocaine. Centac had known about Ramos almost from the start, because his name had shown up on US Customs reports that linked him to earlier, highly suspicious voyages of the *Mitzi Ann* and the *Mary C.* But Centac had had nothing on Ramos, no lever it could apply—until Armando Un talked.

Finding Ramos was easy because he was on probation on drug charges, and he was required to report every week to his parole officer. In early November 1985, after keeping one such routine appointment, Ramos was intercepted in the street by Singleton and Alvarez, and "invited" to go to Centac's office. Once there, Ramos listened for less than an hour to the detectives' recital of what Centac knew, and guessed, before he said: "I'll cooperate." And Ramos, like Un, looked at Centac's collection of photographs, and had no difficulty at all in picking out the same ensemble of corrupt cops: Armando Estrada, or *Chino,* "the Chinaman," as they called him, because he looked vaguely Oriental; Román Rodríguez, his partner; Rodolfo Arias, known to them as Rudy; Osvaldo Coello, as massive as Rudy, and, in their view, at least as mean; Armando García, known as "Scarface" because of a childhood injury, whose father was also a fully paid up member of the conspiracy; and, Arturo De La Vega, the best-educated and least likely bad apple of them all.

It still was not enough. While nobody challenged the correctness of Centac's case—and, by now, the alarm bells had been rung at city hall, within the upper echelons of the Miami PD, and, of course, at the state attorney's office—there was universal uneasiness at the likely outcome of asking a jury to decide between the word of serving police officers and two self-confessed drug traffickers who would testify only if they received immunity. There was particular concern that one of the alleged ringleaders of the conspiracy, Rudy Arias, had a personnel docket crammed with commendations. He had been celebrated for his bravery in tackling a would-be bank robber who had pulled a submachine gun; Arias had sent him sprawling with a haymaker punch. In July 1985 he had been selected as

"Officer of the Month" for Miami *and* Dade County. He was currently front-runner for "Police Officer of the Year."

What Centac needed was truly incriminating evidence against Arias and the rest; preferably *self*-incriminating evidence.

Un and Ramos both agreed to assist in collecting such evidence, and Un in particular showed all the zealousness of a convert, determined to prove he was telling the truth. Given what they knew about the character of the Miami River cops, this was an act that required some courage.

The corrupt members of the Little Havana midnight shift knew that some or all of them were under suspicion. What they did not know—and this was Centac's edge—was that Un and Ramos had been "flipped" by Centac. Thus, Un and Ramos were in a unique position to gather incriminating, tape-recorded evidence—if they could do so without being detected. If they were detected, then, in Centac's view, there was a very good chance that Un and Ramos would not live long enough to testify against anybody.

The art of secretly tape recording a conversation to the standards demanded by a court of law is much more complicated than Hollywood, and television programs such as *Miami Vice,* would suggest. Radio microphones, which transmit a conversation to a recorder some distance away, are relatively easy to disguise and simple to hide. But transmission is unreliable, because of the risks of electronic interference, and the quality of the recording can be too questionable for the courts to accept. A microphone *and* a recorder, connected by wire, make for a more dependable device but one that is obviously more difficult to conceal on the body and easier to detect—particularly for police officers who know all about "wires" and where best to hide them.

So, it was with some trepidation that in the early hours of November 28, Alvarez allowed Pedro Ramos to go to a meeting with Estrada wearing a "wire." The recorder was strapped to Ramos's ankle—rather than the small of his back—and the wire leading to the microphone was taped to the *back* of his leg, in the hope that if Estrada frisked him it would be in routine police fashion, down the *sides* of his legs. Even so, Alvarez insisted that Ramos also wear a concealed radio microphone, so Centac could monitor the conversation—and be ready to move in the moment that anything went wrong.

The meeting took place in the parking lot of a shopping center across from the *Quisqueya* bar that Ramos used to own. Centac rented an empty second-floor office overlooking the parking lot, and set up videotape equipment to obtain visual evidence of the meeting—in vain as things turned out, because the camera's view was blocked by a tree, and all it was able to record was the rear end of Estrada's patrol car. But the microphones picked up every word.

Ramos had been primed to say that he had been called in for an interview by Centac and that he was worried:

Ramos: Haven't some of the other partners talked?

Estrada: No one, no one, no one, no one, no one, no one, no one. . . .

And later in the conversation:

Estrada: You go with your lawyer. I'm telling you that this has happened to several people, people who know us, and it is to ask the same shit because they [Centac] don't have a fucking thing, and they are trying to probe. You know, do me a little favor: You don't know a fucking thing. 'Do you know him? Do you know him?' 'No, only from seeing him on the street.'

Ramos: No, no, no buddy. Take it easy.

Estrada: 'Did they work for him?' 'No, no. I don't know any policeman who worked for anyone.' Luis can't talk because Luis is dead. The only ones who can talk are the ones who are alive, okay?

The results were sufficiently encouraging that, a week later, Alvarez sent Un to talk to Estrada. He, too, was doubly wired for sound, and although this time there was no convenient place for Centac to hide a video camera, the detectives were able to "eyeball" the meeting from a car made to look as though it had broken down on the I-95 expressway. Another car waited around the corner in case of trouble.

"Clintino"

There was an unexpected bonus in that when Un turned up at the rendezvous in Little Havana, he found Armando García ("Scarface") sitting in a patrol car, and while the two men waited for Estrada to arrive, García gratuitously incriminated himself: "They [Centac] don't have a fucking thing, buddy. . . . There is nothing. They're going to have to suck our dicks." (Later, when the tapes were presented to a jury, defense attorneys attempted to have such obscenities erased from the transcripts because they did not sit well with the image of clean-cut police officers, which is what the attorneys wanted the jury to see. The trial judge refused, noting dryly that if the profanities were removed, there would not be much left for the jury to listen to.)

When Estrada arrived at the rendezvous—and García departed—Un's hidden microphones picked up some startling admissions. Estrada boasted of lying to "fucking Alex" Alvarez. Estrada reassured Un that: "No one knows. The important thing is the river, forget about the rest. . . ." With some ingenuity, Un set Estrada up for what became one of the most damning pieces of evidence against him—an admission that the midnight shift would have killed Luis Rodríguez, if somebody else had not beaten them to it:

> *Un:* . . . He had to be killed, that's what you told me. If they hadn't happened to kill him . . .
> *Estrada:* We would have killed him.

Estrada's main concern was that Un, and Ramos, should leave town: "for the two of you to get fucking lost," as he put it. Un assured him they intended to do that, and Estrada said: "You know that we will always be grateful to you for the rest of our lives, to you and Pedro." Finally one last warning: "Listen buddy, just like a tomb."

The microphones picked up the sounds of Estrada's departure; then, a very happy Armando Un, singing.

The next candidate for self-incrimination was Estrada's partner, Román Rodríguez, whom Un pretended to bump into by chance in Coconut Grove. Rodríguez duly made damaging admissions, but as Un pushed him for more, he became suspicious. To the alarm of Centac's detectives, monitoring the con-

255

versation from a nearby "bug van," Rodríguez wanted to know why Un was wearing "that fucking shirt: are you cold?" and he started to undo the buttons. Un simply slapped his hand away before Rodríguez could discover the microphones that were taped to his chest, but it was a nasty moment. Afterwards, Centac decided that was enough: "We're not going to risk it any more," said Singleton.

By then he believed that his team had accumulated more than sufficient evidence to justify arrest warrants for the six officers Un and Ramos had identified. Thanks to leads they had provided, Centac had found—in Miami, New York, and Boston—thirteen victims of drug rip-offs and persuaded them to cooperate. (Some were more than enthusiastic: when a New York black, who rejoiced in the name of Winston Churchill Riley, was asked to look at photographs of suspects, he demanded: "Show me people, man, people." He was told he would have to be patient.) While Alvarez and Plasencia had concentrated on witnesses, the remaining Centac detective, Joe Díaz, had been following a paper trail that led him to truly damning financial evidence, evidence that the officers had been on epic spending sprees way beyond their legitimate means. Finally, Centac knew that at least Estrada, and probably the others, had acquired safety deposit boxes in which to keep some of the booty. Estrada had urged Un to do the same, promising him: "Not even the federal government can get in there." (He was wrong. In late February 1986 Alvarez, Plasencia, and Díaz went to a branch of the Florida National Bank with a court order to open Estrada's two boxes. They contained a total of $264,600 in cash, on which a police sniffer dog named Moose found ample traces of cocaine.) Therefore, in mid-December, Singleton went to press his case with the chief assistant state attorney.

In six years, Trudy Novicki had somehow managed to give birth to four children while, at the same time, becoming head of the state attorney's Organized Crime Division. Her office walls were littered with drawings by her children of the "Love to Mommy" variety, and it more resembled a day-care center. But that benign impression was illusionary: Novicki was an exceptionally tough and determined prosecutor who had been assigned to the Miami River case because of its importance and its sensitivity. She was as anxious as Singleton to see corrupt cops put behind bars.

But there was a serious political obstacle: the need to save face at the Miami Police Department. Under normal circumstances, the accepted convention is that police forces wash their own dirty linen. And in normal circumstances, the investigation into the Little Havana midnight shift would have been conducted by Miami's Internal Affairs department, or the new PRIDE (Professional Review and Investigation Detail) unit, which had been set up in October 1985 to investigate the theft of $150,000 from the vice squad's safe and other corruption. But although most of the midnight shift's crimes had been committed on Miami's turf, the boundaries of the city are quirky, and Jones Boat Yard happened to be a few hundred yards beyond Miami's limits, in unincorporated Dade County; hence the involvement of Centac.

Miami PD had cooperated with Centac's investigation, but nevertheless the scandal that was about to break was certain to be a bitter pill for the city to swallow. So it was deemed "essential" that Miami PD be seen to be cleaning its own house: the PRIDE unit had its own arrests to make and should be allowed to go first; Centac would have to wait.

By the time PRIDE made its move it was Christmas Eve. Al Singleton, who is tough but also sentimental, agreed with his men to delay the arrests of the midnight shift officers: "Let them have Christmas at home," he said. So it was not until after the Christmas holidays that Alex Alvarez, as lead investigator, took his choice as to which of the suspects he would arrest. At 6:16 A.M. on December 27, on what was for Miami a bitterly cold morning, he knocked on the door of Officer Armando Estrada: "I was expecting you," said Estrada.

In due course, the first six "Miami River Cops," as they were inevitably dubbed, were joined in jail by a seventh: Ricardo Alemán, whose eye-opening girl friend revealed his enthusiastic use of "Master Badge," and of his boast that he had been paid $100,000 to "babysit" the cocaine stolen at Jones Boat Yard. But, by the accounts of Un and Ramos, that still left rotten apples in the barrel, more crooked cops still in uniform. "Worrying, isn't it," said Singleton.

Nor did it take long for those on both sides of the bars to work out who it was who had betrayed them, in spite of Centac's efforts to hide Un and Ramos's identities by strenuously referring to them in all court pleadings only as "Witness No. 1" and "Witness No. 2." The first hint of danger came in late January 1986, when a uniformed Miami police officer, posing as a homicide investigator, attempted to persuade the Department of Motor Vehicles to give him a photograph of Armando Un. Then Un reported that he had been telephoned at home by an anonymous caller speaking Spanish, who told him he would be paid $2 million if he stopped cooperating with the authorities; $1 million up front, the balance when he had demonstrated his "sincerity." A few days later, Un became convinced he was being followed by a Miami PD van. The day after that, he found a note on the windshield of his car, with a telephone number and an invitation to call it, to discuss "a friend in common." Meanwhile, Centac was told by an informant that there was a contract on Un's life.

Centac decided to take Un into protective custody, and he was ensconced in a house in South Miami where he was guarded twenty-four hours a day by armed Metro-Dade police. That turned out to be a sensible precaution for in March 1986, three months after their arrests, the original six "Miami River Cops" plotted in jail to have Un killed.

They had obtained the "statement of facts" accompanying the indictment against them, which described their criminal "enterprise" and revealed the secret tape-recordings that Un and Ramos had made. The statement did not reveal who had made those recordings but their suspicions immediately focused on Un. They made a pact to stick together and, in Arias's words "be tough." They resolved to hire a hit man to kill Un, and then standing in a circle, holding hands, they shouted a defiant chant: "Enterprise! Enterprise! Enterprise!"

The killer they hired was named José Martínez. He was recommended by Carlos Pedrera, a former Miami police officer. Osvaldo Coello told his fellow defendants Martínez was "a punk" but Pedrera denied it: "Look, he's the real thing," he said, "he just killed a family member of mine." Martínez was hired for $100,000; the down payment of $50,000 was provided by the father of Officer "Scarface" García.

By then Arias and Coello had been released on bond and together with García's father and Carlos Pedrera they met Martínez to hand over a photograph of Un and his address. Martínez assured them he knew "how to do it." And, some time later, Arias received a coded phone message—"you sonofabitch"—from Pedrera, claiming the "hit" had been made. Arias says he thought to himself: "Wait 'til Alex Alvarez finds out, that skinny piece of shit of a detective, that his star witness is dead."

But Martínez had merely arranged to have revolver shots fired at Un's house, and then disappeared with his $50,000 fee to California. The truth began to sink in when Coello and Arias casually asked a patrolman who worked that sector, "Have there been any murders lately?" "No," he said, "it's been very quiet."

It was to be well over a year before Centac even knew of the half-hearted effort to kill Un and, by then, there had been other, more serious attempts to kill witnesses.

Meanwhile there was serious concern for the safety of the members of Centac and, in particular, for "Clintino," Alex Alvarez, who appeared to have earned the deep and personal animosity of the arrested officers and their families. According to Un, Estrada had long-since threatened to have the detectives "eliminated" if they got too close to the truth. And when Alvarez went to arrest Rudy Arias at his home, Arias's wife shouted after him: "You laugh now, Alex, but I'll live to spit on your grave, and I hope you die. I'm crying now, but your wife will cry more than me." As a first precaution, all the members of Centac pulled their personal files from department records, and removed their home addresses and details of family relationships. They also set up a system where a computer "tagged" any calls made to Metro-Dade about the Miami River case, and recorded information about who had made the inquiry. And Metro-Dade's repository was instructed to refuse to issue any files about the Miami River case without Centac's knowledge and approval.

Alvarez took to changing his route to work and alerted his children's schools to report any suspicious behavior. All of the family's documentation was switched to his wife's maiden name, including their subscription to *The Miami Herald,* in case anybody—including reporters—attempted to obtain his address from the paper's subscription department.

Alvarez covered his tracks well. Later, when the families of the Miami River Cops set out to trace the home addresses of jurors, prosecutors, and members of Centac by arranging for their license plate numbers to be run through the police computer, the only address they failed to get was that of Alex Alvarez.

17

Wages of Sin

As Centac's investigation into the Miami River case had become more and more of an open secret, a letter circulated within the Miami Police Department offering membership in a club: COP, or Cuban Officers in Prison. One of the supposed benefits of membership was the unlisted telephone number of Miami attorney Roy Black. It was meant as a joke but, during the winter of 1985, Black received calls from a number of Miami police officers who felt reason to be concerned. He kept a log of the time and date of each call. And when Centac finally made its arrests, Black agreed to represent the first of those indicted officers on the list to have called him: Román Rodríguez.

Black had a formidable reputation in Miami as a kind of legal Houdini, and news of his involvement in the case was met with despondency by a columnist for *The Miami Herald:* "Convicting a policeman of any crime is difficult, and there are precious few prosecutors who can't be eaten alive by defense attorneys of Roy Black's caliber. Don't be surprised if some of the cops are acquitted." At Centac, and at the state attorney's office, the reaction was more ambivalent. While Black's intervention guaranteed that the prosecution of Rodríguez and his colleagues would be neither easy nor swift, it also served to confirm Rodríguez's guilt: Roy Black's services in drug cases do not come cheap; where, if he was innocent, could a young police officer like Rodríguez have possibly obtained the means to pay lawyer's fees that might easily amount to $250,000?

But there was anger, too. Alex Alvarez, who intended to become a lawyer himself one day, was outraged that "prominent members of this community" could and would accept the proceeds of drug trafficking to defend "dirty cops." "I could never do what Roy Black does," said Alvarez. "I don't know how he sleeps."

It was the lure of water that first drew Roy Black to Miami, not fat fees paid in advance. Offered the chance to study at Columbia University Law School and an athletic scholarship to the University of Miami, he chose the latter because he was a keen swimmer with an intensely competitive bent. Study of the law took second place until Black met his mentor, Professor Phillip Hubbart, when Hubbart became his evidence professor at the university's law school. Black passed the Florida Bar exam with the highest marks of his year. In January 1971, when Hubbart was elected Dade County's public defender, Black accepted his offer of a job at $8,500 a year, and the opportunity to participate in a small revolution.

Miami's explosive population growth had been accompanied by a rise in crime that was modest compared to what was to come, but which, even so, had overwhelmed the judicial system. Before Hubbart's arrival, the public defender's office—staffed by older attorneys who only went to the office twice a week—coped with the backlog by plea bargaining most of its cases. As Hubbart remembers, with some scorn: "None of them lasted more than five or ten minutes. They were tried like traffic cases."

Hubbart became a "talent scout" who persuaded "kids out of school" to work with him, for meager salaries, and on a full-time basis. The experience, which Black compares to that of interning at a large public hospital, was considered so valuable that even law graduates who had never considered criminal defense work saw the opportunity and grabbed it.

Hubbart shared Black's competitive instincts, which was one of the things that attracted the two men to each other. Hubbart believed in winning, any way he could within the law, and swapping leniency for guilty pleas was not his idea of victory. He changed the policy of the public defender's office from one

of compromise to one of aggressive advocacy, a creed he in-
stilled in Black and his other young assistants. And having
urged them to conduct each trial as if their lives depended on
it, and as if they were being properly paid, he gave them their
heads.

Black teamed up with another of Hubbart's former pupils,
Jack Denaro, and together they set out to learn everything they
could about the creative practice of criminal law. They sat in
on trials to study other attorneys' techniques, and after their
own trials they asked judges to critique their performance:
"What were our mistakes, judge? What did we do right?" They
studied blood serology, and forensic medicine, and the finer
points of fingerprinting, and, Black in particular became a dis-
ciple of Melvin Belli, whom he regarded as the master of
demonstrative evidence. They studied notable British trials of
the nineteenth century and every modern-day precedent set by
the higher courts of the United States. They pioneered the use
of videotapes, at least in Miami, and persuaded the courts to
admit them as evidence. After not much more than a year,
Black was named in a poll as one of the top ten criminal defense attorneys in Miami. And by then, the public defender's
office in Dade County was winning far more cases than it was
losing.

People who worked for and with them say the partnership
was magical. As Harold Smith, their intern, describes it: "It was
as if Mozart had met Brahms: each recognized the genius in
each other." Black was the scholar, exquisitely prepared on the
legal minutiae; Denaro, who had turned to law after initially
studying for the priesthood, was the passionate advocate whose
courtroom rhetoric could move mountains and juries. Either
one of them could win cases that most defense attorneys would
plead. Together, they were practically indomitable.

Denaro remembers an atmosphere, encouraged by Hubbart,
of "total immersion" in every case they accepted. He and Black
would take an exhaustive number of depositions and interview
witnesses, often in dangerous areas of the city. Denaro says
that, in many ways, it was the detective work that he found
most appealing.

Black's particular skills and enthusiasm lay in the area of

psychology. He read voraciously and would confound the prosecution's expert witnesses with his knowledge of their standard
textbooks—an invaluable talent when, as often happened, he
and Denaro were faced with overwhelming evidence of a client's guilt, and the only possible defense was that of insanity.

They never shied away from unpopular causes. One of
Black's clients, for whom he pled insanity, had beaten a young
English tourist so badly that, in the police report, the eighteen-
year-old, fair-skinned girl was described as a "50-year-old
black hooker." And as implacable opponents of the death penalty, Black and Denaro saved from the electric chair a Jamaican man who had ritually sacrificed an eleven-year-old boy
over a toilet bowl, as though it were an altar—an act he claimed
had been ordered by God. To prove he was genuinely insane,
Black and Denaro obtained a court order to have their client
taken off the antipsychotic drugs the prison authorities were
using to subdue him, and then, on Christmas morning, took a
video camera into his cell to capture his pseudoreligious rav-
ings; he was declared incompetent to stand trial.

As Black recalls, the practice of criminal law had been "kind
of staid" in Miami until he and Denaro realized that they were
limited only by their imaginations. Once, when prosecutors
sprung a demand for one of their client's fingerprints to be
taken in court, the two public defenders calmly removed his
socks, put them on his hands, and claimed it would require a
search warrant before his prints could be taken. The judge,
unsure of precedent, dismissed the case. And when the fate of
another of their clients hinged on whether a federal agent
could identify him in court, Denaro successfully muddied the
waters by sending *the client* to serve the agent with a witness
subpoena; disarmed by the circumstances, the agent failed to
recognize him.

At the state courthouse in Miami, the two young defenders
became legendary for their legal cunning, and they became
known as BlackanDenaro, as though they were one. They tried
more than forty cases together, and, even when their seniority
afforded them an office each, they chose to continue sharing.

In 1975 they opted to leave the public defender's office and go
into private practice together. By and large their trade re-

Rudy Arias, one of the ringleaders of the corrupt police officers who worked on the Little Havana midnight shift. But for his arrest he would have been nominated as Miami's "Officer of the Year."

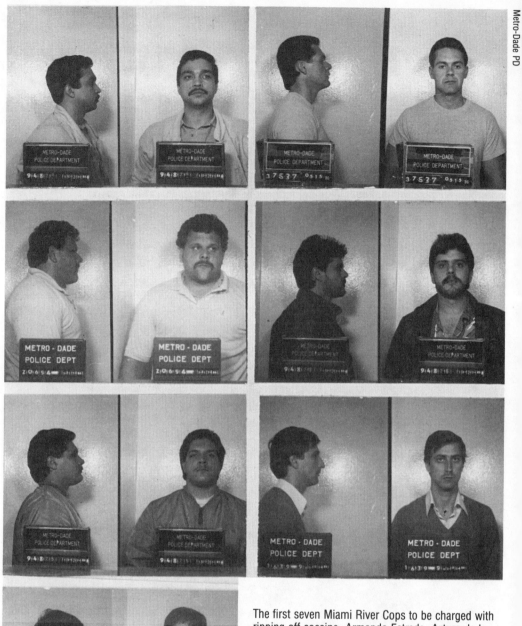

The first seven Miami River Cops to be charged with ripping off cocaine. Armando Estrada, Arturo de la Vega (*top row*), and Rudy Arias and Román Rodríguez (*second row*) all pled guilty. Armando García (*third row, left*) became a fugitive. Ricardo Aleman (*third row, right*) survived two trials but was convicted at a third. Osvaldo Coello (*bottom row*) fled but was captured in the Bahamas.

Centac 26—the four Metro-Dade Homicide detectives who realized that Miami PD was riddled with corruption. *Left to right*, Sergeant Al Singleton, Joe Díaz, Alex Alvarez, and George Plasencia.

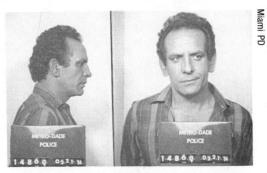

Luis Rodriguez, a small man with big ideas who ended up dead in a pine box.

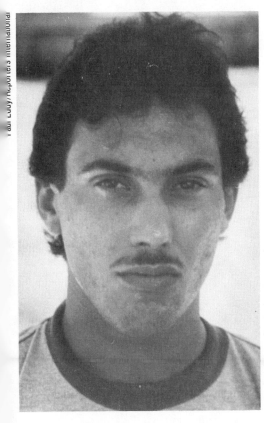

Faustino Martinez told Centac how his father, Pedro, had drowned in the Miami River.

Roy Black, a leading Miami defense attorney. There are precious few prosecutors he cannot eat alive.

Jorge Ochoa, leader of the Medillín Cartel, the largest criminal conspiracy in the world.

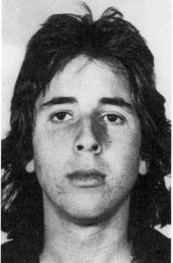

Fabio Ochoa, Sr., known to all as Don Fabio, and for his love of horses.

Juan David Ochoa, eldest of the three brothers and exceptionally reserved.

Fabio Ochoa, Jr., ordered the murder of Adler "Barry" Seal when Jorge was in prison.

Gonzalo Rodriguez Gacha, a Bogotá associate of the Medellín Cartel.

Pablo Escobar, an alternate member of the Colombian House of Representatives, legendary social benefactor in Medellín, and, when the Cartel came to be formed, second in importance only to the Ochoas. He got his start as a petty thief.

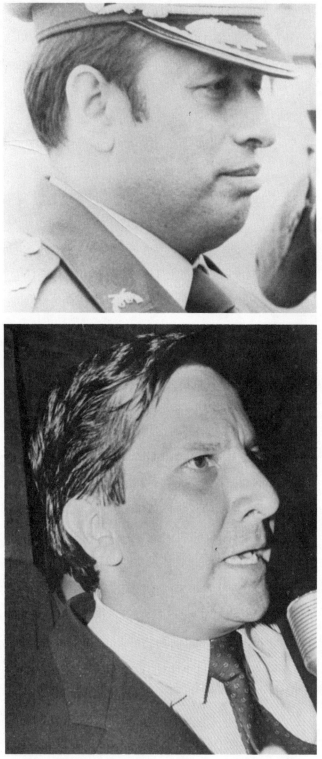

Colonel Jaime Ramírez Gómez (*left*) perhaps the most competent police officer in Bogotá and certainly one of the bravest, was given carte blanche by Justice Minister Rodrigo Lara Bonilla (*below left*) and told to hit the traffickers where it would hurt most. Ramírez led the raid on the massive *Tranquilandia* cocaine complex (*seen from the air, right*) which was equipped with executive offices, bunkhouses to accommodate up to one hundred people, a clubhouse for pilots, a huge canteen, several storage rooms for chemicals, food, parts, and medicines, and two adjacent workshops for automobile repair and airplane maintenance (*below right*). Most of the workers and guards escaped but left behind an array of weapons (*far right*).

Both the justice minister and Colonel Ramírez paid for their temerity with their lives. *Below*, Minister Lara's bullet-ridden car.

Rough Justice: the inscription above the door of Bogotá's Palace of Justice reads, "Colombians: Arms have given us independence. Laws will give us freedom." In truth, Colombia's cocaine traffickers have made a mockery of the law. *Above*, security forces prepare to retake the Palace of Justice after it had been seized by gunmen who began executing supreme justices. In the massacre and the subsequent battle, more than one hundred people died.

mained the same in that they tended to represent those least likely to secure an adequate defense. For the most part, they continued to be paid from the public purse, offering themselves as CAAs—Court Appointed Attorneys—to indigent defendants who, by the nature of their alleged crimes, needed more thorough advocacy than the overworked staff of the public defender's office could possibly offer. Many of their victories left other people uncomfortable: for example, the extraordinary acquittal of a mother charged with drowning her three-year-old son in a bathtub—the second of her infants to suffer such a fate. Black and Denaro would justify what they did by arguing that those accused of the most heinous crimes were most likely to be shunned by society and denied their rights, and therefore most in need of a strong defense; *any* defense within the law.

But in 1978, after three years of the partnership, Black and Denaro agreed to split up. It came as no surprise to many observers. For while Denaro had treated the partnership as though the frugal restraints of the public defender's office still applied, Black, on the other hand, had begun to surround himself with the trappings of a successful big city lawyer. He wanted a "decent office," computer systems, researchers, and a library. Denaro hated spending money. "I used to brag that I was the only lawyer in town who tried to keep the overheads up," said Black. As Harold Smith, their former intern, put it: "Roy was putting in mahogany. Jack wanted plywood."

So Black acquired a new partner, Frank Furci, a trained lawyer but one who also had a master's degree in business administration. Furci took over the front office, organizing all of the "support systems" that Black wanted. He also took over the finances of the practice, imposing a proper scale of fees and payment schedules to replace Black's haphazard system of "gentlemen's agreements" that were not always kept. That did not prevent Black from sometimes taking the cases of people who could not afford his fees, and he would even do *pro bono* work. But from then on, Black would also defend, with all of his skills and legal cunning, those people who could best afford his fees and pay them up front: drug dealers.

Before the Miami River Cops case his more notorious clients

had included "Amílcar" León, Centac's first target, and Griselda Blanco, the "Ma Barker" of Medellín and the cocaine trade, and the reputed sponsor of the Dadeland Massacre. Black had no hesitation in taking Román Rodríguez as a client, and advised another defense attorney to become involved in the case: Black said it was "an-us-against-the-world kind of case" and one that a criminal lawyer "ought to die to get his hands on."

He dismissed out of hand the notion that there was something immoral in representing a corrupt cop, saying: "I do not see it as my job to clean up the police department." His job, by his philosophy, was to provide Rodríguez with the best possible defense, to fight as though his own life depended on it, and to win—any way he could within the law.

From the time of their arrests, the Miami River defendants had decided they would sink or swim together, and their individual lawyers therefore formed a defense team, sharing strategy and resources. None of the other defense attorneys was as prominent as Roy Black, but three of them did bring exceptional credentials to the case in that they were all former prosecutors from the state attorney's office who, until they switched sides, had specialized in prosecuting drug traffickers. And one of them, Samuel Rabin, Jr., had a very distinctive edge: until he switched, he had been assigned as full-time prosecutor to Centac.

At Rabin's farewell party a few months before, Al Singleton had told him there were no hard feelings: "We hope you make a million dollars," said Singleton. "See you in court."

But neither Singleton nor his men could really stomach the idea of their once-crusading prosecutor taking "dirty money" from "dirty cops." Nor were they comforted when Rabin hired a private detective to investigate and, if he could, undermine Centac's case. The investigator Rabin recruited was Centac's creator, Raúl Díaz.

When Díaz had been forced to quit Centac and had gone into self-imposed exile as the afternoon shift commander at Miami International Airport, his body, accustomed if not addicted to so many years of stress, was unable to cope with the change. Díaz became very ill: his immune system broke down and he was hospitalized with body sores and severe stomach problems. He also became extremely depressed.

It was a good moment for him to have been approached by two former narcotics detectives from Metro-Dade, Juan Cayado and Tom D'Azevedo, who had left the police department to go into the investigation business for themselves. They set out to convince "the best cop in Miami" to stop wasting his time at the airport and join them. They offered to loan him money so that he could buy into their partnership, and to guarantee other loans that would get him a house and a decent car. They also promised him a salary and a share in the profits that would eclipse what he earned as a police lieutenant.

So Díaz joined the grandly named InterContinental Detective Agency, which would not meet most people's perception of a private eye enterprise. ICDA is equipped with computer systems and the paraphernalia of high-tech surveillance and communications, and it has a staff of about forty people, and "field offices" in Jacksonville and Tampa. Much of the business that supports all of that comes from big corporations and public entities that employ ICDA to investigate fraudulent worker-compensation claims. But much of it—at times as much as 70 percent of their business—comes from criminal defense attorneys, and, inevitably in Miami, most of that work concerns drugs. Díaz and his two partners have found themselves working, albeit indirectly, for some very major traffickers—including the Ochoa family and Carlos Lehder. It is not a situation they are entirely comfortable with, and it has brought them considerable animosity from some of their former colleagues in law enforcement, and, in particular, from federal prosecutors. Still, there is a Porsche, and a BMW, and a Thunderbird in ICDA's private parking lot, and, inside the office, a strict set of rules laying down "What We Will Not Do." One of the rules is that they will not work directly for criminal defendants, but only through their attorneys. The fact that so many of those attorneys also once pursued the traffickers they now serve eases any qualms that Díaz and partners may have.

Even so, Díaz was uncomfortable when Rabin asked him to

take on the Miami River case, not least because he quickly came to believe that the seven defendants were guilty. He agreed, he says, because he was close to Rabin and fond of him—indeed, had chosen him to be Centac's first prosecutor—"and this was Sam's first big case and I wanted to help him." But, as a condition, he and Rabin also agreed that there would be no attempt, at least by ICDA, to attack Centac's integrity; Díaz would merely test the strength of Centac's case.

At the defense team's early meetings, held at Roy Black's impressive offices overlooking Biscayne Bay, the obvious strategy that emerged was one of attack. The prosecution would undoubtedly rely heavily on the testimony of Armando Un and Pedro Ramos who, as members of the conspiracy, were damaging witnesses, but also vulnerable ones: they, too, had benefited from the crimes, yet they were not being prosecuted; it might be possible to convince a jury that they were lying "to save their own skins."

But in the Miami River case, this routine defense tactic of attempting to discredit "tainted evidence"—what defense attorneys are prone to call "evidence that has been bought with promises of immunity"—faced a considerable obstacle. Whatever else they may have lied about, Ramos and Un were clearly *not* lying about the raid on Jones Boat Yard: the raid happened and it was carried out by men who claimed to be police officers and who gave every appearance of being so. The defense team gave Raúl Díaz the job of attempting to explain away that difficulty.

It turned out to be ridiculously easy. Díaz sent his investigators to the stores in Miami that specialize in supplying uniforms and paraphernalia to the twenty-eight separate police departments that exist in Dade County and, with no questions asked, they were allowed to buy complete uniforms, gunbelts, holsters, and epaulets. They did not pretend to be police officers; they did not have to. Only once were they asked who they were and even then, having told the truth, they were allowed to buy what they wanted.

And to rub it in, Díaz sent two attractive female staff members from ICDA to the headquarters of the Miami Police Department, where they asked the desk sergeant how they could obtain Miami PD shoulder badges. The sergeant sent them along to Public Affairs, which said, "No problem"—and, without question or hesitation, handed out six badges, as though they were souvenirs.

So, Díaz proved, just about anybody could obtain the means to pose as a Miami police officer. It was, as Díaz knew, a total red herring, but a seductive one—and perhaps enough to cast into the mind of at least one juror the seed of "reasonable doubt."

That Díaz was willing to do that, that he would attempt to sabotage Centac's case, says a great deal about the bitterness and cynicism he felt towards "the system." Just how bitter and how cynical became clear when Díaz walked into Roy Black's offices for one of the strategy meetings to discover that the defense team had gained a new member: the diminutive Doug Williams. Díaz took one look at his nemesis, the man whom he blamed for the orchestration of the campaign that had destroyed his police career, and walked out of the room, pursued by Rabin.

"Sam, what the fuck is he doing here?" Díaz demanded. Rabin explained that one of the defendants, Osvaldo Coello, had fired his original attorney and replaced him with Williams. "Well," said Díaz "then I'm going to get the hell out of the case."

Rabin begged him, as a personal favor, to put up with Williams: "Please, just tolerate him." Williams took Díaz into a side office and attempted to persuade him that they should declare a truce, "for the greater good." Díaz felt an almost irresistible urge to point out to Williams that they were alone in a room on the fourteenth floor of a building with windows that opened, but he held his tongue.

In the end, Díaz agreed to let bygones be bygones, temporarily. And during the months leading up to the trial the truce held, though largely by virtue of the fact that Díaz reported his progress directly to Rabin and had almost nothing to do with the other attorneys.

But when the trial finally got underway, Díaz learned that the defense wished to call him as an "expert witness," one who is qualified by experience and qualifications to give his opinion on the stand. He was to be questioned on a subject about which he was undeniably an expert—the management, and risks, of police informants. But, the attorney who was going to qualify him, and seek his opinions, was Doug Williams. Once again, Díaz threatened to quit, but once again he was pacified by Rabin. He even agreed to have lunch with Williams to discuss his testimony, and it was a surprisingly amicable meeting until, towards the end, Williams said he had one question to ask: Was it true that Díaz had attempted to have Williams killed? "No," said Díaz. "If I had, you would be dead."

In the Miami River trial, Williams duly qualified Díaz as an expert witness by asking him to describe to the jury the details of his "illustrious career," and obtained his expert agreement that informants could, indeed, be unreliable. Not once did either of them so much as hint that Williams had done his best to destroy that illustrious career, nor that he believed that Díaz's use of informants was highly improper.

Afterwards, after Díaz had shaken hands with his old friends and colleagues at Centac, and they had all agreed there were "no hard feelings," Díaz was asked why he had allowed himself to be manipulated.

"Because I've learned," he said. He paraphrased a passage from a book, Miles Copeland's *The Game of Nations,* in which the vice-president of what was then the United Arab Republic addresses a group of graduating army cadets: It was important to remember, he said, that war was a game in which the individual participants were not concerned with overall victory, but with not personally losing; their objective was to remain in the game. Díaz said that in the War on Drugs, he had lost sight of that, and gone for overall victory, and, consequently, he had lost. He was, he said, no longer so naive: "The whole thing's a game. It's all a fucking game."

18

We, the Jury

The trial of the Miami River Cops, as it was inevitably dubbed by the local media, began on September 29, 1986, in the federal courthouse for the Southern District of Florida, where the central courtroom is dominated by a huge mural. It portrays a rather romanticized cross-section of Miami's community going about its work, with the figure of black-robed benevolent Justice at the center. It was originally commissioned by Judge Halstead L. Ritter in the mid-1930s, who ensured that the artist painted his likeness into it. Unfortunately, Judge Ritter was impeached before it could be completed and the likeness of Justice was repainted: it apparently bears an uncanny resemblance to Ritter's successor.

It also bears a passing resemblance to fifty-four-year-old Judge Kenneth Ryskamp, the newest recruit to the federal bench in South Florida who had been sworn in only three months before. Ryskamp had been a civil lawyer who specialized in appellate work, and this was his first major criminal trial. It proved to be a deeply frustrating experience for him.

The trial was held in an extraordinarily circus-like atmosphere; and what happened during the seventeen weeks and four days that it lasted had almost nothing to do with justice, and everything to do with theater.

The defendants' mothers, fathers, wives, cousins, aunts, uncles, babies, and friends kept constant vigil in the precincts of the court every day, sending out for hamburgers and sandwiches and regular supplies of Cuban coffee. They huddled together, glaring defiantly at any intruder who crossed the invisible line to their courthouse territory. It was as if they had decided to create a Cuban "wake."

The trial attracted enormous media interest. Reporters and crews from four English-speaking and two Hispanic television stations, radio, the wire services, and the two local newspapers were often swollen in rank by courtroom artists and print and television journalists from out of town. As they gathered during each break to lobby defense attorneys for quotes and the chance of an "exclusive" interview with one of the defendants, there was, at least in the early stages of the trial, a large measure of agreement with the much-stated view of the defendants' families, that the government's witnesses were worthless.

They were dismissed in the same breath as the three "dopers" who had drowned in the Miami River: So what? (This feeling, that the killing of "a doper" is not the most heinous of crimes, is shared by a lot of people in Miami, including police officers, jurors, and even some members of the judiciary. In a state that enthusiastically endorses the death penalty, not one of the killers that Centac has captured has yet been sent to the electric chair. Al Singleton of Centac understands the community's ambivalence, and he and his men joke about it. "But I thought *we* cared," said Joe Díaz. "Why do you keep sending us to the funerals?" "To take surveillance photographs," said Singleton.)

The defense attorneys presented a civilized front, at least superficially. They dressed in sober suits and those who possessed expensive Rolex watches, so much in evidence during pre-trial hearings, took the precaution of removing them from the jury's view; as Black explained it, no need for the jury to be reminded of the "commercialism" of the lawyers' trade. But, ranged en masse, they conveyed the impression that nothing very serious was at stake here, and they sometimes resembled nothing more than a group of naughty schoolboys. More than once, Judge Ryskamp had to admonish them for a lack of decorum.

They would sometimes recreate the day's events in the form of a soap opera that they called "As the River Runs." They called the small room set aside for their use "the clavo," which literally means "the nail," but which in the drugs trade is a term used to describe secret compartments of the kind installed on the *Mary C.* They gave each other and the prosecutors nicknames: Roy Black was "The Professor"; Doug Williams, perhaps because of his stature, was "Brainy Smurf." And Sam Burstyn, another member of the defense team, who specialized in histrionics, who threatened a witness, and who received regular rebukes from the judge, was known, appropriately, as "Wild Man."

Prosecutor Russell Killinger, who had the unenviable task of presenting the government's financial evidence, was called, behind his back, "Dr. Insomnia." And Trudy Novicki, always carefully referred to as *Miss* Novicki, was nevertheless the butt of much courtly banter: when, for example, she introduced photographs of one of Little Havana's sleazy bars, the defense attorneys suggested that she drop by for "ladies' night."

The mood was pervasive, and though the seven defendants dressed conservatively—to give what Black described as "that image of nonviolence"—and had shed their gold jewelry, the changes proved to be cosmetic. There were occasional flashes of midnight shift hooliganism. Outside the courtroom, Osvaldo Coello pretended to point a gun at one of the government's witnesses, and said: "We're going to burn you on the street." Coello would also attempt to intimidate the prosecutors. "Hey, Killinger," he said in a loud stage whisper, "you'd better get your shit together." And when Pat Sullivan, the third member of the prosecution team, encountered Coello, Rudy Arias, and Arturo De La Vega in the men's room, Coello said: "Let's beat his ass, boys."

At least once, the behavior of the defendants threatened to have very serious consequences. The prosecutors learned that Román Rodríguez was using marijuana and Quaaludes in jail and, under their influence, had told a fellow prisoner that it was "funny as hell" that the three Miami River victims had died. He admitted taking part in the raid on the *Mary C* because, he said, he needed the money. Rodríguez also confided that he had used his uniform to commit other robberies.

The government rushed to produce the prisoner as a witness

and Roy Black was required to spend all of one night researching the legal issues, "cursing my fate and Pat Sullivan and my client," until he could construct an abstruse legal argument that persuaded the judge that the witness should not be heard.

And throughout it all, the families performed like a Roman gallery, cheering and jeering, and roundly denouncing the *chivatos*—"snitches"—to anyone who would listen. When Judge Ryskamp finally warned that any further intimidation of witnesses would constitute contempt, the families contented themselves with taunting Alex Alvarez, who always bore the brunt of their animosity. They were delighted when Doug Williams told the jury that the entire case resulted from some petty ambition of Alvarez to win promotion to sergeant: "What could have been a bigger feather in his career cap than to go and bag a load of cops?" said Williams.

For some of the families, the expensive skills of their attorneys were not enough. Some of them were adherents of Santería, a centuries-old Afro-Caribbean religion which has a large following in Miami and which involves gods and deities and the worship of natural forces, and an array of powders, colognes, and rituals—including animal sacrifice. It is designed to invoke "white magic," to prevent harm. So when one of the defendants faced the possibility of having his bond revoked, courthouse cleaners found chicken heads and talcum powder scattered in front of the courtroom door. It worked.

But perhaps a more powerful influence throughout the trial was the mother of Arturo De La Vega, a partner of Rudy Arias on the midnight shift. A tired, careworn woman, Fe Llerena had been abandoned by Arturo's father "when he was forty-three days old," as she would say, and she had raised Arturo on her own, by working as many menial jobs as she could fit into a day. By dint of hard work, she was able to send him to a respectable private school in Miami, and although remarried, still worked long hours in a cafeteria at Miami International Airport. She attended the trial between shifts.

Her air of saintly suffering was made all the more effective when she slipped and fell on the courthouse steps, injuring her leg. In a plaster cast, and using a stick, Fe Llerena took to using her disability to entice jurors into the courthouse elevator, where she would embrace them and show them photographs of "my boy." And having learned that the foreman of the jury had lost his job because of the duration of the trial, she stopped him on the street and told him she was trying to find him another one.

Neither Fe nor some of the other mothers were prepared to leave anything to chance, however. Though the names of the jurors were supposed to be secret, and they were known only by numbers, the families easily discovered that juror number 72 was Olga Albarrán Fernández, and they found out where she lived—indeed, on one occasion she was given a ride home by one of the relatives. Olga's daughter was lobbied to urge her mother to vote for acquittal. And in mid-trial, Fe Llerena, along with the mothers of Armando Estrada and Armando García, went to the woman's home on Miami Beach to plead with her. "Don't worry," Olga told the assembled mothers. "Un and Ramos should be hanged! I'm not going to convict."

Defense attorneys of Roy Black's caliber do not go willy-nilly before a jury of their clients' peers, and the jury of which Olga Albarrán was part had been selected with enormous care. After two hundred jury trials in his seventeen-year career, Black said that, with one exception, he has never lost a case in which he was able to use sophisticated jury selection techniques. To help Black and other defense attorneys in such efforts, there are specialist firms such as Trial Consultants Inc., which is whom the defense team in the Miami River case hired to help select the jury.

Because of the enormous publicity the case had received in Miami, it was always going to be difficult to find an impartial jury, and, in early pre-trial hearings, Judge Ryskamp was lulled into agreeing that a pool of 275 potential jurors should be asked to fill in a questionnaire. The questions were supposed to elicit each person's knowledge about the case, and detect any possible bias. But what the defense had in mind went far beyond that.

The questionnaire produced by Black and a psychologist from Trial Consultants ran to sixteen pages and asked one hundred-twenty-eight questions—only fourteen of which had anything remotely to do with the events on the Miami River: "Do you feel that a person should pay heavily for their mistakes?";

"What is your frank opinion of defense attorneys?"; "What can be done to lower the crime rate?"; "Please share your thoughts and feelings about the Hialeah politician accused of corruption"; "Would you invite a politician into your home that you did not know? Why or why not?"

Whether by chance or design, the questionnaire was delivered to the court by Black on the day of the mailing deadline for sending out, and there was little time for the judge or the prosecutors to review it. It was only later, after many of the potential jurors had been reduced to shambling confusion, that Judge Ryskamp declared some of the questions to be "totally worthless," while others were so abstruse they would require an expert in law to answer them. He blamed himself for allowing it.

But for the defense, the exercise was far from worthless. Trial Consultants analyzed the responses and gave each potential juror a rating from "good" to "very poor," along with a brief description. For example, of juror number 22, Trial Consultants said: "1. Has very traditional strict values; 'right is right, wrong is wrong'; 2. Honesty is important to her; 3. Believes drug trafficking is a big problem; 4. Thinks if the government brings a case, the person(s) are probably guilty. Rating: Poor." Of juror number 3, on the other hand: "1. Creative thinker—definitely not one of the crowd; 2. Was a victim—state handled the case poorly; 3. Punitive; 4. Thinks prosecutors are over zealous sometimes and defense attorneys preserve people's rights; 5. Honest; 6. Thinks the P.O. are not guilty!!! Rating: Good." Only occasionally was the verdict ambivalent: "Believes they [the defendants] were probably framed—wants to be on this case to protect the innocent; she is either nuts or a great juror. Rating: ?"

Armed with the completed questionnaires and their experts' recommendations, the defense attorneys sat down to decide among themselves which of the candidates they should attempt to get onto the jury and which should be kept off. In general they favored blacks because research conducted in Miami in the late 1970s showed that blacks were fiercely antigovernment, and that their enmity for the government was even greater than it was for Hispanics.

Hispanics, on the other hand, were regarded warily because, as Black explained it: "They're extremely conservative, right-wing, anticommunist, very patriotic, very pro-government, very anti-crime and very embarrassed when there's a Latin defendant." And, perhaps because of that, the defense overdid it: their first choice for a jury was almost entirely black and, after some agonizing, they decided to go through the selection process again.

There were some "knock-down, drag-out fights" between the attorneys. Black remembers one potential female juror, a religious fanatic, whose "outrageous" answers to the questionnaire reduced a defense team meeting to chaos. Some of the attorneys felt the prosecution's case was so strong that they had nothing to lose. As Black paraphrased their argument: "If we put this nut on the jury, you never know what she might do. Jesus may come to her in the middle of the night and say, 'They're all innocent.' " The woman was not selected, but later, during the trial's bleaker moments, one of the attorneys would pipe up: "I told you we should have left the nut on the jury!"

But there was one important criterion on which all of the defense attorneys agreed: that they could not afford to have on the jury anyone "with any modicum of intelligence," as Black put it. They wanted people who knew almost nothing about the community in which they lived, who were totally without curiosity, "who don't read the papers, who don't know current affairs, who know nothing about what's going on around them . . . stupid people."

The defense team used all of the twenty-one challenges it was allowed to get the jury it wanted. It was made up of six blacks, three Anglos, and three Hispanics—including Olga Albarrán Fernández.

She had protested from the start that she would have problems attending the trial, because her sister was ill with cancer, but when told that each juror would receive $30 a day, she was persuaded. However, it soon became clear that she had no interest in the proceedings. She looked alternately bored and distracted, and pointedly ignored much of the prosecution's evidence. Eventually, the judge admonished her for writing what appeared to be her Christmas lists during testimony.

When the judge discovered that Olga's daughter had sat in court throughout, and that Olga had invited her into the jury room during recesses, he was obliged to admonish her again, this time formally. He was unable to do so directly, however, because she did not understand English sufficiently well to know what he was talking about without the services of an interpreter.

There was every reason to remove her from the jury and replace her with one of the four "alternates" who had been selected at the beginning of the trial as replacements in case any of the original jurors should become indisposed. But that did not suit the defense attorneys at all. For in the process of so carefully selecting the jurors they wanted, they had exhausted their challenges; the "alternates" were not of their choosing and, in Roy Black's words, "were not favorable towards us."

So Black and the others "fought tooth and nail to keep Olga on the jury," by persuading the judge that she was not "insane and illiterate." In that endeavor, there were days, he said, when "we felt we were at the Battle of the Somme."

In the end it was Olga who decided she had had enough. On January 8, 1987, after three and a half months of evidence and argument, the jury retired to consider its verdict; and on the judge's orders, was sequestered in a hotel. Olga objected— pleading her sick sister again—and offered the bemused judge the idea: "I go to another place for night." Forced to accept the government's hospitality, she later tried to hand in the key of her room to US marshals, having complained, in a chaotic handwritten note, that she had not been allowed a television and a telephone in her room. And when the jury returned to court, to ask if it could rehear some of the evidence, Olga arrived singing. She sat down for a while, then suddenly got up, saying *me voy*—"I'm off"—and, to the astonishment of the judge and attorneys, started walking out of the courtroom.

But by then, it did not matter. Black had discovered that Congress had recently passed an obscure amendment which said that a juror who withdrew *during deliberations* need not be substituted with an alternate—and Black had his legal arguments well-prepared. He was absolutely certain that if Judge Ryskamp had known about the amendment earlier, Olga would have been replaced by an alternate before the jury retired. Now it was too late; the Miami River Cops would be judged by *eleven* of their peers.

As Marc Nurik, a member of the defense team, was fond of saying, the prosecution needed twelve votes (or, after Olga's departure, eleven), whereas "I just need one." Because the verdicts of federal juries must be unanimous one dissenting voice is enough to cause a mistrial, and while that is hardly the same as an acquittal, in the Miami River case it was the best the defense attorneys could hope for; something close to victory.

In Olga's absence it was handed to them by juror number 199: William Rountree, a seventy-six-year-old retired chef who dabbled as a private investigator, and who was also something of a professional juror: he had, by his own estimates, served on more than a dozen juries and been foreman three times. Throughout the eleven days of jury deliberations, the screams and shouts that were heard coming from the jury room were provoked largely by Rountree's refusal to agree with his colleagues about anything. The sixty-four separate counts on which the jury had to pronounce were sufficient cause for confusion and dissent, but ten of them could at least agree on 80 percent of their verdicts, which were mostly "Guilty." Not Rountree. As he later announced with pride: "I was the holdout from the start." And no amount of pleading or cajoling would make him change his mind.

After a week of this, the jury attempted to return nonunanimous verdicts, and was sent back to try again. Four days later the foreman sent the latest in a series of increasingly despairing messages to the court: "Judge Ryskamp, We have reached an impasse in our deliberations. Some, we have agreed unanimously and some we are *definitely dead lock*[ed]. Could part of the defendants be judge[d] as a hung jury?" The judge urged them to keep trying.

And, after just one more day, it seemed there had been a miracle. The jury said it had reached agreement on two of the seven defendants, and this time the verdicts were unanimous: Armando Estrada and his partner, Román Rodríguez, were cleared of a total of nineteen charges, but both were found guilty of racketeering, conspiracy, and the raid at Jones Boat Yard. In a courtroom filled to capacity—and guarded by more than thirty marshals who had been bussed in for fear of violence—the clerk of the court was instructed to poll the jury, one by one, to confirm that was their verdict: "No," said Rountree, firmly. Polled a second time, Rountree still said "No." Taken to the judge's chambers along with Estrada and Rodríguez and the attorneys, Rountree changed his mind several times. He said that Estrada and Rodríguez were certainly guilty of the raid at Jones Boat Yard—but so were the rest of them and he did not see why they should get away with it. Judge Ryskamp had no choice but to declare a mistrial.

Roy Black, the veteran of two hundred jury trials, said he had never seen anything like it, "and neither, I suspect, has anybody else."

Outside the federal courthouse, police snipers watched from rooftops in case the Colombians whose cocaine the midnight shift had stolen might decide to take the law into their own hands. Those defendants who were free on bond, and the faithful families, pushed their way through the crowds, some of them shouting "Party! Party!"

That night, at one of the more exclusive nightclubs in Coconut Grove, the defense attorneys gathered to also toast their victory. Sam Burstyn, "Wild Man," in ebullient form, said: "What a game! They were all as guilty as hell, of course."

At a somber gathering in a German bar in Coral Gables, the members of Centac and the prosecutors cried into their beer, and cursed the system. They vowed they would not give up. They said they would try the case again, and "next time it'll be even better."

The question was, would the witnesses still be alive?

In all, Rudy Arias, Armando Estrada, Armando García, Arturo De La Vega, Román Rodríguez, and Osvaldo Coello, along with others, constructed six separate plots to kill or have killed witnesses against them. In addition to the abortive attempt on Un's life, which they sponsored soon after their arrests, they also conspired to murder:

> A fellow Miami police officer who testified that De La Vega said he wanted to "take down" a man whom he saw driving an expensive Mercedes and wearing a diamond-studded Rolex;
>
> A fifty-year-old Colombian woman from whom De La Vega had

stolen a kilo of cocaine. Her life was spared only because she agreed to take a bribe not to identify De La Vega in court;

Alejo Cossio, a builder to whom Arias had given $172,000 in cash "under the table" for a new house. The crooked cops feared that Cossio's testimony against Arias could damage all of them. At one of the daily lunches they took together during the trial, Arias, De La Vega, Coello, and Ricardo Alemán decided killing the builder would be "a piece of cake." Cossio's car license number was run through the police department's computer to establish his address. His house was then placed under surveillance by a contract killer who accepted $40,000 from the Miami River defendants to "do Cossio." Fortunately, Cossio did not go home.

And, in early February 1987, two weeks or so after the mistrial, five of the defendants met at the law offices of Sam Burstyn, "Wild Man," and decided they could not afford their attorneys' fees for a second trial. Instead, they agreed to establish a fund to which they and other unindicted former police officers contributed, to finance a second attempt on the life of Armando Un and to kill the other key witness, Pedro Ramos.

Arturo De La Vega, Osvaldo Coello, Armando García, and another former member of the midnight shift, Raimundo Betancourt, made the first attempt on Ramos themselves. They staked out a video store in Hialeah, where they had been told he was expected, on two successive days, armed between them with guns that included a KG-99 semi-automatic rifle, a shot-gun, and a MAC-10 .45-caliber submachine gun equipped with silencer. Had Ramos shown up, their plan was to take his bullet-riddled body to the home of prosecutor Trudy Novicki, and dump it on the hood of her black Volvo car.

Injustice in Miami is not cheap. Between them six of the Miami River cops paid their defense lawyers more than $1.6 million in fees and expenses, much of it in cash. (The seventh defendant, Ricardo Alemán, had a court-appointed attorney paid for out of public funds.)

To honest cops and prosecutors in Miami it is a cause of despair that reputable attorneys, what Alex Alvarez describes as "prominent members of this community," demand fees their clients cannot possibly afford to pay—unless they are guilty.

The irony, and the ire of honest cops, increases when prominent lawyers take vast fees from police officers who, if they can pay, *must* be corrupt. For if the lawyers do their work well and gain acquittals, the logical consequence is that their crooked clients can return to uniform and regain the power and authority they have already abused. True, in the case of the Miami River cops that would never have happened because, to his credit, Chief Clarence Dickson made it clear he did not care what the jury thought: he said he would resign as police chief before he would accept any of the seven men back onto the force. But not all police chiefs are as forthright as Dickson (or as foolhardy perhaps: Dickson was immediately hit with a civil lawsuit by Rudy Arias, alleging defamation) and it seems perverse—reckless even, for the community in which they live—that responsible people should use their considerable skills to defend and, if they can, exculpate corrupt police officers. The lawyers in the Miami River Cops case did not set out to right injustice but to cause it—for cash.

The lawyers were not alone in accepting what was, in effect, drug money. Builders, bankers, realtors, retailers, and car salesmen took huge cash payments from apparently ordinary working cops, with no questions asked; relatives, wives, and girl friends benefited from the rip-offs and either knew where the money was coming from or did not inquire; friends and colleagues in the Miami Police Department accepted generous gifts and looked the other way. In all, there were dozens, if not scores, of people in Miami who knew or suspected what was going on, yet nobody said a word.

That silence is the more extraordinary because there were not seven "dirty" cops in Miami. As events would prove, the real number was nearer *seventy*.

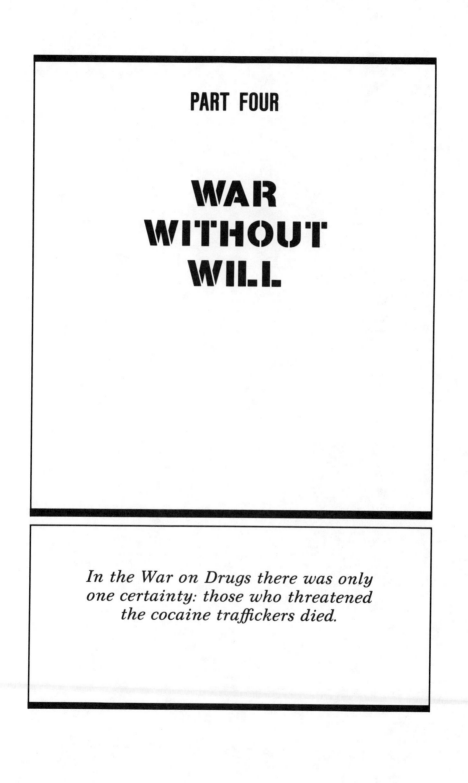

PART FOUR

WAR WITHOUT WILL

In the War on Drugs there was only one certainty: those who threatened the cocaine traffickers died.

19

The Cartel

If the profits from cocaine trafficking can buy widespread silence in Miami; if some of the best American lawyers will take drug money to thwart justice (or, in the case of the Miami River cops, at least delay justice); if, in a city swarming with law enforcement agencies, as many as one in ten of the local police officers are corrupt, and nobody notices; if a so-called friendly nation can flagrantly facilitate the flow of cocaine into the United States, and get away with it; if the American government declares all-out war on drugs and, five years on, is losing that war—what hope is there for Colombia?

The Colombians who dominate the cocaine trade do so from within the borders of Colombia, and the failure of the Colombian government to stop them has created enormous impatience and cynicism in Washington. The demand that Colombia should do more to curtail the traffickers is tempered only by Washington's suspicion that the Colombian government does not wish to do more—because of cocaine's importance to the country's economy. Since a senior official of the central bank in Bogotá freely admits the "sad but unequivocal reality" that drug money keeps the economy going, there is, surely, a measure of ambivalence in the Colombian government's attitude. The question is, even if their was greater determination in Bogotá, could the government do more?—or is it now too late?

As the DEA's Miguel Walsh said in his prescient paper on

cocaine trafficking published in 1979, there were regions of Colombia where the traffickers commanded "more power and respect than the central government." Since 1979 there has been a significant increase in the traffickers' power and though respect for them may have waned it has been replaced by something far more potent: fear.

For the last seven years Colombia has been embroiled in an undeclared civil war between the authorities and the traffickers, and what might be called their allies of convenience. The traffickers have not won every battle and they have suffered serious setbacks, but the reality is they have been winning the war and continue to do so: for every loss and every retreat they have been forced to make, there has been a subsequent advance and a victory. It is probably true that the Colombian cocaine mafia is better organized today than it has ever been, and the trafficking ethos never more entrenched.

The story of how and why Colombia lost—or, at least, is losing—its own "war on drugs" provides an object lesson in the limitations of democratic government when it is confronted by ruthless, implacable opponents who go armed with the lure of fabulous profits.

On a November morning in 1981, Carlos Lehder left his home on the outskirts of Armenia to drive the ten miles to his *La Posada Alemana* resort to check on the progress of the construction work. After making the rounds, he next headed for *Hacienda Pisamal,* the 700-acre *finca* which he hoped to transform into a cattle ranch. In those days Lehder felt no need for bodyguards, and the only person with him was his driver. They were a couple of miles from the city's outskirts when they were forced to stop by a car that appeared to have broken down, blocking the road. As Lehder and his driver went to offer help, two men appeared from behind some bushes, brandishing guns: "Don't move," they said. "This is a kidnap."

The driver was tied up and gagged, and Lehder was bundled into the back of the car. But he had not been immobilized and, as the car sped away, Lehder began kicking and punching and somehow managed to open one of the rear doors and roll out of the car. It stopped, one of the men got out and, from a distance of some fifteen yards, he fired several shots at Lehder, hitting him once below the chest.

He must have thought he had killed him because he said: "Let's go. This sonofabitch is gone." But Lehder was found in time by workers from a nearby building and taken to the *Clínica Central del Quindío,* where it took him almost two weeks to recover. The day he was discharged, ten well-armed men escorted him from the hospital.

Meanwhile, on the morning of November 12, 1981, some 120 miles away in Medellín, other would-be kidnappers mingled with thousands of students on the campus of the University of Antioquia. The university is funded by the state, and it has always fostered the kind of left-wing radicalism that gave birth to the nationalist guerrilla movement, M-19, formed in the early 1970s, mainly by disenchanted college students and university professors. On that November morning, M-19 entered the kidnapping business by seizing one of the more unlikely students of such a proletarian university: Martha Nieves Ochoa Vásquez, one of the three daughters of Don Fabio Ochoa.

Kidnapping is practically endemic in Colombia but rarely if ever before had the victims been major drug traffickers or their offspring. And M-19's adoption of extortion as a means of raising funds was another new development and, for drug traffickers, a disturbing one. There are three major guerrilla groups in Colombia, and any number of splinter factions, and if the Ochoas had paid a ransom for Martha Nieves, they might have set a trend that could spread.

The Ochoas did not pay. Instead, their response was to call the first-ever meeting of all of Colombia's most influential traffickers, all of whom, because of their vast fortunes, were now potential kidnap targets. It was held on December 1, 1981, in Cali, the sprawling capital of Valle province, southwest of Medellín—and an appropriate venue since it was one of the main bases for M-19.

Within days of the Cali meeting, hundreds of thousands of fliers were distributed throughout Colombia, handed out at busy city intersections and dropped from helicopters into crowded soccer stadiums. Their contents announced:

1. At an emergency meeting, held only a few days ago, 223 mafia bosses met exclusively to discuss the issue of kidnapping. The mafia is aware that several kidnappings have taken and will be taking place throughout the nation;

2. Kidnappings have been carried out both by common criminals and subversive elements, with the latter trying to finance their activities by targeting people like us, whose hard-earned money has brought progress and employment to this country, and much-needed schools, hospitals, etc.;

3. At said meeting, the 223 mafia bosses, representing every region of the country, agreed to finance this endeavor through personal contributions of 2 million pesos each [approximately $20,000], which, put together, add up to 446 million pesos [then worth approximately $4.4 million]. In our effort to fight the practice of kidnapping, these resources will be used to pay for rewards, execution of perpetrators, and equipment;

4. At said meeting, we also agreed to create an operative group called MAS [*Muerte A Secuestradores*—"Death to Kidnappers"] which will be under the direct control of the mafia;

5. Each boss has registered ten of his best men, and, therefore, a total of 2,230 individuals will be involved in the initial operations;

6. As from this date, these individuals are on the alert, and will be carrying out the executions of all those associated with the practice of kidnapping, whether common criminals or subversives;

7. Kidnappers will be executed in public: they will be hanged from trees in public places or shot by firing squads. They will be duly marked with a small cross which is the symbol of our organization—MAS;

8. Our action will cover all kidnapping cases that occur as from this date. These cases will be investigated directly by our people;

9. A 20 million peso reward [approximately $200,000] has been created for those who, personally and directly, provide us with information on kidnappings;

10. This information can be reported to any boss or member of our organization, all of whom are widely known in this country;

11. Those kidnappers who are arrested by police will be executed in prison; if their whereabouts cannot be established, our people will act on their colleagues or the nearest relatives.

MAS—Operative Group of the Mafia

Please do not destroy this communiqué; exhibit it in a public place.

The "mafia" was as good as its word. The manhunt which MAS unleashed to find the kidnappers of Martha Nieves was exceptionally brutal, even by Colombia's standards. Ten M-19 guerrillas were kidnapped and tortured, and two of them—who were on the Colombian army's "most-wanted" list—were handed over to the military commanders amidst widespread publicity. In Medellín, MAS invaded homes and shot suspected guerrillas—but also trades unionists, old ladies, young children, horses, pigs, and chickens. Mere sympathizers of M-19 were abducted from the university, tortured, and, if they were lucky, sent home in their underwear. After a few weeks of this, M-19 effectively surrendered: on February 17, 1982, three months after her abduction, Martha Nieves was released unharmed.

And, at least for a while, M-19 no longer regarded drug traffickers or their families as fair game. Instead the "mafia" and the guerrillas reached an accommodation whereby M-19 received money and weapons and, in return, performed chores for the traffickers: guarding their jungle strips, for example, and carrying out occasional contract killings—including at least one in Miami. The two groups had nothing in common, of course, except for their mutual hatred of America.

The much more significant alliance to emerge from the kidnapping threat was between the traffickers themselves. Before the Cali convention that created MAS, they had operated as distinct and often rival groups which were usually based on close ties of blood, marriage, or friendship. But the success of their death squad clearly demonstrated the benefits of cooperation in the common interest, and it led to a lasting bond between some of the major "families."

The Ochoa family and Pablo Escobar had cooperated with each other since at least 1981, and, sometime in 1982, they formed what they called *Medellín & Compañía* and took into that enterprise a third partner, Gonzalo Rodríguez Gacha, a trafficker from Bogotá who shared Don Fabio's extreme devotion to horses. They divided up responsibilities: Rodríguez

Gacha, who had started out in the trade working with prominent coca growers and paste manufacturers in neighboring
Peru, ensured ever-increasing supplies of the basic ingredient;
Escobar took overall charge of cocaine production; Jorge Ochoa
and his two brothers took responsibility for transportation of
the finished product to the United States, distribution, and
money laundering.

They each provided these services not merely for themselves
but also for scores of other smaller groups. The Ochoas, Escobar, and Rodríguez Gacha became known as *los dueños del
cupo*—"the holders of the quota"—who allotted coca paste to
others for refining. The "company" also entered into cooperation agreements with numerous subcontractors, of which the
most important was Carlos Lehder's group, which specialized
in transportation.

The result was a loose federation that embraced literally
thousands of people—the Cartel: without doubt, the largest and
the most profitable criminal conspiracy in the world.

The first manifestation of this new-found cooperation was a
construction project which the Cartel undertook deep in the
province of Caquetá, in southern Colombia, which is isolated
from the rest of the country by thick rain forests and an intricate system of rivers. There, on an island measuring 6.2 square
miles, in the middle of Caquetá's Yarí River, the Cartel decided
to establish new facilities for manufacturing cocaine. Traditional cocaine laboratories, or "kitchens," usually located in
suburban Medellín, Cali, and Bogotá, were ramshackle affairs,
poorly equipped, and capable of producing only five to ten kilos
at a time; the idea this time was for something a little grander.

Throughout late 1982 and a good part of 1983, hundreds of
manual workers were recruited in Medellín and Bogotá, and
flown down to Caquetá, lured by the pay of $100 a month (three
times the minimum wage in Colombia) and the promise of a
regular free trip home. Essential equipment and tools were
ferried to the island by helicopter and on barges, to allow the
laborers to first clear the forest and then construct a long landing strip. Once the initial work was completed, cargo planes
arrived with more tools and building materials, electrical generators, and communications equipment.

They built three separate camps on the island. The first to be completed was called *Tranquilandia,* apparently because it was so isolated that nobody was likely to disturb its peace. It had executive offices, bunkhouses to accommodate up to one hundred people, a clubhouse for pilots, a huge canteen, several storage rooms for chemicals, food, parts and medicines, and two adjacent workshops for automobile repair and airplane maintenance.

The second and third camps were essentially workplaces— gigantic cocaine laboratories that were christened *Villa Coca* and *Coquilandia.* A network of boardwalks linked them to the living quarters of *Tranquilandia,* and to the main runway and six other airstrips that were added to the complex.

Air-conditioning equipment was installed in most of the buildings. Bathrooms were tiled and equipped with ceramic toilets and basins. Sleeping quarters were furnished with new bunk beds and mattresses. For entertainment, workers were provided with video-cassette recorders, table games, and an assortment of American porn magazines. Large refrigerators and dishwashers were installed in the main kitchen, and railings hung from the ceiling to hold several hundred pounds of dried meat. Near the kitchen, a pigpen and a chicken yard were erected. Two rooms, one in *Tranquilandia* and the other in *Villa Coca,* were converted into medical clinics.

The complex became operational in 1983 with the arrival of laboratory technicians, camp supervisors, and a general manager. They began producing more than four tons of cocaine per week, and twenty tons per month. Whenever they topped those production quotas, workers were treated to turkey dinners.

Planes flew in daily from northern Colombia carrying German and American-made ether and other chemicals, and left fully loaded with cocaine, refueling at *Hacienda Veracruz,* Jorge Ochoa's farm on Colombia's northern coast, before continuing their journey to the United States. Other aircraft arrived from Bolivia with coca paste and cocaine base. Large boats delivered fuel and livestock from San Vicente del Caguán, the nearest frontier town. Helicopters brought in food supplies from Neiva, the nearest provincial capital, and ferried workers in and out.

Within the camps there was strict discipline. "Reserved area.

Do not enter without proper authorization from the kitchen," one sign read. "Please keep this place tidy," read another. Menial workers, or *lavaperros*—"dogwashers"—who were paid the minimum wage, were not allowed to talk to technical personnel, or discuss the comings and goings at the complex among themselves. Perhaps frustrated by the rule of silence, they began leaving graffiti on the walls and doors to express their feelings. "Life is a jungle," said one philosophical message, "and we all have to engage in a battle for life; a battle that often makes us prone to accidents." A more banal protest scrawled on a toilet wall read: "Shitting is prohibited here."

Protection for the complex was provided by a unit of the Communist Revolutionary Armed Forces of Colombia—FARC —another guerrilla group with which the Cartel had reached an understanding, and which had been active in Caquetá for decades. The unit was heavily armed, and it established and rehearsed security and evacuation procedures in case *Tranquilandia* should ever be attacked.

Nothing so large and elaborate could possibly escape notice for long, and *Tranquilandia* neatly demonstrated both the power and the arrogance of the Cartel. Escobar, the Ochoas, and the rest thought they could get away with it, just as they had got away with the excesses of MAS, because they believed they had nothing to fear from the Colombian government. They believed this because both of the major political parties in Colombia had accepted hefty donations from them, and because nobody in Colombia had yet abandoned the absurd fiction that Escobar and Ochoa were anything other than successful "industrialists" and "businessmen." Indeed, in March 1982, Escobar had been elected as an alternate congressman to the House of Representatives. (Every member of the House and every senator in Colombia is elected with an alternate, in case he or she becomes indisposed.)

But not long after *Tranquilandia* went into full production, Colombia gained a new minister of justice who was not in the pocket of the traffickers, and who, with the help of the Americans, was determined to expose them. As the Cartel was soon to discover, his animosity ran very deep and, at least towards Escobar, it became extremely personal.

Rodrigo Lara Bonilla was born to be a politician. After graduating from law school in Bogotá, he returned to his hometown of Neiva to become its mayor at the age of twenty-three. In 1974, when he was only twenty-eight, he was elected to the Senate, and he was a leading activist in the ruling Liberal party. When he and others grew weary of the Liberal establishment, he helped to form the breakaway New Liberalism party, which did sufficiently well in the 1982 elections to be given one cabinet post in the new Conservative government of Belisario Betancur Cuartas. There was never much doubt that Lara was the New Liberal who would get the job.

He was appointed justice minister by President Betancur in August 1983. The news caused shock waves among all of those politicians who had taken money from drug traffickers because Lara had long threatened to expose them. Now that he was in a position to do so, they hastily mounted a counterattack.

On August 16, 1983, barely a week after his appointment, during a debate in Congress, Lara was accused of accepting drug money to finance his own political campaigns. To prove it, supposedly, his opponents produced a cancelled check and a tape recording, secretly made, of an ambiguous conversation between Lara and a drug trafficker named Evaristo Porras. Ironically, most of that conversation concerned Pablo Escobar's activities as a drug trafficker, and it was not lost on Lara that all of those engaged in the attack upon him were associated in some way with Escobar. But for most people, that was lost in the uproar: "So now the birds are firing at the guns," said Lara.

The attack was skillfully constructed and might have done fatal injury to Lara's reputation. Fortunately for him, however, before the debate could end, the ABC television network in New York revealed the imminent broadcast of a documentary on cocaine trafficking, and invited reporters to a preview. What they saw, and what some of them reported back to Colombian newspapers, was the first public identification of alternate Congressman Escobar as a major trafficker. (The program also identified the Ochoas and Carlos Lehder.)

Suddenly Escobar found himself in an unwelcome spotlight. A Bogotá newspaper, *El Espectador,* began to probe Escobar's criminal record, and also pointed out that two policemen who had arrested him in 1976 had been killed, and that the case file against him had been mysteriously "misplaced."

Encouraged by what he perceived as support from *El Espectador,* Lara ordered the case reopened, and Escobar was eventually forced to withdraw from politics. The American Embassy in Bogotá cancelled Escobar's tourist visa. A Medellín judge ruled that Escobar should be detained because there was strong evidence that he had, indeed, had something to do with the murder of two detectives. Another judge later rescinded the arrest warrant, of course—but then a Customs tribunal began to investigate Escobar for the illegal importation of exotic animals, to wit, elephants and camels for his private zoo.

Lara increased his public attacks against Escobar, naming him as a founding member of MAS. Escobar sued him for libel, claiming: "I'm just a victim of a persecution campaign." There was some truth to that. Lara said the battle was not between drug traffickers and the government, but rather between "Escobar and me."

Throughout this period, Lara's office phones were constantly tapped and his conversations were recorded; to prove it anonymous callers would play the recordings back to him. He received death threats on his private phone and police uncovered an assassination plot against him. Undaunted, Lara pressed on. The narcotics unit of the National Police was then headed by Colonel Jaime Ramírez, perhaps the most competent police officer in Bogotá and certainly one of the bravest. He had briefly worked in Medellín and had assembled detailed profiles of the major traffickers, but there had never been the political will to allow him to use them. Now there was: Lara gave Ramírez carte blanche, and told him to hit the traffickers where it would hurt most.

In 1983 the Colombian government had placed strict controls on imports of ether and other chemicals necessary for the production of cocaine (after the DEA had claimed only 2 percent of Colombia's ether imports were used for pharmaceutical purposes). But shipments from the United States and West Germany were still entering the country illegally and, with the help of the DEA, Ramírez set out to trace them. The breakthrough in the joint investigation came on November 22, 1983, when Francisco Torres, a Medellín businessman operating an import-export business in Miami, walked into the Newark, New Jersey, offices of J. T. Baker Chemical Supply Co., and attempted to order thirteen hundred 55-gallon drums of high-grade ethyl ether—equal to almost half Colombia's annual ether imports.

Ethyl ether, a surgical anesthetic, is best known today as the single most efficient solvent used in cocaine manufacturing. In the United States a 55-gallon drum sells for about $300. In Colombia, following the government's crackdown on imports, one drum was worth $5,000.

There were—and are—only a small number of manufacturers of ethyl ether, most of them in the United States and West Germany. And in America at least, ether manufacturers have unwritten agreements with the DEA to tip the agency off about "suspicious" customers. So when Francisco Torres, the little man from Medellín, attempted to buy from J. T. Baker enough ethyl ether to process sixty-six *tons* of cocaine, and said he would pay $300,000 in cash, and asked for the drums to be unlabeled, and said he would accept delivery anywhere in the United States or Canada, J. T. Baker stalled Torres—and immediately informed the DEA.

Ten days later, on December 2, Torres received a telephone call at his office in Miami from Melvin Schabilion, who described himself as a representative of North Central Industrial Chemicals (NCIC) of Chicago. In fact, Schabilion was a DEA agent, and NCIC was an undercover operation of the DEA's Chicago field office. (The name chosen for the supposed chemical company was an inside joke: NCIC actually stands for National Crime Information Center, the FBI's repository for its millions of criminal records.)

Schabilion told Torres the NCIC was in a position to supply him with the ether he had been unable to get from J. T. Baker and, on December 6, Schabilion and Harry Fullet, another undercover agent, traveled to Miami to discuss the details. Torres met the agents at a Ramada Inn near the international airport, and thoroughly incriminated himself. He said he needed the first three hundred drums of his order before the end of the month and, since the ether was going to Colombia, the drums should be falsely labeled to defeat import controls.

No problem, said the undercover agents—a message Torres doubtless passed on when he telephoned a number in Barranquilla, Colombia, that is listed to Armando Bravo-Muñoz, the owner of a small airline who, in the DEA's view, is a functionary of the Medellín Cartel.

When, on December 14, Torres went to Chicago to make the final shipping arrangements he candidly told agent Fullet the ether was going to be used for cocaine processing, but that his role was limited to buying and transporting the chemicals. The following day he paid Fullet and Schabilion $15,000 in cash as a down payment, and instructed them to label the drums as ethyl formate and ethylene glycol. He added that his clients were willing to purchase "as much ether as can be provided."

The DEA's first shipment of ether to the cartel, sent via New Orleans, consisted of seventy-six 55-gallon drums, two of which were equipped with electronic transmitters the size of cigarette packs. They were packed in Styrofoam and, together with battery packs, concealed in a false bottom welded into each drum. Thin filaments acting as antennae ran up the sides of each drum, and transmitted a signal on a pre-set frequency that allowed satellites of the National Security Agency (NSA) to pinpoint their precise location.

When the cargo reached Colombia, the satellites enabled the DEA to trace it: first, to *Hacienda Veracruz*, Jorge Ochoa's vast cattle ranch near Barranquilla; next to the isolated province of Caquetá. Colonel Ramírez had already established—again, with the aid of American satellites—a startling increase in radio traffic in Caquetá province, and now another satellite obtained the first photographs of the *Tranquilandia* complex, revealing airstrips that were in almost constant use.

In conditions of extreme secrecy, Ramírez planned an operation, code-named *Yarí '84*. He assembled a specialized group of thirty-four police and army officers, supported by two helicopters and a small plane, and devised a detailed strategy to raid *Tranquilandia* on Saturday, March 10, 1984. Only a handful of people knew: Lara, the minister of defense, the director of the national police, Ramírez, and his closest aides.

But on March 9, Ramírez's brother, a retired major with the National Police, was resting at his Bogotá home when the doorbell rang. His unexpected visitors were four men, wearing cowboy hats and boots. One of them said: "Listen, Major, your brother is about to disturb our work, and we would like him not to do that." Baffled, the major told them he did not know what they were talking about. "Listen," the man said, "just tell him that we have 400 million pesos [then worth approximately $3 million] for him, which we will deposit anywhere he wants, if he just stays put."

Major Ramírez called his brother's house, but it was too late: the colonel's wife said he had left Bogotá for the weekend, on business.

The raid on *Tranquilandia* took place as planned at two o'clock on Saturday afternoon. It was not entirely successful. When the raiding party was landed by helicopter at the far end of the main runway, it encountered heavy armed resistance from FARC guerrillas, and Ramírez and his men were unable to prevent several helicopters from taking off. Over one hundred people fled across the river in boats or by using an ingenious system of ropes specifically designed for rapid escape. Only forty-five "dogwashers," including four women, were arrested. No major drug traffickers, nor even the complex manager, were caught.

But what Ramírez and his men did find was the largest cocaine facility in the world. At the *Tranquilandia* camp, they confiscated 2,500 kilos of pure cocaine, 19 machine guns and rifles, hundreds of rounds of ammunition, 1 mortar, 7 portable radios, 27 military uniforms, 4 electrical plants, 1 motorcycle, 2 vehicles, 4 tractors, 55 drums of ether, and 3,000 units of other chemical ingredients. At *Villa Coca* they uncovered 4 fully equipped laboratories, 3,500 kilos of cocaine base, 30 more kilos of pure cocaine, 2,000 drums of ether, 4 small airplanes, and 1 helicopter. At *Coquilandia,* they found 5,500 kilos of cocaine, 15 laboratories, 4 electrical plants, 5,000 drums of ether, 3,500 plastic cans, 4 ovens, 4 drying trays each heated by 500 bulbs, 10 washing machines, vast amounts of fuel, other chemicals, several hundred rolls of masking tape, and thousands of plastic bags. The street value of the cocaine alone was estimated at

$1.2 billion. When the raiding party dumped the cocaine into the Yarí River, its waters turned white.

A more careful search of the "executive offices" at *Tranquilandia* produced ledgers and documents linking the Ochoas, Pablo Escobar and Gonzalo Rodríguez Gacha to the complex. Other documents detailed the arrival of chemicals and the purchases of coca base and paste, showing that Armando Bravo-Muñoz's Aviaco Airlines flew equipment, workers, and chemicals to *Tranquilandia.* Colombian police also found the general manager's diary, which contained a warning: "This is the property of Guillermo León Ochoa [assumed, by the police, to be related to the Ochoa family]. Don't steal it, and don't pretend that it has been lost. Thank you."

Tranquilandia gave the Colombian government a field day and, for once, the US government could genuinely rejoice. For Ramírez, however, there was a bitter aftertaste. Through talking to his brother, he realized there had been a leak, and he eventually came to suspect one of his closest aides. Unable to prove anything, he simply fired the man. A few weeks later, the burnt and mutilated body of the aide was found outside Bogotá, together with the bodies of two unidentified females. As with most drug-related murders in Colombia, these homicides remain unsolved.

Colonel Jaime Ramírez would eventually pay for his temerity: he was murdered outside Bogotá on November 17, 1985, while returning from a weekend outing with his family. But the immediate blame was laid at the door of the justice minister.

Seven weeks after the raid, on the evening of April 30, 1984, Lara was returning home from work in his official Mercedes when a red Yamaha motorcycle pulled up alongside the right rear window. The man riding pillion opened fire with an Ingram .45 submachine gun, and Lara was hit eight times. The impact of the bullets almost tore his head from his body.

The fleeing *asesinos de la moto* threw a hand grenade at Lara's bodyguards, but their bike skidded on a bend and they fell off. One broke his neck and died instantly. The survivor said they had been hired in Medellín, where they were told they would be "bumping off" someone who owed money for cocaine.

A Bogotá judge who investigated Lara's assassination found evidence that Escobar, the Ochoas, and Rodríguez Gacha were behind it, but before he could prove that, he, too, was killed.

The government reacted with enormous anger. Carlos Lehder's extradition order, which had gathered dust on the presidential desk for months, was promptly signed by President Betancur—though, by then, Lehder was nowhere to be found. A state of siege was formally resurrected (it had been in effect, for other reasons, for most of the previous thirty years), unleashing an "unprecedented" crackdown against the Ochoas, Escobar, and Rodríguez Gacha. But they had also disappeared—except for Don Fabio, who handed himself in to the police in Medellín. He was taken to Bogotá for questioning, but was later released for lack of evidence.

It turned out that the others had not fled very far. On May 26, less than four weeks after Lara's assassination, the leaders of the Cartel met in secret with Colombia's attorney general, Carlos Jiménez Gómez, in the Soloy Hotel in Panama City. The traffickers had met the attorney general three times before, always in secret, to discuss the possibility of a grant of amnesty. In Panama, they handed him a formal, type-written proposal, which they asked him to deliver to President Betancur and to the American Embassy in Bogotá. In some respects the memorandum was remarkably frank. It said, in part:

> It has taken a very long time to set up our organizations, and it would take ten years or more to replace them. Today, these organizations control approximately 70 to 80 per cent of the world drug trade.
>
> Even if Colombia is willing to withdraw from the drug trade, the total elimination of the problem will only be achieved by crop substitution in Bolivia and Peru and through extensive campaigns against abuse in countries with a drug problem.
>
> Our market share currently represents an annual income of $2 billion, part of which is fed back into Colombia.
>
> Those of us who control cocaine smuggling do not take part and have not taken part in coca production in the country or in the distribution of *basuco.*
>
> Putting an end to drug trafficking in Colombia will lead, in the

short term, to price increases in the consumer markets, reduction in quality, and marketing problems, and, as a result, to a decrease in the number of users.

Dismantling the trafficking apparatus cannot be total. There will always be minor smugglers trying to move the product in small quantities via travellers using luggage, false heels, etc.

And then, some necessary dissimulation:

Our organizations have no direct or indirect responsibility in the assassination of Doctor Rodrigo Lara Bonilla.

We do not have, nor do we acknowledge, any links with the rebel groups. Our activities have at no time tried to replace the democratic and republican form of government in Colombia. It is therefore unfair to talk about the existence of the narco-guerrilla, a vicious and suspicious concept promoted before the death of Doctor Lara Bonilla.

The political activity of some of our members was exclusively motivated by a desire to fight the extradition treaty signed with the United States of America.

In the memorandum the Cartel offered to close down cocaine laboratories and illegal airstrips; pull out of all stages of smuggling in which it admitted it was involved; help the government with anti-drug campaigns; withdraw from politics; and repatriate their fortunes. In return, the Cartel asked for the safe return of its leaders to Colombia as free citizens. But it also demanded the revision of Colombia's extradition treaty with the United States, and the suspension of all current extradition proceedings. Finally, the memorandum asked that the US government be informed of the plan, which, the Cartel said, would in the end "benefit the American people."

The American embassy in Bogotá did not see it that way, wisely. It leaked the news that the attorney general of Colombia was, apparently, in cozy consultation with notorious drug traffickers, and the resulting uproar prevented the Betancur government from even considering the Cartel's offer.

That was just as well, because the Cartel never had any intention of abandoning its lucrative industry. At precisely the moment it was, supposedly, negotiating with the attorney general at the Panama "summit," it was simultaneously finalizing other plans that would deal with the consequences of Lara's murder, and allow business to continue much as before.

20

"Our Most Costly Failure"

On June 14, 1984, less than three weeks after the abortive "summit" in Panama, Jorge Ochoa; his wife, María Lía; and their baby daughter, María del Mar, arrived in the Spanish capital of Madrid to begin a new life.

Before leaving Panama, Ochoa had obtained a fresh identity: a passport, an identity card, a driving license, and credit cards, including American Express and Diners Club, all in the name of Moisés Moreno Miranda. He even bought a marriage certificate for Moisés Moreno Miranda and María Lía Posada Echeverría showing their wedding date as September 9, 1983; he kept it in a little black folder of family photographs. There was no need to change María Lía's identity. She traveled on a Colombian passport bearing her maiden name.

In their first few weeks in Madrid, Jorge and María Lía spent their time rebuilding their lives with style. Their first major acquisition, purchased in María Lía's name, was a house in Pozuela de Alarcón, a fashionable suburb of Madrid, which had a swimming pool, tennis courts, and a discotheque. Ochoa bought a new Mercedes-Benz, in which he toured Madrid and its environs in search of other real estate investments, and he found and purchased a second home, a spacious apartment in Calle Miguel Angel in the heart of the city. Meanwhile, María Lía shopped for fine jewelry and designer clothes, and works of art such as a Miró lithograph that she bought for the drawing room of their apartment.

When they had settled down, their frequent outings were made possible by Solange, a Bolivian maid and au pair, who adored and cared for the couple's baby daughter. Most often the Ochoas chose the company of another South American couple, also newly arrived in Madrid: a wealthy Venezuelan by the name of Gilberto González Linares and his wife Gladys. They had taken a pleasant apartment in Calle General Oráa, close to the Ochoas' apartment, and had also bought two other large apartments and what seemed to be a small fleet of Mercedes. Gilberto was not, of course, the Venezuelan he pretended to be: his real name was Gilberto Rodríguez Orejuela, the son of a little-known and impoverished Colombian painter. Rodríguez controlled a small empire of discount pharmacy stores, banks— in Colombia and Panama—and radio stations. Most of his brothers and sisters, their spouses, and their grown-up children—among them lawyers, economists, accountants, and company directors—worked for his growing *Grupo Rodríguez,* which also included Cali's best soccer team. According to the DEA, he had obtained the means to acquire that empire by distributing tons of cocaine throughout the United States. And he, too, had fled Colombia after the assassination of the justice minister.

From their new base in Madrid, Ochoa and Rodríguez studied the relatively unexplored European cocaine market, and made plans to buy a large ranch in Badajoz, near the border with Portugal, to use as a center of operations. Teodoro Castrillón, one of Ochoa's lieutenants and a trusted "son," was sent to England, Germany, Spain, and Holland to establish contacts within the growing Colombian communities in those countries, and to develop infrastructures which would mimic the cocaine distribution networks in the United States.

Meanwhile, in Latin America, other members of the Cartel put the finishing touches to reorganization plans that were designed to cope with the temporary difficulties in Colombia, and to suit the times. The problem was that, for once, the United States government knew exactly what they were up to.

Jorge Ochoa and other leading members of the Cartel knew him as Ellis McKenzie, but his real name was Adler Berriman

"Barry" Seal. Although he was known as the most prolific drug smuggler in his home state of Louisiana, the authorities there had never come close to proving his guilt. Seal delighted in provoking them: he would walk up to narcotics agents in New Orleans or Baton Rouge, and say: "You dumb sonofabitch, you'll never catch me."

He was the eldest son of a Louisiana candy wholesaler, and had been passionate about flying since childhood. He made his first solo flight at age fifteen, and got his first job as a pilot towing advertising banners. After a brief stint with the US Army Special Forces in Vietnam, he was accepted by Trans World Airlines (TWA) as a flight engineer, and, at twenty-six, he became the youngest 747 pilot in the nation.

It was while flying for TWA that Seal agreed to transport a shipment of plastic explosives from Miami to an anti-Castro group in Mexico, but the "buyer" turned out to be an under-cover federal agent, who arrested him. Although charges were subsequently dismissed, the incident cost Seal his job with the airline. So, in 1977, he began working as an independent avia-tion consultant, traveling extensively throughout Latin Amer-ica, where a friend introduced him to a group of Colombian marijuana traffickers. After a couple of trial runs, he knew he had discovered a new career: "Smuggling was so simple, so anonymous, and so lucrative that it eventually became my sole occupation," he later said. In 1981, in Medellín, he was enrolled by the Ochoa family to fly less bulky but much more profitable shipments of cocaine.

In his seven years as a smuggler, Seal made more than one hundred clandestine flights into the United States without being intercepted. His services came to be in such demand by the Cartel that, eventually, he hired other pilots to help him. He bragged that he made as much as $50 million.

He raised to an art form the so-called "sea-spray height" flying technique, keeping his aircraft so close to the water that spray from the waves misted the windshield. He also pi-oneered a new aerial smuggling route that avoided both the Bahamas and Florida by exploiting what he called the "lax radar coverage" over the Gulf of Mexico, from eastern Texas to the Alabama-Florida state line. Since most of the flights were at night, Seal equipped himself and his pilots with powerful night-vision goggles, at $5,000 a pair, that magnified available light 50,000 times. He and his men air-dropped duffel bags full of cocaine at predetermined locations in Louisiana, where waiting helicopters took them on to their final destination.

Seal also oversaw part of the distribution process in the United States, coordinating between the Cartel in Medellín and its representatives across the country. He was frequently to be seen in Baton Rouge, where he lived, with a bag full of quarters making simultaneous calls from adjacent pay phones. To stop the anxious Louisiana authorities from listening in, and to further infuriate them, he used a voice scrambler.

But for all his cleverness, Seal eventually fell victim to every trafficker's occupational hazard—an informant who needed to save his own skin. In late 1982 the informant told the DEA in Miami about some of Seal's activities and an agent named Randy Beasley telephoned colleagues in Baton Rouge and said: "Hey, I got a guy, he's a pilot, he's from Baton Rouge and they call him *El Gordo"* (The Fat Man—Seal, at 5 feet, 9 inches, weighed 250 pounds). "Boy, we know who you got," said Baton Rouge. "And, if you've got him we're going to come down and kiss you."

As a result, in February 1983 a grand jury in Fort Lauderdale, Florida, indicted Seal on charges of smuggling 200,000 Quaaludes and of conspiracy to distribute, and possess with intent to distribute, drugs. Out on $250,000 bond, Seal spent much of the next year trying to negotiate a deal with the DEA and the US attorney's office, but nobody would listen to him. In February 1984, Seal went to trial and was convicted. With sentencing set for May, Seal flew to Washington without telling his own attorney, and asked to see staff members of the vice-president's task force. They would only agree to meet him on the street, but then, impressed by what he said, they escorted him to the DEA's headquarters where Seal revealed some of what he knew about the Medellín Cartel. He also volunteered to act as an undercover operative, and provide evidence against the Cartel's leading members It was an extraordinary offer: for the first time, the DEA had a "CI" with access to the very nerve center of the conspiracy: Don Fabio Ochoa's *Finca La Loma,* the house on the hill.

On April 7, 1984, Barry Seal flew from Miami to a landing strip in northern Colombia accompanied by another pilot, Félix Bates, who did not know that Seal was now a spy. They proceeded to Medellín, where at the Ochoas' hillside house they met Jorge and his two brothers, Fabio, Jr., and Juan David, and Pablo Escobar. The Ochoas wanted Seal and Bates to transport fifteen hundred kilos of cocaine "as soon as possible," and then return for another fifteen hundred kilos—two vast shipments by the standards of that time.

But something even more startling was to emerge from that meeting: Jorge Ochoa told Seal that he had acquired a 6,000-foot landing strip in Nicaragua that he wanted Seal to inspect. He claimed that the Sandinista government had agreed to enlarge the airstrip and build a hangar there, and to allow these facilities to be used for the transshipment of drugs. According to Seal, Ochoa said that although the Cartel did not particularly share the Sandinistas' political philosophy, "they serve our means and we serve theirs."

During the next two months, Seal shuttled back and forth between Medellín, Panama, and Miami, meeting with Ochoa and Escobar, all the while gathering intelligence about the Cartel that was of incalculable value to the DEA. On one of his visits to Panama, Seal was introduced to Pedro Capell, the Cartel's chief accountant. In Miami, Seal met Carlos Bustamante, Escobar's distributor in the United States, who told him he was running five hundred kilos of cocaine a week through the Auto World car dealership on Miami's South Dixie Highway. Seal introduced two of "my men" to Bustamante, who did not even suspect that they were DEA agents; the first, and probably the last, US government men to infiltrate the Medellín Cartel.

And, most dramatic of all, Seal met the Cartel's man in Managua, Federico Vaughan, who described himself as a high-ranking functionary of the Nicaraguan government, and who US intelligence said was the senior aide to the minister of the interior, Tomás Borge. On May 20, 1984, Seal and his co-pilot, Félix Bates, flew to Managua, where Vaughan took them to the Los Brasiles airstrip, twelve miles northeast of the city. Vaughan told them that they could land there to refuel without impediment and he gave them an identification code that would allow for their recognition by air-traffic controllers at the Sandino International Airport.

It was sensational stuff, and it is not difficult to imagine the excitement it caused at the DEA, and in the higher echelons of the American government. All that was now required was proof.

Unfortunately, the Ochoas' desire to move the first fifteen-hundred kilo shipment of cocaine "as soon as possible" was continually thwarted by mishaps and events. Just hours before Seal and Bates were due to leave for Colombia to pick up the load, one of the engines of their airplane failed during a test flight. The operation was canceled a second time when the assassination of Lara, the justice minister, made things too hot. Next, Bates had to pull out of the scheme when his wife was arrested for cocaine possession. On May 28, when Seal and a new copilot finally made it to Colombia, and collected the cocaine, their plane crashed on take-off, almost killing both of them. Seal blamed Carlos Lehder, who supervised the loading, because he forced Seal to leave at gunpoint, despite the exceptionally muddy state of the airstrip.

And on June 3, 1984, after Seal had finally managed to transport the cocaine from Colombia to Nicaragua in a new plane provided by Jorge Ochoa, things went dramatically wrong when he attempted to resume his journey to Florida. Having refueled and waited until it got dark, Seal took off and followed the flight plan, which led him a mile north of Managua, where he was supposed to head east, out over Lake Managua and toward the Atlantic Ocean. But there was an air curfew in effect that night, and when soldiers on the ground heard the noise of the plane, they assumed the Contra rebels had launched an air attack, and then opened fire. Seal's aircraft was hit in the left engine, and unable to control it, he decided to turn back "to save the aircraft and probably my life." He radioed the airstrip he had taken off from, but nobody answered. He then broadcast a Mayday alert, and landed at Sandino International Airport, where he and his copilot were promptly arrested by

Sandinista soldiers. According to Seal, they were held in a "torture chamber" near the terminal until Federico Vaughan arrived to obtain their freedom.

Pablo Escobar was in Managua, and so too was Gonzalo Rodríguez Gacha, and they decided that Seal should return to the United States to find a new aircraft in which to transport the cocaine. They also asked him to purchase and bring back to Managua some sophisticated radio equipment, and $500,000 in spending money.

It was an opportunity that the American government found too good to resist. On June 25, when Seal flew back to Managua, it was in a Vietnam-vintage C-123 cargo plane, painted in camouflage colors and which Seal named "The Fat Lady." A few days earlier, at the Rickenbacker Air Force Base in Ohio, technicians from the CIA had installed a remote-controlled 35-mm camera, hidden inside an electronics box that was mounted on a bulkhead facing the rear cargo doors. When the plane landed at Los Brasiles, and men dressed in the uniforms of the Sandinista soldiers began loading the cocaine, the remote-control device Seal had been given did not work. But Seal was able to operate the camera manually, covering the noise of the shutter as best he could, and the pictures he took included one that showed Pablo Escobar and a man who was later identified by the CIA as the high-ranking Nicaraguan functionary, Federico Vaughan.

When Seal returned safely to Florida, it was these grainy images, and not the cocaine he also brought, that caused the excitement. Three days later General Paul Gorman, head of the US Southern Command, was able to state with confidence, in a speech to the American Chamber of Commerce in San Salvador, that: "The traffickers in drugs are conduits for subversion. The *commandantes* in Nicaragua are involved in those movements." It was an extraordinarily hasty revelation to make, because Seal was still gathering evidence for the DEA, and still shuttling back and forth to Nicaragua.

And, inevitably, it got picked up. In mid-July, the DEA learned that *The Washington Times* was about to publish detailed accusations against the Sandinistas, based on Seal's mission, and quoting "US government sources." Seal was actually in mid-air, on his way back to Nicaragua, when the news came through. He was hastily recalled, and an undercover radio operator in Nicaragua who had been assisting Seal was advised to flee.

The Washington Times story was published on Tuesday, July 17, 1984. The next day other newspapers revealed that the DEA had incriminating photographs of the Sandinistas, and information from "a pilot." Horrified agents of the DEA could only scramble to arrest Carlos Bustamante and other members of the Cartel in Miami before they could flee—and wonder at the rank stupidity of the "Sandinista bashing" that had ruined their case. "We had hoped to go a lot further with it," said one of them. "Today was not our best day."

However, a few weeks later, in August 1984, Fernando Martínez Cos-Gayón, head of the Madrid Drug Squad, began to receive disturbing reports from his "cocaine team." An investigation into bands of Colombians, who seemed to be muscling in on the traditional local dealers, had turned up evidence of bigger fish than the Spaniards alone could handle. Intercepted telephone calls and other intelligence had revealed that high-level Colombian traffickers were living in Spain and directing the movement of significant amounts of cocaine, unheard of for Spanish consumption. And Spanish authorities had received an anonymous note saying that one Jorge Ochoa was living in Madrid under an assumed name.

Deeply disturbed, Cos-Gayón went to the American Embassy in Madrid in late August to see Jimmy Kibble, one of the DEA's two undercover agents stationed in Spain. Kibble had helped the Spanish police on many occasions, usually by posing as a London buyer which, despite his Hispanic looks and his strong New York accent, he does remarkably well. When Kibble reported the news to Washington, in his words, "bells went off and phones started ringing."

When Kibble subsequently reported that the Spanish police had located Ochoa, the Department of Justice and the US attorney's office in Miami both told Kibble to press them, to "go out and arrest this man right away." Kibble refused. The Spaniards wanted to watch Ochoa for a while, to see where he might lead them, and Kibble told the Justice Department: "We don't want to spoil the relationship we have with them. They've played ball with us. Give them a chance. These are very competent police people so they aren't going to lose Ochoa."

And though the Justice Department was deeply unhappy with the delay, and Kibble's telephone never stopped ringing, within weeks Ochoa had inadvertently led the police to Gilberto Rodríguez. As a result, Kibble now had New York and California on the phone as well, clamoring for Rodríguez's immediate arrest. Again Kibble refused. He pointed out that if he had obeyed his original orders, they would have lost Rodríguez. And again he was proved right. In November Cos-Gayón came to him a third time with a third name: Teodoro Castrillón, Ochoa's lieutenant, who had been building distribution networks in Europe.

On November 15, 1984, Cos-Gayon finally gave the order, and Ochoa and Rodríguez, together with their wives, were arrested in Calle General Oraa close to the American Embassy in Madrid and near to Rodríguez's own apartment. The four Colombians were all charged under the antiterrorist act—charges that were not to stick, but which allowed Cos-Gayón to keep them at the Puerta de Sol police station for seven days of interrogation.

For María Lía, Ochoa's wife, it was a terrifying experience, her first encounter with the US "bogeymen" who, she became convinced, were out to get her. "I was interrogated by Spanish police, but the American agents were there in the police station, telling the Spanish police what to ask," she said. María Lía found her interrogation perplexing: "They kept asking me about the guerrillas, about the M-19, and I kept saying I didn't know them or anything about them." (The American agents in the police station were Jimmy Kibble and Billie Mockler, a DEA agent from New York who had headed the investigation into Rodríguez for the previous seven years. Kibble laughs at the thought that they had anything to do with the interrogation: "Mockler," he said, "doesn't even speak Spanish.")

Afterwards, María Lía was transferred to Yesería women's prison, where she was held for six weeks, a period so dreadful that she could not bear to think about it afterwards. María Lía was Jorge's second wife. An unassuming, pretty woman from Medellín, she was then twenty-eight years old but—tall and thin, with long dark curly hair, pale skin, and delicate features—she looked much younger. Before her arrest, she claims, she was a naive girl from a Colombian mountain town who knew nothing of life and less of *narcotráfico* and guerrillas. The experience certainly seemed to have unhinged her: once released, she spent the next year or more moping in her luxurious Madrid flat, too listless to go to the shops or galleries, too downhearted to make conversation with anyone. She refused to read newspapers, in case they contained anything about Jorge: "The newspapers just print the terrible things the Americans say about us," she said.

Meanwhile, after their interrogations—which produced very little—Ochoa and Rodríguez were removed to prison cells in Alcalá-Meco, Spain's toughest jail, ninety minutes by car from Madrid, which has neither sanitation nor central heating, and where prisoners are made to stand isolated in their cells for hours on end. From there, they began to wage a propaganda war against the Spanish police and the DEA. Almost every day, Spanish newspapers carried stories that the two Colombians had been denied their rights in the police station, interrogated by DEA agents, and offered their freedom if they would denounce the Sandinistas as drug-traffickers. These stories sent Jimmy Kibble and his DEA colleagues into a white rage.

While María Lía contemplated the possibility of life without Jorge, the real American "bogeyman" arrived in town. Roger Yochelson, a squarely built man with a pockmarked face, who wore pinstriped suits with brown leather cowboy boots, was a lawyer from the Justice Department in Washington who had been dispatched to Madrid to secure the extradition of Ochoa and Rodríguez to the United States. He was a staffer at the Office of International Affairs, which dedicates 80 percent of its time to extraditions. Yochelson dealt with the Spanish- and Portuguese-speaking countries, plus Canada and Israel, and of his extradition cases about 60 percent concern drugs, usually cocaine.

Yochelson's job was to liase with the Spanish authorities which, in turn, had to satisfy the courts in Madrid of the validity of the charges that Ochoa and Rodríguez faced in the United States. The job of persuading the courts otherwise fell to a small army of Spanish and Colombian lawyers—including experts on extradition, and constitutional and criminal law—who were assembled at a cost to Ochoa that American officials in Madrid estimated to be several million dollars.

But it was not only money that brought them together. The American evidence against Ochoa depended almost entirely on sworn statements made by Barry Seal. And while such evidence should have been more than sufficient to demonstrate that a *prima facie* case existed—all that is normally required to win extradition—it was complicated, and ultimately compromised, by what became known as the "Nicaraguan Factor."

Enrique Gimbernat Ordeig was a highly respected lawyer in Madrid who had never before taken on a drugs case: his more usual concerns were with drafting a new Spanish penal code, and writing learned articles on abortion, rape, the death penalty, antiterrorist laws, and the Palestinian problem. But Gimbernat could not resist adding his considerable clout to Ochoa's cause because he became convinced that the real target of the US government was Nicaragua. He did not believe Seal's "fishy" allegations, but that was not the point. He claimed that President Reagan had telephoned Spain's prime minister to press for Ochoa's extradition and that the attorney general, Ed Meese, had met with the Spanish justice minister, and that other Spanish ministers were similarly put under pressure by their US counterparts. "The ministers in turn telephoned the judges to put pressure on them," said Gimbernat. "This is really scandalous. It is a crime under our criminal code: an attack on the independence of the judiciary.

"I just do not understand it. Why is the US so interested in this case, unless it is because they want to incriminate Nicaragua? In Spain it has been treated as a matter of state: some leverage must have been applied, some high-level political issue, some treaty, something to do with withdrawal of personnel from US bases. I don't know. But I do know that I have never seen anything like it."

While Barry Seal's remarkable cooperation with the DEA had won him friends in Miami and the promise that he would not be sentenced to more than ten years imprisonment for smuggling Quaaludes, his relations with the authorities in Louisiana worsened distinctly. "Miami thinks the guy is the greatest thing since sliced bread, which is usual, because he's helping them," said Al Winters, chief of the Organized Crime Strike Force in New Orleans. "And Baton Rouge thinks he's the worst drug dealer in the history of Louisiana." Rumors that Seal had made close to $700,000 during the Nicaraguan operation, and had been allowed to keep it to cover his expenses, did not help matters.

Stanford Bardwell, the US attorney in Baton Rouge, was determined to press charges against Seal in Louisiana, and negotiations with Seal's attorney, and with the US attorney's office in Miami, failed to produce a compromise. So Seal, as arrogant as ever, devised a self-defense strategy. He contacted John Camp, an investigative reporter at WBRZ Television in Baton Rouge, and explained his plight: that while he was considered a vital witness in one federal district, he was hunted in another. The net result was a one-hour documentary, entitled "Uncle Sam Wants You," which aired on November 19, 1984— by coincidence, four days after Ochoa's arrest in Spain.

In it Seal, who wore combat fatigues and sunglasses, was extremely disdainful of Baton Rouge law enforcement agents, and produced a witness to argue on camera that the Louisiana authorities were trying to get him, "whatever it costs, whatever it takes."

It had some effect in that the authorities in Louisiana did eventually give Seal a deal: he pled guilty to two token counts, one of smuggling cocaine and one of money laundering, in return for which he was guaranteed a penalty that would match whatever was imposed in Florida when he was sentenced for smuggling Quaaludes.

But his television defense went awry. Bardwell, the US Attorney for Baton Rouge, was furious; two Baton Rouge narcotics agents attacked by Seal in the documentary sued the television station; and, in Medellín, Colombia, Jorge Ochoa's younger brother, Fabio, learned the real identity of the pilot he knew only as Ellis McKenzie.

Max Mermelstein was a thirty-four-year-old, overweight man from Brooklyn with an associate's degree in applied sciences who later became chief engineer at the Sheraton Hotel in San Juan, Puerto Rico. By 1978 he had settled in Miami and gone into business for himself importing shoes into Miami from Spain. Around the same time, he developed a more lucrative sideline, providing false documentation to Colombian drug traffickers who wished to reside in the United States. One of those he helped was a Colombian named Rafael Cardona Salazar who, in time, became the principal representative of the Medellín Cartel in Miami. The two men became friends, and Mermelstein asked Cardona to be the godfather of one of his children. That was despite the fact that Cardona had killed a man in his presence, and that Mermelstein felt he could never refuse any request Cardona made; if he did, he believed, his wife and children would be in danger.

And at Cardona's behest Mermelstein went willingly to Colombia to meet Jorge Ochoa and Pablo Escobar. The first thing he learned was the leaders of the Cartel did not allow anybody to use the word "cocaine" in their presence—though they thought it a "harmless vice" that was making them multimillionaires.

Mermelstein would later say that all of the Ochoas he met at Jorge Ochoa's *Hacienda Veracruz* were cordial, soft-spoken, and well-mannered—none more so than Jorge. For example, when Fabio, his younger brother, drove Ochoa and Mermelstein to the ranch's private airstrip in a pickup truck, and it was raining, Jorge insisted that he be the one to sit in the back and get wet. "That's the type of person he is," Mermelstein said. And Jorge repeatedly asked Mermelstein if he was happy, and satisfied with the Ochoas' hospitality. Mermelstein then came to the conclusion that the most feared leaders of the Medellín Cartel were simple people who understood all "the proper values."

He found the Ochoas to be modest in their habits; only occasionally would they drink a glass of wine with their meals. Pablo Escobar, on the other hand, enjoyed drinking—though not excessively—and was always "elegant and eloquent."

Upon his return to Miami, Mermelstein became a trusted servant of the Cartel under Cardona, overseeing transportation arrangements, scheduling flights, counting inventory, and planning distribution of cocaine and collections of monies. He was told by Cardona that there were only two ways to cease his employment with the Cartel—go to jail, or be killed.

In December 1984 Mermelstein attended a meeting at a house in northeast Miami that Cardona used alternately as an office, a stash house, and even a cocaine laboratory. Among those present was a man known to Mermelstein only as Cano, who had just arrived from Medellín bearing a message from Fabio Ochoa, Jr., and a Betamax video cassette. It was a copy of "Uncle Sam Wants You," which the group assembled in Cardona's house watched in silence. When it was over, Cano said he had been sent to Miami by Ochoa and Pablo Escobar to ensure that Seal never testified: "This *pajarito*—little bird—has to be located as soon as possible," he said.

Cano said that the Cartel would pay $1 million to have Seal kidnapped, or $500,000 for his murder. Turning to Mermelstein, Cardona said: *"Compadre,* you make the arrangements. You are an American. I don't want any Latins in Baton Rouge. They would stick out like sore thumbs."

Mermelstein was given a series of details: the approximate whereabouts of Seal's home in Baton Rouge; the types of cars both he and his secretary drove; a description of each of the aircraft he owned; and the names of his favorite restaurants. Cano also mentioned that Seal was married and that he had children. Mermelstein said he would not have anything to do with the killing of women and children, but Cardona interrupted: "If it has to be done, it has to be done."

Cardona then telephoned Fabio Ochoa in Medellín and told him that Mermelstein was going to take care of the *pajarito*. Fabio asked to speak to him. He thanked Mermelstein and wished him good luck: "You know, it's necessary," Ochoa said. "McKenzie [Seal] is the only one who could testify against Jorge and Pablo. So we want you to do what's necessary." Mermelstein then talked to Pablo Escobar, who told him: "We're backing you up on it." Mermelstein was asked if he needed any money. "It would come in handy," he said.

A few days later a Cartel representative in Miami handed him $100,000 in cash to cover his expenses, and Mermelstein began looking for somebody to carry out the contract. An American trafficker who had once boasted to Mermelstein that he could "take care" of any necessary homicides proved to be as good as his word and recommended a man named Bob Dragin. In the last week of January 1985, Mermelstein and Dragin flew together to New Orleans, where Dragin rented a car, and drove alone to Baton Rouge. Mermelstein stayed firmly put in New Orleans: "I wanted to stay as far away as possible," he said. "It was Dragin's responsibility."

But try as he might, Dragin could find no trace of Seal in Baton Rouge. Cano's information turned out to be a lot less precise that it had seemed, and though Dragin kept watch on the various addresses he had been given, he could not be sure that he was watching the right buildings. Eventually he insisted that Mermelstein join him in Baton Rouge, and they toured the town together, to no avail.

Back in Miami, Mermelstein arranged for Cano to be sent over from Colombia to aid the hunt, because he had spent time with Seal in Baton Rouge and could identify his haunts. In mid-February 1985, Mermelstein and Cano traveled to Baton Rouge, where they found Seal's secluded house, his office, and several of his favorite restaurants. They did not, however, find Seal.

As Mermelstein was made fully aware, there was growing impatience in Medellín. Cano said that Fabio Ochoa had contacted his brother in jail in Spain, and that Jorge had agreed that Seal must be silenced, and the Cartel wanted results. Mermelstein appealed for patience. He said it was not practical to go and kill Seal in his house unless everybody else there was also killed, and "I'm not about to do that."

One of the Cartel's men in Miami did not understand Mermelstein's squeamishness. His name was Miguel Vélez, and he had previously worked as a "hit man" for Griselda Blanco. He was one of the perpetrators of the Dadeland Massacre, and he told Mermelstein: "It wouldn't bother me at all. I'd just go in and take everybody out." He seemed upset that he had not been offered the contract on Seal, and he said he was going to talk to Fabio Ochoa about it.

Max Mermelstein made one more futile trip to Baton Rouge before he was arrested in Florida in June 1985 for drug trafficking. To save himself, he told the authorities what he knew about the plot to kill Seal, and Mermelstein, together with sixteen of his relatives, was immediately placed in the US government's Witness Protection Program.

So, too, was Seal, and he hated it. For fifty days, he was kept in an underground room ten feet by twelve feet, in the basement of the federal courthouse in Miami. It had no windows and only a fluorescent light, a bed, a television set, and a bathroom. He could hear no outside noise and received no visits from family and friends. He was then taken to Las Vegas, Nevada, for two weeks, and housed in the basement of an abandoned rifle range. From there, he was transferred to what the federal authorities called his "permanent protection facility," where he was allowed to exercise for one hour a day. His wife and children attempted to visit him, but their names were not on the permitted visitors' list, and they were not allowed to see him.

His miserable incarceration continued until October 30, 1985, when Seal was taken back to Florida to finally be sentenced for smuggling Quaaludes. He expected the worst—ten years' imprisonment, which was the maximum allowed under his cooperation agreement—because Judge Norman Roettger had made it very clear at previous hearings that he regarded Seal as "evil." And Seal could take bets that Louisiana would double his sentence, by matching what Florida gave him to the very last day.

But Judge Roettger astounded everybody: "Promises of cooperation don't cut any ice with me at all, and the only time I let anybody out of jail entirely . . . is when their cooperation rises to the level where they have put their life in a position of peril. And when they do that, then I think they deserve to be suitably rewarded." Seal's sentence was "time served and three years probation." In other words, he was a free man.

In Louisiana, federal Judge Frank Polozola, a forty-four-year old law-and-order enthusiast and a devout Catholic, was outraged: "If I had the remotest idea, the slightest idea, Mr. Seal would not receive a jail sentence in Florida, under no circumstances, absolutely under no circumstances, would I have accepted this plea agreement," Polozola told Seal and his lawyers when they appeared before him in December 1985. "As far as I'm concerned, drug dealers like Mr. Seal are the lowest, most despicable type of people I can think of. In my own opinion, people like you, Mr. Seal, ought to be in a federal penitentiary. You all ought to be there working at hard labor. Working in the hottest sun or the coldest day wouldn't be good enough for drug dealers like you."

Under the deal he had approved, Polozola had no choice other then to give Seal probation, but setting the conditions was another matter. He ordered that Seal must get his personal approval to travel outside Louisiana: "You don't go any place, any place, without getting my personal written approval in advance," he said. Noncompliance would make Seal liable to five years in prison. And, said the judge, "as a further condition of probation, the defendant shall reside at the Salvation Army Community Treatment Center, 7361 Airline Highway, Baton Rouge, Louisiana, for a period of six months." The judge's order allowed Seal to leave the hostel during the day, but he had to return at six o'clock sharp every evening: attempting to find Barry Seal would no longer be a matter of chance.

One month later, on January 21, 1986, the Audiencia Nacional—the supreme court—in Madrid reversed an earlier decision by the lower courts, and ordered Jorge Ochoa extradited to the United States to face cocaine charges. Three days later in Baton Rouge, Seal's attorneys went before Judge Polozola and stressed that their client was the government's only witness against the "notorious Colombian trafficker," and that forcing him to live at the Salvation Army hostel would "place Mr. Seal in a life-threatening situation." But a counter-motion, filed by US prosecutors, disagreed: "The government does not see how residing at the Salvation Army imposes any more of a threat than Mr. Seal residing at his home."

Judge Polozola, by now much calmer, suggested that Seal should re-enter the Witness Protection Program, but he refused. He was therefore ordered to immediately enter the Salvation Army hostel, and he did so that night. "I'm a clay pigeon," he said, and he was right.

Luis Carlos Quintero Cruz, a small man with dark skin and a distinctive Indian face, left Medellín in early February 1986 and traveled to Mexico. He hired a *coyote*—someone who specializes in smuggling aliens into the United States—and, under cover of darkness, crossed the Rio Grande and disappeared into the Texas night. He headed for New Orleans, where, on February 17, he met up with a group of other Colombians at the Airport Hilton Hotel. The group included Miguel Vélez, the Dadeland killer who had been so perplexed by Max Mermelstein's squeamishness. Quintero was handed a MAC-10 submachine gun, a package of ammunition, and a silencer. Meanwhile, one of the other Colombians bought a 1982 gray Buick for $6,500 in $100 bills, which was registered in the name of Mary L. Cook. Then Quintero took a cab to the Jay Motel on Airline Highway in Baton Rouge where he rented Room 228 for $15.91 a day. The motel had no restaurant and the room had no telephone, but it did have a balcony with an uninterrupted view of the parking lot of the Salvation Army hostel.

For the next two days, Seal's comings and goings from the hostel were carefully chronicled, though he did not know it. He may have been distracted by a demand from the IRS for $29,-487,718 which, it was alleged, he owed in back taxes. On February 19, he was also advised that his pilot's license had been revoked because he was a convicted felon.

Just before 6 P.M. that evening, the gray Buick, with Vélez at the wheel and Quintero as passenger, pulled into the Salvation Army parking lot. The two men got out of the car and stretched their legs and Quintero strolled towards three large "drop boxes" the Salvation Army provided for those who wished to donate clothing. He was carrying a folded raincoat, which he placed inside one of the boxes. He remained there while Vélez repositioned himself behind the wheel of the Buick, and started the engine.

At six o'clock sharp, Seal drove into the parking lot in his white Cadillac, and terminated a conversation he was holding on his cellular telephone with an aviation consultant in Phoenix, Arizona. "I'll call you back from the building," Seal said. He backed his car into a spot near the drop boxes. Robert Lane, a destitute who did odd jobs at the hostel, was about to tell him that he had taken up two parking spaces when Quintero reclaimed his raincoat, removed from it the MAC-10, and pulled the trigger for two seconds. Seal slumped over the front seat of the Cadillac. He was bleeding profusely, his hands covering his ears as if he had tried to block out all sound. Three bullets had hit Seal in the left side of the head, passing through his skull and severing the cerebrum from the brain stem. A fourth bullet had furrowed his scalp. A fifth had struck his left upper arm, fracturing the bone, passing through and shattering a rib. A sixth had torn through his chest. Major B. T. Lewis ran from inside the hostel and despite the fact he could see a hole passed clean through Seal's head, he asked: "Barry, can you hear me?"

In one sense, Barry Seal's murder may not have been strictly necessary. In Colombia, Jorge Ochoa's lawyers arranged for him to be charged with exactly the same offenses that he faced in the United States. They then claimed in Spain that since the charges were equally serious, and since Ochoa was a Colombian national, he should stand trial in his own country, rather than America, and, by a vote of two-to-one, the supreme court agreed. But by then Seal, the only willing witness against him, was dead.

And so, on a stiflingly hot Saturday night in July 1986, María Lía Ochoa was abruptly told that, finally, she could go home. Her Bolivian au pair, Solange, fussed over last-minute arrangements, although suitcases and cartons of belongings accumulated over two years in Spain had stood packed in the hallway for several weeks. A male relative drove with her to the airport where they joined a gathering crowd, waiting for her husband to arrive.

That night in Madrid, Jimmy Kibble of the DEA could not help recalling the day in 1984 that he and the Spanish police celebrated their spectacular arrest of Ochoa: "I really thought the Spanish government could deliver Ochoa if they wanted to; there are ways of getting what you want," he said. But that was before Washington introduced the "Nicaraguan Factor" which turned Ochoa, of all men, into a "political prisoner," thus confusing a perfectly straightforward extradition case.

Jorge Ochoa was brought to the airport in a black Seat van escorted by six police cars and two motorcycle outriders. TV crews and the few stray reporters who were not fooled by an announcement that Ochoa would leave Madrid the following day, jostled for a glimpse and a word with Spain's most famous prisoner. A deep line of security guards denied them even a view.

After nearly two years in prison he looked a paler version of himself, but he had the same stocky frame carried in the same cocksure manner that had led the DEA to cast him as their "Number One Creep."

Ochoa changed Spanish for Colombian handcuffs—a contingent of Colombian police had flown in that morning—and greeted his wife and their chattering five-year-old daughter. He then climbed the steps of the waiting Avianca plane, which took off at 2:45 A.M. None of those who watched it go were in any doubt that what awaited Ochoa in Colombia was almost-certain freedom.

That Saturday, in far-off Maryland, Roger Yochelson of the Justice Department, who had expected a long lunch and a party at the expense of the DEA to celebrate Ochoa's extradition to the United States, complained bitterly to Sherpa and Miju, the two cats that share his life and home in Bethesda. Later he said: "For the kinds of quantities his organization moves, for his total disregard for the despair caused by drugs, because he is directly and indirectly responsible for murders, rapes, and torture, that man should have spent the rest of his life in an American jail. The fact that he may live in a big hacienda and does not see these atrocities himself doesn't matter an iota."

21

Rough Justice

The Colombia that Jorge Ochoa returned home to had, in his absence, lost almost all of its enthusiasm for confronting the Cartel head on. Many judges and politicians were no longer willing to accept the risks. An American official in Bogotá said: "Who can blame them, when the only alternative is death?"

Just how far the Cartel was willing to go to defend itself had become chillingly clear in November 1985, when the supreme court in Bogotá prepared to deliver its verdict on the constitutionality of Colombia's extradition treaty with the United States. That much-maligned treaty had been signed into law when Colombia's president was out of the country, and its critics—drug traffickers, of course, but also some of the most respected members of the legal profession—argued that nobody other than the president had the authority to sign an international treaty. The twenty-four justices of the supreme court refused to consider the matter for several years, and a dozen or so traffickers were extradited to America—albeit at a slower pace than the US authorities would have liked. Eventually, however, the supreme court agreed to consider the issue. It was heavily rumored in Bogotá that the vast majority of the justices was in favor of upholding the treaty.

On Wednesday, November 6, 1985, a bus painted in the colors of the Bogotá Telephone Company approached the downtown district of Bogotá through a maze of narrow streets where turn-of-the-century buildings lodge an unlikely assortment of museums, shabby bars, primitive barbecue restaurants, and law offices. When it reached the Palace of Justice—which is relatively modern—the bus entered the underground garage and came to a halt by the entrance to the elevators. The doors of the bus opened, and some forty to forty-five well-armed men and women from the M-19 guerrilla movement prepared to launch their assault.

It was approaching noon, and many of the 250 people in the building—among them justices, members of the council of state, secretaries, lawyers, and visitors—were making themselves ready for lunch. Without warning, the guerrillas burst onto the first floor and quickly overwhelmed the few guards that were on hand. They moved to the main entrance—overlooking the Plaza de Bolívar, Bogotá's central square—and shut and locked the heavy bronze doors. Everybody inside was now a hostage.

Shouting "Long live Colombia! Long live M-19!" and firing machine guns, they took the building's four floors one by one. They forced their way into offices, where they ordered anybody they found to lie down on the floor with their hands on their heads. Some people ran into the toilets and attempted to hide; others took refuge in closets; others just crouched under their desks.

The leader of the group was forty-eight-year-old Andrés Amarales, one of the founders of M-19, who took it upon himself to round up all the justices found in the building, most of whom were at a meeting called to discuss the extradition treaty. While the rest were held under guard, Amarales took the president of the supreme court, Alfonso Reyes Echandía, to a telephone and forced him to call the speaker of the House of Representatives and President Betancur. Amarales wanted both to come to the Palace of Justice to face a "people's trial" for having "betrayed the fatherland." Instead, Betancur sent his elite antiterrorist squad. When their assault got underway, Amarales began slaughtering the justices; Reyes was one of his first victims, shot in cold blood.

The attack by the security forces succeeded in freeing many of the hostages, but those members of M-19 who survived it retreated to the third floor with the remaining captives and prepared to make their last stand. By nightfall, almost the entire building was ablaze.

President Betancur waited until 2 P.M. the following day before ordering the final assault. An army tank pushed its way through the bronze entrance doors followed by foot soldiers obliged to fight a pitched battle with hand grenades and machine guns. By the time it was over, all of the guerrillas were dead—with the possible exception of a handful who might have slipped out of the building with some of the hostages. Eleven justices were killed, either executed by M-19 or shot in error by the army. In all, more than one hundred bodies were recovered from the rubble.

In the aftermath, it became clear that during the siege M-19 had selectively and systematically burnt court documents concerning several pending extradition cases. And, without exception, all of the murdered justices were known to be staunch supporters of the extradition treaty. In a communiqué released after the attack, M-19 said that one of its purposes had been to denounce the existence of a treaty which had delivered "a mortal blow to our sovereignty."

Colombian and American law enforcement agents became convinced that the hand of the Cartel lay behind that savage onslaught. Any lingering doubts were extinguished when a justice who had survived the attack, and who had remained a supporter of the treaty, was gunned down in Bogotá. Few people ever doubted that, when a new supreme court was constituted, those who replaced the slain justices would think long and hard before they voted to allow extradition.

In the middle of August 1986, Jorge Ochoa prepared for his first taste of Colombian justice. Since arriving from Spain, he had been held in Bogotá for thirty days, but was then transferred to Cartagena, friendlier territory, to answer the charge that he had illegally imported bulls into Colombia. On the eve of his arrival a group of the family's bodyguards caused a disturbance in Cartagena, and had themselves put in the city jail for unruly behavior, thus making themselves available to provide Ochoa with any protection he might need.

Ochoa duly appeared before a young and inexperienced magistrate who found him guilty of the charges and sentenced him to two years in prison. But then, pending an appeal, he released Ochoa on bond of $11,500, despite the fact that Ochoa still faced the vastly more serious drug charges on which he had been extradited from Spain. The magistrate said that Ochoa must report to the court twice a month. Ochoa thanked him, and left with his entourage.

The government launched a "nationwide hunt" for Ochoa but to no avail: the joke in Medellín was that the police had searched every building, except the one that Ochoa was in. The justice ministry demanded an explanation from the Cartagena magistrate, who said he had not been aware that Ochoa was facing any other charges. He lost his job, but he is alive; he was widely rumored to have acquired a fortune.

In Miami, federal prosecutors drew up a massive new indictment, based largely on the evidence of Max Mermelstein, which charged all three Ochoa brothers, Pablo Escobar, Gonzalo Rodríguez Gacha, Carlos Lehder, Rafael Cardona, and others with every crime they could think of. And in Washington, Congress approved a reward of $500,000—the largest government bounty ever offered—for information leading to Jorge Ochoa's arrest. In Colombia, nobody came forward to claim it.

But in Medellín, of all places, somebody did come forward to claim the much smaller reward the Colombian government had offered for the arrest of any number of *narcotraficantes,* including Carlos Lehder. In February 1987, Lehder *was* arrested, and extradited to the United States with almost indecent haste. The circumstances surrounding that uncommon event are curious and, for the cynically minded, suspicious.

Like most other leading members of the Cartel, Lehder left Colombia after the assassination of the justice minister, and he, like Ochoa and Rodríguez Orejuela, went to Spain. But despite the claims of American prosecutors, Lehder was never a member of the inner circle, and certainly not of sufficient stature to be regarded as a *dueño de cupo*—a holder of the quota. He was an important and prolific smuggler for the Cartel, but he was also exceptionally wild and indiscreet; a loose cannon rolling on deck, who could be much more trouble than he was worth.

It was not for nothing that his colleagues took to calling him *El Loquito Carlos*—"Carlos the Mad Man."

So Lehder was not part of Ochoa's new life in Spain, which is why he was not trapped by the police's surveillance of Ochoa. When Ochoa and Rodríguez Orejuela were arrested in Madrid, Lehder fled across the border into Portugal. From there, thanks to the connection of Jemel, his wife, he went to Havana, where he was given safe haven for two weeks. He was then told to leave Cuba, apparently for "offensive behavior."

In December 1984 he resurfaced briefly in Mexico, where he made provocative statements about Colombian politics and drug enforcement efforts. In early 1985, he re-entered Colombia illegally, and would occasionally hold court for foreign journalists. In April 1985 Lehder narrowly escaped an army raid on the cattle ranch in the eastern plains of Meta province where he was living, and left behind 350 kilos of cocaine, $1.6 million in cash, and nine of his bodyguards. Unrestrained, in September, he gave an interview to a newspaper in Cali in which he vowed to become a revolutionary hero: he said he was about to join a dissident faction of the M-19, which had joined forces with a left-wing organization of peasants. By Christmas, however, Lehder was back in Medellín, attending holiday parties given by members of the Cartel.

At one of those parties, Lehder shot and killed a man he attempted to seduce, and who insulted him. The victim was one of Pablo Escobar's favorite bodyguards. Whether that was sufficient to cause Lehder to be betrayed by the Cartel is an open question. What is not in doubt is that he *was* betrayed—and Lehder, for one, certainly blames Escobar and the Ochoas.

In late January 1987 a man walked into the office of a high-ranking police officer in Medellín and asked how much he would get if he told the authorities where to find "one of the *capos* you're looking for." He was told that although the government had approved the payment of rewards for information there was, as yet, no budget to provide them. "I won't tell you, then," he said. "Think about it. I'll call in again in a few days."

When he returned he was told that the government had still not been able to provide any money, but that the US Embassy in Bogotá was willing to pay $50,000 for reliable information.

For that sum, he disclosed where the *capo* was hiding, though he did not name him.

As a result, at dawn on February 4, 1987, Major William Lemus of the Rionegro police and thirty-five of his men raided the *Finca Berracal* in the small town of Guarne, some twenty miles from Medellín. As they approached the house, a startled guard opened fire with a machine gun, but as soon as he saw their uniforms he dropped the weapon and ran; he was shot in the buttocks. A dozen young men, all in their underwear, emerged from the house and also tried to flee, but Lemus threatened to shoot them too. "Hold your fire," said another man who appeared in the doorway. "I'm Carlos Lehder."

While Lehder and his young friends posed for a photograph, looking for all the world as though they were the victims of some prank, Lemus called his superiors in Medellín and said: "The Virgin has smiled on us. We have captured Carlos Lehder."

The police called the mayor of Medellín, who in turn spoke with the minister of defense in Bogotá. At 10:45 that morning, the president of Colombia asked the justice minister if Lehder could be extradited immediately. Before noon, a DEA plane was on its way from Florida.

That afternoon, Lehder was taken to Bogotá by the Colombian Air Force and at 5:07 P.M., he was put aboard the DEA's Turbo Commander. Before midnight, less than eighteen hours after his arrest, Lehder was in Tampa, Florida, in an American jail.

There had never been anything like it—and what added to the uniqueness of the event is that there was no outcry over Lehder's extradition and, for once, no retaliation. It was as if the Cartel was happy to see him go, and grateful for the respite which his arrest provided: while the United States celebrated its rare victory, the Ochoas, Escobar, and Rodríguez Gacha were allowed to live in comparative peace.

Anybody who thought that things had really changed in Colombia should have attended the trial of Gilberto Rodríguez Orejuela, who had been arrested with Ochoa in Madrid, and who had also been extradited to Colombia. Unlike Ochoa, Rodríguez Orejuela was kept in jail for a year, in Cali, though it was not a great hardship. Other inmates ran errands for him and the prison director referred to him as Don Gilberto. His cell resembled a hotel suite because he was allowed to equip it with whatever luxuries he chose. On the occasion of a festival, known as the Day of the Prisoner, it was, inevitably, Rodríguez Orejuela who hosted the unforgettable party that was attended by, among others, the state governor.

His trial, when it eventually took place, was a farce. The main witness against him was a DEA agent who did not speak fluent Spanish. He was therefore provided with an official interpreter, who did not speak fluent English. She apparently found it impossible to convey the detail of his evidence, and the agent spent much of his time on the witness stand with his face buried in his hands, in some attempt to contain his disbelief. The trial was held not in a courtroom but in the judge's office, which could barely hold the participants, let alone the representatives of the press and television who would travel from Bogotá. (The local media entirely ignored the trial.) Rodríguez Orejuela would direct the TV crews as to when they could and could not run their cameras. His first decision each day was the menu for lunch, and he would instruct one of his attending aides what food to buy. When lunchtime came, the improvised courtroom was turned into a canteen and Rodríguez Orejuela would invite the judge to join him; rarely did the judge decline.

In July 1987 Rodríguez Orejuela was acquitted of all the charges against him, a decision which carried a double benefit since it meant that he was both a free man in Colombia and immune from extradition to the United States on those charges, no matter how violently the Americans might protest.

And anyway, by then the reconstituted supreme court had decided, by one vote, that Colombia's extradition treaty with the United States was unconstitutional. The Colombian government attempted to repair the flaws in the legislation that had created the treaty, but, in June 1987, the supreme court rejected it for the second time. That night in Medellín, Cali, and Bogotá there were loud all-night parties. "They celebrated the news as they do when they crown [successfully complete] a trip," said one observer in Medellín. "For them, it was the best crowning they ever had."

In light of the supreme court's decision, Pablo Escobar's attorneys inquired of the ministry of justice as to whether he was still a wanted man. The ministry said that the arrest warrant against Escobar was no longer active; nor, indeed, were the warrants against more than a hundred traffickers whose extradition the United States had requested.

In quiet celebration, Pablo Escobar placed discreet advertisements in national newspapers announcing that he could now be contacted at his old address, the elaborate *Hacienda Nápoles.*

And five months later, in late November 1987, Jorge Ochoa, the most wanted member of the Cartel, gave the clearest possible demonstration of the Cartel's power—and of the powerlessness of the Colombian authorities.

On November 21, Ochoa was stopped at a police checkpoint between the cities of Cali and Palmira, some 165 miles southeast of Bogotá, for driving a white Porsche at 110 MPH in a 55-MPH zone. He showed the police his own identity documents and made no serious attempt to evade arrest. He was taken into custody by the army in Cali and then transferred to a high-security military camp in Bogotá.

In Miami, news of Ochoa's arrest was greeted with great excitement. The DEA seriously believed Ochoa would be extradited in the same fashion as Carlos Lehder, and the Metro-Dade Police Department was asked to send a "green and white," a patrol car, to Homestead Air Force Base in southern Dade County to await his arrival. Initially, there was cause for optimism. Enrique Low Murta, recently appointed Colombia's minister of justice, had pledged he would "keep extraditing" drug traffickers to the United States and, after Ochoa's arrest, Low told American embassy officials in Bogotá that he was "actively seeking" ways to give them Ochoa. But Low soon changed his tune. Within days of Ochoa's arrest he announced that Ochoa had to serve the twenty-month prison sentence he had been given for illegally importing bulls: "Colombia's claim comes first," Low said. He added that the government would "continue to study" the possibility of eventually extraditing Ochoa "in accordance to the law."

Then on December 29, 1987, a Medellín judge named Cecilia Cadavid Montoya received a visit from Jorge Ochoa's two brothers, Fabio and Juan David, and Pablo Escobar. What passed between the three traffickers and the judge is not yet a matter of public record but the following day Judge Cadavid issued a ruling that, in the words of a subsequent government inquiry, "paved the way" for Ochoa's release from prison. Armed with that ruling Ochoa's lawyers in Bogotá filed a writ of habeas corpus and, just after dusk on December 30, he walked out of La Picota prison. He was driven to Guaimaral airport, ten miles north of Bogotá, where he boarded a private jet. By the time arrest warrants were issued for Ochoa, his two brothers, Pablo Escobar, and the other leader of the Cartel, Gonzalo Rodriguez Gacha, all of them had vanished.

At least one member of the Colombian government took great offense at that affront. Attorney General Carlos Mauro Hoyos Jimenez had opposed the traffickers but always "with tact and discretion," as one of his friends put it; for example, he did not support a new extradition treaty with the United States. But in the light of Ochoa's escape Hoyos had second thoughts. He gave interviews to reporters in which he said that because the Colombian justice system was evidently "powerless to control the traffickers," they should after all be sent to the United States to stand trial.

It was a brave but foolhardy stand to take. On January 26, 1988, while on a visit to Medellín—his home town—Hoyos was kidnapped and executed. His body was found gagged, blindfolded, and handcuffed. He had been shot ten times in the head. In a telephone call to a Medellín radio station, a man claiming to represent *los extraditables* said: "The war goes on. I repeat, the war goes on."

22

Reagan's War

uis "Kojak" García's final accomplishment as a drug smuggler, in November 1982, was the successful importation
into Miami of 360 kilos of cocaine for the Ochoa family. The
cocaine was flown from Medellín to an airstrip in the arid
Guajira Peninsula from where one of Kojak's pilots took it on
to an equally isolated strip in the Dominican Republic, which
lies roughly midway between northern Colombia and southern
Florida. Kojak had leased the strip from the Dominican government, to provide a much-needed crop dusting service in that
desperately poor land. His crop-dusting business always ran at
a loss, of as much as $100,000 a year, but he considered that a
cheap price to pay for what was the perfect "transit stop" for
his planes; as often as he thought prudent, they would break
their journey to the Bahamas at the strip and stay there for
hours or even days, to "change the pattern" and make them
even more difficult to track. The Ochoas' cocaine sat in the
Dominican Republic for four days before it was flown on to
Gorda Cay, from where Kojak's boatmen did the rest. He was
paid $1.8 million for his artful services.

When Kojak subsequently "retired," this was, necessarily,
one of the episodes he described to the DEA, and he told them
what he knew of the Ochoas' representatives with whom he
had dealt. He knew there was a risk in that but he shrugged it
off saying: "No Colombian has gone to jail because of me." Even
so, he took to carrying a gun, a silver-colored .38 "Police Special," and he equipped his house with a burglar alarm.

Nothing happened for almost three years, until a Thursday afternoon in February 1986, when Kojak received a telephone call from Gene Francar, his case agent at the DEA. By that time Kojak had become the owner of a travel agency in Miami and he could obtain airline tickets at a discount: Francar told him to buy two of them and leave town immediately—because, the DEA had learned, there was a contract on his life.

It had been placed by a Colombian named Jorge Morales who, much like Kojak, worked as a subcontractor to the drug trade, specializing in transportation. Using a Miami-based aircraft leasing company, Aviation Activities Corporation, as a front, he flew marijuana and cocaine into Florida, and Kojak had helped him to become established by loaning him a DC-3. Morales also brought in drugs from the Bahamas by boat and, when Kojak quit, some of his boatmen would occasionally work for the Colombian.

Morales was well known to the DEA, and particularly to Gene Francar, who had first arrested him in December 1982 for conspiracy to import marijuana. For reasons that Francar could never understand, the case was later dropped by federal prosecutors, but the DEA arrested Morales again in March 1984: this time he was charged with twenty-one counts of smuggling marijuana and Quaaludes, and, most serious of all, of operating "a continuing criminal enterprise"—a catch-all charge that carries a minimum mandatory sentence of fifteen years imprisonment, without parole. Even then he did not go to jail. To the chagrin of the DEA, Morales was allowed bond—initially of $2 million—his trial was endlessly delayed, and he was given extraordinary freedom by the court to travel abroad. He was granted permission to travel to the Bahamas, Cuba (twice), the Dominican Republic, Panama, and Mexico; the only time the court balked was when he asked for consent to go to Colombia.

Throughout that period Morales continued to smuggle cocaine. The DEA first acquired solid evidence of that in January 1986 when one of its confidential informants, a pilot, reported that Morales had offered him a total of $375,000 to fly three loads of cocaine from Costa Rica—another convenient transit stop—to Great Harbor Cay in the Bahamas. With the DEA's knowledge, he made the first flight, transporting 420 kilos to Great Harbor. The DEA then informed the Bahamian police which, on January 16, raided the island and seized what it reported was only 80 kilos of that load; the rest had simply disappeared.

Perhaps Morales stole it, because the explanation he gave to the Cartel was false and thoroughly malicious. He said that the boatmen he had employed to bring in the cocaine from the Bahamas were all former associates of Kojak: "Black Carlos," Carlos's brother Amado, and another legendary operator who— because of his appearance—was known to everybody in the trade as "Dracula." He claimed that they had ripped off the load, in connivance with Kojak who, Morales said, had an understanding with the DEA that allowed him to carry out occasional acts of piracy in return for his cooperation. Given Kojak's past, it was a story that would have the ring of truth in Medellín, and it was given further credibility by Morales' assurance that he had arranged to have Kojak and the three boatmen killed; in those circumstances, the Cartel would expect no less.

Kojak promised Gene Francar that he would leave town, and he sent his young wife, Neysa, home to pack. He promised her he would follow almost immediately, but instead he disappeared for more than three hours. When he finally arrived at their house late that evening, Neysa was almost hysterical, and Francar was calling every five minutes from a pay phone; that night, of all nights, his home phone was out of order.

Kojak had been to see Black Carlos and had learned something the DEA did not know—that Carlos's brother, Amado, and Dracula were already dead, presumed by the family to have been lost at sea. Their bodies had not been found, but the family's certainty was such that it had already divided Amado's property. Kojak told Black Carlos that for "lost at sea" the family should substitute "murdered." He also told Black Carlos something that was not true: that besides the two of them, Morales had also placed on the "hit list" another boatman who was regarded as being exceptionally hard-headed and who was universally known as *Puntilla*—"Nailhead." He was not a killer but he responded badly to threats against him, and in his briefcase he carried a machine pistol that he had adapted to be capable of firing thirty-six nine-millimeter rounds per second. Black Carlos said he would make sure that Nailhead got the message.

When Kojak finally returned home, he called Francar at the pay phone and told him what he had done. Francar laughed. Kojak said: "Listen, when you play you pay, right?"

He refused to leave town until the following day, because he had a dinner engagement he would not break. He insisted on going to one of his favorite restaurants and, afterwards, he insisted on going home to sleep in his own bed. He did agree to take the precaution of skirting the house a couple of times before pulling into the driveway, and he opened the front door with his gun in hand. Neysa was certain that the side gate to the house had been tampered with, and she was alarmed that their watchdog did not bark. Kojak told her the only thing to fear was fear, and, that night at least, he was right.

The DEA, already annoyed by the delays in bringing Morales to trial and by the remarkable freedom to operate that he enjoyed, was deeply angered by his attempts to have Kojak killed. As Francar put it: "Threatening Luis was not a smart thing to do." Morales was put at the top of the DEA's list in Miami and, using its informant to trap him, the agency developed a new case, of conspiracy to import cocaine. He was arrested at his home in Fort Lauderdale, some twenty miles north of Miami, in June 1986, and this time there was no question of bond: Morales went to jail.

He offered to do a deal but there were no takers. Then, after six months of silence, his defense lawyer made a startling disclosure that, perhaps, explained why the DEA had experienced such difficulty in putting his client in jail: Jorge Morales was not a drug smuggler, he said; what Morales smuggled, on behalf of the United States government, was money and supplies to the contra rebels fighting in Nicaragua. And to prove it, three distinguished witnesses had been subpoenaed to appear for the defense: CIA Director William Casey, Secretary of State George Schultz, and Vice-President George Bush. "Bullshit," said Kojak when he heard of Morales's claims, but it promised to be an interesting trial.

Later on Morales would modify his story, conceding that he had been a smuggler—but that only made his allegations the more sensational. He claimed that a few weeks after his indictment in March 1984, he had been approached by three contras, two of whom identified themselves as CIA agents, with a proposal that was marked by its neat symmetry. They said the CIA would "take care" of his "legal problems" if, in return, Morales would agree to fly weapons to the contras. On the return flights, he could bring drugs into the United States unmolested so long as he donated part of the proceeds to the contras, to enable them to buy yet more weapons for him to smuggle.

And that, according to Morales, is exactly what happened for the next eighteen months. He said that weapons were loaded onto planes, in broad daylight, at either the Executive Airport in Fort Lauderdale, or at Opa-Locka airport near Miami and flown to El Salvador, or Honduras or Costa Rica. On the return flights the planes transported cocaine, tons of it, and Morales claimed that he donated to the contras a total of $4.5 million.

This was no rogue operation, he said: the CIA, the State Department and the White House all knew about it, and, indeed, in May 1986 Morales was due to meet Vice-President Bush to discuss the "secret operation," but the meeting was abruptly canceled at the last moment. (If that claim is true, it is not surprising the meeting was canceled for by then the DEA was closing in on Morales with the utmost determination.) Morales had a high opinion of the vice-president. "Bush is the real president," he said. "Reagan is just a puppet."

Jorge Morales was not the first drug smuggler to claim an alliance with the contras, nor was he the first to contend that the US government, or factions of it, had endorsed and aided a "drugs for guns" policy or, at the very least, turned a blind eye towards it. The rumor had been in the air since 1983 when a smuggler told prosecutors in San Francisco that he was a contra, and that he had given $500,000 of his profits to one of the contra groups, the Armed Forces of National Revolution. And in Miami, there were persistent, if unproven, reports that drugs had been carried on the planes of Southern Air Transport, a locally based cargo airline that was once a CIA "proprietary" and that retained suspiciously close links to the agency. The allegations had been taken up and pursued with some vigor by Senator John Kerry, a Democrat from Massachusetts, but his suspicions were largely scoffed at—until the disclosure of the Iran-contra affair made anything seem possible, and until Jorge Morales put some meat on the bones.

Morales gave names and dates and places, and two of his pilots, who were also in jail, supported his story with detailed descriptions of their own of "drugs for guns" flights which they claimed to have carried out. What gave their combined account a special resonance was two of the people it named, names guaranteed to set alarm bells ringing whenever they are invoked.

John Clarke Hull is a naturalized Costa Rican citizen, originally from Evansville, Indiana, who since 1968 has managed a ranch near San Carlos, which is conveniently close to Costa Rica's border with Nicaragua. Though he vehemently denies it, Hull is widely regarded as a CIA "contract operative" who assists the contras. According to Morales and his pilots, he also assists drug traffickers, and it was on his ranch that some of the return flights were loaded with cocaine.

Even more potent was the second name: Félix Ismael Rodríguez, also known as Max Gómez. Rodríguez was a Cuban who fled to Miami in 1961 when he was nineteen years old to become one of the thousands of exiles recruited and trained by the CIA for the futile attempts to overthrow Castro. Later he carried out "counter-insurgency" missions in Vietnam, and he also worked as a "security advisor" for the governments of Argentina, Brazil, Uruguay, and Bolivia. It was in Bolivia, in October 1967, that Rodríguez earned his enduring notoriety by being present at the final interrogation, and execution, of Ernesto "Che" Guevara. By 1984, when Morales says the "drugs for guns" arrangement began, Félix Rodríguez was at the Ilopango air force base in El Salvador where he became a key figure in Colonel Oliver North's secret efforts to resupply the contras. Rodríguez had direct links to the White House, through the office of the vice-president, and met Bush himself at least twice. Yet, if Morales and his pilots were to be believed, he was up to his neck in the drug business: he had, supposedly, arranged for one of the pilots to fly twelve tons of marijuana directly into the Homestead Air Force Base at Homestead, Florida, and he had personally paid the man his fee of $75,000.

At the last moment, Morales changed his mind about going to trial, and pled guilty to cocaine-trafficking charges in return for a sentence of sixteen years, which was a great deal less than he might have got. But he did not withdraw his allegations, and they sat on the table drawing widespread publicity—and furious denials from the CIA, and the State and Justice departments—but no real investigation.

Could the allegations possibly be true? Jack Blum thought so. He was then the attorney for the International Center for Development Policy in Washington, a group that opposed the Reagan administration's program in Central America, and his opinion of the CIA under William Casey was extremely low. So the center had provided funds for a joint investigation with Senator Kerry's staff, which established, at least to their satisfaction, that the contras had been involved in drug trafficking. The question that remained was, was the American government also involved?

In February 1987 Kerry was finally able to persuade the Senate Foreign Relations Committee, of which he was a member, to launch an official investigation under the auspices of its subcommittee on terrorism, narcotics, and international operations. To placate Republican members of the committee, who thought there had already been more than enough "contra-bashing," Kerry agreed that the investigation should also look at the possible role of foreign governments in drug trafficking, and that compromise bought him an unexpected and unlikely ally: Jesse Helms, the Republican senator from North Carolina, whose particular beef was with General Manuel Antonio Noriega, head of the armed forces of Panama, and the alleged recipient of vast bribes from the Cartel.

The subcommittee's first act was to appoint Jack Blum to direct the investigation (an offer he accepted at some financial self-sacrifice, since senate committees do not pay particularly well; he and his wife agreed that he would take a sabbatical from his law practice "for as long as we could afford it"). Blum was no novice: in 1972, at the age of thirty, he was appointed an investigator and associate counsel to the Senate Foreign

Relations Committee on Multinational Corporations and, during the next four years, he was one of those responsible for exposing the attempts of the ITT Corporation to influence elections in Chile for its commercial advantage. At the same time, he also helped to expose the enormous bribes paid to officials of foreign governments by the Lockheed Corporation.

He was, in short, not entirely naive about the power of money or the perniciousness of corruption when he packed his bags and flew to Miami to begin his investigation into drug trafficking. But nothing in his experience, and nothing he had read, had quite prepared him for what he would find.

Jack Blum interviewed Jorge Morales in the Metropolitan Correctional Center in western Dade County, and obtained documents that tended to corroborate parts of his story. Blum came to believe much of what he said.

Morales's two pilots, however, were another matter. One of them, Gary Betzner, damaged his allegations against the contras and the CIA by also offering Blum his bizarre opinions on the medical uses of cocaine—as an enema, for example. Blum did not believe he would make a credible witness before the Senate: "He's marching to a different drummer," he said. And, though Michael Tolliver, the second pilot, gave a rational account of a "drugs-for-guns" flight he says he made, he could not provide sufficient detail to totally convince Blum.

But at the end of their long question-and-answer session, held at the Buttner Penitentiary in North Carolina, Tolliver said there was another inmate of the prison who Blum should see: a "quiet guy" who "doesn't say much" but who apparently knew a great deal about drugs, the contras, the CIA, and the Medellín Cartel. That night, thanks to Tolliver, Blum met for the first time a man named Ramón Milián Rodríguez; a man whose story helped to convince Blum that America's so-called "War on Drugs" was, in reality, an elaborate game.

That was, of course, the same conclusion that Raúl Díaz had reached—that it was "all a fucking game"—when he was forced to quit Centac 26, and chose to quit the police force, and, in some people's eyes, joined the other side—and there is irony in that. After his visit to the Buttner Penitentiary and his meeting with Milián, Blum became convinced that he had identified not merely the game but also one of its major players: the "cut out" between those nether worlds of espionage and drug trafficking, the "link man" between the Cartel and the CIA—former police lieutenant, Raúl Díaz.

In view of these allegations, it has to be said that Raúl Díaz has an unfortunate knack of knowing the wrong people and of being in the wrong place at the wrong time. His aunt was, in his words, "one of the best operatives the CIA ever had." His first wife's father, to whom he remains extremely close, also worked for the CIA, and was a Watergate burglar. And, through him, Díaz got to know and like the notorious Félix Rodríguez, and has been present at gatherings where, for amusement, Rodríguez has read extracts from the final interrogation of Che Guevara. And where was Raúl Díaz on the day that Félix Rodríguez telephoned the White House to report that one of the planes engaged in the secret contra resupply effort had been shot down over Nicaragua? "In the executive offices," said Díaz, "next door to Oliver North's office." He was there as part of a delegation of minority businessmen, but he did not expect anybody to believe that.

It was also unfortunate, in retrospect, that Díaz should have become a partner of the InterContinental Detective Agency at precisely the moment that Ramón Milián first came to appreciate that he was in very serious trouble.

Milián was an accountant who became a prolific launderer of drug money. According to his version of events, he first crossed the line into illegality in 1979 when, at the age of twenty-eight, he became a money courier for Cuban exiles in Miami, smuggling cash to "conservative causes" in Latin America. When he began to suspect that much of this money was the product of drug trafficking, he said, he informed the CIA. If he is to be believed, the CIA effectively shrugged—and began using Milián to send money down to Latin America to the people and causes which *it* supported.

In 1980, he claimed, he began laundering money for Colombian drug traffickers including the Ochoas and Escobar. As part of his duties, he says, he began delivering approximately $10 million *a month* to General Manuel Noriega, the "strongman" of Panama.

There is no doubt that Milián shipped vast quantities of cash from Miami to Panama: he kept detailed records, which the US authorities subsequently found in his briefcase, which showed that in the nine months between August 1982 and May 1983 he made forty-seven flights to Panama aboard his personal Learjet, and transported a total of $151 million. What would have been the forty-eighth flight was abruptly terminated at Fort Lauderdale International Airport, on May 4, 1983, when US Customs agents raided the plane moments before take-off, and found on board twenty boxes containing $5,449,962.

Milián was never a hero, and after just one hour in custody, he summoned his captors and said: they had no idea what they had stumbled on; at no time before had federal agents faced such a golden opportunity; that he, Milián, was the pre-eminent money launderer in all of south Florida; that his clientele consisted of the most significant traffickers in the region—that they were the "who's who" of the drugs underworld; that he was prepared to shop them, and that he was sufficiently close to "actual operations" that he could provide "strategic intelligence."

When Milián was taken to Customs headquarters in Miami, he proved to be as good as his word and identified from photographs a total of twenty-two Cuban distributors in Miami and their Colombian suppliers. In appreciation, the Customs agents agreed that Milián could go home for the night, rather than spend it in jail, and, misled by their apparent generosity, he agreed that they could search his office without the need for a warrant. That was a mistake: in his office the agents found a duffel bag filled with weapons including an Uzi submachine gun equipped with a laser-scope, and sixty pounds of cocaine which, on analysis, turned out to be 97 percent pure. Milián was re-arrested at his home at three o'clock in the morning; he told the agents he did not understand why they were so mad.

And having secured his temporary freedom on bond of $5 million, Milián would not acknowledge his difficulties. He hired a highly competent defense attorney and, through him, the services of the InterContinental Detective Agency, and he always believed he could avoid prosecution, by making a deal. The bait he eventually offered was his claim that the Cartel was in league with the Sandinista government in Nicaragua, and he proposed that he should be given back his Learjet and the $5 million—both of which had been confiscated—and be allowed to go to Managua, where he would involve the Sandinistas even more deeply. He promised to keep in touch, and to give the United States the evidence it needed to destabilize the Nicaraguan government.

His offer was refused out of hand by Customs agents—which was, perhaps, when Milián first realized that he was in deep trouble. By then Raúl Díaz was a fully fledged partner of Inter-Continental, and, to his eternal regret, he agreed to approach the CIA to inquire if that agency was interested in Milián's proposal.

Díaz took Milián to meet the notorious Félix Rodríguez. According to Díaz, the meeting took place at Rodríguez's home in Miami. And, according to Díaz, Rodríguez was reserved and noncommittal, and told Milián only that he would "check with some people" and "get back to you if they're interested"; so far as Díaz knows, he never did "get back."

But that is not what Milián told Jack Blum. He claimed that while Rodríguez rejected the Nicaraguan proposal, he counter-proposed that Milián should use his good offices with the Cartel to arrange a donation for the contras. And, according to Milián, he subsequently delivered between $9 and $10 million of the Cartel's money to the contras; money the Cartel hoped would secure some tolerance from the Reagan administration.

Blum essentially believed Milián, and his belief was only cemented by his discovery that InterContinental was working for the defense in two remarkable cases: the trial in Louisiana of the Colombians who killed Barry Seal; and, in Florida, for the defense of Carlos Lehder.

In July 1987 Blum issued subpoenas against Díaz and his partners, demanding that they appear before the Senate, and he also demanded most of InterContinental's records. Díaz and his partners declined the invitation to go to Washington, and they hired an attorney with relevant expertise who promised Blum a fight that might last for years. With Milián's consent, they did hand over to the Senate their records on Milián's case, but they insisted that all of their other records were "work product," protected from disclosure by the privilege that is afforded under law to all communications between a lawyer and his client.

The irony of that dispute was inescapable. Díaz and his partners felt they had no choice but to stand behind the shields of "privilege" and "work product" to protect the secrets and rights of precisely the kind of people they once hunted so effectively—and were genuinely offended that Blum should attempt to use the powers of Congress to extract those secrets. Blum, for his part, was morally outraged that Díaz and his partners should employ legal pretexts and a clever lawyer to deny congress evidence of a most cynical conspiracy between drug traffickers, the contras, and the US government.

And that perfectly expresses the dichotomy.

As Jack Blum inquired more and more deeply into the drug-trafficking industry, and the attempts of the US government to curtail it—as he visited and revisited Miami, and California, Texas, New York, North Carolina, and Costa Rica; as he sat in prisons and listened to drug smugglers talk about their "work for the government"; as he listened to Kojak describe how he had bought the Bahamas; as allegations mounted against General Noriega of Panama; as he watched the Miami Police Department founder in a sea of corruption allegations; as he saw for himself the vast gulf between the claims for success of Reagan's War on Drugs and the reality of the flood-tide of cocaine on the streets, and its ever-decreasing price; as he began to comprehend the way in which some informants were given a virtual license to operate; as he calculated the earnings of the members of the Cartel, and the economic power it gave them— Blum came to believe that America was no longer engaged in an all-out battle against a massive conspiracy but that, in a subtle way, it had become part of that conspiracy.

The martin is a bird valued by mankind because it feeds on mosquitoes. But the martin will not eat the mosquitoes' larvae; it has no interest in ridding the world of that on which it depends for nourishment. And similarly—in Jack Blum's view—

communities like Miami, which benefit economically from drugs, and fat-cat lawyers, and bankers, accountants, realtors, and car salesmen, and the massed ranks of law enforcement, and CIA agents who know an opportunity when they see one, do not perceive it as being in their best interests to try and rid the world of drug traffickers.

And often, it seems, the most intense battles in the war on drugs take place not at the front line in Miami, but in Washington: on Capitol Hill where rival law enforcement agencies vie for shares of the appropriations budget, using as ammuniton their ever-growing (but largely meaningless) arrest and seizure figures; between the departments of State and Justice and the often conflicting interests of foreign policy and national security on the one hand, and domestic law enforcement on the other; and at the White House where the rhetoric against drugs, however sincere, is rarely matched by the necessary political will, and never by sufficient funds.

Perhaps the truth is that the Reagan administration fought the wrong war. While it concentrated to the point of obsession on the Sandinistas in Nicaragua and the threat of communism in Central America, forces just as potent, just as threatening to the United States, and arguably more deadly, were able to subvert much of the South American continent: Colombia and Panama for sure; perhaps Honduras, where there is evidence of the Cartel's growing influence; Mexico, where corrupt officials and army officers have been heavily implicated in drug trafficking; Bolivia and Peru, where traffickers control entire regions of those countries; and now Brazil, where the Cartel is becoming increasingly established.

If the Reagan administration had applied the same rage and resources to battling the Cartel that it brought to bear against the Sandinistas; if it had not turned a blind eye to massive drug corruption in Panama and the Bahamas; if in fighting the war on communism in Central America it had not lost sight of the fact that some of its supposed allies in that cause were, in other respects, dangerous enemies, then the outcome of Reagan's War on Drugs might have been very different. As it is, in *that* war, the enemy is literally at the door.

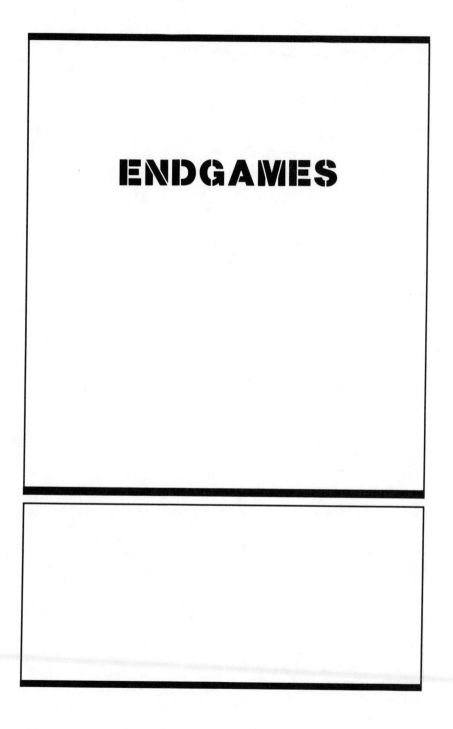

ENDGAMES

I

On a fine spring morning in early May 1987, while the
Miami River Cops waited for their retrial, Rudy Arias
went to San Lázaro Catholic Church in Hialeah to see Father
Luis Pérez. The priest was in a jovial mood and pretended to
shadowbox with Arias, whom he had known since Rudy was an
altar boy. "Come on *gordo* [fat one], tell me what's happening,"
he said. So Arias did. He confessed to the midnight shift's rip-
offs and drug deals. He confessed he had spent part of his share
of the proceeds on maintaining a mistress. And he confessed
that he and other Miami police officers had done their level best
to murder government witnesses. Father Pérez received this
two-hour litany in stunned silence. By the time it was over he
was slumped in his office chair.

When he recovered Father Pérez took Arias into the church
and instructed him to kneel before a statue of Jesus. Then with
Arias repeating each line, the priest prayed for about thirty
minutes. Father Pérez made Arias swear that he would make
no further attempts to kill anyone, and to beg for God's forgive-
ness. He did not, however, encourage Arias to repeat his confession in public or to the police—though Arias was clearly on the
brink of doing so.

And while Arias confessed to his priest, José Martínez, the
professional killer, confessed to Centac that he had accepted a
$100,000 contract from Arias and other Miami River Cops to
murder the government's key witness, Armando Un. Though

that attempt had not amounted to much, "Killer Joe," as Centac called him, had murdered another drug dealer—also at the behest of a Miami police officer—and been caught. Facing the prospect of life imprisonment or even execution, Killer Joe offered a deal: damning evidence against the Miami River Cops in return for leniency.

As a result, at 6 A.M. on Friday, May 8, Arias received a telephone call from Osvaldo Coello, his hulking former colleague on the midnight shift and a codefendant. Coello said he was calling from a girl friend's house; his own home, where he lived with his parents, was "surrounded" by police. He thought they might be looking for him because of home invasion robberies he had committed. Coello asked for the telephone number of Arias's lawyer, Sammy "Wild Man" Burstyn. He said he wanted to find out if, having surrendered, he would be able to get bond. If not, he said, he was going to "play hardball."

An already despondent Arias left the house where he now lived alone; Reina, his wife, had departed after a row, taking with her the couple's young daughter. He went to an auto-body repair shop in Miami where to pass the time he worked as an unpaid mechanic. He was sanding down the paintwork of a car when Reina arrived in tears and said: "They're looking for you, with another arrest warrant." One call to his lawyer, Sam Burstyn, was all it took for Arias to found out why: conspiracy to murder. Burstyn said if Arias surrendered he would try and get him bond.

But when Arias spoke next to Arturo de la Vega he received rather different advice. "Coello's hiding, he's not going to surrender," said de la Vega. "If they catch you go down fighting. Shoot them. Blow them away."

"That's great, but they're not looking for you," replied Arias. "If it was you involved you'd be shitting in your pants."

De la Vega said he did not want to get into an argument about who was tougher. And anyway, he said, Centac *was* looking for him, and he was leaving. "I still have some money left. Keep in touch, call me on the beeper."

Arias spent the rest of the day hiding in a relative's house in Miami Beach from where he spoke to his lawyer by telephone. Burstyn warned if he or Coello resisted arrest, the police had orders to shoot to kill. Arias decided to surrender—and to admit to Centac what he had already confessed to his priest. That night Burstyn and a second attorney, Robert Dunlap, collected Arias from Miami Beach and drove him to Metro-Dade police headquarters where three Centac detectives and three government prosecutors waited to conduct the most critical interview of their entire investigation.

True to his "wild man" reputation, Burstyn began negotiations with a preposterous opening gambit. He said Arias would admit his guilt but only in return for a maximum sentence of seven years. The prosecutors were adamant the *minimum* sentence they would accept was twenty years—unless Arias agreed to "cooperate." If he did that, if he agreed to turn on his friends and former colleagues and testify against them if necessary, he might get as little as ten years.

One by one the three Centac detectives—Alex Alvarez, George Plasencia, and Joe Díaz—made what seemed to Arias to be set speeches, pleading with him to "put an end to this." He let them finish, told them he knew he should "do right" for his family, and then asked to speak to Alex Alvarez alone. Centac's youngest detective, who had been so despised and maligned by the Miami River Cops and their families, could hardly contain his excitement as he and Arias went into another room.

"Do you really want to break this case?" said Arias.

"Yes," said Alvarez.

"I'm willing to cooperate but only if you're willing to work this one down. We're going to take this case to the end. But you better be prepared—I've got some heavy shit. Just don't let me down."

"I won't," Alvarez promised.

And because Alvarez kept his word, and Centac and the FBI pursued every lead they were given, Rudy Arias brought the walls of the Shining City tumbling down.

Centac had believed that as many as twenty Miami cops were "dirty." When Arias was shown photographs of present and former Miami police men and women, he identified sixty whom he knew to be corrupt. Three of those officers, when arrested, also agreed to "cooperate" with the government and some of them named other "dirty cops." Clarence Dickson, Miami's police chief, eventually calculated that one out of every ten officers in his department might be "tainted by corruption." If so, no police department in America has been so devastated since Prohibition; in New York City, for example, the celebrated Knapp Commission inquiry incriminated merely one officer out of every 125. Nevertheless, Chief Dickson was extraordinarily grateful to Arias for his revelations; he described him as "a hero."

Arias regarded himself less kindly. "We became the scum," he said of himself and his corrupt colleagues on the midnight shift. Placed in the Witness Protection Program pending his testimony at a series of trials, he suffered bouts of depression and dangerously high blood pressure. Reina, his wife, rejoined him with their daughter. As she and he attempted to come to terms with what he had done, the family were moved, by his account, at least twenty times in three months. Eventually they were relocated to a place they did not know, and where no one knew them, and Arias was given ample time to consider what would happen to his wife and daughter when, as seemed inevitable, he went to jail.

Even so, he more than lived up to his promise of "cooperation." In September 1987 Arias returned to Miami under guard to testify against Ricardo Alemán, the first Miami River Cop to be retried (for "babysitting" some of the cocaine stolen by police in the raid at Jones Boat Yard). Before taking the witness stand Arias agreed to meet Alemán, who remained convinced he could beat the case against him. Arias told him he was wrong and begged him to make a deal with the government because "if I have to testify I'm going to destroy you." Alemán hugged Arias and cried, but ignored his advice. That afternoon Arias took the stand and testified against his friend for almost four hours, proving himself to be what Al Singleton of Centac described as "the most impressive witness I've ever seen." Alemán's attorney attacked Arias as a "criminal trying to save his own neck" and a man who "makes me want to puke," but the jury was not swayed. Alemán was found guilty of conspiracy to possess cocaine and tax evasion. In February 1988 he still awaited sentencing.

Perhaps because of Arias's impressive debut as the government's main witness, three of the original seven Miami River cops changed their pleas to guilty. Armando Estrada, his nervous partner Román Rodríguez, and Arturo de la Vega—whose ambition to leave town was thwarted by police after a high-speed car chase—all admitted to participating in drug rip-offs. Because they refused to cooperate with the government, the prosecution asked for thirty years in prison for each of them—which is precisely what they got.

The remaining two defendants, Armando García and Osvaldo Coello, fled. García disappeared along with his father, Dagoberto, who had played a significant role in the midnight shift's rip-offs and in the conspiracies to murder witnesses. The Garcías remained fugitives at the time of writing, believed to be hiding in Costa Rica, and protected by their own cunning and whatever García had left of the more than two million dollars he obtained through crime.

Osvaldo Coello fled first to Jamaica and then, having obtained a fake Jamaican passport, to Nassau in the Bahamas where he was finally captured in October 1987. Coello had been unable to resist telephoning girl friends in Miami and he was convinced that the calls were traced by Centac, or that one of the women betrayed him. He was wrong. Coello was betrayed by the Miami man who supplied his fake passport and who—having himself been betrayed by an informant—was given a stark choice by Centac: reveal Coello's whereabouts or go to prison for a very long time.

As Coello had promised, he did not give up easily. When Bahamian police first attempted to arrest him at the Nassau house where he was living, Coello floored two constables with his fists and escaped into a nearby forest—clad only in red bikini underpants—ignoring the warning shots fired over his head. Three weeks later, however, he was lured into a trap set by the police on an isolated dock twelve miles from Nassau. This time there was no escape and Coello surrendered without a fight. The Bahamians set a police dog on him anyway.

Coello returned to Miami in handcuffs, looking ten years older than when he left. He offered to plead guilty in return for a maximum sentence of forty years but his prosecutors would accept nothing less than life imprisonment. Having little to lose, Coello went to trial and Rudy Arias was again required to return to Miami to testify against an old friend. In February 1988, Coello was convicted of most of the charges against him.

The hatred for Arias in the courtroom was palpable, as it had been at Alemán's trial—though this time there was additional cause. In September 1987, Coello's father had committed suicide: having been arrested for shoplifting at a supermarket, Coello senior went home to his wife, locked himself in the bathroom, slashed the veins in his arms with a double-edged razor blade, and bled to death in the tub. Arias had been like a second son to Coello senior, and it was Arias the family blamed for his death. Like the families of the other Miami River cops, they could neither understand nor accept that it was greed that brought tragedy to them all.

They did not despise the crimes the Miami River cops committed—they despised Arias for admitting them. Once when he arrived in Miami to testify the FBI found a sign pinned to the courtroom door: "Judas 1987."

In December 1987 Alex Alvarez, George Plasencia, and Joe Díaz were chosen as "officers of the year" by Metro-Dade PD for their work on the Miami River investigation. Al Singleton, their supervisor, was not formally recognized for his contribution. He shrugged off that slight, saying his detectives deserved the honor and he was proud of them. They thought differently and commissioned a plaque of their own to acknowledge that without him they could not have done the job.

At the luncheon held to celebrate the Metro-Dade award, Centac's detectives wanted the guests at the top table to include Raúl Díaz, Centac's founder. The demand was resisted by some senior Metro-Dade officers, perhaps because they truly believed that Díaz was corrupt, and is now "the most dangerous man in Miami." But Centac insisted. Joe Díaz repeated what he has said a hundred times: "Show me the money he took, and I'll be first in line to arrest him."

So Raúl Díaz was there to join in the standing ovation that his protégés received when they collected their award—much the same award that Miami PD might have given to Rudy Arias two years before, had Centac not arrested him.

II

On his involuntary arrival in Florida in February 1987, Carlos Lehder said he was indigent and could not afford a lawyer—a claim somewhat undermined by the six-thousand dollar Rolex watch he wore on his wrist. After two months, however, Lehder hired José Quiñón, a former state prosecutor who had been part of the Miami River defense team, and Edward Shohat, a prominent Jewish attorney in Miami who disregarded the fact that his new client idolized Hitler and had once proposed that all Jews should be shot. Both Shohat and Quiñón said they regarded the Lehder case as the ultimate professional challenge. "This is the type of case that represents to us the highest mountain and we're going after it," said Quiñón. "This is our Everest." Their combined fee for scaling such heights was rumored (by envious colleagues) to be two million dollars.

The stakes were also high for the prosecution, though in a very different way. Robert Merkle, US Attorney for the Middle District of Florida, was nicknamed "Mad Dog" by his fellow prosecutors for his zeal in rooting out public corruption. In five years his office had indicted more than seventy judges, attorneys, federal agents, state representatives, county commissioners, state prosecutors, local lawmen, and postal workers. Most were convicted but not all, and Merkle's occasional failures led to the assembly of an army of powerful critics calling for his head. "In Merkle's paranoid fantasy, he is Central Florida's sole repository of honesty and character," said an editorial in the *St. Petersburg Times.* And the *Tampa Tribune* wrote: "We urge the Justice Department, respectfully but urgently, to get Merkle out of here." In January 1987 Bob Martínez, Florida's newly elected Republican governor, was aggressively questioned by Merkle when he took the witness stand to defend himself against unsubstantiated allegations of bribery. Four days later the governor called the White House, launching the third campaign in five years to have Merkle removed from office. The campaign would probably have succeeded—but for the arrest of Carlos Lehder.

Merkle assigned himself the case, and the governor agreed to a truce until Lehder's trial was over. As Republican Congressman Bill Young told *The Wall Street Journal:* "This is just not the time to be making political moves when as big a drug case as this is being handled by Bob Merkle."

When Lehder's trial began in Jacksonville in November 1987, the jury was presented with two startlingly different profiles of the man in the dock. According to Merkle's opening statement, Lehder was the would-be "king of cocaine," a politically motivated revolutionary driven by lust for money and hatred for the United States. According to Edward Shohat he was plain "Joe": a rich, brash property developer with a big mouth; not a drug trafficker but a *victim* of drug traffickers who had framed him, and of a vindictive United States government which did not like his politics.

The truth lay somewhere in the middle. Carlos Lehder was never a "cocaine kingpin" in the sense that Jorge Ochoa, and Pablo Escobar, and Gonzalo Rodríguez Gacha were and are. And his absurd political rantings were more the product of opportunism—and, perhaps, his addiction to *basuco*—than revolutionary ideology. But for as long as Lehder was permitted to use Norman's Cay as a transshipment point and a safe haven, he led the effort to flood the United States with cocaine and in so doing he caused irreparable harm.

In his opening statement Merkle promised the jury it would hear evidence that Lehder was allowed to remain on Norman's Cay because he made payments to Bahamian officials and "directly to the prime minister of the Bahamas, still the prime minister, Lynden Pindling." At the time of writing some evidence had been presented but it was clear from what Merkle said that he intended to rely, to a large extent, on the testimony of Gorman Bannister.

There was no doubt Gorman would testify he accompanied his father, Everette, to Colombia to meet Lehder, who complained of Norman's Cay being "closed down" despite the bribes he had paid. There was also no doubt Gorman would testify that whenever his father took money—be it from busi-

nessmen seeking deals, international fugitives, or drug traffickers—Prime Minister Pindling *"always* got his share."

What was in doubt, at least for a while, was whether Gorman
Bannister would be able to testify at all.

The US Marshals Service claims its federal Witness Protection
Program has never lost a customer, but it came desperately
close to losing Gorman.

Having been debriefed by the DEA, and having agreed to
testify at Lehder's trial, Gorman was handed over to the Marshals for safekeeping until his day in court. It was obvious he
needed help to break his fourteen-year addiction to cocaine
and, preferably, treatment at a residential center where he
would not be exposed to temptation. Instead Gorman was sent
to Memphis, Tennessee, where, in his words, "there is more shit
on the streets than I've ever seen." He was given a rented apartment, fake identity, a used car, and three hundred dollars a
week—and left to his own devices.

The inevitable happened when the marshal responsible for
Gorman gave him two weeks' money in one lump sum, and left
Memphis for a vacation. Alone in a city where he had no
friends, no one to talk to, and no support, Gorman spent most
of the six hundred dollars on crack. When the binge (modest by
his standards) was over, Gorman discovered his car had been
stolen in the course of it.

The response of the Marshals service in Washington to Gorman's confession of what he had done was to tell him he was
being "immediately terminated" from the Witness Protection
Program. And, but for intervention of the DEA and Merkle's
office, that is undoubtedly what would have happened.

Even so it was months before Gorman was moved to a place
where crack is not available on almost every street corner, and
placed in a residential rehabilitation clinic. In early 1988, still
awaiting his day in court, he seemed to be benefiting from the
treatment. For one thing, he fully understood that the only person who could break his addiction to cocaine was himself.

III

While he was still operating from Norman's Cay, Carlos Lehder told his wife, Jemel, that he had divorced her in Haiti. He then took a new wife, Liliana García Osorio, a pretty middle-class girl from his hometown of Armenia, whom he married on Norman's Cay—supposedly. The caveat is necessary because there are no official records of the divorce nor of the subsequent marriage. Liliana nevertheless insists she is Lehder's real wife and for supporting evidence points to their five-year-old daughter. She refers to Jemel as "the other woman." Jemel, for her part, says the child cannot possibly be Lehder's because he has an abnormally low sperm count, and, anyway she insists she is still married to him.

The issue became relevant after Lehder's arrest and extradition to the United States because of the near-certainty he would spend most of the rest of his life in prison: Lehder would still be wealthy, even after paying his lawyers, and Jemel and Liliana were both determined to secure what they thought they were entitled to.

To some extent the division was decided by geography. Liliana lives in Armenia, in a mock-Spanish colonial house Lehder bought for her, and she took de facto control of *La Posada Alemana* which, together with Lehder's brother and sister, she hoped to re-open as a tourist resort. Meanwhile Jemel, who lives in New York, gained control of two condominiums in Miami. That left Norman's Cay which, even in its dilapidated state, might be worth three or four million dollars.

Jemel believed that some of the property on the island might be registered in her name and, if so, she wanted to claim it—something she was sure Lehder would approve of. The trouble was, she needed to visit Lehder in prison to get his consent but was afraid that if she did, she too would be arrested. At the very least she feared she would be subpoenaed and forced to testify against him.

We became aware of Jemel's dilemma in September 1987 when we asked to interview her about Lehder and their life together. We made our approach through Luis "Kojak" García, who knew Jemel because she was a childhood friend of his wife, Neysa.

Jemel agreed to be interviewed in Miami, and even volunteered to persuade Lehder to talk to us if we could establish three things: that she was not "wanted" by the DEA; that she would not be forced to testify against Lehder; and, who owned the property on Norman's Cay. The DEA said there was no indictment outstanding against her. To the second question the answer was less clear-cut: certainly, Merkle wanted her to testify at Lehder's trial but the DEA believed that if she was subpoenaed she would be a hostile witness, and worthless; the hope was that, after the interview, Kojak would persuade her to cooperate, as he had persuaded Gorman Bannister. The answer to the third question would have disappointed Jemel, and was not passed on to her. We learned the Bahamian government had begun proceedings to seize Norman's Cay, on the grounds it had been used for illegal activity.

Early in the morning of September 29, Kojak flew to New York City to collect Jemel and accompany her back to Miami, where the promised interview was to begin the next day. She was not at her apartment where they had arranged to meet but Kojak found her at her mother's home. The mother said she had forbidden Jemel to go to Miami. She claimed to have destroyed the collection of documents and photographs that Jemel had promised to bring to Miami. She accused Kojak of being a government agent and delivered a strident tirade against "Yankee imperialism." Kojak's opinion of "communists" was the same as that shared by most Cuban-Americans and it is safe to assume that he did not suffer the attack in silence.

The argument ended when Jemel whispered to Kojak in English (which her mother does not speak fluently) that she still intended to accompany him to Miami, and that the photographs and documents were safe. She said she would meet him at her apartment at 5 P.M.

That afternoon, while waiting for the appointment, Kojak

suffered a coronary occlusion—an obstruction of the coronary artery, cutting off the supply of blood to his heart. He complained of severe chest pains and of losing feeling in his arms and legs but he would not go to a hospital. Instead he kept his appointment with Jemel. This time she was accompanied by an aunt and there was a similar, if less heated, discussion to the one that had taken place in the morning. At the end of it Jemel stalled: she said she might be willing to go to Miami in a few days' time.

Kojak caught the last plane home and reached Miami at about midnight. He said he felt a little better and again refused to go to a hospital. He said he was tired and wanted to sleep. He promised he would go to a doctor in the morning.

At a little after 4 A.M. his heart stopped beating and he fell out of bed. Neysa attempted to revive him with mouth-to-mouth resuscitation, and the paramedics who arrived within ten minutes did manage to get his heart beating again. It was illusory. Luis "Kojak" García was pronounced dead shortly after arrival at Miami's Mercy Hospital. He was fifty-five years old.

Notes and Sources

O ur professional interest in the Cocaine Wars dates back to
1983 when one of us went to live in Colombia and began
chronicling the activities of the Cartel at what was undoubtedly its most turbulent time. And in the spring and summer of
1985, two of us participated in an investigation mounted by *The
Sunday Times* of London into the crucial role of the Bahamas
in drug trafficking, and the activities of Carlos Lehder. Full-
time work on this book began in Miami in October 1985 and
was completed in January 1988.

We had help. Justine Picardie and Dorothy Wade—who, with
us, make up Reporters International—took time off from the
book they were working on to conduct research and interviews
for us in London, and both of them spent extended periods in
Miami. Dorothy Wade carried out all of the research and interviews in Spain. We also recruited the help and experience of
Michael Graham, formerly a crime reporter for the *Detroit
Free Press, The San Diego Union,* and the *Los Angeles Daily
News.* He made inquiries for us in California and conducted a
series of interviews in Miami.

PROLOGUE: *The Education of Jack Blum*

By the time Jack Blum arrived in Miami in March 1987 to begin
his education, we had been based in the city for eighteen
months and knew many of the people who became either his

witnesses or his targets. We exchanged thoughts and ideas with him on that first trip, and witnessed his astonishment. We saw him regularly in Miami and Washington throughout the remainder of 1987.

PART ONE *1. The Kingdom of the Ochoas*

We have never met Jorge Ochoa nor his brothers, though we tried. Even at home in Medellín, "it is very difficult to get to talk to Jorge," said one of his friends. When full-time work on this book began in the fall of 1985, Ochoa had already been in jail in Spain for almost a year awaiting extradition. In late 1985 and 1986 Dorothy Wade spent weeks in Madrid trying to get to him, but the Spanish authorities would not allow it. Ochoa sent a message: "I wish you well with your book."

Our description of the Ochoas and their life-style is, therefore, based on interviews with friends, relatives, and lawyers in Colombia and Spain. They included Juan David Botero, a young lawyer from Medellín who abandoned his local practice for several months to assist Ochoa's defense in Spain. Botero is not a criminal lawyer nor even one of the Ochoas' paid attorneys. He was attracted to the case, he said, by the "Nicaraguan factor," and also by what he saw as the erroneous American view of cocaine trafficking in Latin America: "When they [the Americans] needed gold, we produced gold. When they needed coffee, we produced coffee. Now they want cocaine, so we produce it because they buy it. So cocaine trafficking can never be reduced through law enforcement and repression alone. It needs a social solution."

Another important source on Ochoa was Mario Arango, who performs a peculiar balancing act in Medellín, where he is an author, a lawyer, a journalist, a university professor, and a politician, all at the same time. We spoke to him frequently in both Madrid and later in Medellín, where he was running for mayor. He denies that Jorge Ochoa is a drug trafficker, but he defends Medellín's major industry in light of the economic realities of the region: for Arango, producing cocaine is no worse than manufacturing cigarettes or alcohol.

Other information about the Ochoas came from law enforcement officials, journalists, academics, and ordinary people in Bogotá and Medellín, some of whom know the Ochoas well and have been to their homes. Without exception, all of our informants demanded anonymity.

The quote, "Bomb Medellín . . . ," is from the transcript of an interview with one of the DEA special agents with whom we met regularly in Miami.

Our description of Medellín is based on what we saw.

Our estimate of how many anti-drug government officials, judges, policemen, and journalists have been killed in Colombia is a very conservative one. Other reporters claim the toll is much higher, but we know of nobody who has kept an accurate record.

Our estimate of the amount of cocaine that emanates from Medellín was extracted from DEA reports. It can be no more that an educated guess.

The admission from a senior banker that *narco* dollars are "needed" in Colombia to keep the economy going was obtained in an off-the-record interview with that official. He went on to say: "How else can I explain the continued existence of the 'Sinister Window' at the [Central] bank, where anybody can change dollars for pesos with no restrictions whatsoever and no questions asked?"

Our description of the Cartel and how it operates was compiled primarily from court documents and the testimony of traffickers who, to save themselves, agreed to give evidence. It is obviously true that such testimony is self-serving and we have treated it with caution. The principal sources within this category were Adler "Barry" Seal and Max Mermelstein, neither of whom we met (in Seal's case, because he was killed before he could keep the appointment). The testimony we relied on was therefore taken from: a statement sworn by Seal before Federal Judge James L. King in Miami on November 30, 1984, which was presented to the Spanish government during the attempt to extradite Jorge Ochoa; Max Mermelstein's testimony in the case of *The United States v. Carlos Sarmiento, et al.,* given in Miami on May 28, 1987; and Mermelstein's testimony in the case *State of Louisiana v. Miguel Vélez, et al.,* in Calcasieu, Louisiana, in April 1987.

The "trafficker's bible," written by Carlos Madrid Palacios, was an exhibit in the 1984 prosecution of Carlos Bustamante, et al., and it is to be found in the exhibits file of Case Number 84-493-Cr-KING in the US Federal Court in Miami.

2. The Third Scourge of Mankind

Our history of coca and cocaine was assembled from the vast literature, both published and unpublished, that exists on those subjects. We relied principally on: *Cocaine: Chemical, Biological, Clinical, Social and Treatment Aspects,* by S. J. Mule (CRC Press, 1976); an undated and untitled DEA internal report; "The Role of Coca in the History, Religion and Medicine of South American Indians," by Richard Martin, published in *Economic Botany,* May 1970; *Drugs and Information Control,* by Jerald W. Cloyd (Greenwood, 1982); *The Coca Leaf and Cocaine Papers,* edited by George Andrews and David Solomon (Harcourt, Brace, Jovanovich, 1975); *Big Deal: The Politics of the Illicit Drugs Business,* by Anthony Henman and Roger Lewis (Pluto Press, 1985); "Cocaine Consciousness, the Gourmet Trip," by Jerry Hopkins, originally published in *Rolling Stone* magazine in 1971; *Mama Coca,* by "Antonil," (Hassle Free Press, 1978).

Our account of the visit to Medellín by two federal agents in 1959 comes from Mario Arango's book *Los Condenados de la Coca, el manejo politico de la droga* (Editorial Arango, 1985).

Our description of Medellín as a traditional smuggling center depends largely on interviews with a local writer who has studied the subject extensively. He says of the present generation of traffickers: "We are not talking about geniuses but pragmatists who like to stay on top of things by improvising and taking risks. It's happened here for centuries. What they've done now is apply their drive to the world's most expensive commodity. And from the point of view of free enterprise, there is nothing wrong with it, is there?"

3. Walsh's Warning

Miguel Walsh's prescient paper was classified as "Sensitive" by the DEA and has not been released. Walsh's paper, "A Survey

of Reporting on Cocaine Hydrochloride Production and Trafficking Within and From Colombia," was remarkably comprehensive; it ran to seventy-one closely typed pages and came
with statistical annexes, tables, maps, and graphs. We wanted
to congratulate him but he had left the DEA and was rumored
to be working in one of the unlisted departments of the Penta-
gon; we were unable to trace him.

We did not go to Bolivia. Our description of that country and
the role it played in the cocaine explosion is based on the
knowledge of a senior DEA intelligence analyst whom we interviewed in Washington twice, and also on the work of other
writers. For an understanding of how Bolivia was corrupted by
coca, we relied on *Rebellion in the Veins: Political Struggle in
Bolivia 1952–1982*, by James Dunkerley (Verso, 1984)—easily
the best account to date of Bolivia's turbulent modern history.
According to Dunkerley, René Bascopé, a Bolivian journalist
writing for the left-wing weekly *Aquí*, was the first person to
reveal that the extraordinary expansion of the coca industry in
Bolivia in 1975 was the work of members of the *Asociación de
Productores de Algodón.*

Details of the cocaine smuggling routes were obtained from
Walsh's report. According to more recent studies, the same
routes continue to be used.

For general descriptions of Bolivia, we drew on three authori-
tative portraits of the nation: *Bolivia: Land, People, and Institutions*, by Olen E. Leonard (Scarecrow Press, 1952); *Bolivia: The
Gate of the Sun*, by Margaret Joan Anstee (Paul S. Eriksson,
Inc., 1970); and *Bolivia: A Profile*, by William Carter (Praeger,
1971).

We should point out that there was a similar, though smaller,
increase in the coca harvest of Peru, which rivals Bolivia as the
main supplier for the basic ingredient of cocaine. We chose to
concentrate on what happened in Bolivia because of the overt
involvement of the government in the decision to plant "one
heck of a lot of trees." That quote comes from our interview
with a DEA intelligence analyst in Washington.

The story of the "Papa, come home" telephone call Jorge
Ochoa is supposed to have made to his father may be apocry-
phal but it is widely believed in Medellín. Ochoa's uncle, from

whom he supposedly received sixty pounds of cocaine while in Miami, was murdered in Colombia in 1978. According to a report in *The Miami Herald,* published on November 23, 1987: "The DEA heard speculation that Ochoa had his uncle killed," and then took over his trafficking organization—but we know of no evidence to support that speculation.

The life and deeds of Pablo Escobar remained generally unknown until March 1982, when he was elected to the national assembly as an alternate congressman for Medellín. Up until then, he was seen as a civic benefactor, engaged in public endeavors to help the poor. Only a handful of people questioned the origins of his wealth, and even fewer ventured to say that he was one of Colombia's most prolific cocaine traffickers. His cover was finally blown in 1983—the year we began our research in Colombia—when he became involved in a personal feud with then Justice Minister Rodrigo Lara Bonilla, and investigative journalists from *El Espectador* of Bogotá offered proof of his involvement in drug trafficking. Escobar denied the allegations but never contested them in court. Our description of his present life-style and of his *Hacienda Nápoles* depends on people who know Escobar and the house, and whom we interviewed in Medellín in 1987.

4. Dadeland

All of our information about Raúl Díaz comes from the horse's mouth, so to speak. Throughout 1987 he submitted to innumerable interviews both formal and casual, and allowed us access to his voluminous records and diaries. He was always extraordinarily frank, even about his personal life and his finances. We should make it clear where our prejudice lies: we do not believe he was corrupt, or that his relationship with Ricardo "Monkey" Morales—or any of his other informants—derived from self-interest.

Our description of the blind faith of Monumental Properties is based on articles published by *The Miami Herald* at the time. In a retrospective study published in October 1987, *The Herald* quoted one of the original store owners as saying: "We started out in a valley. It was dead here. During the Cuban missile crisis they shut down US 1. They had army tanks headed down to Key West. . . . I'd drive in the rear lot in the morning and snakes would be sunbathing in the parking lot." Dadeland now comprises 1.4 million square feet spread over seventy-one acres.

Our various descriptions of the mass exodus from Cuba, and its aftermath, are based primarily on interviews with experts in Miami who are acknowledged in the notes for Chapter 12, Fruits of Rage.

Our description of the Dadeland massacre is based on the official police report.

The explanation for the massacre given by Hugo Echeverría Brand comes from a Metro-Dade PD internal memorandum dated November 17, 1982, which recounts the debriefing of Echeverría. The supporting account given by the owner of the pet shop is taken from an internal memo dated August 26, 1982.

The descriptions of the homicides that preceded Dadeland are based on police files. The description of the "Kendall Six" massacre comes from interviews with Detective Joe Díaz.

5. *The Birth of Centac 26*

The difficulties of investigating "drug-related homicides" were described to us in interviews with Metro-Dade homicide detectives. We also relied on a number of Metro-Dade internal memoranda, principally one written on April 19, 1982, headed: "Difficulties in solving Latin drug-related homicides."

Our description of the proposal for Centac 26 is based on the written submission itself. This was the last Central Tactical Unit to be created by Washington, and, when the Centac concept became unfashionable, the unit was officially redesignated as a Special Enforcement Operation (SEO) and given the codename Redrum—murder spell backwards. SEO never caught on with members of the squad, however; they continue to refer to themselves, with pride, as Centac.

We attempted to interview "Amílcar"—Rafael León Rodríguez—in the state prison in central Florida where he is now serving thirty years for the double homicide; permission was refused by the prison authorities. Our description of those homicides and Amílcar's other activities is therefore based on police files. Our description of his pursuit and final capture is based on interviews with Raúl Díaz and detectives Joe Díaz and George Plasencia.

6. Decline and Fall

The numerous allegations of corruption against Raúl Díaz are based on the following documents: two files maintained on Díaz by the FBI, one in Miami and one at its Washington headquarters, both of which Díaz obtained under the Freedom of Information Act; the report of a Disposition Panel of Metro-Dade PD, dated August 4, 1983, in which fourteen charges against Díaz were considered—and rejected, as "unfounded" or "not substantiated"; a separate report by another Metro-Dade PD Disposition Panel, dated November 14, 1983, which rejected four serious allegations against Díaz, but which sustained a fifth allegation that he had attempted to influence Nancy Cid (formerly Nancy Lamazares) "in the manner in which she was to respond to questioning, if she had been subpoenaed to testify" before a grand jury.

We also obtained a copy of the original transcript of the tape-recorded conversation between Díaz and Nancy Cid.

Our descriptions of Centac's detectives are based on interviews with them, interviews with some of their colleagues in Homicide, and personal observation.

The descriptions of Monkey Morales, and his role in the Sixteenth Street caper, come from our interviews with Raúl Díaz, court records, and contemporaneous reports in *The Miami Herald.* As we have indicated in the text, we also owe a debt to John Rothchild for his article on Monkey Morales, published in *Harper's* magazine in January 1982. Rothchild is an extremely witty writer, but also a perceptive one, and a diligent researcher; in the course of our inquires about the Monkey, we found his footprints were everywhere.

Our assertions about Juan Cid come from the findings of the two Disposition Panels that heard the complaints against Díaz, interviews with Díaz, and testimony contained in Juan Cid's file to be found in the records of the Federal District Court in

Miami. At the time of writing, Cid was in prison awaiting trial—in Lafayette, Louisiana, for drug trafficking, and in Miami, for filing false tax returns and for interstate and foreign commerce violations. We attempted to talk to Cid's attorney, Douglas Williams, but he declined to discuss his client's case, or any matter concerning Raúl Díaz.

7. Enter the Task Force

Our descriptions of the South Florida Task Force are based on its own publicity and contemporary newspaper reports. Stanley Marcus, who was selected to run the US Attorney's Office in Miami, later became a federal judge and was replaced by his deputy, Leon Kellner.

Our assertion that the Task Force has comprehensively failed to halt the flow of drugs into South Florida is based on countless interviews in Miami with federal drug agents and narcotics detectives; in more than two years, we did not meet one who believed that America had come anywhere close to winning "the war on drugs." We also relied on our regular conversations with drug smugglers, both boatmen and pilots, most of whom we met through Luis "Kojak" García. It may seem curious that smugglers would talk to reporters—especially in the presence of Kojak, somebody they knew was an informant for the DEA—but the plain fact is they did so willingly, so long as we stayed away from specifics, and observed the fictional understanding that they had, of course, "retired"; we took it as a measure of their confidence. Black Carlos was one of those who spoke to us. His offer to prove to the DEA the ineffectiveness of Blue Lightning was made in Kojak's house.

Our claim that cocaine is more openly available in parts of Miami than cigarettes is literally true. They don't sell tobacco on street corners in Coconut Grove; they do sell crack. Perhaps that is why, according to a Dade County grand jury report, 90 percent of those arrested for criminal violations during 1986 were found to have drugs in their system; the comparable figure for New York and Washington, D.C., was 65 percent.

We interviewed Luis Fernández and Preston Lucas on a regular basis, and our colleagues, Dorothy Wade and Justine Picardie, went out onto the streets with them to watch them work their magic. Both of them described to us the ever-growing supply of cocaine on the market and their inability to do anything about it. Lucas found this particularly dispiriting; in late 1987, after four years of undercover work, he went back into uniform.

PART TWO 8. *Kojak*

We met Luis "Kojak" García and interviewed him for the first time on the day we arrived in Miami in October 1985. At the end of that interview, and in a gesture of what turned out to be typical generosity, Kojak handed over the first draft of a manuscript he had written about his life, and some sixty hours of tape recordings in which he described his drug-trafficking activities. Once we had absorbed that material, he submitted to innumerable interviews and provided documents and photographs; he introduced us to many of his former "employees"; and he became our (unpaid) consultant and guide to the drug trafficking business. When he and we were in Miami, there was hardly a day that we did not see him. We were with him on the day that he learned a contract had been placed on his life, and we were with him when he died, of a heart attack, on September 30, 1987. It is is literally true that this book could not possibly have been written without him.

All of the episodes involving Kojak come from him though, where possible, we obtained confirmation of key events from his former associates, boatmen and pilots.

Our recent history of drug trafficking in the Bahamas depends primarily on the report of a Commission of Inquiry that was appointed by the Bahamian government "to inquire into the illegal use of the Bahamas for the transshipment of dangerous drugs destined for the United States" in November 1983. The commission's report was submitted in December 1984.

Detective Superintendent David Stockley described Kojak as "truly evil" in an interview in London with Justine Picardie.

Assistant Commissioner Howard Smith denied receiving bribes from Kojak, but the Commission of Inquiry did not believe him. He was subsequently charged and Kojak agreed to go to the Bahamas to testify against him. However, when Kojak arrived in Nassau for Smith's trial, in February 1986, the attorney general refused to sign an agreement that would have given Kojak blanket immunity against prosecution—and he in turn refused to testify against Smith. The charges were dropped, and Smith was allowed to resign from the police force.

9. The Men Who Stole Paradise

In early 1985 after the Commission of Inquiry's report was published, the Insight team of *The Sunday Times* of London launched an investigation into the Pindling government. The resulting 20,000-word article, entitled "Paradise Lost," was published by *The Sunday Times Magazine* on September 29, 1985. One of us led that investigation and one of us participated in it, and much of the information contained in this chapter derives from it. We gratefully acknowledge our debt to the other reporters who worked on that investigation: Will Ellsworth-Jones, Andrew Hogg, Tim McGirk, and Peter Murtagh.

When Gorman Bannister decided to "defect" to the United States, he first approached Eileen Carron, the editor and publisher of *The Tribune* in Nassau who, at some risk to herself, had done as much as anybody to expose corruption in the Bahamas. Mrs. Carron would not and could not pay the money that Gorman was asking for his story, but she put him in contact with Ira Silverman and Brian Ross of NBC Television News, whose explosive revelations about what had happened on Norman's Cay had led to the setting up of the Commission of Inquiry. Ross and Silverman in turn brought Gorman to us, and though we could not and would not pay Gorman for his story, we did agree to finance his "escape": with the help of *The Sunday Times* of London, we provided him with an airline ticket; we paid his food and hotel bills for the eight days it took to debrief him; and, we gave him $5,000 to enable him to make overdue alimony payments to his ex-wife, and, supposedly, to rent an apartment to "begin a new life."

When, in the course of our debriefing, it became clear that Gorman could provide evidence against Carlos Lehder—then awaiting trial in Jacksonville, Florida—we introduced Gorman to Kojak, who, with great skill, persuaded him to meet agents of the DEA. The DEA persuaded Gorman to agree to testify against Lehder and arranged for him to be given a new identity and placed in the federal Witness Protection Program.

But before that could happen, and while Gorman was still in our informal custody, he "escaped" from the Miami hotel where we had installed him, and disappeared. It took us more than twenty-four hours to find him, and we would not have done so without the help of Kojak and Gene Francar of the DEA, who joined us on a search of some of the more unappealing areas of Liberty City and Coconut Grove. By then, Gorman had spent some $1,500 on crack and other illegal drugs, all of which he had consumed. We confiscated what remained of the $5,000, and insisted that he agree to enter the Witness Protection Program immediately, and seek medical help to fight his drug addiction. We remained in frequent contact with him throughout this period and grew extremely fond of him. At the time of writing, he had graduated from the rehabilitation program, and was about to testify at Lehder's trial.

All of the descriptions and quotations attributed to Gorman in the text come from the transcript of our tape-recorded interviews with him.

Our biography of Sir Lynden Pindling is based on the research of Will Ellsworth-Jones of *The Sunday Times*, who interviewed the prime minister twice during the summer of 1985. The details of Everette Bannister's career come from Gorman.

Our assertion that Robert Vesco became involved in drug trafficking is based partially on Gorman's testimony, and on the word of Carlos Lehder's wife, Jemel.

10. Devil's Island

Our description of Norman's Cay comes from Tim McGirk of *The Sunday Times*, who visited the island with photographer Frank Herrmann for four days in July 1985. Their escort and guide on that expedition was the indomitable Professor Richard Novak, who described his adventures of the Lehder era to McGirk and one of the authors.

Our biography of Lehder and the story of his triumphant

return to his native Armenia was provided, in part, by a local journalist in Armenia, Jorge Eliécer Orozco, who, as a correspondent for *El Tiempo* of Bogotá and the nationwide radio network *Radio Cadena Nacional,* watched Lehder's rise and fall over a period of six years. We have talked to Orozco and studied his book *Lehder: El Hombre*—"Lehder: The Man"— published by Plaza & Janes in Bogotá in 1987.

We also relied on Jemel Lehder, his wife. As we describe in the section, "Endgames," Kojak spoke to her on our behalf on two occasions shortly before he died in September 1987.

The description of how Lehder obtained his foothold on Norman's Cay comes from Carl Hiassen and Jim McGee of *The Miami Herald,* who researched and wrote an excellent series of reports on the Bahamas entitled "Nation for Sale." Hiassen and McGee were extremely generous to us in providing information—and, incidentally, Hiassen is, without doubt, the most perceptive professional observer of Miami; for anybody who wishes to understand the city his regular column in *The Herald* is required reading.

The testimony of Ed and Emilie Ward is taken from the transcripts of their evidence given to the Commission of Inquiry, as is the account of Norman Solomon.

"That was when we were on the same side," is a quotation taken from the transcript of one of our interviews with DEA agents in Miami.

Timothy Minnig's account is taken from his evidence to the Commission of Inquiry, and a follow-up interview with Minnig by Will Ellsworth-Jones of *The Sunday Times,* conducted in the summer of 1985.

Our description of Lehder's continuing activities on Norman's Cay comes from contemporaneous reports in *The Tribune,* and evidence given to the Commission of Inquiry. Our assertion that some members of Pindling's cabinet believed there was truth in NBC's allegations comes from our interviews with those ministers.

The allegations of "Tommy" Maillis are based on our interviews with him. In the spring of 1987, we learned that Maillis had shown the compromising pictures of Pindling to a DEA agent in Miami. Through intermediaries, we contacted Maillis in Greece, where he was a fugitive, and he agreed to meet us for "exploratory talks." *The Sunday Times* of London financed that expedition, and sent along the present editor of its Insight team, Andrew Hogg. Since he knew Maillis, and could test his claims, we also asked Kojak to accompany us.

We met Maillis in Athens and then accompanied him to his home island of Kalymnos where, for four days, we attempted to reconcile our differences: he was determined to tell us nothing without payment of some vast if unspecified sum; we were determined to extract what he knew without paying him one red cent. In the end, we probably got the better of the negotiations in that Maillis did tell us a little of what he knew, and we did not pay him. We acknowledge that there are enormous gaps in his story, which he declined to fill, but we are certain of two things: Maillis did work for the CIA and he did obtain highly compromising photographs of Pindling.

Our description of Maillis's role in "Operation Grouper" depends on the testimony of government witnesses given at Maillis's trial.

11. "If You Play, You Pay"

Our description of Lehder's activities in Armenia depends, primarily, on Jorge Eliécer Orozco. The description of the Bannisters' visit to *La Posada Alemana* comes, obviously, from Gorman.

Kojak's dealings with Everette Bannister, which both he and Gorman described, have been emphatically denied by Bannister. The Commission of Inquiry did not believe Bannister, and he, too was subsequently charged; however, when the Bahamian government refused to give Kojak the kind of comprehensive immunity he sought, he also declined to testify at Bannister's trial, and Bannister, like Assistant Commissioner Howard Smith, was acquitted of all charges. At the time of writing he remains what he has always been: a wheeler-dealer of remarkable stamina, and one who appears to enjoy a charmed life.

Our description of the events concerning Frank Barber depends on Kojak and agents of the DEA.

We talked to Gene Francar of the DEA on a number of occasions, and he read the manuscript of this book prior to its publication. That does not mean he approves of its contents, but he did say: "You've got it close enough."

PART THREE *12. The Fraternal Order*

Our account of the Miami River affair is based on three primary sources: an exhaustive examination of some twenty-eight volumes of statements, depositions, reports, and exhibits that the trial produced; detailed and repeated interviews with the detectives of Centac; and the alarmingly frank confessions of Rodolfo "Rudy" Arias. We also attended the Miami River Cops trials and most of the pretrial proceedings.

Our description of the voyage up the Miami River is based on the testimony of one of those who made it, Pedro Ramos.

We had originally intended to include much more about the history of Miami, until we discovered that Miami was suddenly in vogue and generating more books on the subject than any city library could stock. By that stage we had spent some time at the Historical Museum of Southern Florida and talked to many historians and "pioneers," including Thelma Peters and Joe Pero. Arva Moore Parks was helpful in pointing us in the right direction. Our very brief history of Miami is based on that research.

Our description of the career of Pedro Martínez comes primarily from his son, Faustino, whom we interviewed three times. So, too, does the description of how Centac became involved in the case and received the first indications that Miami PD was riddled with corruption.

The litany of other police corruption is based primarily on the contemporary reporting of *The Miami Herald,* though Jacqueline Quintana's account comes from the Centac detectives who interviewed her and from the evidence that she gave at two trials—the first in state court in Miami where Ricardo Alemán was acquitted of all nine charges, to the amazement of one of his own defense attorneys.

The judge who said "We are literally on the ragged edge of anarchy," said it in the presence of Richard Capen, publisher of *The Miami Herald.* Capen included it in a column he wrote for that newspaper, but he would not name the judge.

The quotations and opinions of Geoffrey Alpert come from two interviews he granted us.

During the twenty-seven months we spent in Miami working on the book, our base was in Coconut Grove and our description of what happens there is based largely on what we saw.

Bernard Garmire's experience as Miami's police chief was so disturbing and painful to him he would have preferred to forget it. Nevertheless, he agreed to see us in Phoenix, Arizona, and talked about those embattled times for two days. However, not all of the anecdotes of that period come from him, for we also spoke at length to officers who served under him including: Richard Witt, now chief of police at Hollywood, Florida; Major Newell Horne, retired to his home state of Georgia; Major Adam Klimkowski, now retired; Assistant Chief Kenneth Fox, now a Miami realtor. Hunter George, who covered the police department for *The Miami Herald* during some of that period and who is now executive editor of *The News and Observer* in Raleigh, North Carolina, also helped us, and he is the "local journalist" quoted in the text.

We should say that Garmire disputes the account we give of the meeting at which he announced to his senior staff that they had caused his wife's stroke. He says he can remember no such occasion, and that those staff members would not have had "the intestinal fortitude" to offer to buy his airline ticket home.

The account of Walter Headley's reign at Miami PD is based on contemporary newspaper reports, *Criminal Justice in Miami 1896–1930* by Paul S. George, an unpublished doctoral thesis for Florida State University, 1975, and an interview with Headley's son, Jack, who also served in the Miami PD for twelve years, and who loaned us his father's collection of memorabilia.

Our description of then Mayor Maurice Ferré is based on numerous interviews with fellow politicians, city officials, and senior police officers who, on this subject, wish to remain anonymous; they do not lightly dismiss his alleged study of the works of Machiavelli. Ferré himself granted us one interview. (In November 1987, he attempted to regain the mayor's seat, running on his record. He reached the runoffs against the incumbent mayor but was overwhelmingly defeated.)

13. Fruits of Rage

The description of the murder of Arthur McDuffie is based on interviews with Marvin Dunn, an associate professor at Florida International University who studied the causes and consequences of that brutal act for his excellent book, *The Miami Riot of 1980,* coauthored with Bruce Porter (Lexington Books, 1984).

Whilst there is little doubt that McDuffie's murder had racial overtones, and blacks in Miami had more than enough cause to feel that they were discriminated against, we should enter the caveat that the beating of McDuffie came at the end of a high-speed chase. He had, allegedly, failed to stop at a red light and "gave the finger" to a watching police officer. In the resulting chase he led more than one dozen patrol cars through the streets of downtown Miami at speeds sometimes exceeding 100 MPH. Sergeant Al Singleton, now with Centac, was one of the Homicide investigators who became involved with the McDuffie case, and he points out that, in that kind of situation, the adrenaline builds up so that by the end of the chase, the officers are in a high state of excitement. In his words, "You're liable to take a beating whether you're black, white, or yellow." His view is that in McDuffie's case "the assault just got totally out of hand."

Our description of the riots themselves depend on Dunn—who did his personal best to damp them down—and interviews by Justine Picardie with a number of leaders of the black community in Miami, including: Georgia Ayers, John Bennett, T. Willard Fair, Thelma Gibson, and George Knox, who was at the time of the riots Miami's city attorney.

The Mariel boatlift and its aftermath were extensively documented and our general description of it depends on: *Why? The Cuban Exodus* by Professor Juan Clark, for the Union of Cubans in Exile; *After Mariel: A Survey of the Re-Settlement Experiences of 1980 Cuban Refugees in Miami* by Clark, Portes, and Manning; *The Cuban Refugee Problem in Perspective,*

1959–1980, prepared by Sylvia Castellanos for the Heritage Foundation; and Wayne S. Smith's account, *The Closest of Enemies* (W. W. Norton, 1987); Smith was chief of the US Interests Section in Havana at the time.

In addition, Dorothy Wade and we interviewed a number of Mariel refugees, including Mario Jardón, Pedro Peña, and Dinorah Alonso; Estrella Benítez, who helped to organize the boatlift, and Professor Juan Clark. We also interviewed Dr. Jeffrey Silbert and Bob Stephenson, respectively, the executive director and the special projects assistant of the Dade-Miami Criminal Justice Council, who have made detailed studies of the boatlift's consequences; and various experts within and on the Cuban community in Miami including Herbert Levin of Radio Suave, Josefina Carbonnell, Xiomara Casado, and Mercedes Sandoval.

The specifics of our account on the Mariel boatlift come from an interview with Larry Boemler, now an assistant chief at Miami PD, and Sergio Pereira, who was Dade County manager until October 1987, when he suspended himself because of allegations that he had purchased stolen clothing from a store run out of a duplex in Miami that was also patronized by other senior officials of the state, county, and city. In late November 1987, the charges against Pereira were dropped, and he was reinstated. In February 1988, he resigned.

The account of the tragedy involving Shanreka Perry is based on Justine Picardie's interview with her, and Marvin Dunn's book.

14. Panic at City Hall

Our account of the debacle that led to the mass hirings at Miami PD depends on Bernard Garmire, Richard Witt, Maurice Ferré, Geoffrey Alpert, and, crucially, interviews with Robert Krause, who was at the time head of Human Resources for the city of Miami; with Kenneth Harms, who was police chief during that time; and with Howard Gary, the city's first and to date only black city manager.

We do not pretend that their accounts were in agreement on what happened and why; we have made our own judgments.

We also obtained a copy of a twenty-three-page memorandum that Harms wrote to Gary protesting his firing, in which he set out the history and, in his view, the causes, of their extraordinary battle.

There is at least one serious omission from the list of people we interviewed in our attempt to make sense of these tangled events: the current police chief for the city of Miami, Clarence Dickson. Dickson was distinctly annoyed with an article we wrote in the course of our research that previewed the Miami River Cops trial and that included derogatory remarks Harms had made about Dickson. Harms subsequently denied to *The Miami Herald* that he had made those remarks, but the fact is that he did, to our colleague Michael Graham.

15. *The Little Havana Midnight Shift*

Rodolfo "Rudy" Arias began talking to us, disingenuously, after the Miami River Cops trial, and began dropping what we took to be hints that he was prepared to make a deal with the government. In April 1987 he agreed to a detailed background interview, and took us on a tour of some of the Little Havana bars that had featured so prominently in the trial. A short while afterwards, Arias was rearrested and charged with attempts to kill government witnesses. Once he had agreed to plead guilty to the charges against him, and cooperate with the government, he also talked and wrote to us. Our account of the activities of the Little Havana Midnight Shift is based on what he has told us, but also on court records and on the knowledge and suspicions of Centac.

16. *"Clintino"*

Much of the information in this chapter, including the description of Centac's first meeting with Officer Armando Estrada, comes from Alex Alvarez's lengthy depositions given when the Miami River Cops case was due to be tried in state court. It was partly because the state system allows prosecution witnesses to be deposed, and the fact that the prosecution intended to call more than one hundred witnesses, that the decision was made to drop the state charges and move the case to federal court.

The snag was that, in so doing, the homicide charges against Officers Estrada, Rodríguez, and García had to be dropped because there is no such charge under federal law; instead, the three officers were charged with depriving the three victims of the raid on Jones Boat Yard with their civil rights—to wit, "their right to life."

Alvarez and George Plasencia described for us the frustrating and often heart-stopping process of secretly tape-recording Estrada, Rodríguez, and García.

Miami PD's PRIDE unit lasted for about a year before being disbanded. The missing $150,000 from the vice squad's safe has yet to be found.

The description of the death threats come from court records; the description of the methods Centac used to preserve their personal safety from Alvarez and Al Singleton; the allegation that the families of the Miami River defendants used a corrupt member of the police department to run the license tags of prosecutors and detectives came from Rudy Arias.

17. Wages of Sin

Roy Black was the primary source for the defense team's strategy, though most of the other attorneys also spoke to us on a formal and informal basis. Black provided us with a copy of the bulletin that circulated within Miami PD before any officer was charged. It reads:

> Tired of long hours? Tired of low pay? Tired of driving year-old cars? Tired of promises by your F.O.P.?
>
> Join an organization that will stop all this. Join an organization of macho men that gets results! Join the C.O.P.—CUBAN OFFICERS IN PRISON!
>
> This organization is men that have a Porsche in every driveway. Our goals are oriented towards the officers' benefit. We propose the following:
> 1. Full automatic weapons for every officer.
> 2. Nameplates with changeable letters.
> 3. Uniforms that are brown on one side and blue on the other.
> 4. Badges with removable titles.

5. Free assortment of patches of every department, including velcro backs.

6. I.D. cards with mustache overlays.

The dues are only a modest $5,000.00 per week. This will be easily affordable once you become an active member.

Officers becoming members prior to arrest get a 25% discount with that famous bail bondsman, J.J. Welch, and also get Roy Black's unlisted phone number. The dues also include a two kilo safety deposit box. A two bale deposit vault is also available for a slight fee.

For members who wish to deposit $150,000.00 of City of Miami pre-owned cash or more, we have special security. These will, of course, be charter members.

Instead of the usual dull, hum drum meeting hall, we have purchased the Pavillion Hotel. We furnish the party set-ups at no charge—straws and razor blades.

At the end of each fiscal year, we will take a roll call. A status report on each member will be read. Members that have been given 15 years or more will be awarded lifetime membership status. All members not indicted or convicted will be promoted to Major or above.

A plaque proclaiming your membership will be given to you when you join the C.O.P. You can proudly take this home to your house and place it on your wall—so all seven families can read it.

Make your amigos proud—become a *COP* today.

(The C.O.P. is an equal opportunity employer)

For recollections of Black's tenure as a public defender, we talked to Appellate Judge Phillip Hubbart, his former partner Jack Denaro, and their former intern, Harold Smith. Diane Goldner of *The American Lawyer* magazine wrote an excellent profile of Black that was invaluable.

Raúl Díaz's partners at the InterContinental Detective Agency, Juan Cayado and Tom D'Azevedo, described to us what the agency does, and how Díaz became a part of that operation. Our account of Díaz's involvement in the Miami River Cops case depends on him, a supporting account from Roy Black, and what we observed.

18. We, the Jury

The history of the mural in the central courtroom of the federal courthouse in Miami comes from *Knights of The Fourth Estate,* by Nixon Smiley (E. A. Seemann, 1974).

We attended the pretrial hearings, and the trials of the Miami River Cops, and our descriptions of it depend on what we saw, and on conversations with defense attorneys, prosecutors, and family members. Rudy Arias was the source for our allegations about jury tampering.

Roy Black provided us with a copy of the questionnaire sent to the jurors, his experts' analysis of the jurors' responses to certain key questions, and a selection of his and Trial Consultants' notes on individual jurors.

We attended the defense attorney's celebratory party, and report what we heard. The description of Centac's more somber gathering comes from Al Singleton.

PART FOUR 19. The Cartel

Our description of the Cartel is based on what we saw in Colombia, scores of interviews and conversations, and hundreds of clippings from Colombian newspapers that we began collecting in 1983. We saw for ourselves the growing power and influence of Colombia's traffickers, and followed, day by day, the well-publicized battle between Justice Minister Lara and Pablo Escobar; it was always easy to predict that it would end in Lara's death.

One of us was also in Colombia when the entire country was up in arms over the news of the secret "summit" in Panama between the heads of the Medellín Cartel and the attorney general of Colombia, and we obtained a copy of the Cartel's written "peace offer."

Francisco Javier Torres Sierra, who inadvertently led the DEA and the Colombian police to *Tranquilandia,* pled guilty to conspiracy charges in Miami and was sentenced to five years. Our account of the DEA's sting operation is based on the sworn affidavit of Special Agent Carol Cooper.

We closely monitored the work of Colonel Jaime Ramírez, and we obtained a copy of his official report describing the raid on *Tranquilandia,* on which our account is largely based. However, after Ramírez's assassination, we reconstructed some key events with the help of his brother, Major Francisco Ramírez, who is not afraid of the traffickers because he is dying of leukemia.

20. *"Our Most Costly Failure"*

When Dorothy Wade was in Madrid in 1985 and 1986, she was privy to the Ochoas' struggle to stop Jorge from being extradited to the United States. She accompanied the family to court, observed Ochoa's lawyers at work, and talked to family friends and relatives. She studied all police records pertaining to Ochoa's arrest and interviewed Spanish and American law enforcement agents working in Madrid, including Jimmy Kibble. She interviewed Roger Yochelson in Madrid and, later, at his home in Maryland.

Meanwhile, we studied thousands of pages of court documents in the United States in order to piece together the structure of the Medellín Cartel and roles allegedly played by each one of its top members. A *Miami Herald* six-part series on the Cartel published in November and December 1987, which included an exclusive interview with Max Mermelstein, was also helpful.

Our account of Barry Seal's adventures in Nicaragua depend on his statements and testimony. We should acknowledge that doubts have been raised as to the veracity of Seal's claims of Nicaragua's involvement in drug trafficking. Articles published in *The Village Voice, The Nation,* and *The Wall Street Journal* have raised the prospect that the Sandinistas were "framed" by the CIA, and that Seal's supposed flights to Managua never took place. The evidence says otherwise. Throughout the period he was working on "the Nicaraguan connection," Seal was closely supervised by two DEA agents in Miami who are as apolitical as it is possible to be, and the notion that they would conspire to "frame" the Sandinistas is, in our view, simply absurd: they monitored his flights and his telephone calls to Managua, and they say that Managua is where he went, and Managua is where he called to.

What is in doubt is the real identity of Federico Vaughan. The claim that Vaughan was a senior official of the Nicaraguan government depends primarily on Seal, and he only knew what Vaughan told him. The Sandinistas have always denied Vaughan's existence. The fact remains, whoever he was, and whatever his position, he had sufficient clout to get Barry Seal out of jail after his plane had been shot down.

For information regarding Seal's battle with Miami and Louisiana courts, and his murder, we relied on interviews with DEA and FBI agents, court records, and on a four-part series on Seal's life and death written by *Miami Herald* reporter Jeff Leen and published in October 1986. Our understanding of Seal's disappointment with the federal Witness Protection Program came from a motion filed by one of his lawyers in the District Court in Fort Lauderdale on October 2, 1985.

21. Rough Justice

Colombians are very critical of themselves, and when we asked lawyers for their opinions of their criminal justice system they were extremely candid. Some of them offered to give us a guided tour of Bogotá's courts, and when we took it we easily understood the assertion that the whole system was "a joke." We entered one courtroom where a judge, modestly dressed in his everyday clothes, presided over a homicide trial that in no way resembled a serious attempt to administer justice. The prosecutor, sporting an open-collar shirt, swiveled in his chair, smoking a cigarette and drinking soda from a bottle. The three-member jury looked aimlessly at the ceiling with no apparent interest in the arguments of one of the defense lawyers, whose table was partially covered by half-eaten sandwiches. The defendant paid no attention to the proceedings whatsoever, while his relatives chatted among themselves and exchanged snacks. "And this is a showpiece," said our knowledgeable guide.

In cases like these, we were told, juries almost inevitably vote for acquittal—for fear that if they don't, they will be the next victims. The judges share that fear: "They don't make enough money to live decently, they don't make enough to buy a car, they are not important enough to deserve decent protection," said our guide. "If you want to see the bottom line, go to one of their office bathrooms: there is no toilet paper, no soap, no towel. It's a shame. Under those circumstances, who isn't going to have a price?"

Our description of the attack on the Palace of Justice depends on contemporary newspaper accounts and follow-up interviews with officials in Bogotá, as does our account of Carlos Lehder's capture and abrupt extradition. Our account of Rodríguez Orejuela's trial is based on the reporting of one of the journalists who attended it.

22. Reagan's War

Together with Donald Berry, a visiting colleague from London, we were Kojak's reluctant dinner guests on the night the contract was placed on his life, and our description of the events is based on what we saw. In the following days and weeks we inquired into Jorge Morales's case and examined his file at the federal courthouse in Fort Lauderdale; like the DEA, we failed to understand why he was not in jail. When Morales was finally arrested, we learned of his claims, and the claims of his pilots, from published reports in *The Miami Herald,* broadcast interviews on the CBS Television program "West 57th Street," and from Jack Blum.

When Ramón Milián Rodríguez made his sensational claims, we became minor participants in the drama since, by coincidence, we were with Raúl Díaz at the InterContinental Detective Agency when Jack Blum's subpoenas arrived. For a brief period, we acted as informal intermediaries between Díaz and Blum, and what we describe in this chapter is based on what we saw and on what we were told.

ENDGAMES

Our account of Rudy Arias's confession is based on his and Centac's recollections and Arias's testimony at the second Miami River Cops trial, which began in December 1987. Initially there were six accused: Arturo de la Vega and Osvaldo Coello, who were defendants in the original trial; Raimundo Betancourt, Omar Manzanilla, and Mario Carballo, three more

Miami police officers named by Arias as having participated in the rip-offs; and Raúl Rojas, a drug dealer. Betancourt and Rojas changed their pleas to guilty before the trial began, De la Vega changed his plea after the jury had been selected, and Manzanilla admitted his guilt after Arias had testified. Coello and Carballo were eventually convicted by the jury.

The calculation that no American police department has been so damaged by corruption since Prohibition comes from a report in *The Miami News,* which quoted its sources as Professor Lawrence Sherman, president of the Crime Control Institute in Washington, D.C., and criminologist James Fyfe of the American University, also in Washington. The Knapp Commission investigation into the New York Police Department— which is twenty-seven times larger than Miami's force—resulted in 218 officers being suspended or fired. Chief Dickson was quoted by *The News* as anticipating that up to 100 Miami police officers would be implicated in the scandal.

The detail of Osvaldo Coello's capture in the Bahamas comes from Centac, as does the account of his father's suicide.

The "Judas 1987" sign was found pinned to the courtroom door during Ricardo Alemán's trial.

Joe Díaz's loyalty to Raúl Díaz is shared by Al Singleton and George Plasencia (Alex Alvarez did not join Centac until after Raúl Díaz had resigned from Metro-Dade PD).

The remarks attributed to Edward Shohat and José Quiñón about why they took Carlos Lehder's case are taken from a report in *The Miami Herald.*

Our account of the squabble between Lehder's two "wives" in based on the reporting of Colombian investigative journalist Gonzalo Guillén, who described to us his lengthy interview with Liliana in Armenia, and Kojak, who had two substantial discussions with Jemel on our behalf prior to going to New York to collect her.

The events of Kojak's last day were related to us by him, in a series of telephone calls from New York.

In addition to those people identified in the text, and those listed in the notes for each chapter, there were a large number of others who granted interviews or who helped us obtain background information. Those we can acknowledge are:

George Adams; Luis Alvarez; William Anderson; Paul Andrews; Don Askew; Charles Blowers; Luis Botifoll; William Cullom; Miller Dawkins; Bill Deac; T. Van Edsall; Tom Ferguson; James Fleming; Joan Fleischman; Olgar Garay-Ahern; Hank Green; Ed Howett; Felix Huertas; Cleve Jones; Alberto Jorge; Rosario Kennedy; Charles Kimball; Renée Krause; Raymond LaCombe; Robert Lamont; Manuel Lasaga; Stephen Loffredo; Jan Luytjes; Jorge Mas Canosa; Jim Millerick; Jim Mullens; Peter Nelson; Lorna Nones; César Odio; Skip Pearson; Matt Pritchard; José Quiñón; AnaBelle Ramos; Jacqueline Ramos; Tomás Regalado; Angela Rodríguez; Juan Román; Paul Silverstein; Stephanie Slewka; Don Thompson; William Thompson; Bill Turner; Miñuca Villaverde; Arthur Vincent; and George Yoss.

Acknowledgments

F our of the reporters who worked on this book previously worked for *The Sunday Times* of London. Andrew Neil, *The Sunday Times*'s editor, respected our ambition to strike out on our own and despite our desertion from his newspaper, supported this project with understanding, encouragement, and money. We are deeply grateful for his help.

Donald Berry, formerly managing editor of *The Sunday Times,* provided advice and wisdom.

Len Gowland and Hazel Whitnell were with us in Miami when we were attempting to complete the manuscript, and Kojak died. Their support and practical help during that difficult period kept us sane.

Sallie Coolidge was our editor for much of the project, and a true friend.

Stuart Speiser and Charles McManus, of the New York law firm Speiser & Krause, supplied crucial legal advice without which we would not have been able to complete our work.

W. W. Norton and, in particular, Donald Lamm and Starling Lawrence, are the kind of publishers every author should have. The faith they displayed in this book, and in us, was extraordinary and there are no words to adequately thank them. We are grateful to Patty Peltekos, who edited the manuscript, improved our literacy, and saved us from countless errors. (Any errors that remain are our sole responsibility.)

Dinorah Alonso took care of us in Miami, and we could not

have managed without her. Lore Croghan, Linda Melvern, and Fran Miller were constant friends and also indispensable.

Finally, we wish to thank Robert Ducas, our business manager in New York, and Jeanie Curtiss, his assistant. Robert obtained the initial finance for this project; he arranged refinancing when the project ran into trouble; and, throughout the project's life, he provided daily succor, advice, support, and criticism. It is literally true that he made this book possible. If it has merit, much of the credit belongs to him.

Paul Eddy, Hugo Sabogal, Sara Walden
Miami, January 1988

Index

The letter *n* after a page number indicates an entry in the Notes and Sources.

389

Index

INDEX

INDEX

Index

Index